Recollections of
Marshal Macdonald
Duke of Tarentum

Marshal MacDonald (Duke of Tarentum)

Recollections of Marshal Macdonald Duke of Tarentum

The Napoleonic Wars as Experienced by a Renowned French Military Commander

Jacques Macdonald

Recollections of Marshal Macdonald Duke of Tarentum
The Napoleonic Wars as Experienced by a
Renowned French Military Commander
by Jacques Macdonald

First published under the title
Recollections of Marshal Macdonald Duke of Tarentum
Edited by Camille Rousset
Translated by Stephen Louis Simeon

Leonaur is an imprint of Oakpast Ltd
Copyright in this form © 2011 Oakpast Ltd

ISBN: 978-0-85706-571-1 (hardcover)
ISBN: 978-0-85706-572-8 (softcover)

http://www.leonaur.com

Publisher's Notes

The opinions of the authors represent a view of events in which he was a participant related from his own perspective, as such the text is relevant as an historical document.

The views expressed in this book are not necessarily those of the publisher.

Contents

Introduction	7
Introduction by M. Camille Rousset	23
Life at Sancerre	25
First Campaign	34
Macdonald Appointed Adjutant-General	44
Ordered to Walcheren	53
Operations on the Rhine	60
Ordered to Italy	64
Insurrections in the Country	73
Rising in Tuscany	83
The Marshal in Danger	92
Plans for Retreat	102
Landing of Napoleon	109
Napoleon Elected Emperor	115
Warnings and Defensive Measures	120
An Incomplete Success	127
Advance to Raab	136
Battle of Wagram	140
Annex to Chapter 16	153
Evacuation of Styria	156
Blockade and Surrender of Figueras	163
Preparations for the Russian Campaign	167

A Terrible March	174
Disorderly Retreat	181
Commencement of the Retreat	192
Discouragement	203
The Enemy Cross the Rhine	213
Campaign in France	220
On the Marne	231
Abdication of the Emperor	236
Decision of the Allies	246
Attitude of Napoleon	255
Reported Flight of Napoleon	264
Delivery of the Treaty	271
First Steps towards Unpopularity	278
Indifference of the Government	288
Landing of Napoleon	292
Retreat	299
Ney's Desertion	310
Plan of Escape	319
An Inconvenient Loss	327
The News of Waterloo	335
Mission to Paris	342
Marshal Macdonald takes the Command	351
Mission to Lyons	358
Appendix	368

Introduction

Jacques Étienne Joseph Alexandre Macdonald, Duke of Tarentum, was the son of a Uist crofter, Macachaim. The Macachaims of Uist were a far-off sept of the Macdonalds of Clanranald. The future Marshal's father was educated at the Scots College in Paris, and was for some time a tutor in Clanranald's household. Owing to his knowledge of French he was entrusted with the duty of helping Flora Macdonald to arrange the escape of Prince Charles. He accompanied the Prince to France, and obtained a commission in Ogilvie's regiment of foot. In 1768 Vall Macachaim, or Neil Macdonald, as he was called in France, retired on a pension of thirty pounds a year. On this pittance he brought up his family at Sancerre.

The future Marshal was born at Sedan on November 17, 1765. He was educated for the army at a military academy in Paris, kept by a Scotchman, Paulet, but, owing to bad mathematics, he was unable to enter the Artillery and Engineering School. This failure came as a bitter blow to the keen young soldier, who, after reading Homer, already imagined himself an Achilles. But in 1784 his chance came; the Dutch, threatened by the emperor Joseph II., had to improvise an army, and Macdonald accepted a pair of colours in a regiment raised by a Frenchman, the Count de Maillebois. A few months later the regiment was disbanded, as the Dutch bought the peace they could not gain by arms.

The young officer, thus thrown on his own resources, was glad to accept a cadetship in Dillon's Irish regiment in the French king's service, and at the moment the Revolution broke out he was a sub-lieutenant in that corps. Owing to emigration and the fortune of war, promotion came quickly. Macdonald also was lucky in having a friend in General Beurnonville, on whose staff he served till he was transferred to that of Dumouriez, the commander-in-chief. As a reward for his services at

Jemmappes and elsewhere he was made lieutenant-colonel, and early in 1793 his friend Beurnonville, who had become War Minister, gave him his colonelcy and the command of the Picardy regiment, one of the four senior corps of the old French infantry. The young colonel of twenty-eight could not expect to be always so favoured by fortune. Dumouriez's failure at Neerwinden and subsequent desertion to the Allies cast a cloud of suspicion on his protégé at a moment when to be suspected was to be condemned. Luckily, some of the commissioners from the Convention could recognise merit, but Macdonald spent many anxious months amid denunciations and accusations from those who grudged him his colonelcy.

To his intense surprise he was at last summoned before the dread commissioners and told that, for his zeal, he was to be promoted general of brigade. Overcome by this unexpected turn of fortune, he wished to refuse the honour, and pleaded his youth and inexperience, and was promptly given the choice of accepting or becoming a "suspect" and being arrested. Safe for the moment, Macdonald threw himself heart and soul into his new duties, but still denunciations and accusations were hurled against him. Fresh commissioners came from the Assembly, and it was only their fortunate recall to Paris that saved the general from arrest. Then came the decree banishing all "*ci-devant*" nobles. Macdonald, fearing after this order that if he met with the slightest check he would be greeted with cries of treachery, demanded written orders from the new commissioners confirming him in his employment. These were refused, as also his resignation, with the curt reply, "If you leave the army we will have you arrested and brought to trial."

In this dilemma he found a friend in the representative Isore, who, struck by his ability and industry, took up his cause, and from that moment Macdonald had nothing to fear from the revolutionary tribunal. In November, 1794, he was quite unexpectedly gazetted general of division in the army of Pichegru, and took part in the winter campaign against Holland, where he proved his capacity by seizing the occasion of a hard frost to cross the Vaal on the ice and surprise the Anglo-Hanoverian force at Nimeguen. A few days later, during the general advance, he captured Naarden, the masterpiece of the great engineer Cohorn. Proud of his success, he hastened to inform the commander-in-chief, Pichegru, and was greeted by a laugh, and, "Bah! I pay no attention now to anything less than the surrender of provinces."

The blasé commander-in-chief a week or two later himself performed the exploit of capturing the ice-bound Dutch fleet with a cavalry brigade and a battery of horse artillery.

After serving on the Rhine in 1796 Macdonald was transferred in 1798 to the Army of Italy, and sent to Rome to relieve Gouvion St. Cyr. When war broke out between France and Naples, the troops in Southern Italy were formed into the Army of Naples under Championnet. The commander-in-chief overrated the fighting qualities of the Neapolitan troops and thought it prudent to evacuate Rome. Macdonald was entrusted with this duty, and was further required to cover the concentration of Championnet's army. The hard-headed Scotchman had, however, gauged to a nicety the *morale* of the Neapolitan army, and, although he had but five thousand troops against forty thousand Neapolitans, under the celebrated Austrian general Mack, he engaged the enemy at Cività Castellana, defeated them, followed them up, drove them out of Rome and over the frontier, and practically annihilated the whole force. Unfortunately he wrote a comical account of the operations to his chief, who, having no sense of humour, felt that his evacuation of Rome had, to say the least of it, been hurried and undignified. Championnet therefore greeted his victorious lieutenant with the words, "You want to make me pass for a damned fool," and no explanations could appease his rage. So bitter became the quarrel that Macdonald had to resign his command.

By February, 1799, Championnet had fallen into disgrace with the Directory, and Macdonald was gazetted in his place commander-in chief. When he arrived in Naples and took up his command the situation seemed quiet. But the far-seeing soldier read the signs of the times. The elite of the French army was locked up in Egypt. Austria and Russia were bent on extinguishing France and her revolutionary ideas. Accordingly the general at once set about quietly concentrating his troops to meet an invasion of Northern Italy by the Allies. With his keen military insight he desired to evacuate all Southern Italy, retaining only such fortresses as could be well supplied. But the principle of keeping everything gained the day. Still, on the news of Schérer's defeat at Magnano by the impetuous Suvaroff, the Army of Naples was ready at once to start for the north, and set off to try and pick up communication with General Moreau, who was re-forming the Army of Italy at Genoa. The idea was that a concentrated movement should be made against the Allies through the Apennines. Unfortunately there existed a bitter rivalry between the Army of Italy and the Army of Naples.

Consequently on June 17th Macdonald found himself with twenty-five thousand men near Piacenza, in the presence of the enemy, with no support save two divisions of the Army of Italy, which had come in from Bologna, and whose commanders were jealous of his orders. Still there was always the hope that Moreau might after all be coming to his assistance, and accordingly he determined to stand and fight. In the action of June 17th, owing to the lack of co-operation from one of the attached divisions, the general was ridden over by a division of the enemy's cavalry. Carried about in a litter, he directed all movements during the 18th, and held the enemy at bay along the mountain torrent of the Trebbia.

On the 19th he determined to take the initiative, but, owing to the collapse of the attached division which formed his centre, he had to fall back on his old position, which he held throughout the whole day. During the three days' fighting on the Trebbia the French had lost a third of their men and nearly all their officers. Still, early on the morning of the 20th the retreat was effected in good order, save that one of the attached divisions under Victor started so late that it was overtaken by the enemy and abandoned all its guns. But Macdonald at once returned to its aid and saved the artillery, for, as he sarcastically wrote to Victor, "he found neither friends nor foes." Both sides had run away.

The Battle of the Trebbia brought into notice the sterling qualities of the French commander, and when he was recalled to Paris he found that military opinion was on his side and that Bonaparte himself highly approved of his conduct. "Thenceforward the opinion of my *amphitryon* was settled in my favour!"

Macdonald's next employment was in command of the Army of the Grisons, whose duty was to cover Moreau's right rear in his advance down the Danube, and to keep up communication with the Army of Italy in the valley of the Po. It was in the performance of this duty that the Army of the Grisons crossed the Splügen Pass in winter in spite of glaciers and avalanches, a feat immeasurably superior to Bonaparte's task in crossing the much easier Great St. Bernard Pass, after the snows had melted. Unfortunately for Macdonald, Bonaparte believed him to belong to Moreau's faction. After Hohenlinden the future emperor, who was afraid that Moreau's glory would outshine his own, placed all that general's friends on the black book. Further, owing to his outspokenness, Talleyrand had conceived a hatred of the hero of the Splügen. Accordingly, he found himself in deep disgrace.

First he was exiled as ambassador at Copenhagen, then his enemies tried to get him sent to Russia in the same capacity, but he refused to go, and for the next few years lived the life of a quiet country gentleman on his estate of Courcelles le Roi.

Like most of the generals, Macdonald was by now comparatively well off, for the French government, on the conquest of a country, had allowed its generals to take what works of art they chose, after the commissioners had selected the best for the national collection at the Louvre. The general's share as commander-in-chief at Naples had been valued by experts at thirty-four thousand pounds. Unfortunately, however, this booty and many masterpieces which he had bought himself were all lost in the hurried march north that ended in the battle of the Trebbia.

It was not till 1809 that Macdonald was summoned from his retreat. In that year the emperor needed every soldier of ability, with the Spanish ulcer eating at his vitals and the war with Austria on his hands. Accordingly, at a day's notice, he was ordered to hurry off to Italy to help Napoleon's stepson, Prince Eugène, who was opposed by an Austrian army under the Archduke John.

On arriving in Italy the old soldier found that Prince Eugène, unaccustomed to an independent command, had opened the gate of Italy to the Austrians by his impetuous action at Sacile. The French troops were in complete disorganisation, and the slightest activity on the part of the Austrians would have turned the retreat into a rout. Prince Eugène, who was without a spark of jealousy, and in reality a man of considerable character, greeted his mentor with delight. Macdonald at once pointed out that it was unnecessary to retire as far as Mantua, because the Archduke would not venture to penetrate far into Italy until a decision had been arrived at between the main armies on the Danube. Under his careful supervision, order and discipline were restored among the French troops on the line of the Adige.

The news of the French success at Eckmühl and Ratisbon automatically cleared the Austrians out of Northern Italy. During the pursuit the general had to impose on himself the severest self-control, because, though Prince Eugène invariably accepted his advice, the disaster at Sacile had for the time broken his nerve, and, again and again, he spoiled his mentor's best combinations by ordering a halt whenever the enemy appeared to be going to offer any resistance. It was hard indeed to accept subsequent apologies with a courteous smile, when it was success alone that would win back the emperor's favour. But at last patience had its reward: while the viceroy himself pursued the main force of the enemy, he detached his lieutenant with a strong corps to take Trieste and to pick up communication with Marmont, who was bringing up the army of Dalmatia. Macdonald was given *carte blanche*.

Trieste and Görz were taken; the junction with Marmont was speedily effected, and the combined forces hurried on towards Vienna. The great entrenched camp at Laybach blocked the way. Macdonald had not the necessary heavy artillery with which to capture it. He determined therefore to make a threatening demonstration by day and slip past it by night. But at ten o'clock in the evening a flag of truce arrived offering a capitulation. "You are doing wisely," said the imperturbable Scotchman; "I was just going to sound the attack."

At Gratz he overtook Prince Eugène's army at the moment that the ill news of the battle of Aspern-Essling arrived. Then came the summons to hurry to the assistance of the emperor. After marching sixty leagues in three days the Army of Italy arrived at nine o'clock at night on July 4th at the imperial headquarters at Ebersdorf. During that night it crossed the Danube, under cover of the terrific thunderstorm which hid the French advance from the Austrians.

On the afternoon of July 5th it fell to the lot of Macdonald to attempt to seize the plateau which formed the Austrian centre. As the general well knew, the emperor had been mistaken in thinking that the enemy were evacuating their position; still, he had to obey orders, and night alone saved his cruelly shaken battalions.

Next day was fought the terrible Battle of Wagram. At the critical moment of the fight, when the emperor heard that Masséna, on his left wing, was being driven in on the bridge-head, amid the confusion and rout he ordered Macdonald to attempt by a bold counterstroke to break the enemy's centre. The Austrians were advancing in masses, with nothing in front of them, and the bridge, the only line of retreat, was threatened. To meet this situation Macdonald deployed four battalions in line, at the double; behind them he formed up the rest of his corps in two solid columns, and closed the rear of this immense rectangle of troops by Nansouty's cavalry. Covered by the fire of a massed battery of a hundred guns, he discharged this huge body of thirty thousand troops against the Austrians, and in spite of vast losses from the enemy's artillery, by sheer weight of human beings he completely checked the Austrian advance and broke their centre. If the cavalry of the Guard had only charged home the enemy would have been driven off the field in complete rout. Still unsupported, the column continued its victorious career, taking six thousand prisoners and ten guns, the only trophies of the day. Next morning the hero of Wagram, lame from the effect of a kick from his horse, was summoned before the emperor.

Napoleon embraced him with the words, "Let us be friends." "Till death," replied his staunch lieutenant. Then came his reward. "You have behaved valiantly," continued the emperor, "and have rendered me the greatest services, as, indeed, throughout the entire campaign. On the battlefield of your glory, where I owe you so large a share of yesterday's success, I make you a Marshal of France. You have long deserved it."

After the ratification of peace, the emperor created his new Marshal Duke of Tarentum, granted him a present of sixty thousand *francs*, and presented him with the Grand Cordon of the Legion of Honour. Having at last regained the emperor's favour, the marshal had never again to complain of lack of employment.

From Wagram he was sent to watch the army of the Archduke John; thereafter he was appointed commander-in-chief of the Army of Italy. In 1810 he was despatched to Spain to take command in Catalonia. Like his fellow Marshals, Macdonald hated the Spanish war, which was a war of posts, and devoid of glory. But he showed his versatility by capturing, without artillery, the stronghold of Figueras.

It was while suffering from a bad attack of gout after this success that he was summoned from Spain to Tilsit, to command the corps comprised of Prussian troops which was to join the Grand Army in its advance into Russia. As he graphically put it, "I had left my armchair in the fortress of Figueras, I left one crutch in Paris and the other in Berlin."

The Duke of Tarentum's duty was to guard the *tête-du-pont* at Dunaberg, near the mouth of the Dwina; consequently he was spared a great many of the horrors of the terrible retreat. Still, he had his full share of troubles, for the Prussians deserted him and went over to the enemy. So confident was he of the loyalty of his subordinates that this desertion took him quite unawares, and, in spite of warnings, he waited for the divisions to rejoin him, declaring that, "My life, my career, shall never be stained with the reproach that I have committed the cowardly action of deserting troops committed to my care."

Fortunately his eyes were opened by letters which he intercepted. With a handful of troops he escaped to Dantzig. On returning to

Paris Macdonald was greeted with a cold reception by the emperor, who thought that the desertion of the Prussians was due to his negligence. But the marshal's character was soon cleared and a reconciliation followed. In the campaign of 1813 it fell to the lot of the Duke of Tarentum to watch the Prussian army under Blücher in Silesia while the emperor operated against the Austrians round Dresden. Whilst thus employed he was defeated on August 26th at the Katzbach. The Prussians had established themselves on the heights at Jauer. Macdonald attempted, by a combined frontal attack and a turning movement, to dislodge them. Unfortunately the rain came down in torrents, the French artillery became embedded in the mud, the infantry could not fire, the cavalry could not charge, and a hurried retreat alone saved the Army from absolute annihilation, for, as Macdonald wrote in his despatch:

> The generals cannot prevent the men from seeking shelter, as their muskets are useless to them.

The repulse at the Katzbach did not weaken the emperor's esteem for the marshal, and a few days later he sent to inquire his views of the general situation. With absolute courage he told the truth. The situation was hopeless; the only wise course was to evacuate all garrisons in Germany and retire on the Saale. Unfortunately, such a retirement would have meant the loss of Napoleon's throne.

On the third day of the Battle of Leipzig, in the midst of the action, Macdonald was deserted by all the Hessian troops under his command, and, at the same time, Marshal Augereau, who was supposed to cover his right, withdrew from the combat. Accordingly, the marshal retired with the remnants of his corps to the Elster, only to find the bridge blown up. Dragged along by the crowd of fugitives, he determined not to fall alive into the hands of the enemy, but either to drown or shoot himself. More fortunate, however, than Prince Poniatowski, he managed to cross the river on his horse. Once safely across, he was greeted by cries from the other bank, "*monsieur le Maréchal*, save your soldiers, save your children!" But there was nothing to be done; no advice could he give them save to surrender.

The Duke of Tarentum was mainly instrumental in saving the remnants of the army which had managed to cross the Elster. Going straight to the emperor, he laid the situation before him, ruthlessly tore aside the tissue of lies with which the staff were trying to cajole him, and, by his force of will, compelled Napoleon, who for the time was quite unnerved and mazed, to hurry on the retreat to the Rhine. It was entirely owing to the marshal that the Bavarians were brushed aside at Hanau, and that some few remnants of the great army regained France. In the famous campaign of 1814 Macdonald fought fiercely to drive the enemy out of France. His corps was one of those which the emperor summoned to Arcis sur Aube. There again he had to tell Napoleon the truth and convince him that the enemy were not retreating, but were in full advance on Paris. When the emperor tried to retrieve his mistake by following in the rear, the marshal was in favour of the bolder course of advancing into Alsace and Lorraine, and of raising the nation in arms, and thus starving out the Allies by cutting off their supplies and reinforcements; and no doubt he was right, for the *Czar* himself said that the Allies lost more than three thousand troops in the Vosges without seeing a single French soldier.

When Napoleon reached Fontainebleau he found that he had shot his bolt. So tired were his officers and men of continual fighting that, when ordered to charge, a general officer in front of his men had called out, "Damn it, let us have peace!" Consequently when Macdonald and the other Marshals and generals were informed that the Allies would no longer treat with Napoleon, they determined to make him abdicate. The emperor, on summoning his council, found that they no longer feared him, and refused to listen to his arguments. Hoping to save the throne for his son, he despatched Caulaincourt, Ney, Marmont, and Macdonald to the *Czar*, offering to abdicate. The best terms the commissioners could get from the *Czar* were that Napoleon must give up all hope of seeing his son succeed him, but that he should retain his imperial title and should be allowed to rule the island of Elba. The *Czar* magnanimously added, "If he will not accept this sovereignty, and if he can find no shelter elsewhere, tell him, I say, to come to my dominions. There he shall be received as a sovereign: he can trust the word of Alexander."

Ney and Marmont did not accompany the other commissioners with their sorrowful terms; like rats they left the sinking ship. But Macdonald was of a strain which had stood the test of the '45, and his proud Scotch blood boiled up when the insidious Talleyrand suggested that he should desert his master, telling him that he had now fulfilled all his engagements and was free. "No, I am not," was the stern reply, "and nobody knows better than you that, as long as a treaty has not been ratified, it may be annulled. After that formality is ended, I shall know what to do."

The stricken emperor met his two faithful commissioners, his face haggard, his complexion yellow and sickly, but for once at least he felt gratitude. "I have loaded with favours," he said, "many others who have now deserted and abandoned me. You, who owe me nothing, have remained faithful. I appreciate your loyalty too late, and I sincerely regret that I am now in a position in which I can only prove my gratitude by words."

After Napoleon started for Elba, Macdonald never saw him again. Like all his fellow Marshals, except Davout, he swore allegiance to Louis XVIII., looking on him as the only hope of France, but, unlike the most of them, he served him loyally, though, as he truly said, "The government behaved like a sick man who is utterly indifferent to all around him."

As a soldier and a liberal he could not disguise his repugnance for many of its measures. As secretary to the Chamber of Peers, he fought tooth and nail against the government's first measure, a bill attempting to restrict the liberties of the peers. The king summoned the marshal and rebuked him for both speaking and voting against the government, adding, "When I take the trouble to draw up a Bill, I have good reasons for wishing it to pass."

But the old soldier, who had never feared to speak the truth to Napoleon himself, was not to be overawed by the attempted sternness of the feeble Bourbon. He pointed out that if all bills presented by the king were bound to pass, "registration would serve equally well, since to you belongs the initiative," adding with quiet sarcasm, "and we must remain as mute as the late Corps Legislatif."

The Chancellor stopped him as he left the king's presence, telling him he should show more reserve and pick his words.

"Sir Chancellor," said the marshal, "I have never learned to twist myself, and I pity the king if what he ought to know is concealed from him. For my part, I shall always speak to him honestly and serve him in the same manner."

When neglect of the army, the partiality shown to favourites, and the general spirit of discontent throughout France tempted Napoleon once again to seize the reins of government, Macdonald was commanding the twenty-first military division at Bourges. As he says, "The news of the emperor's return took away my breath, and I at once foresaw the misfortunes that have since settled upon France."

Placing his duty to his country and his plighted faith before the longings of his heart, he remained faithful to the Bourbons. It was the marshal who at Lyons vainly endeavoured to aid the Count of Artois to organise resistance to Napoleon's advance. It was he who showed the king the vanity of Ney's boast that he would bring back the emperor in an iron cage, who impressed on him Napoleon's activity, and who persuaded him to retire northwards to Lille and there attempt to rally his friends to his aid. Ministers and king were only too thankful to leave all arrangements to this cautious, indefatigable soldier, who supervised everything. Through every town the monarch passed he found the same feeling of apathy, the same tendency among the troops to cry "*Vive l'Empereur,*" the same lack of enterprise among the officials. Typical of the situation was the sub-prefect of Bethune, who stood at the door of the royal carriage, one leg half-naked, his feet in slippers, his coat under his arm, his waistcoat unbuttoned, his hat on his head, one hand struggling with his sword, the other trying to fasten his necktie. The marshal, ever mindful of Napoleon's activity, had to hurry the poor king, and Louis' portmanteau, with his six clean shirts and his old pair of slippers, got lost on the road. This loss, more than anything else, brought home to the monarch his pitiable condition.

"They have taken my shirts," said he to Macdonald. "I had not too many in the first place; but what I regret still more is the loss of my slippers. Some day, my dear Marshal, you will appreciate the value of slippers that have taken the shape of your feet."

With Napoleon at Paris, Lille seemed to offer but little security, and accordingly the king determined to seek safety in Belgium. The marshal escorted him to the frontier and saw him put in charge of the Belgian troops. Then, promising to be faithful to his oath, he took an affectionate farewell of the old monarch with the words, "Farewell, sir; *au revoir,* in three months!"

Macdonald returned to Paris and lived quietly in his own house, refusing to have any intercourse with Napoleon or his ministers. Within three months came the news of Waterloo. Thereafter, against his will, but in accordance with orders, he joined Fouché, who had established a provisional government. Fouché, who knew the importance of outward signs, sent him off to try and persuade the returning monarch to win over the army by mounting the tricolour instead of the white cockade. But the king was obstinate; the marshal quoted Henry IV.'s famous saying, "*Paris is worth a mass.*" The king countered with, "Yes; but it was not a very Catholic one." But though the king would not listen to his advice he called on him to show his devotion. The imperial army had to be disbanded—a most unpopular and thankless task, requiring both tact and firmness.

At his sovereign's earnest request, Macdonald undertook the duty, but with two stipulations: first, that he should have complete freedom of action; secondly, that he should be in no way an instrument for inflicting punishment on individuals. Immediately on taking up his appointment at Bourges, the marshal summoned all the generals and officers to his presence, and informed them that, under Fouché's supervision, a list of proscribed had been drawn up. His advice was that all on this list should fly at once. That same evening police officials arrived in the camp to arrest the proscribed; playing on the fears of the *mouchards*, he locked them up all night, alleging that it was to save them from the infuriated soldiery. Thus all the proscribed escaped; but neither Fouché nor the Duc de Berri cared to bring the old soldier to task for this action. So the marshal was left to work in his own way, and by October 21, 1815, thanks to his firmness and tact, "the bold and unhappy army, which had for so long been triumphant," was quietly dissolved without the slightest attempt at challenging the royal decision.

The marshal did not mix much in politics. The king, at the second Restoration, created him arch-chancellor of the Legion of Honour. This post gave him considerable occupation, as it entailed the supervision of the schools for the children of those who had received the Cross, and he was for long happily employed in looking after the welfare of the descendants of his late comrades-in-arms. In November, 1830, the plea of the gout came opportunely at the moment of the commencement of the July monarchy, and the marshal resigned the arch-chancellorship and returned to his estate of Courcelles, where he lived in retirement till his death, on September 25, 1840, at the age of seventy-five.

It was a maxim of Napoleon that success covers everything, that it is only failure which cannot be forgiven. Against the Duke of Tarentum's name stood the defeats of Trebbia and the Katzbach. But in spite of this, Napoleon never treated him as he treated Dupont and the other unfortunate generals. For Macdonald possessed qualities which were too important to be overlooked. With all the fiery enthusiasm of the Gael, he possessed to an unusual degree the caution of the Lowland Scot. Possessed of great reasoning powers and of the gift of seeing clearly both sides of a question, he had the necessary force of character to make up his mind which course to pursue, and to persevere in it to the logical issue. In the crossing of the Vaal, in the fighting round Rome, in the campaign with Prince Eugène in Italy, before and after Leipzig, and in his final campaign in France, he proved the correctness of his judgment and his capacity to work out his carefully prepared combinations. His defeat at the Trebbia was due to the treachery of the general commanding one of the attached divisions; the rout at the Katzbach was primarily due to climatic conditions and to the want of cohesion among the recently drafted recruits which formed the bulk of his army. On the stricken field of Wagram, and in the running fight at Hanau, his inflexible will and the quickness with which he grasped the vital points of the problem saved the emperor and his army.

The only black spot in his otherwise glorious career is the battle of Leipzig. Long must the cry of *"monsieur le Maréchal,* save your soldiers, save your children!" have rung in his ear. For once he had forgotten his proud boast that he never deserted troops entrusted to his command. Like the emperor and his fellow Marshals and most of the generals, for the moment he lost his nerve; but he could still, though humbly, boast that he was the first to remember his duties and to try and save the remnant of the troops who had crossed the Elster. Duty and truth were his watchwords. Once only he failed in his duty; never did he shirk telling the truth. It was this fearless utterance of the truth more than any connection with Moreau which was the cause of his long years of disgrace; it was this fearlessness, strange to say, which, in the end, conquered the emperor, and which so charmed King Louis that he nicknamed him "His Outspokenness."

R. P. Dunn-Pattison

> GENERAL MACDONALD,
> ONE OF THE MOST INTREPID MEN
> WHO EVER APPEARED IN OUR ARMIES,
> EXPERIENCED, SHREWD, COLD,
> AND KNOWING HOW TO MAKE HIMSELF OBEYED.
>
> THIERS

> BECAUSE I CANNOT FLATTER, AND SPEAK FAIR,
> SMILE IN MEN'S FACES, SMOOTH, DECEIVE, AND COY,
> DUCK WITH FRENCH NODS AND APISH COURTESY,
> I MUST BE HELD TO BE A RANCOROUS ENEMY.
> CANNOT A PLAIN MAN LIVE, AND THINK NO HARM,
> BUT THUS HIS SIMPLE TRUTH MUST BE ABUSED
> BY SILKEN, SLY, INSINUATING JACKS?
>
> SHAKESPEARE.

Introduction
by M. Camille Rousset

In the month of May, 1825, the sexagenarian Marshal Macdonald, left a widower for the third time, was plunged in the deepest grief. By his previous marriage he had only daughters; the last marriage, solemnized scarcely four years before, and which had terminated so sadly, left him a son, heir to his name. It was for this child still in the cradle that, far from Paris, far from the conventional consolations and condolences of the Court, the Marshal undertook—not to distract, but to occupy the isolation caused by his sorrow—to note down the various stages of his long and glorious career. He did not pretend to write memoirs; they are merely recollections destined for the child who was alone to see them in the future.

Sixty-five years have elapsed since they were penned; more than fifty have come and gone since the Marshal died, (as at time of first publication), and his grand-daughter, the Baronne de Pommereul, has thought that, in the interest and for the advantage of history, as well as for the reputation and fame of her ancestor, the moment has come to lift the veil which, until now, has covered these *Recollections*, and has entrusted to me the task of revealing them to the public. It is a great honour, for which I am grateful to her. I could not help feeling respectful emotion as I turned over those pages impregnated with sincerity, and which breathed forth truth like a refreshing perfume. On no occasion, nor in any presence, did Macdonald conceal his thoughts, even when with the greatest of men, with Napoleon or with Louis XVIII.

There is no single erasure or alteration in this manuscript of 472 folio pages; there are consequently a few incomplete sentences, of which it has been found necessary to restore a word or two. With these exceptions, and with the omission of a few intimate details of precious interest for the family, but not for anyone unconnected with it, the text has been treated with the respect it merits.

    Paris.   C. R.

CHAPTER 1

Life at Sancerre

Courcelles-le-Roi[1] May 16, 1825.

The idea has occurred to me, my son, of beginning this sketch of my life for you, without caring to know when it will be finished; nevertheless, I set to work, having for guide and assistance nothing but my memory. I let my pen travel on and write these lines, as you will observe, in the simplest and most familiar style possible. Truth needs no adornment, and, moreover, I am not writing for the public; these lines are not intended for the light of day. I write in haste from an old habit of never leaving anything till tomorrow; besides, my return to Paris cannot long be postponed, and once there, I shall have no time to continue this work, as I am contemplating a journey of six weeks or two months, in order to see the three kingdoms of the British Empire, with which I am unacquainted, and to visit my father's birthplace in the Hebrides.

Paris, June 1, 1825.

You and my family will probably be surprised, and justly, at finding among my papers as yet no special recital of my campaigns, not even a diary; I owe you some explanation upon this point.

Twenty years ago I had ample leisure, as I was not being employed,[2] but I had recently acquired Courcelles. It was the first time that I had owned an estate, and it was but natural that I should wish to enjoy all its pleasures. Surrounded with books

---
1. Situated in the department of the Loiret.—Translator.
2. After the trial of Moreau, in which a futile and unjust attempt was made to implicate Macdonald, he remained five years in disgrace, and was not recalled to service until 1809.

on agriculture, I discovered attractions hitherto unknown to me. I forgot the papers locked up in my chest, and all my fine schemes for writing my military life were temporarily abandoned. If Heaven prolongs my desolate existence,[3] I will include in this narrative an account of my military career, and of the different ranks that I have held. As for events, they are written in every history of the time; but beware of them, especially upon any subject connected with me, for histories, narratives, and biographical notices must be affected by our recent troubles, and consequently by the passions of men and by party spirit; however, impartial history will someday avenge those who have fallen victims.

I have never had reason to reproach myself, nor have I ever had to blush for any circumstance in my life. I received an untarnished name. I transmit it to you, feeling sure that you will keep it pure. My conscience during a long and active life has nothing to reproach me, because I always followed three safe guides: Honour, Fidelity, and Disinterestedness; and I like to believe that my guides will be yours also.

Courcelles-le-Roi, August 6, 1825.

My rapid journey has been brought to a satisfactory conclusion. The coast of France looked to me like the Promised Land. I have once more seen France, my beloved country! This is the first anniversary of your birth. What joy and happiness that event caused us! But, alas! how many regrets and painful memories have come since!

I ought to tell you something about your family upon your father's side. I alone can give you details, which I knew but imperfectly, but which, in the course of my travels, I collected on the spot. Your paternal grandfather was born in 1719, in the parish of Coubry, or Boubry, in South Uist, one of the Hebrides.[4] He was educated in France at the Scotch College at Douai, and was probably destined for an ecclesiastical career. I know not what were his tastes, or wishes, but I do

---

3. He had just lost his third wife, mother of the son to whom these recollections are addressed. She was Mademoiselle de Bourgoing, and had previously married her cousin, Baron de Bourgoing. She had two children by the Marshal: this son, Alexander, afterwards Duke of Tarentum, and a daughter who died in infancy.—Translator.

4. I learn from Mr. John Macdonald, of Glenaladale, whose father accompanied the Duke on his journey to the Hebrides, that the district in which the Marshal's father was born was that of Houghbeag. See also note on next page.—Translator.

know that, after completing a brilliant course of study, he returned to the place of his birth. Thence he was summoned by Prince Charles [Edward] Stuart, styled the Pretender.

Throughout the disastrous expedition of 1745 my father attached himself to the good and bad fortune of the Prince, like a loyal Scotsman. The cup of their common misfortunes, and of so many others besides, was filled by the loss of the Battle of Culloden, near Inverness, in 1746. The details of this disastrous event are written in history, and it would be superfluous to repeat them here; but what are less known are the results that this unhappy affair had upon the life of the Prince, who was compelled for several months to seek shelter in caves and barns, in order to save his head, upon which a price had been set. He wandered from island to island, guided by my father, until at last a heroine, Flora Macdonald, of the Isle of Skye, succeeded in baffling their pursuers, and exposed herself in order to assist their flight on board a French man-of-war. Miraculously saved, they reached France. (See note below). Your grandfather was put into Ogilvy's Scotch regiment, and the Prince never gave him another thought!

> *Note:*—'Marshal Macdonald used to remit money to his relatives in Uist, and one of his cousins visited him in France at his request. In 1825 the Marshal visited Great Britain, and was everywhere received with distinguished honour, both by the Government and people. The cordiality of his reception in London was only equalled by that of his reception in Edinburgh and Inverness. He visited the field of Culloden, and expressed strong disapprobation at the Highlanders for engaging the Royal troops in such a place.
>
> 'Marshal Macdonald visited the Western Isles in a revenue cruiser placed at his disposal by Government, accompanied by Mr. Ranald Macdonald, Writer to the Signet in Edinburgh, who was a son of Macdonald of Boisdale, a scion of the Macdonalds of Clanranald.
>
> 'The Marshal walked from the ford at Lochdar to Houghbeag, a distance of ten miles. On coming in sight of the river he exclaimed:
>
> '"That is the river Hough! I know it from my father's description! Many a salmon has he caught there!"
>
> 'He sent for all his relations in the neighbourhood. When his blind old uncle was brought to him, he embraced him affec-

tionately, saying:
'"You dear old man, how like you are to my own father!"
'He addressed his relations in French and broken Gaelic, they answering him in Gaelic, for none of them could speak any English. He distributed sums of money, varying in value among them, giving to some £20, and to others larger amounts or fixed annuities. He took earth from the floor of the house where his father was born, and potatoes from the garden, and these he placed in a bag and carried home with him to France. He planted the potatoes in his garden, and gave orders that the earth should be placed in his coffin after his death.
'From Houghbeag he crossed the hills to Glen Corrodail to visit the cave in which Prince Charlie and a few faithful followers lived for six weeks after Culloden. It is a walk of about two hours over very rough roads; but the Marshal, then about sixty years of age, travelled the mountains with ease.
'From Corrodail he re-embarked on board the cruiser that had brought him to the island. Many persons are still living who saw the Marshal when in Uist. They all describe him as a man of about the middle height, well built and muscular, but not stout. They say that he resembled in form, features, and voice, his kinsfolk in Uist, but in complexion they differed, he being dark and sallow, and they fair and ruddy.
'Flora Macdonald and Neill MacEachann were remotely, but very remotely, connected, through the Clanranalds. Flora was nearly related to the Clanranalds, and by the Lady Clanranald of the day she was much beloved and admired, as indeed she was by all who knew her. She was not born, as many people, even natives of Skye, suppose, in the island of Skye, but in the island of South Uist, on the farm of Mitton. Some six miles farther north is Houghbeag, where Neill MacEachann, father of the Marshal, was born.'—Note by Mr. Alexander Carmichael, of Edinburgh.

After the peace of 1763, nearly all the foreign regiments were disbanded. Among them was Ogilvy's, and your grandfather, proscribed in his own country, and abandoned in this one, was reduced to live upon the modest pension of three hundred *livres* (about £30). Almost immediately afterwards he made what, in military parlance, is called a 'garrison marriage'; that is to say, he wedded a girl without any fortune. Your grandfather had settled himself at Sedan, where I was born [November 17, 1765], when he was invited by Lord Nairn, proscribed like himself, to the little town of Sancerre [near Bourges]. The cheapness of living, and probably of the wine, which is good, had determined these gentlemen to settle there; other Scotsmen had preceded them.

In this retreat, with his friends and his books, he consoled himself for the cruelty of fortune. He was very studious, well versed in the Greek and Latin tongues, which he spoke easily, as well as French, English, and Gaelic, his native language. He never saw his country again, although in 1784 an Act or Amnesty was passed by the English Parliament, permitting fugitives to return. My father died at Sancerre in 1788, in all probability from the effects of a fall he had had some years previously, and which had dislocated his hip, which had been badly set by an inexperienced surgeon. I was at that time quartered at Calais. One of his compatriots, Mr. MacNab, undertook to represent me. He collected all his books and papers, with the intention of restoring them to me. Among them I should certainly have found many details about my family, and about the events of which your grandfather had been both witness and victim; but MacNab, at that time corporal in the Bodyguard, was, like so many others, seized during the Revolution, arrested and imprisoned. His papers and mine were carried off, and are lost forever. I have these unlucky details from himself.

I have little information about your paternal grandmother. I only know she was of good family. She was born at St. Omer, but as her father, a soldier by profession, was a stranger in the town, nobody remembered her, and I could obtain no information when I caused inquiries to be made.

Unfortunately, while I was moving from garrison to garrison, your grandfather and grandmother had, two or three years before the death of the former, differences of so serious a nature that they voluntarily separated. I fancy that your grandmother, perhaps embittered by trouble, had some slight affection of the mind, but it was scarcely noticeable, and certainly not so apparent to others as to me. She retired to Fontainebleau, where she ended her days twenty-five or twenty-six years ago. Your grandfather was very gentle, she was quick-tempered; she was a great talker, he was naturally silent. I have heard him, however, talk very well; his memory was well stored, full of anecdote, and he was a good musician, playing the violin; he was much esteemed and sought after by the society of that time.

They had four children, two boys and two girls; two died at an early age, my sister and I have survived. Your aunt was educated in a convent at Rouen, and married a Swiss doctor at Soleure, who afterwards gave up the 'fruitless science of Galen,' became a soldier, and was killed, holding the rank of Lieutenant-Colonel, at the passage of the Beresina, in the fatal expedition of 1812. They left three girls and a boy, who is now in India, in command of a company of *Sepoys* at Pondicherry, (at time of first publication). One of the daughters is a nun; the eldest married Major-General the Viscount de Saint-Mars, and the second Colonel de Couëssin, attached to my staff. They are all living, (as at time of first publication), and have children. Your aunt, after the death of her husband, Colonel Weltner, settled at Beaulieu, near me, and died there two years ago, (as at time of first publication).

My early studies had been somewhat neglected at Sancerre. I was sent to Paris to a school kept by Chevalier Pawlet (*sic*). His foreign name caused the proscription of the tutor, and his establishment was suppressed at the beginning of the Revolution. I had profited fairly well by his instruction. Before going thither, I had been destined for the Church, in the hope of obtaining a canonry at Cambrai. But my military tastes were developed by my studies and surroundings, and especially by Homer, the reading of which set my brain on fire. I thought myself an Achilles!

They wished to make an engineer of me, and I was encouraged to study mathematics. Two comrades and I had to undergo an examination; we failed, and were sent back for another year; but in the interval powerful patrons, Prince Ferdinand de Rohan, Archbishop of Cambrai, Countess d'Albestrop, Lady Mary and Lady Lucy Stuart, obtained for me, in 1785, a lieutenancy in Maillebois' regiment, then serving the Dutch.

The seven United Provinces formed at that time a republican federation, which on more than one occasion had fought successfully against states much stronger than herself. This time she had to face her neighbour, the Emperor of Austria, Sovereign of the Netherlands, who had quarrelled with her on behalf of Antwerp and Ghent, for the free navigation of the Scheldt. The Dutch, trusting in the defences which gave them safety—their good fleet, their frontiers surrounded by rivers, and their bristling fortresses—maintained only a small standing army but threatened as they were at this moment, they were seeking everywhere for generals, officers, and men.

On hearing of my appointment, and the object for which the regiment was being raised, I was nearly beside myself with pleasure. My head was already crammed with books upon the art of war, with histories of sieges, campaigns, combats and battles. I was already planning out various schemes of attack and defence, and flattered myself that I should reap at least a colonelcy in this campaign, and that in the next I should become a rival to the great Turenne. Such were my ideas when I first put on my uniform at the beginning of 1785, and started with a number of other officers for our corps at Nimeguen, Arnheim, and Bois-le-Duc.

You will easily conceive with what ardour I commenced the work of training my men. I had learnt the rudiments at Chevalier Pawlet's school, which was organized upon the lines of military schools, enjoying some of their prerogatives, notably the privilege of receiving officers' commissions, without counting those granted to such as passed from there into the special colleges for the artillery and engineers.

You will experience, I hope, my son, the real joy that is caused by a first uniform and a first commission; and although I have reached the highest rank, I assure you, in perfect sincerity, that my colonelcy was the crowning point to me.

My new brother officers and I thought of nothing but how soon we could take the field against the Austrians. All our conversations turned upon this subject, so full for us of charm and attraction, whereon we each founded his ambition, his promotion, and his fortune, when we learned with deep chagrin that peace had been concluded, and that our regiment would be disbanded. The Dutch thus justified the sarcasm of Frederick the Great, who on one occasion inquired of their ambassador how matters were going with them.

'Very well,' was the answer. 'We shall hold our own against the Emperor.'

'Nonsense!' replied the King. 'I know exactly what will happen: you will give a *tip* (*pourboire*) 'to his Imperial Majesty, and there will be an end of the matter.'

This opinion, though expressed in jest, was found to be borne out completely when the treaty was published.

In the statute ordering the regiment to be raised of which the Count de Maillebois was colonel (as well as commander-in-chief of the Dutch forces), a *proviso* had been inserted that, in case of peace and consequent disbandment, the officers should receive as pension half their pay, on condition of spending it in the country, or a sum down, equivalent to four years of the said pension, with permission to leave the country at their pleasure. It was not a very large sum, for the Dutch, a frugal people, had only eight months in their financial year, each month containing six weeks.

After taking the advice of my father and patrons, I returned to France. They then put their heads together to save me from living in idleness at Sancerre, where I was wearing out my uniform by showing it off at Mass and vespers on Sundays, and to the country people on market days. Everyone made way for me, and this could not fail to increase my stock of vanity.

It was very difficult to be reinstated in a regiment in the service of France. Government seems to have viewed with displeasure the custom prevalent among our officers, of leaving their rank in their .own army for a superior rank in the Legion. The Austrian minister had made representations, and, in order to give no justification for the suspicion of connivance, the French Minister refused to reinstate those who had willingly abandoned their ranks; *à fortiori* he would refuse to give even a sub-lieutenant's commission to the others. They were, however, permitted to begin their career as gentlemen-cadets, according to the established rules.

These obstacles were pointed out to me, together with the necessity of coming to a decision. I did not hesitate. The lazy life of Sancerre wearied me. I had had a taste of life in garrison; the work, exercises, parades, inspections, manoeuvres, which bored so many others, especially the old officers who had fought in America, were attractive to me. Count Arthur Dillon, who fell a victim to the Revolution, after having served it loyally, offered me a cadetship in the regiment that bore his name, of which he was proprietary Colonel. I put on the red coat; a white *aiglet*, distinctive mark of the gentlemen-cadets, took the place of my lieutenant's epaulettes. I am bound to admit that it was not without a heavy heart that I took this courageous resolution, nor without a lively feeling of grief, which, (however, diminished upon my hearing that I should soon be made an officer. That was a crumb of comfort, certainly, but it seems to me a very long way off, seeing that up to the rank of captain promotion only went by seniority, that there were several cadets above me, and that the list of officers was very long. Some of these were there as substitutes, etc. Modifications have now been introduced into the laws governing promotion, more favourable to talent, and especially to patronage.

I thus spent several years continuing my studies, and always keenly interested in my profession. I had chosen my friends well; they also were fond of work. They were good musicians and draughtsmen. I have always regretted that I could do no more than scrape my fiddle. I had begun too late, and my masters, independently of their bad method, knew little more about it than I did. My other amusements were fencing, dancing, and the theatre. My taste for music and good acting had helped me to store my memory; it became stronger while I was employed in Italy. It is an advantage to a young officer to be able to play an instrument; the best society is always open to him, especially if to his talent he joins good breeding and education, as well as good behaviour.

The Revolution broke out; every officer's brain was in a ferment; no one dreamed of anything save war and promotion. The camp of St. Omer, where I was with my regiment, was able, by means of meetings and conventions, to free itself from the severe and humiliating discipline to which the council of war wished to subject all regiments and officers.

At the period when the officers obtained their long leave, I profited by mine, at the end of 1790, to go to my sister at Andrézy, and to St. Germain. I was at that time a lieutenant, a little bit of a musician, and, though I could only scrape my violin, I was presented in several houses, and voted passable.

A young and pretty Creole[5] reciprocated the attentions I paid her. I offered her my hand, which was accepted; her mother gave her approval, but the father's consent was yet to be obtained. He was a wily fox, who had amassed a fortune in the West Indies, and was more than economical, not to say stingy. The only fortune I could offer was my youth and my military prospects; he wanted something more solid. He politely refused my proposal, but I would not take 'No' for an answer. We set Colonel Beurnonville, afterwards a Marshal of France, to work; he was well acquainted with the family, and had the ear of the father, who was his wife's uncle. The latter, who was afraid of the colonel, though he had declined my offer, thought fit to make inquiries among the patrons already named, and whom I had mentioned to him. At last, worried and tormented, he finished by giving his consent to our union, which was celebrated on the 5th of May, 1791. From that time to the day of his death he was very kind to me; he became very fond of me, and I honestly reciprocated his affection.

---

5. Mademoiselle Jacob, by whom he had two daughters, the Duchesse de Massa and the Comtesse de Perregaux. See Michaud, *Biographic Universelle*, art. *Macdonald.*—Translator.

CHAPTER 2

First Campaign

The Revolution made giant strides; war seemed imminent, and I was recalled to my regiment. Hostilities broke out at the beginning of 1792. Beurnonville received a command, and took me as his *aide-de-camp*.

There had been considerable emigration among the officers of the army, and particularly among those of my regiment. Efforts were made to induce me to go, too; but I was married, and very much attached to my wife, who was near her confinement. These were surely good reasons! Besides, I cared nothing about politics.

The campaign opened, and its first start was not fortunate; there was no feelings of camaraderie and a great deal of insubordination. General Dumouriez came to take command of the northern frontier; his headquarters were at the camp at Maulde, then under, the orders of General Beurnonville. He gave me several commissions, which I carried out satisfactorily, and wished to keep me near him, with the rank of Captain. Beurnonville, seeing that it was for my interest, strongly urged me to accept. Gratitude and friendship compelled me to refuse, and I resisted, but ended by submitting to reiterated pressure, the more readily that he and I should still continue in the same *corps d'armée*.

I will enter here into no details of the events of the war, even so far as they concerned me personally; they have passed into the domain of history, and to do so I should have to write memoirs, which is not at all my intention. Perhaps I will collect them some day, if I can find time and my papers; but now I have too much to do, and my career has been too full to admit of my undertaking such a lengthy task.

Some months later, General Dumouriez received orders to join the Army of the Ardennes. He took up his quarters at Grandpré, then at St. Menehould, called VALMY, or *Camp de la Lune*. The Prussians attacked him there; he resisted; the enemy retired.[1] I was not forgotten amid the numerous promotions that took place. I was made lieutenant-colonel, now called *chef de bataillon*. General Dumouriez left orders with Beurnonville, who was lieutenant-general, to lead a body to the assistance of Lille, and went himself to Paris to devise the ulterior plan of action. I followed him thither.

After a short stay, we rejoined the army assembled under the ramparts of Valenciennes. The plan decided upon in Paris was to invade Belgium. For the execution of this enterprise the commander-in-chief caused reconnaissances to be made all along the frontier, and his *aides-de camp* were sent to the principal points of attack, in order to report upon the strength of the troops opposed to him. He was to decide from these reports where to concentrate his troops and commence the main attack. He sent me to Lille. I accompanied the reconnoitring party sent to Tournai, and commanded by General Lamarlière.

Our men were now to meet an enemy for the first time face to face, upon his own ground. We were not to provoke a pitched battle; our chief object was to gauge the strength of the enemy by the resistance opposed to us. We were very superior to them, besides which a strong reserve, following us at a distance, had orders to support our movements, or to cover us in case of a repulse. This was the last part played by this troop, commanded by Lieutenant-General la Bourdonnaie in person; he bore the title of general-commanding, but was subordinate to Dumouriez, who was a 'General of the Army' (*General d'armée*), a rank corresponding to that of Marshal, which title had been abolished, though such as already bore it were allowed to keep it.

At the first shot, our reconnoitring party broke and fled to Lille, carrying with them the panic that had seized them. However, the enemy did not deploy more than twelve hundred men of all arms and two pieces of cannon, and I am confident that they had no more at that particular spot. Vainly did we try to stop our runaways; but the enemy did not advance much, and the reserve, on being brought up, made a good stand.

I reported the event, which was absolutely the second Pas de Baisieux on the frontier.[2] The generals were kind enough to quote the

---

1. Had the Marshal, who wrote very rapidly and never re-read what he had written, looked over this brief but pithy passage, he would doubtless have found more to say concerning the Argonne campaign.
2. An allusion to the rout of April 29, 1792, after which the fugitives, hurrying from Baisieux to Lille, massacred their general, Theobald Dillon.

efforts I had made to carry out the mission with which I was charged, as well as my demeanour during the skirmish, and, in truth, I was able to render some services upon this occasion. The receipt of complete intelligence satisfied us that the enemy's forces, commanded by Duke Albert of Saxe Teschen, were drawn up before us in an entrenched camp upon the heights of Mons and Berlaimont, covering the latter town, and General Dumouriez resolved upon giving battle.

After all our preparations were made, the army advanced and took up a position parallel to that of the entrenched camp. Orders were given along the lines for a general attack at noon on the following day. Every watch was set by that of the general in command. Feints were to be made upon the principal points on the frontier, and at the same time. It was somewhat late for a battle, but the plan had been regulated by the march of General d'Harville, who was bringing 10,000 men from the camp at Maubeuge, and was to turn Duke Albert's left wing.

A discharge from the twelve-pounder battery announced the hour of noon. The army advanced upon the enemy, and opened the attack with plenty of determination.[3] The firing became very brisk, and the resistance obstinate. Obstacles such as entrenchments, *epaulments*, *abattis*, and *chevaux de frise*, favoured the defence; they were troublesome, but not insurmountable. However, our lines began to reel, and even to fall back. Dumouriez was at hand with a remedy; but General d'Harville, who was to support our right and turn the enemy's left, did not arrive, notwithstanding repeated orders to him to hasten his march. Our left did not advance; the general went to discover the reason, and recognised the difficulty of forcing the Austrians' right. Our advanced guard, commanded by Beurnonville, on the right of the line, had just been repulsed; a second charge had produced no better result. Our centre was stationary, and losing many men. The Duc de Chartres, who was commanding it, received orders to try to pierce that of the enemy, or so to fix their attention as to prevent them from withdrawing any men, while, with a few fresh troops, whom he would himself command, Dumouriez would make another effort on his right.

I had just informed him that the head of General d'Harville's column had appeared at last, but that he would require some hours and a little rest before he could execute the movement required of him, in order to turn the enemy's left from the formidable position it oc-

---
3. Battle of Jemmappes, November 6, 1792.

cupied. Dumouriez left me with the Duc de Chartres, who desired me to bring him a regiment of dragoons left in reserve. While this regiment was coming up, we saw Dumouriez and Beurnonville rush forward at the head of the advanced guard, and, after a feeble resistance on the part of the Austrians, we saw our men crowning the heights. This rapid and decisive attack, coupled with the advance of D'Harville on our extreme right, appeared to decide the enemy to retreat, as they did not wish to expose themselves to having the road to Brussels closed against them, an operation which was clearly indicated by the movement of this body. The Duc de Chartres, as soon as he perceived the progress and success of the advanced guard, ordered his troops to charge. The positions so long defended were overcome, and I myself led the regiment of dragoons at a gallop to the heights, where they still found some work to do; but we only entered Mons the next day, after the Austrians had evacuated it.

During the battle, Beurnonville received orders summoning him to take command of the Army of the Moselle. Dumouriez, who had appointed him lieutenant-general, and hoped to keep him with his army, was displeased at this arrangement, and I was very vexed at it. However, there was nothing for it but to obey, and Beurnonville took leave of us, promising not to forget me.

The army continued its march, skirmishing as it went, and took up winter quarters on the Meuse and the Roër, instead of pushing on to the Rhine. Dumouriez started for Paris, permitting me to accompany him. He only remained there long enough to plan the invasion of Holland, and prolonged my leave.

While Dumouriez was subduing the fortresses on the Dutch frontier, the army left on the Roër and Meuse was surprised in its cantonments, and sought to rally on the hitherward side of Liège. Dumouriez received orders to hasten there. All officers on leave were ordered to join, and I was preparing for my departure, when I learned that Beurnonville had arrived in Paris, and had been appointed War Minister. I went to see and take my leave of him; but he retained me, and a few days later presented me with an appointment as colonel of the Picardy regiment. Two important promotions in six months surely ought to have satisfied the most boundless ambition! I had no right to expect such a rapid rise, and was consequently the proudest and happiest man in the world. I could only hope, supposing that there had been any favouritism or any friendship on the part of Beurnonville, that the regiment I was about to command would not find me unworthy of such a rank, especially as it was one of those that I had supported during our reconnoitring expedition near Tournai.

We soon had news of the loss of the Battle of Neerwinde, and of Dumouriez's retreat. His enemies declared that treason had been at work; from that moment he was lost, and the important services he had rendered in Champagne, Flanders, and Belgium were forgotten. Such is the fate of men who serve revolutions! Mine only hung by a thread.

Scarcely had I crossed our frontier when I met bands of fugitives returning to France, and screaming national songs at the top of their voices. I reached Brussels, where I found the staff not yet recovered from the confusion consequent upon the loss of the battle. No one knew whither the troops had betaken themselves, especially the Picardy regiment. Dumouriez was covering the army, or what remained of it, with the rear-guard, which was on its way back from Louvain, so I waited for him. Some hours later I was told that an officer had come from my regiment for orders; I sent it into temporary quarters in the neighbourhood of Tournai.

I saw Dumouriez on his arrival. He reproached me, as he had previously done Beurnonville, with having abandoned him. I answered that the friendship of the latter for me had caused him to reward and encourage some small efforts on my part, and that no doubt, under more fortunate circumstances, he (Dumouriez) would have obtained an appointment for me. I added that I was not abandoning him, as my regiment formed a part of his army. This reasoning soothed him. He talked over our unlucky position with me, begging me to hasten to my post, and desiring me to do my utmost to keep my regiment together, and to preserve it from the bad influences caused by the disorder into which everything had been thrown. I embraced him, and departed; each of us had tears in his eyes. Little did we think that this was our last farewell.

I reached my quarters, and made myself known, to the indignation of a lieutenant-colonel, who exclaimed to all who would listen to him that the most outrageous injustice had been done him by the appointment of a superior officer. He asked for leave, which I granted him, and he never reappeared.

As our retrograde movement continued, we did not stop till we were once more on our own territory. General Miaczinski's brigade, to which I belonged, came to Orchies. I was struck by the half-heartedness of the enemy, who never attacked us.

A few days later, while at dinner, a corporal of my regiment came to tell me that the War Minister was changing horses at the posthouse, and desired to see me immediately. Surprised at this unexpected arrival, I went to him. After embracing me, he presented me to four commissioners from the Convention, who questioned me as to our retreat. I was unable to give them much information, as I had only arrived a few days previously, a statement which was confirmed by the minister. They were in a hurry to go on and fulfil their mission, the object of which was not disclosed to me. I questioned Beurnonville, but he also was discreet; he recommended me, however, to hold my regiment in readiness, as he would review it on his return from the headquarters at Boues de St. Amand.

Next morning Miaczinski sent for me. I found him in great spirits. His room was full of officers, one of whom was reading aloud to the General a despatch that had just arrived. I gathered simply that the War Minister and the commissioners had been seized and taken to Tournai. Miaczinski ordered me to have my regiment under arms, adding that he would shortly send me further instructions. In a few minutes an *aide-de-camp* brought me verbal instructions to take command of the camp, to set the troops in motion, and march upon Lille, whither the general would precede me. I sent forward my quartermasters,[4] and we followed. A halt being necessary, I stopped at Pont-à-Marcq. Fresh orders from the general desired me to hasten my advance, and we started again. On the road, some of my officers informed me of what had happened at St. Amand; our general had made no secret of it, and it had gradually leaked out to the regiment. They tried to discover what I thought; my answer was simply that we had to obey orders without troubling ourselves about future events.

The head of the column had just reached the Faubourg des Malades (a suburb of Lille), when I received a note from Miaczinski ordering me to stop wherever this note reached me, to provide refreshment for my men, and not to leave them. They had just reached the glacis of the fortress. I ordered them to face about, according to the regulations, and pile their arms. No victuals! I sent to Lille for some. The gates and barriers were shut, and the drawbridges raised. This circumstance led me to the conclusion that something very unusual was taking place in the town, seeing that the gates of a fortified town are not shut, except for form's sake, on the arrival of a fresh garrison. The proximity of the enemy could not account for it, for we on the

---

4. Officers charged with the duty of furnishing provisions and lodgings.

glacis were a goodly number of defenders. While I was discussing this strange reception with some of my officers, I was informed that a municipal official wished to see me. I went to him, and found him in considerable agitation. He told me that the council, assembled at the town-hall, wished to see me. I answered by showing him the note from the general, in which I was ordered not to leave my troops; that I presumed that the object of this municipal invitation was to concert measures for food and quarters; that the general was there as well as my quartermasters; that they should address themselves to him; that I only held the command in his absence; that I would send a captain in my place, who would bring me back his orders.

Our disasters, which extended the whole length of our frontiers, and especially in the north, were all laid at the door of the leaders, and the policy of the day was rather to sacrifice them than to accuse the number of cowards who had brought them into such straits. That is why Dumouriez was declared a traitor to his country. A decree of accusation had just been issued against him. The four commissioners whom I have mentioned were sent to carry it out at headquarters, and to bring Dumouriez to the bar of the Convention. Beurnonville was ordered to reorganize the army, of which he was to take command. Dumouriez, however, had been warned, and had taken such measures that, after an excited discussion with these gentlemen, he had caused them to be arrested and carried to Tournai. Here they were handed over to the enemy, with whom he had made a secret treaty whereby he was to be supported in his march upon Paris to upset the Convention.

After this *coup d'état*, trusting too implicitly upon the affection of his army, he divided it into several columns, which were to march upon the capital from different quarters, and, wishing at the same time to secure the northern strongholds, he ordered Miaczinski to take possession of them. The latter, who had a cause of complaint against the commissioners, who had treated him very abruptly at Orchies on the preceding evening, because a detachment that was to escort them was not ready at the moment they wished to start, was enchanted at the prospect of having his revenge. He imparted his orders and all that had happened to those who were about him, and one of these, St. Georges, his friend, accompanied by the courier who had brought Dumouriez's orders to Miaczinski, started immediately for Lille and warned the authorities of the danger threatening their town, and all the others in the department. Such were the reasons that had decided them to shut their gates. Poor Miaczinski, urged by a double desire to avenge himself and to lose no time in executing his orders, hastened thither, and thus rushed blindly on his ruin. He was to have had an interview with the general officer in command of the place, but the latter, warned by the information of St. Georges, hastened to join the civil authorities, who promptly took all the measures rendered necessary by the difficult circumstances in which they were placed.

While awaiting the return of the captain whom I had despatched into the town, I learned the details of all that had happened at St. Amand, and the orders that had been given in consequence. My officer returned without any instructions for me. Night was coming on. The men, who had heard something of what was going on, put various interpretations upon the news, but I paid no heed to them. I was, however, in the utmost anxiety as to my position and that of my men, who were loudly complaining that they had a worse reception from their fellow-countrymen than they would have had from foreigners. They were ravenously hungry. This state of affairs could only end in a crisis, when they cried to us from the walls that the troops were to march to the Faubourg de la Madeleine, where we should find rations, tents, victuals, etc.; but that we must go round the glacis, as the gates were not allowed to be opened.

The men accordingly started, marching in a disorderly manner, which I could see from some distance off, but for which I could not account, until I came close up to them, when I discovered the reason. It was impossible to bring this multitude into order, so I contented myself with accompanying them. On reaching the gate of the Faubourg de Fives, we found the barrier of the glacis closed. We summoned them to open it, but our demand was refused. A voice from within the gate added that the colonel of the Picardy regiment was to come at once to the assembled council. My grenadiers mutinied, and replied in the negative, adding that if their colonel went they would go too. This was refused. I had nothing to reproach myself with. I at once determined upon going alone. The soldiers then raised very alarming cries, declaring, among other things, that these —— had killed their poor *Capet* (Louis XVI.), and so on. They also began to shout, 'Long live the King!' I addressed them with severity, threatening them and pretending that I could recognise individual voices, which frightened them; and I then extracted from them a promise to remain quiet until my return. The barrier was opened for me, but I was not even allowed to take with me a servant to hold my horse.

On passing under the gateway I was surrounded by about thirty men. The officer in charge said to me:

'Colonel, don't be afraid.'

'I have never been afraid of an enemy,' was my answer 'why should I fear Frenchmen?'

I put several questions to him, but could get no intelligence.

I entered the great vestibule of the town-hall. All the authorities were assembled. The meeting was public, and a considerable number of inhabitants were present; profound silence reigned.

The president interrogated me. His first question was as to my Christian name and surname, rank, etc. I answered him.

'Are you in command of the troops on the glacis of the town?'

'Yes, in the absence of General Miaczinski, who must be here.'

I looked round for him, but failed to see him.

'By whose orders have you come?'

'By those of the general I have named.'

'Can you show us his order '

'It was given by word of mouth. We were in camp. The General sent for me as the senior colonel, and ordered me to put my men under arms. I obeyed, and immediately afterwards an *aide-de-camp* came and told me, on behalf of the general, to march my troops forward to this town, whither he would precede me.'

'Did he tell you the reason for this movement?'

'No.'

'What did you think?'

'That, having entered this territory, provision was to be made to safeguard the different places, and that we were intended to defend your town.'

'What do your men say?'

'I cannot conceal from you that they are discontented. The grief caused by their reverses, the privations they have endured during the retreat, their fatigues, needs, devotion, all tended to make them anticipate help from their fellow-citizens; but, instead, they meet only distrust. They are saying very unfitting things, and I have had considerable difficulty in appeasing them. In order to calm them I said that in all probability you desired to concert with me as to the best means of satisfying their pressing wants, and that I would not delay in bringing them good news. Unless such be the case, I cannot answer for any disorders or excesses which they will most certainly commit.'

I called upon the officer who had come with me, and who had

witnessed my efforts to calm the irritation of the men who had put their trust in me. He endorsed all that I had just said, and even went beyond it.

The president, who at first had addressed me very severely, seemed much appeased by my speech, and, when the officer had concluded his report, said to me:

'Colonel, return to your post: keep order among your men. Lead them to the camp of La Madeleine; you will there find provision for all your needs. Orders have been given that nothing should be left unprovided.'

I saluted the assembly and returned to the Faubourg de Fives.

'Well, my friends 'I said to the soldiers on my arrival, 'I knew that it was simply to discuss your needs.'

They all began to cry, 'Long live the Republic!'

Such is the inconstancy of the multitude.

'Forward!' I cried; 'we shall soon find plenty.'

But what was my disappointment and theirs! On reaching the place we found nothing. I sent to the town, and an answer was returned from the ramparts that it was too late that night, but that it should be attended to in the morning. On receiving this answer, I could no longer control my men. They broke away and dispersed, so much so that not a single soldier was left to guard the flag of the regiment, which I myself had to carry to the inn where I lodged.

I passed a wretched night, thinking over all the disorder that might be brought about by such a state of things. Fortunately, there was less of it than might have been expected; but the town authorities were very much to blame—hunger has no ears. Early next morning I caused the assembly to be sounded, and a few hours later I had gathered together nearly all my men. I was again summoned into the town, but this time I went with less anxiety. Fearing a fresh outbreak during my absence, I ordered that the men should remain under arms.

The meeting at the town-hall was less crowded, but I quickly perceived that the feeling was less friendly than it had been the previous night when I left the town. However, I was soon reassured by the advent of my friend Dupont,[5] adjutant-general, an old comrade in the Maillebois regiment, charged by the authorities to settle with me all military details. We decided upon provisional cantonments until all that was necessary for a camp should be distributed.

---

5. It was this General Dupont who afterwards capitulated at Baylen, and became War Minister at the first Restoration.

CHAPTER 3

Macdonald appointed Adjutant-General

Meanwhile, all the movements ordered by Dumouriez had been paralyzed. He himself ran great dangers, and was compelled, to save his head, to throw himself into the arms of the enemy, with whom, according to the admission made by himself in his memoirs, he had been treating secretly.

General Dampierre, who succeeded him, sent General Lamarlière to take command of Lille and of the northern frontier. Immediately upon his arrival someone prejudiced him against the Picardy colonel, whose name he did not even know. He was 'suspected.'[1] The general sent for the colonel, and when I appeared, great was his surprise. He had not forgotten the Pas de Baisieux, where he had noticed me; and without further explanation said to me: 'Return to your post; I will vindicate you.' This magnanimity touched me. He himself became shortly afterwards 'suspected,' and fell a victim, although innocent.

More commissioners came to Lille from the Convention. They were also biased, as General Lamarlière had been, against me. One of them had served as captain in my regiment, and had but recently left it. He was an intimate friend of the lieutenant-colonel who was so vexed when I arrived to take over the command. This man chanced to be in Lille, profiting by the leave I had given him. He also took advantage of his friendship with the commissioner to try to have me removed as a 'suspect,' owing to my having been *aide-de-camp* to Beurnonville and Dumouriez, the former of whom had also become 'suspected' since

---

1. Persons supposed not to be thoroughgoing revolutionists were commonly known as 'suspects.'—Translator.

his arrest.

My conduct underwent severe inquiry. Poor General Lamarlière justified it, adding that I had ceased to be *aide-de-camp* some four or five months previously. As they could not injure me on that score, they proposed to appoint me adjutant-general (now called staff-colonel), a rank corresponding to that which I already held. My good friend Lamarlière spoke to me about it, pointed out the danger of a refusal, and, regarding mere objections as equivalent to consent, announced my acceptance, without my leave, to the commissioners. The deed of appointment was then and there drawn up, for they had plenary powers, and worded in very complimentary terms, based upon my excellent conduct, my patriotism, etc.

Possessed of this document, I went straight to the general, and, while thanking him for his kindness, declared that I could not take advantage of it; that in the eyes of the army it would appear that I was incapable of commanding a regiment; that my susceptibilities were wounded, my honour compromised, and that I would rather be deprived of my command altogether; that he, whose own feelings were of the keenest and most honourable, could, better than anyone else, feel for my position; that I already owed so much to him that I should be glad to increase my debt by another service, and, as I saw that he did not insist, I added:

'Besides, it will be just as much to the interest of the commissioners as to mine to let this affair go no further, seeing that the dullest individual will easily understand that they are acting in private and not public interests' (they had appointed the lieutenant-colonel to succeed me). 'Moreover, this officer is unpopular with the regiment; he is narrow-minded and ill-tempered.'

I ended by saying that, if they thought I should make a good adjutant-general, I considered that I could render more service at the head of a regiment.

'By the way,' I exclaimed, 'why should they not give him the title they have conferred upon me? He wants to be colonel. Well and good, his ambition would be gratified.'

This idea had not occurred to Lamarlière. It seemed to strike him, and he said:

'Give me the letter containing the orders, and your commission. I will take them to the commissioners, and beg them to make the exchange you propose.'

'No, certainly not. I cannot part with them. They are much too flattering, and, besides, they are my justification.'

The commissioners could find no serious objection to the plan proposed by the general. It was adopted, and I was left in peace.

I occupied myself seriously, with ardour and activity, in exercising and drilling my regiment, and in accustoming it to warfare by marches and reconnaissances on the frontier. The enemy occupied the adjacent woods, and I sometimes obtained some little successes in skirmishing. Other corps followed my example, and we thus accustomed our men to see and face the enemy. I forgot to say that my regiment had been divided. I had but one battalion; the second was with the Army of the Moselle, and the commissioners had appointed a colonel to it. All communications ceased between us as soon as our accounts were settled.

Another captain belonging to the regiment, named Béru, who was away on leave, returned to Lille. He was also an intimate friend of the commissioner, and was by him made general-of-brigade, and had command, under Lamarlière, of the troops collected in our camp. Thus I saw one of my subordinates put over my head; however, I made the best of it, and set the example of obedience.

The new general came to the camp with some prejudices against me. A straightforward explanation ensued; he was honest, and we became and remained friends. Shortly afterwards General Lamarlière was deprived of his command, arrested, and taken before the revolutionary tribunal, to which he soon fell a victim. I regretted him deeply. My superior captain succeeded him with the rank of general-of-division, and I was appointed general-of-brigade.[2]

This came upon me like a thunderbolt, as, although for several months past I had performed the duties of the office, I had not had the responsibilities attaching to the rank. I represented that I was youthful and inexperienced, but they would not listen. I had to bow to their decision under pain of being treated as a 'suspect,' and arrested. I resigned myself accordingly. My captain, now general-of-division, who had also made some representations on his own account, was not listened to either, so we agreed to help each other.

I was charged with the command of the frontier from Menin to Armentières, and my quarters were fixed at Lannoy, if I remember rightly, for I have no map at hand.

---

2. Macdonald received this appointment from Houchard, commander-in-chief, and it was confirmed by the representatives with the Army of the North, Levasseur and Bentabole, August 26, 1793.

Partial and simultaneous attacks were made almost daily during August at Linselles, Commines, Blaton, Pont-Rouge, etc., and almost invariably terminated in our favour, which gained me some reputation. These attacks were but the prelude to a real onslaught, which the enemy at last made, advancing with a large body of troops against my lines. Linselles, Commines, and Blaton were all carried at once. The general-of-division and I consulted together. He sent me some reinforcements, raised his camp at La Madeleine, marched upon Linselles and Jupon, Commines and Blaton. Having made all my dispositions, I charged the enemy with the bayonet. They retreated; we pursued eagerly. We regained possession of the two places, and our success was crowned by a large number of killed, wounded, and prisoners. We got ten pieces of cannon, all the ammunition, baggage, etc.

Affairs went otherwise at Linselles, where we lost the same number of guns. My poor general was in despair. He came to see me, and I consoled him as best I could; and before he left me we learned that the enemy had retired from Linselles, which comforted him. We entered Lille in triumph with our captures, so as to dissipate the bad impression caused by the reverses at Linselles. Everyone hailed us as victors; my troops who had taken part were intoxicated, and, to say the truth, I enjoyed the moment as much as anyone, though as modestly as I could. My name appeared honourably mentioned in the official despatches, and this caused me to be regarded as an important person, and roused jealousy and enmity against me.

After these events I daily harassed the enemy, but they had caused so much vexation to the general-of-division that he asked permission to retire, which was granted.

The four Commissioners, to my great bliss, had been recalled or sent elsewhere; they were replaced by another, who, having heard of my success at Commines, and other partial successes, wished for my personal acquaintance. I went to Lille, where he received me with civility, returning my visit a few days later; the outposts thought he was making an inspection. In this interview he expressed to me his desire to be present at a little brush with the enemy. I undertook that he should see one, and promised to let him know the day, hour, and place at which it should occur.

The enemy had replaced by fresh troops those which had been lately worsted, and among the newcomers was a regiment commanded by the Duke of York. Their men swaggered considerably, and gave themselves great airs, and I determined to give them a lesson. Having made my preparations and taken all precautions, I sent word to the commissioner, who arrived in hot haste towards the end of the brush. He saw the rout of the enemy, and a good many prisoners taken, after we had killed and wounded a considerable number. He heard balls and bullets whistle past him, and was beside himself with joy. I asked leave to quote his name in my report; he himself drew one up in which he praised me, and was not too modest about his own share. Finally, when the action was over, and my troops were recalled, he complimented them, gave me the kiss of fraternity, and said aloud that I might count upon him till death. Such protection was by no means to be despised during those horrible times of revolutionary crises, and I thought myself safe from all anxieties, whatever denunciations might be brought against me from any quarter.

I have said that the general-of-division had retired: while awaiting the appointment of his successor, the general in command at Lille held his place. The successor came at last. He was General Souham, who struck up a friendship with me which still endures. Feeling quite easy about the point where I commanded, he turned his attention to the others, and left me a free hand. Security was re-established upon part of the frontier, and I was determined to see that it was respected.

It was then that the good idea occurred of amalgamating all the volunteer battalions, whether of old or new formation, with the regulars, putting two of the former to one of the latter, and I was charged to carry out the operation; but such confusion reigned that nobody seemed to know where these battalions were quartered, because, as it transpired, if they did not like the place where they had been sent, or if it did not suit them, they moved on somewhere else without giving any notice, so that I was ordered to travel through all the neighbouring departments, in order to send in as many battalions as possible to Lille.

While these events were in progress, two new Commissioners Extraordinary arrived, with greatly extended powers. I had been denounced to them; their first act was intended to be my disgrace, arrest, and eventual arraignment before the revolutionary tribunal at Arras, from which no one ever escaped.

I admit that I had made a terrible enemy of a republican and superlatively revolutionary general by laughing at him for cowardice in a skirmish at Menin. He had become the butt and laughing-stock of the troops, even of those who shared his opinions. It was he, moreover, who had denounced and ruined poor General Lamarlière; but Divine justice allowed him to perish eventually by the same means.

Another enemy whom I strongly suspected was a former and very bad comedian, now a general commanding a revolutionary army,[3] who used a seal engraved with a guillotine, but who nevertheless simulated some friendship for me. His functions, however, and his intimacy with the other, left me no doubt, and I received a warning. I despised these men too much to pay the least attention; I was wrong, and too self-confident, for in those terrible times a clear conscience, upright conduct, without blot or blemish, were no guarantees; they only excited jealousy by making others ashamed.

General Souham fought loyally and generously against the accusations, denunciations, etc., and succeeded in staving off the execution of the warrant against me until the return of the commissioners, who were to go to Dunkirk in order to see and hear me. I was in ignorance of all that was being plotted against me, and was quite comfortable in my quarters, when the general sent for me and told me of all that had happened. He then added:

'Look here, you are done for; therefore consider what steps you had better take, and decide quickly, for you are going to be suspended from duty.'

He then advised me to put myself out of the reach of the warrant, the execution of which was only postponed. The commissioners, in granting the delay, had imperatively demanded that my command should be taken from me, and that Lille should be my temporary prison. Therefore it was open to me to go abroad. But if I did, what should I do? What would become of me? I should have found numerous enemies among the emigrants, who never forgave those who refused to join them in 1791.

I then had recourse to the papers given to me when I was appointed adjutant-general, and which I had kept.

'They will be no use to you,' said Souham. 'The very men who signed them are now "suspects" themselves.'

'There is my friend the warlike commissioner,' said I. 'I will go and see him.'

'He!' replied Souham. 'Why, he was present at the discussion. I called upon him to speak up for you, but he was silent.'

'Never mind,' I answered; 'maybe he was intimidated by the presence of his colleagues and superiors. I should like to try him, and

---

3. It was not the revolutionary army of Ronsin and Rossignol, which was specially attached to the northern district.

perhaps inspire him with a little pluck, if he wants it.'

'Go and try,' was the answer, 'and then come back to me.'

I departed in search of my friend.

'Look here! you know that I have fallen into disgrace, and I have come to ask your help. I thought that my conduct and services would save me, but I learn that damaging suspicions have been sown broadcast by enemies who remain in shadow, concealed like those whom we are fighting every day.'

'Indeed!' he replied. 'Do you wish me to speak quite openly to you? I tell you you are not a republican, and I neither can nor will mix myself up with you.'

'But,' I answered, 'I have not changed, as far as I know, since the day when we met on the frontier at the skirmish at Commines; and on that occasion you assured me publicly——'

'I remember what you mean,' he said roughly, interrupting me; 'but times are changed,' and thereupon he turned on his heel.

I returned directly to Souham and related this conversation to him. He implored me to take some steps for my safety.

'They are already taken,' I said. 'I will be, if necessary, one of the thousand victims sacrificed daily. I shall remain.'

'But have you thought it over carefully and weighed all the consequences?'

'Yes.'

I was right in acting as I did. The Commissioners Extraordinary were recalled to Paris from Dunkirk, and I was sent back to my post and forgotten.

I continued to maintain respect for the frontier under my command, which was considerably extended. In it was included all the territory between Armentières and the sea, and my headquarters were moved to Cassel. Although I was only general-of-brigade, I had eleven of the same rank under my control, and about forty thousand men scattered over this long frontier-line, which vastly increased my responsibility.

I had made representations with a view to being relieved, for, notwithstanding this force, scattered as it was, we were weak everywhere. A promise had been given me that I should be replaced by the first general-of-division who should arrive, and I experienced great satisfaction when he was at length announced to me. I was to have returned to my former quarters, but my destination was altered, and this change of plans was coloured by a representation as to the necessity of retrieving some checks that one of my comrades had received. As a matter of fact, this comrade had started in his military career with the rank of general, and his troops had no confidence in him. I took his place, and my command extended from Menin to Tournai.

About this time serious thoughts arose as to the advisability of assembling the whole army and taking the offensive. For this purpose a new commander-in-chief[4] came down, accompanied by two Commissioners Extraordinary. A decree had just been published ordering all 'nobles' to move thirty leagues from the frontiers, to quit the army and Paris. Under these circumstances I ought to have retired. I had furnished the headquarters staff with all the information in my possession upon the frontier, the enemy, their strength, positions, weapons, etc. My services and conduct had also been mentioned with praise, and the commander-in-chief begged the commissioners to retain me, and exempt me from this measure. They desired me to come to them, and informed me that, by virtue of their plenary powers, they required my services. I answered that I wished nothing better, and that they might count upon my zeal and my efforts, but that they should give me a written commission. I added that, should we have the misfortune to meet with reverses, I should assuredly be accused of treachery, and of having remained with the army in order to secure its defeat, notwithstanding the decree of expulsion. Despite my arguments, they refused to satisfy me, whereupon I said:

'Very well, then. I shall send in my resignation.'

'If you leave the army, we will have you arrested and brought to trial.'

I had no choice but to submit, so, I remained where I was, in spite of the twofold odds against me.

Success alone could ensure my position and save me. After various ups and downs, Victory at length declared herself for us. I took the most important share in the engagements at Lannoy, Roubaix, Tourcoing; at the Battle of Hooglède, where I was alone in command;[5] at the capture of Ypres, Menin, Courtrai, Ostend, Ghent; at the passage of the Scheldt, and of the canal at Mechlin; then at the taking of Antwerp; at the Battles of Turnhout and Boxtel; at the capture of Bois-le-Duc, which the Dutch did me the honour of attributing to me because I had been in their service and garrisoned there, though

---

4. General Pichegru.
5. At the Battle of Hooglède, fought on the 26 *Prairial*, year iii. (June 13, 1794), Macdonald commanded the centre.

in truth I did nothing but cover the besiegers; and finally at the passage of the Meuse and the taking of Nimeguen.

The Waal stopped us. We took up quarters for the winter, which promised to be very severe. Mine were temporarily at Kronenburg. While there I received, most unexpectedly, and, above all, without wishing for or desiring it, my commission as general-of-division,[6] and my quarters were shifted to Nimeguen.

---

6. 8 *Frimaire*, year iii. (November 28, 1794).

CHAPTER 4

Ordered to Walcheren

Pichegru, the new commander-in-chief, being ill, had retired to Brussels, and the command was meanwhile made over to Moreau, the senior general-of-division; the latter's division was added to mine, which extended my command from Fort St. André to Urdingen, where I joined the left of the Army of the Sambre and Meuse, now in position on the Rhine. We took advantage of this interruption of operations to revictual our troops and reorganize them, and to train and discipline our recruits.

We had no means, no possibility of crossing the Waal, a considerable river, whose right bank was defended by fortified dykes. The forts of Knodsenburg, opposite Nimeguen, and Kekerdam, opposite Kronenburg, were well armed. We constantly exchanged shots along the entire line; from one point of view this meant a considerable waste of ammunition from another, however, it gave us a valuable chance of familiarizing our new recruits with the fire of the enemy.

The frost came to our assistance. I had the ice sounded two or three times a day. As regards provisions we were unfortunately situated; our communications with our stores at Antwerp and Bois-le-Duc were cut off, the bridge had been destroyed, and the country between the Meuse and the Waal was exhausted, while we could only get very slender resources from our right towards Cleves. I myself was reduced to regimental bread and cheese, and that only irregularly. The Nimeguen shopkeepers had closed their doors, as we could only offer them *assignats*,[1] which they would not accept. We were compelled, therefore, to leave our present quarters and cross the river in search of plenty.

---

1. Paper-money.—Translator.

All my preparations for crossing the river were made, and instructions given to start at the first signal. The ice was thickening, and we observed that the enemy were making ready to retire, as we imagined, when I suddenly received intelligence that they had evacuated Thiel, opposite Fort St. André. I saw with my own eyes a cannon being removed from the right bank. Never doubting that a retreat had been determined upon, the Central in command at that point received orders to cross the river, now sufficiently frozen, and to follow the enemy, who had taken the direction of Arnheim. I signalled to the rest of the troops that they were to attempt the passage at the points indicated. All the columns moved forward simultaneously at break of day, and crossed the river, almost without resistance, somewhat above and below Nimeguen. The stream had not frozen in the middle of the town. As soon as I could distinguish through the fog the head of the first column nearing the fort by the dyke, I caused several skiffs that I had previously prepared to be launched, and crossed to the other side with two companies of grenadiers'. The fort had just been evacuated. I ordered my men to pursue slowly, so as to give time for all our columns to come up with us, and for the cannon to pass. That was the difficulty. The small ordnance was brought up without trouble, then the larger, and finally the howitzers.

During this operation we heard a violent explosion, which made the very ground tremble. It was, as I imagined, the enemy blowing up their magazines and setting their camp on fire. Fearing lest this terrible explosion might astonish the troops, I sent the generals, who had come to take my orders, to their posts, desiring them to explain this event, which signified the absolute retreat of the enemy, and to watch our right, while I took upon myself the charge of the centre.

They arrived just in time, for a hot and well-sustained fire had broken out. My troops were engaged and attacked by a considerable force. The right division had only succeeded in putting one regiment across, and was repulsed on the left bank of the river; but the general who had provisional command of this division arrived with two other brigades, rallied the first, and finally, after a severe struggle, broke the enemy's ranks. The intermediate division, which was mine, had left its place, and so had the centre, where I was; we were without news from the left. I advanced my lines as far as the Linge, the point which I had named in my orders as that at which we were to concentrate.

This day brought about two important results: first, it facilitated the invasion of Holland by separating her cause from that of her allies, who were forced to evacuate the country; secondly, it put into our hands at least a hundred pieces of cannon, with which the dykes and fort of Knodsenburg, which served us as a *tête-de-pont*,[2] were armed, besides ammunition and a large number of prisoners.

This event proves that in war it is necessary on many occasions to trust to chance; for I repeat now what I said at the time, that I owed more to luck than to wisdom, although success is generally supposed to depend upon plans, schemes, and arrangements. On this occasion the evacuation of Thiel seemed to me the evident result of a retrograde movement, whereas in reality that movement was caused by a misunderstanding. The general commanding my left wing had conscientiously carried out his instructions, and begun his march, when he met the evacuating body, who, having notified their retreat, received injunctions to return to the post they had quitted. But it was too late—the place was already occupied. The two bodies marching in contrary directions met, and an engagement was the result; but, notwithstanding the numerical superiority of their adversaries, our men kept their ground.

The successful crossing of the Waal above and below Nimeguen, together with the advantages gained by my extreme right, which took the offensive after its first brigade had been repulsed, checked the enemy who were opposed to them and broke their lines. Our success was complete. Shortly afterwards the enemy's corps sent to Thiel was recalled to Arnheim. This is a very simple explanation of the reasons that caused my left to remain stationary; it could not come up or set out for the Linge until the following day.

I went to Nimeguen to make my report. The commander-in-chief[3] and the commissioners came to meet me. I was almost ashamed to receive their congratulations, because chance had had a much greater share in the success of the day than my combinations, which, as a matter of fact, were founded upon the apparent retreat of the forces opposed to me, who in reality had no idea of such a thing; but the manner I had adopted in spreading out my lines, and the various points I had attacked, had made the enemy believe that they were bearing the brunt of the whole French army, while their own was scattered over a wide extent of territory.

Next evening, towards dusk, we made a reconnaissance in the direction of Arnheim. The noise and shouting that we heard, combined

---

2. Works covering the approach to a bridge.
3. Pichegru had returned from Brussels.

with the accounts of some deserters and country folk, confirmed our unanimous opinion that a general retreat was going on, and the commander-in-chief gave his orders in consequence. We were, however, too weak to pursue the enemy, invade Holland, and surround the strongholds at one and the same time. This condition of affairs was explained to the commissioners, and they were requested to write to their colleagues with the Army of the Sambre and Meuse, to which we had now come very close; while our commander-in-chief asked his colleague[4] to lend him for the time two divisions to replace those under my command. This request, approved by the commissioners, was granted without delay, and I quitted my position in order to strengthen my left.

A general movement had been caused on the one side by the enemy's retreat, and on the other by the general advance of the army. I crossed the Leck at Amerungen without meeting any enemies, and advanced towards Amersfort, after having turned the lines of the Greb, armed with two hundred guns. The Dutch troops were drawing away from their allies, but being too weak to make a stand against us, they retired into fortresses or distant provinces.

None of our corps remained long bivouacked. They only needed a few hours' rest, for great emulation existed as to who should first reach and take Amsterdam. I did not waste any time, but I had a diagonal line to follow, while the others could march straight ahead. The floods were out and the roads under water, but that was no obstacle, on account of the frost. I arrived in front of Naarden, one of the strongest places in Europe, on the ice. This is the masterpiece of Cohorn, emulator and rival of Vauban;[5] but the water, the principal defence of the place, was now useless. I invested it, and ordered the gates to be opened. The garrisons had orders to commit no act of hostility, to offer no resistance, and to make the best terms possible. They therefore parleyed with us.

The cold was very sharp, and we warmed ourselves at our bivouacs on the ice. My injunctions were to agree to everything, provided that the place were handed over to me on the spot. The articles of capitulation were at length signed, and I took possession of the town. As I

---

4. General Jourdan.
5. Cohorn (1641-1704) the famous Dutch engineer and General of artillery, and afterwards Governor of Flanders. He defended Namur against Louis XIV. Vauban (1633-1707) fortified Dunkirk, Lille, Maestricht, Ghent, etc., and was created a Marshal of France by Louis XIV.—Translator.

reached the gates, a Dutch officer, who had just been replaced by one of ours, and who was drunk, threw himself at the feet of one of my *aides-de-camp*, exclaiming:

'Brave republican, I owe you my life!'

Observe that we had fired neither cannon nor musket, and that we had not even drawn our swords from their scabbards!

At sunrise next day, leaving a strong garrison at Naarden, I started for Amsterdam, and on the road learned that the capital of Holland had been occupied by our troops the previous evening. Mine thus became useless, so I sent them into cantonments, going myself to Amsterdam to take the news of the capitulation of Naarden, and to receive fresh orders. On arriving in presence of the general in command, I presented him with the signed articles. He answered jokingly:

'I pay no attention now to anything less than the surrender of Provinces!'

As a matter of fact, and since the general capitulation of the Netherlands, with the exception of a few places still held by the enemy, my conquest decreased in importance, whereas under other circumstances it would have redounded to the credit of the general who had succeeded in subduing it. It was against this very place that Louis XIV., himself there in person, in the zenith of his power, had failed.

I received orders to move upon the Yssel, to occupy Harderwick, Kampen, Zwolle, Zutphen, Deventer, and to replace the troops of the Sambre and Meuse Army at Arnheim. The enemy retreated at our approach.

The weather had become milder during my short stay at Amsterdam, and the thaw had begun. It was thawing rapidly when I reached the Yssel, and the ice had broken in several places, causing a dyke to burst. The bridge of boats at Kampen could not be removed, and the ice accumulated round it. Half my men had already crossed; the remainder had halted, on learning from the inhabitants that they could only cross at imminent risk, as the bridge must infallibly be carried away. At this moment I came up. Reflecting that the troops already on the other side ran a great risk of falling into the hands of the enemy, I determined to chance it, and gave orders to advance, rapidly crossing the bridge, which was already much strained. The bridge bore us because the waters that had carried away the dyke on the right bank had found an outlet, and were spreading over the country; but then we incurred another danger, that, namely, of inundation. However, all my men got safely across; we reached higher ground, and escaped with nothing worse than wet feet.

Having thus carried out my orders, I received fresh ones to drive the enemy out of the provinces of Frisia, Groningen and Drenthe. This portion of the campaign was very difficult because of the thaw; the roads were shocking, and for the most part under water. The country through which we were marching was perfectly flat. We had to redouble our speed and activity, so as to prevent the enemy from fortifying and victualling Groningen, Delfzyl, and Coevorden. Frisia, owing to its situation, had been already evacuated, but the inhabitants of Groningen came to me, imploring me to hasten our march, and to deliver them from our common enemies, as they expressed it; in making this request they were almost asking for a change of enemies, although my troops kept most rigorous discipline. My advance-guard entered the town as the enemy quitted it. We pursued, overtook, and defeated their rear-guard near Delfzyl. At the same time I heard that Coevorden had opened its gates, and I extended my line as far as the Ems, which the enemy had recrossed. We respectively took up our positions on either side of the river, having, both of us, great need of rest.

While I was inspecting my lines, I was informed of the march of the Prussian army, and shortly afterwards a messenger with a flag of truce brought me a letter announcing that the latter Power had just concluded the Peace of Basle;[6] but as I had no official notification, I at once communicated with the commander-in-chief, who was also in ignorance of the event. I asked for large reinforcements, and meanwhile kept a very strict lookout. Two fresh divisions were sent to join and precede me, and these would not have been too many had the first news of this unexpected peace proved untrue, because the Prussians would have effected a junction with the allied army that I already had in front of me. We at length received confirmation of the news, to the joy of both sides.

The line of demarcation laid down by the treaty followed the right bank of the Rhine and the Ems to its mouth; the Prussians took the place of their former allies on this bank, while we occupied the left. Territorial divisions were formed, of which I had command of the first, composed of the provinces of Drenthe, Frisia, and Groningen, and I established my headquarters in the town of that name.

After three months' rest, of which we all stood in great need, I was called to the command of the provinces of Overyssel and Gueldres,

---
6. The treaty of peace between France and Prussia was signed on the 16 *Germinal*, year iii. (April 5, 1795).

and later on to Utrecht and Holland.

Zealand being at this time threatened by the English,[7] I was ordered to go either to Middleburg or Flushing, whichever I preferred, in the island of Walcheren, and a most unhealthy country. Five-sixths of my men were soon down with fever, and I was so violently attacked that, in fear of my life, I was ordered back to France to recover. All the events I have just described occurred in the years 1794-5. It was towards the end of the latter year that I returned to France, where my fever, which had been somewhat checked before I left Flushing, seized me again at the end of six weeks.

By the end of the summer, 1796, I had recovered, and was ready to return to my duty, when I had the pleasure of greeting Beurnonville, who had just been exchanged and restored from his captivity. The command of the army in Holland had been given to him. He offered to exchange with me. I refused from a mistaken sense of delicacy, on account of our friendship, fearing lest this preference should prejudice other generals against him.

Scarcely had I returned first to Flushing, and then to Middleburg, when, coming back from a tour of inspection round the island, I was again seized with fever, and notwithstanding all the measures employed, especially quinine in large quantities, it could not be subdued until the following spring, when the doses were trebled, and I was removed from that horrible climate.

My friend Beurnonville had his headquarters at Utrecht. He summoned me thither to recover. I had to diet myself very severely; but my relapses, though still acute, were but the prelude to a fresh attack, which I believe has remained unparalleled. Beurnonville was away at the time. On hearing of the danger I was in, he hastened back at once. At length skill and perseverance checked the fever, and I was sent to pass my convalescence at Deventer, in Overyssel, where troops were assembling for the manoeuvres at Gorssel. They were put under my command. I spared no pains to instruct and train them, and thus got much exercise, which was good for my health. Beurnonville came to inspect us.

---

7. The attack on the island of Walcheren by the English was deferred until 1809.

CHAPTER 5

Operations on the Rhine

We foresaw that we should be called ere long to play a part in the events that were in progress on the other side of the Rhine. The Army of the Sambre and Meuse was comanded by General Jourdan, that of the Rhine by General Moreau; each acted without any concert or consideration for the movements of the other. The new campaign had opened brilliantly and decisively, but this, unfortunately, did not last long. A clever and well-designed feint on the part of the Archduke Charles of Austria deceived General Moreau. The Archduke unexpectedly crossed the Danube at Donauwerth, and fell, with overwhelming numbers, upon the right flank of the Army of the Sambre and Meuse, which was on the Rednitz, while that which General Jourdan was pressing back from the Rhine suddenly turned and attacked in front. The inequality of numbers and the great extent of ground occupied by the French army compelled a retreat. Prompt succour was necessary.

In September, 1796, the camp at Gorssel was raised and set in motion, as well as another division of the Army of the North stationed in Belgium. The latter advanced to the *tête-de-pont* at Neuwied, while, with the former, I advanced to the enormous entrenched camp at Düsseldorf. During our march the Army of the Sambre and Meuse, being hard pressed, fell back upon the Lahn, which position it endeavoured to hold until our arrival.

General Castelvert, who commanded the Belgian division, was ordered to put himself in line on the right of this army, in touch with the division temporarily under the command of General Marceau, which extended along the right bank of the Lahn as far as its mouth. General Castelvert's orders, in case the enemy should force the passage of the river, were to retire to the *tête-de-pont* of Neuwied, and to preserve that post on the Rhine at all costs. For this he was to answer with his head. Completely engrossed with this responsibility, he learned that the enemy had taken possession of the town of Nassau, and, without reflecting that this town was situated on the left bank, and that its occupation was consequently immaterial to his position, he hastily retreated to the *tête-de-pont* without giving notice to General Marceau,[8] and thus left absolutely uncovered the extreme right of the Army of the Sambre and Meuse, which that very day was defeated and compelled to retire. This army, of course, threw all the blame upon Castelvert, and there is no doubt that he had committed a serious blunder in compromising the position. The excuse that he made to me is too curious not to be quoted.

'Why,' I asked him, 'did you retire without being compelled to do so, and without giving any notice?'

'There!' he replied. 'Of course they want to throw all the blame for their defeat upon the Army of the North; but they were dying to have an excuse to get away, and as they were retreating eight leagues, surely I had a right to retreat ten, and be d——d to them!'

He was recalled.

I advanced from Düsseldorf to Mülheim, but the enemy left us quiet on the Wupper and the Sieg. General Beurnonville succeeded General Jourdan, bringing with him imperative and reiterated orders to take the offensive; but besides the lateness of the season, the Army of the Sambre and Meuse was not really in a condition to advance; it had scarcely anything. A tacit understanding was arrived at between the two opposing Generals to the effect that the troops should have a rest on condition of ten days' notice being given on each side should either Government order the reopening of hostilities. I took up my quarters on the right bank of the Rhine, extending my left to the line of demarcation settled by the Prussians at the Treaty of Basle. I established my headquarters at Düsseldorf, and thus we passed the winter.

In February, 1797, I recrossed the Rhine, in order to execute a mission in Belgium, leaving my command at Düsseldorf to General-of-Division Desjardins, and that of my titular division to General-of-Brigade Gouvion. In my absence the troops of the Army of the North were *echeloned* from Düsseldorf to Arnheim. I rejoined at Nimeguen.

---

8. This general was mortally wounded on September 20, 1796. His remains rest by treaty in a few feet of French territory in Germany on the banks of the Rhine. The spot was recently visited, we believe, by President Carnot, the head of the present Republic.

Hostilities broke out afresh upon the Rhine. General Hoche was in command of the Army of the Sambre and Meuse, when he died suddenly. I have never heard that the cause of his death was satisfactorily cleared up. It was said that he had been poisoned by an opposing faction. This *corps d'armée* of the North, under my orders, returned to the Rhine; but on the road we heard of the Treaty of Campo Formio, which stopped the Armies of the Rhine and of the Sambre and Meuse in the midst of their successes.

A political revolution occurred in Paris,[9] and General Augereau came to take command of the three armies combined under the name of the Army of Germany. He reviewed us at Cologne, and was struck with the smart appearance of the Army of the North, directly under my orders. Instead of praising it, he said:

'I observe and understand that these troops are drilled in the Prussian manner, but I will soon put a stop to that.'

A halt was called before the march past. The soldiers crowded round the new commander-in-chief. His dress was startling; he was covered with gold embroidery even down to his short boots, thus contrasting strongly with our simple uniforms. He related his Italian campaigns, spoke of the bravery of the troops, but without even mentioning the leader of that army.[10] He said that the soldiers were very well treated there, and that there was not a man among them, bad character as he might be, who had not ten gold pieces in his pocket and a gold watch. This was a hint to our fellows.

On one occasion the theatrical manager came to offer him a choice of plays. Augereau insisted on something very revolutionary, and chose, if I remember rightly, either *Brutus* or the *Death of Cessar*.[11] General Lefèbvre, who had held the command temporarily, was his principal lieutenant. Trigny, commandant of Cologne, had offered his carriage, in the hope, probably, that the commander-in-chief would give a seat in it to his wife. This idea, however, never seemed to occur to the latter, so Trigny very respectfully suggested it. Lefèbvre, seated beside General Augereau, put his head out of window, and inquired:

'What did you say?'

Trigny repeated his proposition.

'Go to blazes!' replied Lefèbvre; 'we did not come here to take your wife out driving!'

---

9. The *coup d'état* of the 18 *Fructidor*, to which Augereau had given his support.
10. General Bonaparte.
11. Both by Voltaire.

Lefèbvre, who had not the remotest acquaintance with literature, applauded heartily with his clumsy hands, believing that the play had been written that very morning in honour of the occasion. He kept nudging me with his elbow, and asking:

'Tell me, where is the chap who wrote this? Is he present?'

On the conclusion of peace, I think in November, I returned to Holland. General Beurnonville was recalled. General Dejean, who held the command provisionally, made it over to me, and I exercised it through the winter, until the moment when General Joubert came to take it over permanently, and I received orders to go to Paris.

CHAPTER 6

Ordered to Italy

In the spring of 1798 I was ordered to betake myself to Italy. The Egyptian expedition was prepared and ready to set sail. I had no doubt that at Milan I should receive orders to go either to Genoa or Civita-Vecchia. I had been able to gain no intelligence in Paris, but on arriving I found, with pleasure, that the expedition had already started.

Italy was denuded of troops. They had all been embarked, but more were expected from the interior of France. General Brune, who was in command, allowed me to make a journey to Rome and Naples. I passed two well-employed months in the first-named city, but was refused permission to enter Neapolitan territory, as I was both a Frenchman and a soldier. I returned to Milan, whence I made various excursions, one of which was nearly fatal to me. I was almost drowned while bathing in the canal at Mantua. General Delmas, then in command, rendered me every service that friendship could suggest—he has since been killed in Saxony—and Mayer, now general, saved my life.

Shortly afterwards I was sent to Rome to take up a command under General Gouvion St. Cyr. He was, I believe, at that time engaged in a quarrel with the Commissioners of the Directory; he was recalled, and I succeeded him.

The Roman States had been erected into a republic, and were then in a state of ferment. Their neighbours, the Neapolitans, were threatening. Austria sent the famous General Mack to command their army, while she herself was preparing to break the Peace of Leoben. Partial insurrections and considerable risings took place, especially at Terracina. I suppressed and kept them under. These events were merely the precursors of much more serious and important matters. I administered the country under the eye of the commissioners, but not in blind accordance with their wishes or authority, although the latter was very limited.

I had but 12,000 men under me, but they were good, trustworthy troops. In my correspondence I informed the Government and the commander in-chief of the army in Italy of our situation. I begged for speedy reinforcements, but no one would believe the danger imminent, albeit it was apparent. I had arranged my men so as to be ready for any emergency. The Neapolitans were organized under no less a chief than General Mack, whose reputation was almost European (and who by no means justified it, whether at the head of the Neapolitans, or later on when in the command of the Austrian army), and at that time he had not the difficulties to contend with that he had in later years.

An 'Army of Rome' was created in Paris and a leader appointed to command it,[1] and a few battalions were ordered down from the north of Italy.

The Neapolitans, to the number of 70,000 or 80,000 men,[2] marched to the extreme points of their frontiers, which I caused to be watched and guarded by small picquets. Everything pointed to a speedy outbreak of hostilities.

The commander-in-chief, Championnet, arrived in Rome while matters were in this position, and with the assurance, given him by the Directory, that the Government of Naples would not dare to take upon themselves the renewal of the war. Both were mistaken, as was proved by the events of the next few days. I thought otherwise, and had arranged to be able to draw off my troops, evacuate Rome, and re-cross the Tiber. My forces at this point numbered about 6,000 men; the remainder, about the same number, were scattered towards Narni, Sulmona, and Fermo, at the entrance of the Abruzzi.

General Championnet had not been more than forty-eight hours in Rome, I think, when I received intelligence, at eleven o'clock at

1. General Championnet.
2. Such was the calculation of the Neapolitan forces transmitted from divers sources, in particular from the French legation at Naples, since confirmed by prisoners, and made in their very capital itself, and yet a note attributed to General Mack only gives the active and effective army assembled on the frontier as 40,000 men. Perhaps, too, he wished to diminish his forces in order to excuse or attenuate his reverses; perhaps he does not include in this calculation detachments, depots, garrisons, etc. He numbers the French forces at 20,600 men, whereas, at the commencement of hostilities, I had not more than from 10,000 to 12,000 between Terracina and Fermo. We were by no means formidable, and I declare that no preparation was made, no order ever transmitted to me to instigate hostilities with the kingdom of Naples.—Note by Marshal Macdonald.

night, that the Neapolitans had crossed their frontiers without any preliminary declaration of war. I informed the commander-in-chief, and at daybreak we mounted our horses and rode out towards Tivoli, the nearest outlet to Rome. All was quiet there, but I anticipated that the hostile body that intended to invade us at this point was waiting for news of the principal corps coming from San Germano to Velletri through Terracina. With a small detachment, I could easily have kept in check the enemy's troops at the end of the road which crosses the Pontine Marshes, but their principal body would come by the old road. My troops, therefore, retired upon Rome. It was easy to foresee that the Neapolitans would debouch simultaneously from many points on the frontier, and that is exactly what occurred.

The commander-in-chief opened negotiations for the evacuation of the capital and retired, leaving me saddled with the burden of the retreat. I saw among the people signs of an approaching rising, of which, moreover, I had already received warning. I made serious representations to him, to which he seemed at first inclined to give attention. All my troops were drawn up outside the town; the first thing to be done was to complete the victualling of Sant'-Àngelo. I had one or two detachments in the town, a hundred and fifty cavalry on the Piazza del Popolo, and cannon pointing down the three streets which opened on to this space.

I had just returned home to give some orders, when I heard shouting and hooting in the street. I hastened to the window, whence I saw my commander galloping as fast as he could, making for the gate, and taking my cavalry with him. This departure—I soften the expression, and refrain from using one more energetic and more correct—was the signal for the rising that I had foreseen. All stray Frenchmen, whether military, civil, or attached to the Government, were pursued and massacred, and the shops pillaged.

All who could escape the popular fury took refuge in the churches, the large shops, and the fortress of Sant'-Àngelo, and some in my house. My *aides-de-camp* and staff officers were on horseback, trying to convey orders to the troops to re-enter the town, but they could not make a way through the crowd; those generals who could not come into the city were in the same plight.

During this crisis, the danger of which increased with every minute, I summoned the artillery from the Piazza, del Popolo. It was drawn up in front of my door, and several charges of grape-shot were fired; but the gunners, fired upon from the upper windows, abandoned their posts. Every instant brought news of fresh outrages. Communication between one quarter of the city and another, nay, between one street and another, was cut off, when a band of insurgents was seen coming from the Piazza Navona, and marching upon my lodgings. I sent my small guard—twelve or fifteen men—to meet them. They fired several shots, which checked the boldest of them for a moment; but were finally compelled to give way. Seeing them return, I determined to mount my horse and make a way for myself. My guard received orders to re-enter and barricade my house. Sword in hand, we galloped through the Via del Popolo as far as the Piazza di Venezia, receiving some shots here and there, and a serious discharge from the street leading thence to the Palazzo Colonna. One of my suite was killed and one wounded.

Pursuing my road with the intention of rejoining my troops outside the town, I met near the *Forum* the head of the column commanded by General Maurice Mathieu, who, not being able to communicate with me, and having heard what was going on inside the walls, had at once started to effect an entrance. It was the 31st regiment of Infantry, led by Colonel d'Arnaud—now a lieutenant-general with a wooden leg—that had succeeded in making their way.

I returned to the Piazza di Venezia, where I distributed companies at the entrances of all the streets. They kept up a fusillade along the streets at the windows, and swept all before them. Orders were successfully conveyed, and at the end of two hours quiet was restored. No one was to be seen out-of-doors or at their windows, for they were fired upon as soon as they appeared. Fortunately the enemy was still twenty-four hours' march distant, otherwise it is impossible to say what misfortunes might not have resulted from this day.

I still think that, had the commander-in-chief not gone off so inappropriately, or had he left during the night, as I begged him to do, we should have quelled the mob by our presence, for, as I have since learned, they believed that the town was entirely evacuated, and that the Neapolitan troops would re-enter it by the old road.

I took advantage of the quiet of night to complete my arrangements for both exterior and interior. A proclamation was printed and published, which remained without effect; for some hours before dawn groups began to form. I would not, however, give them time to concentrate themselves, and they were easily dispersed by a few charges of cavalry. Tranquillity was maintained, notwithstanding the presence of the enemy, who arrived within sight of our outposts.

I had refused to admit any *parlementaire*, as the town was to be evacuated that evening. Having settled everything, and while the last provisions were being carried to Sant'-Àngelo, which was not included in the convention, while the bread was being baked and distributed as fast as it was ready, I went to the gate of St. John Lateran. On the way I met one of General Mack's *aides-de-camp*, who had been admitted by mistake, and who summoned me to yield up the city. I made him turn back.

On reaching the gate, the Neapolitan colonel, Moliterno, and a general of the same nation, whose name I have forgotten, reiterated the demand with considerable arrogance. I had a detachment of men masking a strong ambuscade, and a battery containing several guns loaded with grape-shot. The officer in command, who had heard the threats uttered by these gentlemen, whispered to me:

'Will you allow me to fire?'

'No,' I answered; 'no fighting today. Tomorrow we may be able to make them regret their impertinence—perhaps even tonight.'

A partial engagement might have spoiled all my arrangements, roused the town afresh, stopped the distribution of rations, and disorganized my ranks. I wished to recross the Tiber without trouble and in broad daylight.

On learning that the food was all distributed and the troops assembled, I gave the signal for retreat, and it was effected in the most orderly manner by the three streets that I have mentioned. Gradually the inhabitants emerged until they appeared in crowds, red cockades in their hats, going out to meet the Neapolitans, but without insulting us. My rear-guard came on slowly, followed by the advance-guard of the Neapolitans. While my columns were crossing the river, I went through the Via del Popolo, in the thick of the crowd, as far as the Piazza di Venezia, unaccompanied save by my *aides-de-camp*, without seeing any signs of insurrection, without hearing any hostile cries. The people had calmed down. The upper classes may have fomented the disturbances of the previous day, but they took no ostensible part in them. Well-disposed people had remained at home, and had even saved many Frenchmen who, but for them, would probably have fallen victims to the insurrection.

When at last all my men had left the city, I sent orders to the commandant of the fortress, which was not mentioned, and consequently not included in the convention relating to the evacuation of Rome, to withdraw all his men, to close his barriers, and to consider himself as besieged by a hostile army. I had entrusted our wounded in hospital to the generosity and humanity of General Mack, and left fifty men to guard them, begging him to replace and send them on to me. After taking all these precautions, I left Rome, assuring our friends and partisans that we should not be away more than a fortnight; and I undertook not to shave my beard during our absence. I kept my word, and wore it for seventeen days.

After leaving Rome in good order, and recrossing the Tiber, I marched all night. I encamped at Monterosi, whence two roads branch off, one to Viterbo, and one to Ancona. There I waited for fresh intelligence concerning the march of the Neapolitans; but after hearing a rumour of a successful engagement at Fermo, on the extreme eastern frontier of the States of Naples, I raised my camp, and chose another at Civita-Castellana, a strong and good position, naturally defended by several ravines and by a castle.

General Mack occupied my position at Monterosi, and advanced to attack me with quite 40,000 men; I had at most 5,000 or 6,000 to oppose to him. I reinforced as well as I could my advance-guard at Nepi, and determined to go out to meet them. The conflict was violent, but the Neapolitans did not make a stand, and retreated. We pursued them as far as their camp, which was still standing, and which they abandoned, continuing their flight to Rome. This was the principal point of attack. During the action three other columns advanced along the old road, on the right bank of the Tiber, passing by Santa Maria di Falori. I retraced my steps, repulsed all partial attacks, and thus dislodged this magnificent and haughty army, with less than 3,000 men engaged. Our gains were considerable: a large number of prisoners, artillery, arms, baggage, the camp, the military chest, etc.

Learning that General Mack had rallied his troops, and was passing along the right bank of the Tiber in order to help one of his columns that was descending upon Otricoli, I, too, recrossed the river at the bridge of Borghetto, and supported my right. It was not until after this change of position that I was informed by my scouts that this column was marching upon Otricoli, where I had established my depots of wounded and my provisions.

This road was my only means of communication with headquarters and with the rest of the army. I was not yet certain that the Neapolitans had occupied Otricoli, and wished to ascertain their strength and their position. With this object I took a strong detachment from my camp at Borghetto and started.

There was so dense a fog that we could not see four yards ahead, but we could feel the presence of the enemy by a tolerably long line of fire, to which our men replied. From the enemy's hesitation I concluded that they were not in very good order. The thick fog was fortunate for both of us: it covered our movements and concealed our weakness, while it hid from us their direction. I made my cavalry charge them, on the chance, along the highroad. A discharge of artillery did not check my men; the enemy's advance-guard were surprised and put to the sword, and a battery of light artillery abandoned.

The mist lifted, and we continued our pursuit with a better light. I then discovered that I was dealing not with regulars, but with assassins, who had foully murdered my sick and wounded. The sight of some of these poor fellows, horribly mutilated, but not dead, increased our fury and thirst for vengeance. Learning that these *banditti* were making for Calvi, we followed them thither, and I at the same time sent orders to General Maurice Mathieu to start from camp immediately with his brigade, so as to cut off their flight to Rome. We surrounded Calvi, situated on a high escarped mountain: we were inferior in numbers, but superior in pluck. The enemy offered to surrender. I answered in these words:

'Lay down your arms, or else run the gauntlet of my troops!'

They yielded to the number of about 7,000 men, commanded by Generals Moesk and ———.[3]

After I had thus re-established my communications, I received orders from the commander-in-chief to join him on the road to Rome; he was starting from Narni. General Mack was also on the way to support General Moesk in his retreat; the latter had written to him not to hurry, that he was in a very strong position at Calvi, and that after having rallied and rested his men he would join him. They apparently counted upon our inaction, and that ruined them. General Mack, warned by fugitives of what had happened, turned back towards Rome; we hastily followed him. I had left General Kellermann at Borghetto with a strong detachment. I sent him orders to march, and to drive before him, sword in hand, all that he found on the road.

These unexpected successes aroused the bitter jealousy of General Championnet, a very brave man, it must be acknowledged, but without much capacity.. He had acquired a certain reputation while with the Army of the Sambre and Meuse, by commanding a division that had taken part in several actions always with success. A clique had

---

3. The second name is omitted in the Marshal's MS.

obtained his nomination as commander-in-chief. He himself was a man of pleasant temper, easy to live with; but he was surrounded by envious, pretentious, and ambitious men, one of whom in particular, Romieux, principal *aide-de-camp*, had the reputation of being the real wire-puller. There was another man, General Bonnami, chief of his staff, who had not borne a very good reputation on the Rhine, where his conduct in regard to money matters had not been always straightforward. These charges were established later on in Naples, and this man had the impertinence to wish to direct and lead operations.

The orders I had received were insignificant, and eventually proved impossible of execution. I had been unfortunate enough to see this from the beginning, and made the mistake of answering:

'Let me know what the complete plan is, I will act accordingly, and do not trouble about the details.'

I spoke really in good faith, having a better knowledge of the localities, and also that confidence which always comes after a success gained over an enemy. The orders I received were timid to a degree, whereas they ought to have displayed courage and dash, which would have been quite justified by our successes, and by the spirit that animated my men as well as myself.

I only discovered these announces from the increasing coldness of our correspondence; mine was gay rather than serious, especially so in those reports in which I related our skirmishes, always brilliant and successful. I joked about them with no other intention than that of showing how little glory was to be obtained from fighting enemies who, a few days previously, had proved themselves both boastful and cowardly. Had they not massacred our sick and wounded at Otricoli, and threatened with a like fate those whom we had left in Rome, together with a detachment of fifty men to guard and preserve them against the fury of the populace? These men had been disarmed and made prisoners contrary to every law of war or of nations; and yet it was Mack, the general with a European reputation, who did these things, who wrote and published the fact! I had given him notice of our precautions, had appealed to his humanity on behalf of our sick, and begged him to send back our detachment after replacing it by another. I was indignant, furious, and in my turn published a general order and an energetic proclamation, which I hope will be considered justified when my correspondence is examined.[4]

When I joined the commander-in-chief on the new road to

---

4. Preserved in the archives of the French War Office.

Rome, he received me with considerable curtness, instead of with congratulation upon our successes, which had already almost annihilated the Neapolitan army. I was much vexed, and an angry explanation ensued.

'You want to make me pass for a fool,' he said.

This speech was clearly produced by vanity.

'What foundation or proofs have you for your statement? How dare anyone suggest that I could display such a want of courtesy to my chief?'

'Here is your correspondence,' he replied.

It had been wickedly misconstrued, and presented to him as satirical instead of as the joke that I had intended it to be. I explained this to him, and he softened somewhat. General Éblé, commanding the artillery, came up at this moment; he was a friend of mine, and explained matters, and the General and I were outwardly reconciled. I then proposed a series of operations whereby we should immediately re-enter Rome (feeling persuaded that the Neapolitans there must be in confusion, which proved to be the case), and cut off the passage of a column which was being pursued by General Kellermann on the other side of the Tiber. Championnet consented.

CHAPTER 7

Insurrections in the Country

I sent forward messengers to inform the commandant of Sant'-Àngelo of all that had happened in the sixteen days that had elapsed since we quitted Rome, and of our approach; we intended to return the following day. I told him to assist us by means of sorties, and to try to seize the King of Naples, who was there, and anyone else that he could lay hands upon; but, unfortunately, he was lulled to security, and asleep. The investment had been raised, and he received intelligence of the misunderstandings in the town by means of our partisans. He was besides overjoyed at having held his own, and, until our arrival, it was absolutely hopeless to arouse him from his sense of safety, and thereby he missed making several important captures. To justify himself, he told me that he was afraid that a trap was being laid for him, that he had suspected my spies of serving the enemy, although there was no mistaking the signs agreed upon between us, especially when my cannon was drawing near and becoming perfectly audible. But such is the pusillanimity of some men; everything frightens and terrifies them when they are not actually kept in leading-strings!

The commander-in-chief, hearing that Rome was evacuated, had preceded me; I was to join him at Ponte Molle. He informed me that a column of the enemy, which had come up too late to cross the town and follow General Mack, who had retired to Albano, had stopped at sight of some of our scouts, and that Bonnami, his chief of the staff, having parleyed with them, had granted them three hours to decide whether to lay down their arms.

'An excellent plan,' I replied; 'nothing could be better devised for the purpose of enabling them to escape by the Présides!'[1]

---
1. The Neapolitan *enclaves* in Tuscany, part of the Stato degli Presidii, which were safely reached by this column.

Our junction with General Kellermann had been meanwhile effected. He, as I have already said, followed, without overtaking, the troop since his departure from Borghetto for Civita-Castellana, because he had taken the old road to Rome, while the others marched in a parallel line with him by Monterosi, Bucano, La Storta, and had taken up a position masked by considerable heights.

General Bonnami came to us, and said with emphasis:

'We have got this troop; within an hour they will have laid down their arms.'

'No doubt,' I replied, 'if they are still there. But do you suppose that a troop with free communication behind it, and commanded by an *émigré*, Comte Roger de Damas, will have the kindness to come and yield to us?'

'Why not?' he retorted. 'I told them they should have no quarter if they did not. And their *vedettes* are still there.'

'What proof is that? Of course they are there to conceal the movements; they will remain there as long as they are left; besides, to carry out your threat, they should be surrounded, and their rear is quite open!'

The commander-in-chief had listened in silence to this conversation, but at last, stung by my remarks, he said:

'Well, let us go and see what has really happened.'

We went, and found exactly what was to be expected, not a creature! Then we had to follow; but the small number of our troops in front were resting, or dispersed, believing that an armistice had been concluded, and mine had halted behind, so that it took us some time to collect a small force of cavalry. At about the distance of a league they came upon a very well-posted rear-guard; a brush took place, but with no result, and, as night was coming on, we recalled the detachment.

I asked for orders, and was told to guard the Ponte Molle and the town; I remarked that the important point was the road to Naples, but was told that it would be attended to. Nevertheless, I sent a regiment to the Lateran Gate, another in reserve to the Coliseum, and the Piazza di Venezia. Thus supported, I went, to see the Torlonias[2] and get some news, as the commandant of Sant'-Àngelo knew nothing, and I re-entered my former dwelling, which I had quitted seventeen days previously. I had kept my promise within two days!

About eleven o'clock the same night, I received news from the

---

2. The Roman bankers.—Translator.

Lateran Gate and from General Championnet that a body of the enemy was advancing on that side; the General himself, in great anxiety, rode up with his staff.

'Make yourself easy,' I said; 'I have seen to everything; my reserves are now marching towards that point. I know the way; let us go.'

But it was unnecessary. On reaching the gate we found that the regiment I had placed there, the 11th, if I recollect rightly, had sufficed to repulse the assailants to the number of 5,000 or 6,000 men, as I learned from some prisoners, led by General Mack in person. This was nearly all that remained to him of the formidable army which had so boastfully declared that in a very short time it would drive us out of Italy. General Mack did not think that we were again occupying Rome, or else he hoped to surprise us, and enable Comte de Damas to get through. This expedition having failed, the general, no longer hoping to effect a junction, gained the road to Capua, and we returned to Rome.

I was just about to get into bed, when a *parlementaire* was brought to me, asking leave for another column to pass through the town on its way from Viterbo to Ponte Molle.

'Are you in earnest in making such a request?' I asked.

'Certainly; they tell me a truce has been proclaimed.'

'You have been misinformed; lay down your arms, that is the best thing you can do.'

'What! lay down our arms? We will defend ourselves. We are in force.'

'Very good,' I said; then, turning to the officer who had introduced this man, I continued: 'Take him back, and give orders from me to the commandant of Ponte Molle to put all these gentlemen to the sword; I am going to bed.'

'Is that your final decision?' asked the messenger.

'Yes, it is.'

'In that case I will surrender.'

I discovered that he was the chief of the band of from 1,200 to 1,500 men, which had been skirmishing about my right flank while we were at Civita-Castellana, and had given us a considerable amount of trouble. Next morning I sent a report of what had occurred to the commander-in-chief, adding that. I had not cared to disturb his slumbers for so small a matter.

A general order emanating from headquarters announced all these happy results; to our great surprise, my division was hardly mentioned, although the army did us justice and gave us the honours of this short campaign; but what will scarcely obtain belief is that the staff received all the promotions and rewards. This injustice and partiality made me as angry as the rest of the army. I went straight to the general, and a second and very sharp altercation followed, but without producing any favourable result for my division, and, as if to punish it for the advantages it had secured, it was ordered to march at the rear of the column. We had to swallow this insult; but a few days later, as we met some rear-guards, they sent us forward to the front again.

We thus arrived at the intrenched camp at Capua, where we received overtures for a suspension of hostilities which tempted the commander-in-chief. I, however, opposed them strongly at the meeting that was called of all the generals-of-division. Nothing was settled that day, but on the following a delay of forty-eight hours was granted in my absence. I was furious; but I had to submit, and made all my preparations for a desperate attack at the expiration of the delay allowed.

The excuse given for this ill-timed concession was the absence of news of Generals Duhesme and Lemoine, who were marching upon Naples by the Abruzzi; but the excuse was a bad one. The terror of the Neapolitans was increasing, disturbance was rife in the country, fear in the capital, the court was fleeing to Sicily; therefore there should have been no cessation of hostilities. This state of things might have been taken for granted even had it not been officially known to exist, and there was every reason, nay, necessity, for advancing to assist our troops in crossing the Abruzzi by the prompt and decisive occupation of the capital, instead of allowing time for a reorganization of the remains of the army, for the defence of Capua and its intrenched camp, and insurrection and rebellion among the inhabitants.

At the conclusion of this ill-advised armistice I ordered a reconnaissance; General Maurice Mathieu commanded it, and I followed to support him. All the Neapolitan outposts gave way, and vanished as fast as their horses could carry them. They gave the alarm in the camp and town, whence the defenders began to retire, when General Mack conceived the idea of sending a messenger with an offer of capitulation. In accordance with an old custom, the advance-guard stopped the officer and conducted him to General Mathieu, who sent him on to me. I, unfortunately, was at some distance supporting a detachment of our troops, who had met with some resistance in trying to cross the Volturno. I was furious, and ordered the attack to be continued.

I desired, and should have been able, had it not been for this circumstance, to force the intrenched camp, cross the Volturno by the bridge, and seize Capua; but the Neapolitans had had time to review their position, and to put themselves behind their intrenchments and ramparts. I was in advance of the reinforcements that I was bringing up, and arrived just in time to see General Mathieu's arm broken by a discharge of grape-shot; at the same moment I received an order from the commander-in-chief to cease firing, and return to my position, just as I had hopes of being able to carry the enemy's camp.

I heard next day that Capua was to be handed over by capitulation, and that an armistice for an indefinite period had been signed, instead of our rapidly occupying the capital. I was bitterly disappointed at being thus balked of a conquest not only easy in itself, and which would have put a crown to our efforts, but which must have produced a striking moral effect in the Kingdom of the Two Sicilies, and in Europe, especially in Italy and Austria. A fresh altercation took place at Capua; as hostilities were at an end, I asked to be relieved of my command, a request that was granted with pleasure and alacrity, and I wrote to the War Minister and to the Directory, asking to be employed elsewhere. While awaiting an answer, I stayed at Capua.

Shortly afterwards the truce was violated, I forget on what pretext. The *lazzaroni*[3] organized themselves for the defence of Naples, the troops were disarmed, General Mack resigned and asked for a passport into Austria, which the commander-in-chief granted. The French Government, however, on being informed of this, refused its consent, caused Mack to be arrested at Ancona, contrary to the law of nations, and taken as a prisoner of war to Paris. On passing through Capua the general paid me a visit; it was five o'clock in the morning, and I was in bed. I was soon up, however, and said to him:

'Well, General, a fortnight ago you would not have caught me napping.'

'Ah!' he replied; 'you did for me altogether at Calvi.' In the course of conversation upon past events, he told me that an attempt had been made to poison him at Capua, and to assassinate him at Naples; he was then very far from well, and I saw him again the following year, in Paris, in the same state.

'How,' I asked at our first interview, 'could a general so distinguished by his talents expose his military reputation as a great tactician by putting himself at the head of such an army?'

'I was urged, entreated by the King of Naples,' he replied; 'I re-

---
3. Neapolitan loafers.—Translator.

sisted, but my Sovereign commanded me. I was compelled to submit; and on seeing the army, well drilled, well organized, well equipped, displaying such devotion, and above all, such determination to make war upon you and to liberate Rome and Italy, I was seduced.'

'Perhaps also,' I added, laughing, 'the prospect of coming into France and to Paris had something to do with it.'

'All that army wanted,' he replied, 'was to have been led by a French general.'

After that compliment he took leave of me and departed. I recommended him to the special care of all our commandants He passed near Gaëta first, as that fortress was yielding to our troops, under General Rey, although it had only been threatened with shells.

After the violation of the armistice, as I have said, the army marched upon Naples; the *lazzaroni* made some resistance, but the city was eventually occupied. Being so near, I could not help visiting it. I spent a week there, and learned what abominable exactions were being levied. I deplored them, and left for Rome, where I awaited my next instructions.

One day, on returning tired from a ride in the neighbourhood, I had allowed myself a siesta, when I was aroused by the arrival of a courier. I looked at the despatch, and, to my great surprise, read my nomination as COMMANDER-IN-CHIEF OF THE ARMY OF NAPLES in place of General Championnet.[5] The Directory, dissatisfied with the want of continuity in the conduct of the campaign, with the armistice at Capua, and with the extortions that had been committed, had decided to recall and make him give an account of his conduct. I am bound to say that this proceeding was too severe, that the greater part of the army was innocent of these iniquities, that they were regretted by everybody; but none had any confidence in the leader whose weakness was universally deplored, so that with truth, and without either vanity or conceit, I may say that great pleasure was manifested in my appointment, especially by those troops that had served under me while I had had the command in the Roman States and during the campaign.

I started and passed General Championnet at Aversa. We neither stopped nor spoke. I knew that a magnificent reception was being prepared for me at Naples; out of modesty I avoided it by arriving at eleven o'clock at night, whereas I was only expected the next morn-

---

5. The decree conferring this appointment bears the date of 25 *Pluviose*, year vii. (February 13, 1799).

ing.

Everything was disorganized. Communications between the divisions were interrupted, and those that occupied Salerno and the places nearest at hand were cut off even from the capital. I rearranged all the communications, reassembled a few scattered troops, and restored order in the town. In order to re-establish confidence and tranquillity, I issued proclamations, backed up by effectual demonstrations. I organized a new government in concert with Abrial, the Commissioner sent by the Directory, a very good and worthy man, afterwards count and peer of France.

I next turned my attention to military matters. Our successes against the insurgents were universal, but no sooner was the insurrection crushed at one point than it broke out at another. Communication with Rome had been frequently interrupted. Large escorts, and even cannon, were necessary generally to ensure a safe journey from Mola di Gaëta and Fondi to Terracina; but sometimes impatient travellers would start alone or with slender escorts, and then fell victims to the banditti and brigands, who inflicted upon them the most abominable cruelties.

I passed several months amid these disturbances, not only in the kingdom of Naples, but also in the Roman States and in Tuscany, whither my command extended; but I succeeded in maintaining perfect order in the capitals, especially in Naples, by means of a national guard that I formed, and of the leader of the *lazzaroni*, whom I gained over by presents, and by conferring on him the rank and distinctive marks of a colonel. I also formed the remains of the Neapolitan army into detachments of troops, in order to employ those among their officers who displayed the greatest zeal for the new order of things that is, for the Parthenopeian republic;[6] but these troops soon betrayed us, giving up the tower of Castellamare to the English, after massacring some of their own officers.

I had resolved to induce Admiral Caracciolo to take service in the new fleet; he equipped a flotilla which secured respect for the port and coasts of Naples, frequently threatened by attempts of the English, who occupied the islands and were stationed in the roads.[7] I had a somewhat acrimonious correspondence with one of their captains,

---

6. Parthenopeia, ancient name of Naples.—Translator.
7. An interesting account of these operations will be found in James's *Naval History of Great Britain*, vol. 2. Naples, Rome, Capua, Gaëta, and Leghorn were occupied by the English naval forces for a time when Macdonald was on the Trebbia.

Commander Throwbridge (*sic.*).[8]

Castellamare was a very important point, and so near Naples that its loss was likely to raise the flagging spirits of the insurgents. They were prepared to band together, and this treachery was the signal; but I lost not an instant, and marched in person upon Castellamare. As I crossed Naples I noticed many people who had already placed the red cockade in their hats. It became necessary now to strike a decisive blow, so as to prevent this rising from gaining ground in Naples, where my garrison was but small (except in the forts, which were well occupied, especially that of Sant'-Elmo, that existed as a standing menace to the town; the fear that this fort might set fire to Naples had acted as a salutary check upon the inhabitants). The insurgents from Calabria and Salerno had advanced to the tower of the Annunziata, and were posted near a brook; I attacked them; to rout and put them to flight was the work of an instant.

While they were being pursued and sabred in all directions, those who held Castellamare took fright; some, after a few discharges of cannon, seeing the English put to sea, rushed into the water to save themselves; the rest yielded; the principals in the rising were shot. The flags of England and Naples still remained flying side by side: I promised a reward of twenty-five *louis* (£20) to whomsoever should bring them to me; half an hour later they were in my hands, though they were not obtained without some loss.

Once more in possession of the tower, I turned the guns upon the vessels and those who had taken to flight. I must say here that the skilful and brave Admiral Caracciolo contributed largely with his flotilla to the success of the expedition. He afterwards fell a victim to the English admiral Nelson, who cruelly and ignominiously caused him to be hanged from the yard-arm of his own ship, a death with which I have always deeply reproached myself, as it was I who overcame his reluctance, and gained him to our side.

After re-establishing order, giving all the commands necessary to put an end to the rising, and pursuing those in flight to beyond Salerno, I re-entered Naples, preceded by the banners and flags of the insurgents, which were burned next day on the Piazza Reale by the public executioner. The red cockades had disappeared, and the heat occasioned by this incident had quite cooled down in the capital.

Still more important events were, however, looming in the distance. Russia was marching an army into Italy to join the Austrians,

---

8. Afterwards Admiral Sir Thomas Trowbridge.

our troops were assembling on the Adige under General Schérer, and hostilities soon began. While these events were in preparation I was not inactive; I concentrated my troops. A fresh insurrection broke out in the provinces; another assemblage was dispersed at Cannae at the mouths of the Ofanto. I attempted to carry out orders by revictualling Malta and the Ionian Islands; convoys started, but not one reached its destination; they were either taken or surrendered.

I begged the French Government to evacuate Naples and Rome, keeping only the fortresses. 'If our troops are victorious on the Adige,' I said, 'they will require to make good their losses; if they are beaten, they will need reinforcements and support. There are no troops nearer to them than mine, and these, in the latter case, will be cut off from all communication. In the former case, supported by the fortresses, I could return and reoccupy the two States.' But the principle of keeping everything, and of not yielding a foot of ground, even to imminent danger, gained the day, and my suggestions were set aside.

Nevertheless, seeing what might come to pass, I continued my preparations, under the pretext of concentration, to parry any attack that might be made on the shores of the Mediterranean, the Adriatic, or the interior. I indicated a place which I had not the remotest intention of occupying, feeling persuaded that I should receive serious remonstrances from various private interests affected; nor was I disappointed. I pretended to give way, and succeeded in having pointed out to me the very place whither I wished to go namely, the neighbourhood of Caserta, on the left bank of the Volturno. No doubt it would have been better from a military point of view to take the right bank, but to do that I should have had to disclose my plan; moreover, I had no army in front of me, and should always have time to cross the river.

I provisioned the forts at Naples, Capua, Gaëta, Sant'-Àngelo at Rome, Civita-Vecchia, Civita-Castellana, and Ancona. Rome was in want of food; famine was beginning to make itself felt there. I sent provisions. The national guard and the *lazzaroni* at Naples were increased; I reviewed them, they took over the duty, and I withdrew my men. I called in the divisions scattered in the provinces, and concentrated all before Caserta, where I established my headquarters. Finally, I caused the miracle of St. Januarius[9] to be worked for our benefit, being myself present on the occasion; I will give a description of it

---

9. The saint whose blood is preserved, and is said to liquefy on special occasions. He was martyred at Naples by the Emperor Diocletian, A.D. 284.—Translator.

later on, as I think that no one has ever been in so good a position to observe it as Commissioner Abrial and myself. I had taken careful measures in consequence of the great concourse of people, and tranquillity was not disturbed. The camp of Caserta was raised, and brought to the vicinity of Naples during the ceremony, and the troops did not return till the evening.

This display of force and other similar demonstrations maintained order in the capital and neighbourhood. The victualling of the forts and fortresses went on quickly, as did also that of Rome; but it was more difficult to keep open communications, especially with the Adriatic provinces; strong escorts were necessary, and flying columns showed themselves everywhere.

While these arrangements and preparations, which excited no suspicion, were going on, I caused all useless matter that could embarrass or encumber the march of an army to be sent to Rome, and thence into Tuscany. The commander-in-chief of the army in Italy had asked for a considerable number of ammunition waggons; they were despatched to him, drawn by horses hastily requisitioned. General Éblé, whose skill is so well known, constructed a pontoon-bridge at Capua in order to facilitate the crossing of the rivers Volturno, Garigliano, and Tiber, which would help us in our march, and enable us to effect a junction with the Army of Italy, supposing it were beaten; or, if it stood in need of reinforcement, would enable us to cross the rivers, or, on the other hand, would be of service to us both alike, supposing we were obliged to retreat.

CHAPTER 8

Rising in Tuscany

While in the thick of these preparations, I heard at one and the same time of the declaration of war, of the loss of a battle,[1] of the retreat of the Army of Italy, and received orders to advance immediately, leaving garrisons in such forts and fortresses as I proposed to retain in the two States, and especially taking steps to keep possession of Rome. My foresight had been of the utmost service. I only needed to recall the divisions concentrated in the provinces of Lecce and Bari and the flying columns. I hastily summoned the members of the Neapolitan Government, who were terror-stricken on hearing of what had happened on the Adige and of my marching orders. I begged them to remain at their posts under the protection of the forts and of the national guard. Not one of them, not one even of my own men, had divined the secret of my preparations. I am not now sure if I even confided them to Abrial, the Government commissioner.

The troops returned by forced marches to camp. Scarcely had those who held Brindisi left it, when the French man-of-war, the *Généreux*,[2] which had escaped from the fatal Battle of Aboukir Bay (1798), came to cast anchor there, feeling convinced that it was yet in our hands. She tried to force an entrance, and was fired upon by such guns as had not been rendered useless. The firing was heard by our retiring troops; they turned back immediately and saved the ship, which set sail again at once, and the troops reached their destination, followed, however, by large crowds of insurgents, who compelled them to face about several times. The latter collected at Avellino, but their proximity was so dangerous for Naples, and kept the camp so constantly on the alert,

---
1. Battle of Magnano, lost by Schérer, who was replaced by Moreau.
2. The *Généreux* was captured by a British squadron in the Mediterranean in February, 1800.

that I determined to attack them. I did so. They made no resistance, and were speedily put to flight. This is the site of the ancient Caudine Forks, where a Roman host laid down their arms and passed under the yoke.

Meanwhile we were hurrying on the victualling of the castles of Naples, and the fortresses of Capua and Gaëta, of the Castle of Sant'-Àngelo at Rome, of Civita-Castellana, and of Civita-Vecchia and Ancona. A certain amount of baggage and artillery, and a pontoon train and other encumbrances, were forwarded to Rome.

I received dismal intelligence of the results of the Battle of the Adige, and of the retreat of the Army of Italy, of risings in the Cisalpine Republic, in Tuscany, in the Roman States, and in the Abruzzi provinces. Every despatch, while informing me of these occurrences, exhorted me to hasten my movements. I was, of course, most anxious to do this, but I could not make greater speed. I had already sent forward some troops into Tuscany, echeloning them from Rome to Florence. A number of empty ammunition-waggons under convoy had started through the Marches[3] for Italy; they were compelled to retire upon Rome. Many of my orders were rendered nugatory, or were misunderstood by other generals, especially by the one in command in the Roman States. No one considered or thought of anything but his own immediate business, without any regard for unity of plan.

Instructions had been issued to the commandants of all the strongholds and castles, which prescribed for them carefully their conduct in every extremity. I told them that they could only be invested, and not attacked, as there were no regular troops to fear, and the Neapolitan artillery had been assembled at Capua. I further told them to collect all the provisions they could about them, and, as far as lay in their power, to be careful how they were used. I added that I would soon come to their relief, imagining that France was about to make great efforts to help the Army of Italy, and that by our junction we ought to be soon able to regain our preponderance and repulse the enemy.

With this object, in the event of our being victorious, or of my being prevented from passing into Tuscany, I had taken endless pains to form a pontoon train, wherewith I could cross the Garigliano and Volturno, after defending the ground inch by inch. My one fear was that I might be unable to effect my junction with the Army of Italy. This army had been repulsed in Piedmont, and the risings, fomented by the enemy, were increasing. General Gauthier, commanding in Tus-

---
3. The Papal States between Romagna and Naples.—Translator.

cany, had but few troops, and the detachments that I had been able to send up were but very feeble reinforcements. My instructions to him were to fall back upon me in case he found it necessary to evacuate the territory.

Having thus provided for the garrisons charged with the double task of ensuring the safety of our numerous sick and wounded, and of providing me with places of retreat in case I were beaten back, I crossed the Volturno, and marched in two columns on Rome, having with me only twenty-four battalions and squadrons. The right column met with severe resistance at Lisola, but succeeded in forcing its way; the left rounded the Pontine Marshes, which I myself crossed, and we reached Rome, whence troops were continually starting for Florence. There I learned that the Army of Italy hoped to make a stand upon the Ticino, which encouraged me; I learned at the same time that a strong detachment which was evacuating the Abruzzi by way of Sulmona had had much difficulty in forcing its way past Rocca d'Anzo. I think it had lost three hundred men, together with artillery, baggage, and provisions; the bridges had been destroyed, and the roads encumbered with obstacles of all kinds that had only been surmounted with difficulty.

I was in a state of terrible anxiety and worry, owing to the position in which I had left so many French people in the State of Naples, so many persons devoted to our cause, who would be exposed to the vengeance of the Court, now in exile in Sicily, if our efforts were to fail. In Rome difficulties of organization occupied me several days, though they did not retard the march of my troops. The risings in Naples had extended over the entire Roman States, as over Tuscany, and, in fact, the whole of Italy was disaffected. Despite my letters and apparent confidence, I had good reason to fear that we should be stopped on the road by this state of things; for our communications, already interrupted on the right bank of the river Po, were interrupted also between Florence and Genoa.

I at length quitted Rome, after encouraging the French authorities, as well as those of the Republic, to show a bold face in these times of difficulty. I left a garrison, a small one I admit, together with a few Roman troops, upon whom I did not count, especially if they once met with a reverse. I left there the pontoon train, baggage, and various things which only encumbered my march. A party had preceded us without an escort, among whom were the family of Méchin. They had all been seized on the road by the insurgents.

General Monnier, who commanded the district of Ancona, the only man who did his duty, had sent to me for instructions. I merely answered:

'You know what honour requires and what the law demands; I leave it to you.'

On the supposition that all my efforts were going to fail, and that I was going to be completely stopped on my march, I intended to occupy a strong position, and to keep the enemy in check as long as I could, for I felt sure that they would never dare to venture into the Roman and Neapolitan Republics as long as the Army of Italy was not obliged to recross the Alps. In the contrary event, I determined to dispute every foot of ground, falling back gradually upon Rome and the Neapolitan forts, to defend myself to the last gasp, convinced that France would spare no efforts to reinforce the Army of Italy, and attempt fresh diversions in order to set us free.

General Moreau, on his side, tried to check the enemy, but mere pluck could do nothing against forces superior in number and flushed with victory. His communications being hampered, he ought, in my opinion, to have managed to stretch out a hand towards me while falling back upon Genoa. This junction could alone have enabled us, if not to resume the offensive, at any rate to await assistance from France; but he preferred to maintain his communications through Piedmont, which was already disturbed, instead of by the Cornice road. This last plan could have served the double purpose of covering that road and of preventing any obstacles being placed in the way of our junction in Tuscany. Instead of executing a manoeuvre at once so simple, so natural, and so useful to our cause, finding himself compelled to abandon the Ticino, he threw himself into Piedmont in order, as it was said, to attract thither the Austro-Russians, and to return by a forced march from Ceva to Genoa, I believe. The latter place capitulated to a band of insurgents, so that, deprived of this outlet, he was obliged to abandon part of his equipment, and to make his way over the mountains.

I had left Rome in the hope that the Ticino would be held long enough for me to effect a junction, and on reaching Florence, or on my way thither, I learnt the position into which the Army of Italy had been thrown. My plan had been bold, hazardous perhaps; but it was of the kind that often succeeds in war. I had never shown all my hand. Communication between Florence and Genoa had been cut off, and it was not safe to trust to the sea; no ship was ready at the port of Lerici, in the Gulf of Spezzia. I knew also that Mantua was, in all probability, invested; it was a very strong position, well garrisoned, I had reason to believe, well provisioned, and commanded by General Latour Foissac, father of the present major-general of that name.

I made for Pistoia, and my first proceeding was to take up a position on the Apennines and guard all the passes. I made an attack on the enemy at Sarzana and Pontremoli. Both places were carried, and communication with Genoa re-established. General Dessole, chief of the staff of the Army of Italy, separated, I forget how, from General Moreau, gave me all the sad details just related. Montrichard and Victor had posted their divisions, one at Bologna, and the other not far from Genoa. I had matured my undeveloped scheme, which was to bring about a junction between the two, if they were placed under my orders, and to precipitate myself from the summit of the Apennines against the enemy's left wing, which was posted in the valley of the Po at the foot of the passes, and the principal body of which was covering Modena.

I communicated this plan to General Dessole, and he approved it, at the same time, however, advising me to suspend its execution until the arrival of General Moreau at Genoa, an event which was shortly to take place. The operation, if successfully carried out, would paralyze the left wing of the enemy, if it did not utterly destroy it, and would separate it from the main army by cutting off its communications with it, and driving it across the Po. Proceeding up the right bank of the river, threatening to proceed to raise the siege of Mantua, I hoped by that means to disengage the Army of Italy by forcing the enemy to retreat along the left bank, after which I should have effected my junction with Moreau at Parma or Piacenza.

Meanwhile, I had made preparations to suppress a rising in Arezzo, but postponed it, as I required all my forces.

It might perhaps have been better to effect the junction by the Cornice; at any rate, it would then have been managed without obstacles, as it eventually turned out; but I think I have already explained that there were not sufficient ships in the harbour of Lerici to transport all the artillery and baggage to Genoa, and the Cornice was then nothing but a mule-track. However, in proceeding to carry out the other plan, we did not neglect to supply plenty of transports in case of defeat, which later on saved our most precious war-material.

If, on the other hand, the expedition succeeded it would bring about results of even greater importance. The gain of a single battle would enable us to reconquer all we had lost, and would put a stop to the insurrections, which would no longer have the countenance and support of the enemy; but to prevent failure, the simultaneous action of both armies was necessary, albeit at a great distance apart. The sequel will show how it failed owing to Moreau's irresolution.

All our reports tended to prove a determination on the part of the enemy to keep their position before Modena, and to prevent the Army of Italy from quitting the passes of the Apennines. Montrichard's division, stationed as I have said at Bologna, as well as Victor's, at Pontremoli, I think, were placed under my command. General Lapoype, with 3,000 or 4,000 men, was at Bobbio. The important matter was to retain Florence and Leghorn in my absence, and the State of Tuscany, being almost in arms, necessitated the presence of a force sufficiently imposing to maintain order and give us security. General Gauthier took the command.[4]

General Moreau, unaware of these exigencies, and imagining that I was marching with all my troops, expected that I should collect about 40,000 men, including those belonging to his army, from Tuscany and Genoa, that is to say, with Montrichard's, Pérignon's, and Victor's divisions; but of the Army of Naples I left in that kingdom and in the Roman States from 14,000 to 15,000 men, including sick, and 4,000 or 5,000 in Tuscany. General Pérignon's division could not act with me, for it was only later, on reaching Piacenza, that I heard that the small body belonging to General Lapoype at Bobbio would be at my disposal. The Army of Naples was now able to take the offensive, as with Montrichard's and Victor's divisions it reached the total of 25,000 men, well equipped.

After so long a forced march as that from Brindisi into Tuscany, the need of a few days' rest, and for repairs to material, clothing, harness, ironwork, etc., etc., will be easily understood. The army therefore took up a position. I had only very doubtful information regarding the

---

4. I think I have made a mistake in quoting the Ticino for the Bormida. It was behind the latter river that Moreau had retired, and whence he was driven during my march from Rome to Florence. It will not seem strange to you, my son, if, writing as I do from memory, after so many years crowded with events, you find here and there little slips that you can easily correct by examining my journals and correspondence, which I have not by me, and which, even if I had them, are in such confusion that they would be no real help to me. Moreover, I am writing for you alone, to give you a sketch of my military career. I shall presently be compelled to have recourse to some of my old journals, because an important event which took place soon afterwards, the Battle of the Trebbia, has given rise to much controversy, and will require more detail.—Note by Marshal Macdonald.

strength and position of the enemy, and it would have been imprudent to risk anything.

We expected, and hoped, that the Mediterranean squadron, commanded by Admiral Bruix, was on its way with a reinforcement of 15,000 men; if this were the case, and they could be disembarked either at Spezzia or Genoa, and there joined to all the men whom Moreau could collect round the town, we might hope for some success, and look forward to repairing our losses; but these rumours were unfounded.

I learned at the same time news that had better foundation in fact, namely, the appearance off Ancona of a Turco-Russian fleet, conveying troops to be disembarked; but I was quite at ease, knowing the promptitude of General Monnier. Besides, the Italian business would have to be settled before the reduction of that town, which would take several months. I thought that I might place the same reliance upon the commandants left in the kingdom of Naples, but shortly after my departure they allowed themselves to be intimidated by masses of insurgents, supported by some English detachments, and yielded one after another.[5] What was not the least unfortunate part of the matter was that they abandoned Fort Sant'-Elmo, giving up their compatriots to the vengeance of their sovereign, and Admiral Nelson did not hesitate to tarnish his glory and reputation by causing the unfortunate Admiral Caracciolo to be hanged at his own mast-head. Other patriots were courageous enough to blow themselves up in the little fort called, I think, the Maddalena, near Naples, on the road to Castellamare. I have never heard that after the French reoccupied this kingdom, which became that of Joseph Bonaparte and Murat, any steps were taken to honour this act of devotion.

While the troops were taking up the positions assigned to them, the work of making and distributing necessary articles was pushed on as fast as possible; provisions were collected, either to cross the Apennines or to fall back upon Genoa. I discussed with General Dessole the advantages and drawbacks of an offensive movement; if Moreau returned to Genoa with the rest of his troops, and we acted in concert, we might count upon a force of about 60,000 men. In any case, I urged upon General Dessole the advisability of sending all ships at his disposal from Genoa to Spezzia, and I sent thither all mine from Leghorn. The event proved that this was a wise precaution.

I had just heard that the citadel of Ferrara had capitulated, and that

---
5. See James's *Naval History of Great Britain*, vol. 2.

Fort Urbino was about to be attacked. General Montrichard was at Bologna. I did not know him personally, but presumed he was a man of talent and courage, as he had appeared to possess a reputation upon the banks of the Rhine, a reputation no doubt usurped, as I learned to my cost. I had praised him, never dreaming that he had been the principal cause of the loss of the commander-in-chief, Schérer, on the Adige, that he had retired from Legnano almost without a blow, thus leaving the passage open to the enemy. This had compelled the unlucky Schérer to retreat, and his original acceptance of the command had been severely commented upon without justice. He was reproached with severity, even with harshness, I know not on what ground. I have never found cause in him for anything but praise, and certainly his misfortunes did not arise from want of skill. During his ministry he had quarrelled with General Bonaparte, and consequently with the Army of Italy. When the latter started for Egypt with its chief, and was replaced by other troops from the Rhine and the interior, the hostile feeling remained, and took root in the Italian soil.

My troops continued their march to take up their position at the mouth of all the passes of the Apennines, and I established my headquarters at Lucca, after deciding with the commandant and the Government Commissioner at Florence upon the best means for keeping open communications in Tuscany. This had become a difficult matter, owing to the partial insurrections, particularly that at Arezzo.

I think I have already said that Pontremoli had been retaken. I caused Sarzana to be occupied, so as to help and support communications with Genoa. I received good news from Naples, but none from any of the fortresses. The squadron under Admiral Bruix, which I believed to be holding the Mediterranean, was at Toulon without any troops. Porto-Ferraio, in the island of Elba, was besieged and clamouring for help, but I had none to give. I begged the General commanding in Corsica to see to it. Want made itself universally felt, even at Genoa. I visited Leghorn. Victor's division came to Sarzana to replace the troops from Naples. I had not been warned of this movement, which necessitated a change of position. The civil agents with the two armies[6] could not agree.

Worn out with these quarrels as much as with my work, and considering it hopeless to bring all parts of the service into harmony it

---

6. The divisions of Montrichard and Victor, put provisionally at the disposal of Macdonald, had not ceased to belong to Moreau's army. They kept alive a spirit of dangerous rivalry with the Army of Naples.

even seemed impossible to keep a friendly feeling between the generals of the two armies owing to their jealousy I explained the situation to the Directory, proposing to it to unite the two under one commander, that of the Army of Italy, at the same time offering to resign and serve in the line. I thus sacrificed myself to the public good, but it was long ere my offer of patriotic devotion reached its destination and I obtained an answer. Meanwhile, the crisis was becoming more acute; something had to be done to stop the advance of the enemy and the constant risings of the people.

CHAPTER 9

The Marshal in Danger

I had concerted a plan with Moreau whereby our armies should join at Parma or Piacenza; he was to follow in person Victor's division, which would debouch near Fortenuovo.

My entire army advanced towards Modena, each column having orders to be in position by the 22 or 23 *Prairial* (10 and 11 June, 1799). Montrichard's and Rusca's divisions, escorting the artillery, were to follow the high road to Bologna. I followed Ollivier's division by Pistoia and Formigine. Orders had been previously given for a simultaneous attack upon the enemy stationed at Modena, with a view to cutting off their retreat. This attack was to take place on the 24th. On the previous evening they attacked our advanced posts at Formigine, and were beaten back.

The troops were full of ardour, and on the morning of the 24th, at a meeting of all the generals, an action was decided upon. I had no news of Montrichard's and Rusca's divisions, and it was difficult to communicate with them. Their cannon ought to have foretold their approach; I heard it in the direction of Fort Urbino. Then I ordered a charge; a furious combat began; my left wing even gave way a little; I sent reinforcements, and then ordered a simultaneous charge of cavalry and infantry. The enemy were routed and dispersed; several regiments laid down their arms. We entered Modena pell-mell with them, encumbered with baggage.

The results of this affair nearly cost me my life. My troops, unable to resist the attractions of the baggage, threw themselves upon it, and began to pillage. I knew by experience that if we halted in our pursuit we should restore courage to the terrified enemy, and make them turn again. Some few shots were to be heard at the other side of the town, almost at the gate; by dint of prayers more than by threats I succeeded in getting together a handful of troops to follow me, and drove off the Austrian sharp-shooters. I was on the road to Bologna; no trace of the divisions coming from that direction. What could have become of them? I sent out a reconnaissance of fifty men, followed by another troop of the same number, to support them if necessary. Just as the latter were starting off at a trot, I heard a cry:

'The enemy's cavalry!'

I looked round, and to the right perceived a thick cloud of dust on a cross-road, with deep ditches on either side, leading into the Bologna road. This body was cut off, and was being pursued by some of our cavalry. I sent the adjutant-general, Pamphile Lacroix, to summon them to yield, promising them that they should not be harmed. At the same moment a body of my grenadiers issued from Modena; I had only to cry, 'Halt! Front!' in order to bar the road. My 'guides' (guards attached to the commander-in-chief) deployed at right angles with this battalion, but unfortunately without observing that a broad ditch separated them from the road, along which the enemy's cavalry were advancing; the guides thought they could attack it in flank. When my battalion was drawn up, I ordered them to present arms, but not fire without my orders, and mechanically passed in front of it, studying the map.

I had advanced a few yards, when I suddenly saw Lacroix throw himself backwards, and fall from his horse. The enemy's detachment was advancing at a rapid trot, whether animated by the courage of despair, pursued from behind, barred in front, with large ditches on either flank, or whether they had not noticed this latter obstacle, I know not. They continued to advance, and were only at a short distance from me, when I wished to turn my horse, and get behind my battalion, so as not to be in their line of fire, and to draw my sword; but a double incident occurred. I was accustomed to carry a stick with a spike at the end, a leather thong passed round my wrist, and the spike resting on my foot; but the case for the spike had been lost, so that, not to wound my foot, I had thrust the end of the cane into my stirrup; thus encumbered, the thong entangled round my right arm, and the left occupied in holding my horse, I could neither reach nor draw my sword, and, in spite of my orders, a shot was fired from the left of the battalion; that sufficed to produce a discharge, though the bayonet would have been enough to do the work.

There I was, therefore, midway between my own troop, which was firing, and the advancing hostile cavalry. My horse was struck, and the shock of the charge threw it with me on its back, and at the same moment I received two sabre-cuts—one on the head, and the other across the right thumb. I was thrown senseless to the ground, and there trodden under foot. I heard afterwards that not one of the cavalry had escaped; they had all been either killed or made prisoners; and such must have been the case, for my guides, having advanced and discovered the obstacle presented by the ditch, had immediately turned and drawn up behind the grenadiers, who were then fighting with the bayonet, and, inspired by the sight of my danger, were giving no quarter. The most surprising—nay, almost miraculous—part of the circumstance is that, although I was the fifth or sixth to pass along the line of fire, only one captain of engineers attached to my staff was killed. Not one of the others was touched, not even by the enemy who collected round me, perhaps as a means of safety, perhaps because I was recognised, as I was wearing the full uniform of a commander-in-chief.

The attentions that were lavished upon me restored me to consciousness. On opening my eyes I found myself in a house, surrounded by generals, among them being Montrichard. I believe this was some three hours after the action. I was suffering horribly, not so much from my wounds, as I had lost a quantity of blood, and was, in fact, covered with it, as from the trampling of the horses, the combat having raged over me.

'This is your doing,' I said to General Montrichard. 'Had your troops taken part in the action, this mischance would not have befallen me; and not an enemy could have escaped had my combinations been carried out.'

His excuse was that, on reaching Fort Urbino, the regiment at the head of his column had no cartridges; that the train of artillery, at the end of both divisions, was still at Bologna, and that they had waited for it to come up.

'What!' I exclaimed, 'regiments campaigning without cartridges? Why did you not discover it sooner? Were they all without them?'

'No; only the leading company.'

'Why did you not throw it aside and let the others take the lead? A little more, and we should have been driven back,' I added; 'and it would have been your fault entirely, as you could and should have made an important diversion.'

He dropped his eyes and made no reply. I should have done well to withdraw his command from him then and there. We should have been saved many disasters caused by him; but he belonged to the Army of Italy, and was only for the time being under my orders. Moreau was vexed afterwards that I did not take this prudent step.

They informed me that the enemy were being followed, and prisoners brought in every moment. I gave orders regarding our position, and was transported to my headquarters at Modena. I was suffering greatly from the bruises caused by the trampling of the horses. The generals-of-division had followed me; I felt that I was not in a condition to continue in command and to lead the army; I offered the succession to the senior among them, who declined, and then to the others in turn. The position beyond doubt was difficult. It was pointed out to me that the main body of the enemy was still distant; that, according to the plan for the junction of the Armies of Italy and Naples, which ought to take place in a few days, and according to the marches calculated both to Parma and Piacenza, they would naturally have a chief in Moreau that I could be just as easily transported to Genoa by Bobbio as by the route we were now following, and even by the valley of the Po, as our success would be assured after this junction. These arguments decided me, and orders were given to continue the movement. We pushed on, therefore, towards the places of rendezvous, manoeuvring on the right towards the Po, and spreading a rumour that we were going to raise the siege of Mantua, and that we were gathering forces for that purpose; this was done in order to attract the enemy to the left bank.

Embarrassed by the prisoners, among whom were some of superior and many of inferior rank, I caused them to be conducted to our outposts at Ferrara, after exacting from them a promise not to serve until an agreement could be arrived at for an exchange of prisoners; the baggage, in order to relieve us, was sent to Fort Urbino. I even gave the officers some pecuniary assistance, although they were at no great distance from their own troops; but far from observing the engagement promised, the Austrians had the bad faith to keep as prisoners the detachment of cavalry sent to escort their officers to a place of safety.

They followed me, having obtained some reinforcements for their broken ranks, but without causing me much trouble. I felt sure that, sooner or later, they would fall into our hands after our junction was effected, which would certainly give us a decisive victory.

General Victor had debouched near Castelnuovo, making for Parma or Piacenza, and driving before him an Austrian division which had taken up a position on the Tidone. It was between these two towns, if I remember rightly, that this general sent me a letter from Moreau, stating that he was still in doubt as to the direction of the rest of his army—whether it should follow Victor, or whether it should debouch near Bobbio, or near La Bocchetta. The day even of his departure for either place was uncertain; but he said it would probably take place on the 20 or 21 *Prairial*, and it was now the 26th, so that allowing for twenty four hours' delay, according to our calculations, and for the possible local difficulties of the march—for he had no enemies in either of the former directions—our junction ought to take place at latest on the 27th or 28th either at Parma or Piacenza.

The only obstacles were on my side; but I had declared positively, perhaps somewhat rashly, that I would surmount them, and I had succeeded, inasmuch as I had defeated the hostile body that awaited me at the outlet of the Apennines without the help of the two divisions that were coming up from Bologna. While waiting for the arrival of the Army of Italy, I rapidly continued my march towards the Trebbia and Tidone, and gave orders that our position should be occupied there without engaging in hostilities, as I had two divisions behind, manoeuvring on the Po, which I had called up in order to bring them into line.

The enemy had sent a detachment into the citadel of Piacenza. We had to guard the entrance, and leave on our side of the town a rear-guard to stop the remains of the combatants at Modena from following us.

My sufferings were severely increased by the movement of the carriage in which I was laid. I anxiously expected Moreau, and could get no news of him. I hastened the advance of the two detached divisions, ordering them to come into line with all speed on the Tidone. It was on the 29th[1] that the others took up their position. Victor's regiment, already in position, had exchanged a few volleys; unfortunately, he had remained in person at Piacenza, where I was myself, but without informing me of the circumstance. He had charged his brigadier-general, Charpentier, with the care of settling his position. Dombrowski's and Rusca's regiments arrived soon afterwards. All had orders not to fight; Rusca, notwithstanding the remonstrances of General Charpentier, insisted upon trying to force the passage of the Tidone; he partly succeeded, but was soon repulsed, in spite of the support of the two

---

1. 29 *Prairial*, year vii. (June 17, 1799), first of the three days' fighting which are together called by the name of the Battle of the Trebbia.

other divisions, who were compelled to take part in this unfortunate skirmish. All three were thrown into disorder.

As I was unable to mount a horse, I had given the command of the four divisions drawn up in line[2] to General Victor, with orders to take up his position on the Tidone and drive the enemy to the other side; but this general had remained at Piacenza, unknown to me. Thenceforward all was confusion, and the disorder that followed the engagement may in great part be attributed to this cause. I could hear the firing at Piacenza, but without being able to foresee or to fear the consequence, as the great allied army could not yet be entirely united, and ought to be harassed on its right flank and rear if Moreau had attacked those points. This was what he most likely had done, as he did not appear on our left, and I had no news either of his march or his direction; the junction was always intended to be the chief object of our movements, especially of mine, with a view to attracting the enemy to me, and distracting their attention when in Piedmont.

This junction was made at least, virtually when I arrived in Tuscany; and had it not been for the difficulty attending the transport of baggage by sea, the troops might have marched together along the Cornice road to Genoa, as has since been done. But the operations in the valley of the Po would have been far more important if the movements of the two armies had been simultaneous, according to the original agreement; and I am still convinced, although it is twenty-five years since the events, that our success must have been infallible had it not been for Moreau's hesitation.

By an inversion of the marching order, the reason for which I have now forgotten, General Salm, who commanded the advance-guard, found himself behind the other divisions that were occupying positions on the Tidone, and which, when routed, fell back upon him and disordered his lines. He had the presence of mind to throw his men to the right of the road, and drew up there in order of battle; the enemy, pursuing eagerly, thus found themselves exposed to a flank fire, which compelled them to retreat. On receiving a report of these events, I ordered them to take up a position between the Tidone and the Trebbia; but it was urged against that proposal that there was no place suitable, and that it would be better to recross the Trebbia, as a large number of fugitives had already done. I consented, although this could only be a rallying position; the torrent was wide and fordable everywhere.

Salm, however, received orders to remain where he was, to cover

---

2. Those of Victor, Dombrowski, Rusca, and Salm.

the army, form his advance guard, and send out scouts. Montrichard and Ollivier, still behind, were desired to hasten their advance, and to come and put themselves into line and support us. It was clear that the enemy, too, had made forced marches, and mustered on the Tidone. But where was the Army of Italy? In what direction? I could not tell!

Until the junction was effected, prudence commanded me not to risk a battle with such unequal forces. I had no choice but to retire; but if I went away, and the Army of Italy debouched from the mountains in the expectation of finding that of Naples, it would in its turn be isolated and exposed to certain loss. What excuse could I give if I did not venture it? Of course, the cry of 'treason' would have been raised. But that would not have been all. It was, indeed, stated in the Army of Italy that I had given battle before the junction from motives of personal ambition. It will be seen from these writings how devoid of foundation was this idea, and, besides, my own condition would have sufficed to prevent that. I passed a wretched night, tormented by the fear of being attacked next morning before all our forces had come up, and also lest we should not be able to repair the disorder that had been caused that evening.

Day broke at last. Acting upon the reports received from the reconnoitring parties, I had myself carried to Borgo Sant'-Antonio, near the Trebbia, and thence along my line, which I found drawn up in good order. General Salm and the other generals came to make their reports and observations. I made a few alterations, such, for instance, as changing the position to be occupied by the advance-guard if it were compelled to retreat; the two divisions behind, which I summoned back by means of a forced march, were to remain in reserve.

All appeared tranquil, and our troops seemed prepared to give the enemy a good reception. I intended to be beforehand with the enemy as soon as my two other divisions arrived, and unless they previously made an attack. General Salm, trusting in his troops and his position, which I wished to preserve as far as possible, had strict injunctions not to engage alone; immediately the first serious demonstrations were made, he was to fall back and take his place in the line. So much did he trust in the apparent tranquillity of the enemy, that he asked my leave to go and spend a few hours in Piacenza; I was less confident, refused permission, and did rightly, for shortly afterwards, through my telescope, I perceived at some distance a mounted troop on the lookout. Salm declared that it was a mounted reconnaissance that he had sent out; I answered that it was facing us, and that if the detachment belonged to us it would naturally turn its back to us; but he would not be convinced. I even sent out to reconnoitre, although I was almost certain of what I had seen.

'Make haste!' I said shortly afterwards to him. 'Gallop to your position; that reconnaissance is advancing, and another troop is coming up behind it. You are going to be attacked; be ready to fall back.'

He went.

Firing soon began, and as from the wooded nature of the ground it appeared that the whole force opposed to us had not appeared, Salm sent to ask me for a company of grenadiers, declaring that with their help he could maintain his position. I took a different view of the matter, and in sending him the battalion asked for, which was to draw up in echelon and support him, I also sent him repeated orders to retire. This, unfortunately, he only did at the last extremity, which very nearly caused us serious loss. At the first gunshot my men were under arms. Our vanguard at length retired; the firing increased. I saw five large columns and a large body of cavalry approaching behind our troops Wounded and fugitives came in in crowds. Salm, hard pressed, continued to retire, fighting as he came; being wounded, he made over the command to General Sarrasin, who, wounded in his turn, gave it to the brave Colonel Lahure, who soon shared the same fate, The men, finding themselves without a leader, and not knowing what position in the line they were to take up, recrossed the Trebbia in disorder at another point, and covered the artillery and musketry that should have protected them. If the enemy, whose advance was continuing, had made an effort at this moment, I know not what would have become of us.

At length my lines got clear, and my batteries opened fire. The Austro-Russians made a vigorous onslaught on my line, and renewed it several times without causing us to move; their strength was great, and their cries and howls would have sufficed to terrify any troops except French ones. At length they drew off; the artillery fire gradually slackened on either side, and ceased entirely about ten or eleven at night.

We had already a large number of wounded. The close proximity of the armies required the utmost watchfulness; we passed the night under arms. The two rear divisions arrived; they required rest. They stopped for the time in the second line, while the first reformed and prepared to take the offensive, if opportunity offered, instead of continuing on the defensive.

Daybreak found the two armies facing each other on either bank of the Trebbia. A cannonade began, but without much effect; it sensibly diminished after a few hours, and finally ceased altogether on both sides. We piled arms, as though a truce had been agreed upon. During the night I had decided upon taking the offensive, regardless of the superior strength of the enemy. My troops were excellent, and the French character lends itself better to attack than to defence. My plans were laid and orders given for nine o'clock in the morning, so that only one signal would have been necessary; but it did not take place until noon, for, notwithstanding repeated orders, it was impossible to get the Montrichard division out of its bivouacs. It did come up at last, but without its general, who remained behind.

At the first movement to arms, the enemy formed a line of battle, and the firing began. My columns boldly crossed the Trebbia and scattered the first line. Unluckily, the Montrichard division, having no leader, sent out a party of sharpshooters, flanked by some cavalry. The enemy's horse, weak at that particular point, made a sally to drive back this body, which was causing it inconvenience; the latter, terror-stricken, fell back upon the division and paralyzed its fire. Montrichard's cavalry, although superior, fell back, and returned in disorder, followed by the enemy, and the whole division was thrown into confusion. I deployed my reserve of infantry to protect them, but the cavalry reserve, having failed to take up the positions indicated for them, so that they might support our weak points, lost time in coming up; the enemy took advantage of this to rally and make a charge.

The gap made by the retreat of Montrichard's division, which I stopped and formed up at the edge of the river, left Ollivier's division exposed to a flank attack. It was compelled in its turn to retreat, as was also General Vatrin on the extreme right, but the movement was effected in good order, and it recovered its position. The same movement was executed upon the left, commanded by General Victor, who had surprised the Russians and thrown them into great disorder.

Meanwhile our cavalry reserves had come up and joined the fray. The confusion into which the enemy had been thrown gave us time to rally and to form up again into a line of defence. The enemy soon renewed the attacks of the previous evening, but found only an immovable wall of steel. Their loss of men was enormous, but unavailing; and at length, wearied and worn out, they ceased their attack and retired to their positions. Night fell, but the cannonade continued on both sides, lest either should forget the presence of the other; but at length it ceased. I received disastrous accounts of our losses. Nearly all our Generals and superior officers were more or less seriously wounded; our loss of men, in killed and wounded, was enormous for so weak an army. Not the least serious part of it was that nearly all our ammunition was exhausted. These events occurred on the 29 and 30 *Prairial*, and 1 *Messidor* (June 17, 18, 19, 1799).

CHAPTER 10

Plans for Retreat

No news arrived of Moreau, nor of the Army of Italy, nor of the detachment from Bobbio, which ought to have come up behind the enemy's right. It was clear from the position of the Austro-Russians in front of us that they felt no uneasiness as to their rear. We had been very much weakened; we had scarcely any general or commissioned officers left, hardly any ammunition, a formidable army before us, the batteries of Piacenza, as well as another considerable one on the other side of the Po, barring our road (the survivors of the battle at Modena, reinforced by some troops from the blockade of Mantua, who had come up on our rear near Piacenza)—such was our situation. We must infallibly be attacked next morning, and if we were beaten, all would be lost. I had done my utmost to effect a junction; my efforts were fruitless.

We had to preserve the remaining two-thirds of the army in order to get out of this very awkward position, and try our fortune elsewhere. It was, of course, painful to leave a battlefield where the Army of Naples had so much distinguished itself, and acquired so much glory; but its safety was the first consideration. The generals having explained to me their fears, the superiority of the forces opposed to them, the want of ammunition and provisions, I reluctantly decided upon retiring from this bloody field, and orders were given for the movement to be made at midnight precisely, on the 2 *Messidor* (June 20).

Our army was to march in three columns, leaving behind the main-guard and outposts to form a curtain to cover their movement, until the enemy attempted to advance, when they were to fall back upon their respective corps. Montrichard's division was sent forward to open up the road that we were to follow towards Parma and Modena. It was necessary to avoid the battery on the Po and to get round Piacenza; a road was made during the night. After I had assured myself that all my orders had reached their destination and would be fully carried out, the army moved noiselessly at midnight precisely to recross the Nura; the point at which the three columns were to join was Cadeo. Scarcely had Montrichard's division gone a few miles ahead of us, scarcely had the right and centre columns passed the Nura and formed up beyond it, when the main-guard appeared, as well as the small body that was observing the castle of Piacenza, followed by the leading troops of the enemy. It would have been very fortunate for us if we could have passed this defile without being harassed; but unhappily Victor's division, which, with the flank company of General Calvin, made up the third column, only started at six in the morning, instead of at midnight.

Thus they lost a start which would have been as valuable to them as it was to the others, and also the precious advantage of putting the defile of the Nura between them and the enemy; the bridges could easily have been defended by a few troops. The enemy, as yet unprepared to attack, noticed this retrograde movement, pursued the column, and discovered that there were only a few scouts left along the whole line.

General Victor was pursued and hard pressed, as I could hear plainly, being only a short distance off; but I imagined that the battle was taking place on both banks of the Nura. An *aide-de-camp* from the general came to beg me for help. In order to rescue him, I caused the whole centre column to recross the river, half to drive back the enemy in front, and the other half to execute a flank attack on their left. We succeeded. Being thus freed, both crossed the Nura once more, and continued, without being much harassed, their movement upon Cadeo, where the three, columns were to join. Those of the right and centre arrived there, but the left tarried; however, hearing no firing, I concluded that the movement was being quietly carried out.

Our troops were resting, when some horsemen appeared at full gallop from the direction of the left column, followed by a crowd of fugitives in such terror that I preferred allowing them to go by to attempting to stop them. A staff-officer of General Victor at length rode up to ask for help. I immediately sent my reserve, but on reaching the point mentioned, it found neither friends nor enemies, only all the artillery abandoned by the column. The troops had been scattered and fled, some into the mountains, carrying alarm to Genoa, others, as I afterwards heard, to Castel Arquato.

One of the regiments lost its flags; I have forgotten how. On hearing of this incident, I sent out a number of artillery horses, and rescued all the guns belonging to the column, which were brought back to me by the reserve sent to the assistance of General Victor, who was nowhere to be found. Then we continued our march without further annoyance till the morning.

General Montrichard, who led the march, informed me that the enemy were in front of him, but not stationary. It was important to secure the passage of the Taro, and I sent him word to hasten his advance. At length I had intelligence from General Victor, who stated briefly that his troops, sorely pressed by the enemy, had dispersed, that the rout had begun, and that, to his great regret, he had lost his artillery; that, unless he received contrary instructions, he should make for Borgo San Donino. That was the very place for which I was bound.

'Set your mind at rest,' I replied, 'as to your artillery. The detachment that I sent to your help, when you begged for it at Cadeo, where I then was, reached the spot where you ought to have been, and found neither friends nor foes; but I caused your guns to be brought in without opposition. I will restore them to you the first time we meet.'

This remark cut General Victor[1] to the quick, and I do not believe he has yet forgiven it.

I have never received a satisfactory explanation of this curious event. One grave fault was that of not quitting the battlefield at midnight, which would have given him six hours' start of the enemy. It seems that later on, while crossing the Nura, some disorder had occurred which had not been repaired, and that the appearance of a few *Cossacks* had sufficed to increase and turn it into a rout; for, although we were but a short distance away, we heard no sound of musketry. I have since heard that Moreau only came down from Genoa by the Bocchetta on the 2 *Messidor*, the very day on which I was leaving the Trebbia, that the Austro-Russians retreated from the Nura, only leaving General Ott with a division, and possibly another small troop, to follow us. If the men of the third column were really as fatigued as General Victor declared, there were certainly no symptoms of it evident in their flight, and they would have been much safer had they held their ground.

On reaching Borgo San Donino, whither Victor had preceded

---

1. Victor Perrin, created Marshal of France in 1807, and Duke of Belluno in 1808, after the Battle of Friedland.

me, I drew up fresh instructions for continuing our retrograde movement. The latter general was to return to the Apennines by the pass through which he had come, and troops were successively to hold all the outlets, menace the flank of the enemy that was pursuing me, and thus cover the march of the rest of the army, which was to make for Modena and Bologna with the baggage, place the guns taken from the enemy in Fort Urbino, draw thence fresh ammunition and provisions, take from the two principal towns sufficient food to last them for the five or six days necessary to cross the Apennines, and go to Pistoia and Lucca.

It was the more important to guard the mountain passes, as it was indispensable that our junction should be effected near Genoa, and, if these passes were left undefended, the enemy, by taking possession of them, might reach Pontremoli and Sarzana before us, and again cut off our communications by superior forces. True, they might have forced these outlets, and thus isolated me from the Army of Italy; I had foreseen this possibility, and determined to defend myself inch by inch. By my marches and movements I should have attracted a large body of troops to me in Tuscany, in the Roman States, even as far as Naples, by relying upon the strongholds. It was with this object that I had brought with me, and left in Rome, a pontoon train to enable me to cross the Garigliano and Volturno.

This movement, however, of the enemy's forces was not much to be feared, for the Army of Italy was certain to be doing something somewhere, and it was not likely that Generals Souvorof and Mélas, leaders of the Allied Armies, would risk themselves between two French armies; prudence, nevertheless, necessitated these dispositions; nothing should be left to chance, and, as time was precious, I lost none in having them carried out.

I sent for General Victor in order to have information from him: first, as to why he had been so late in starting from the field of the Trebbia; and secondly, upon all that had taken place on each side of the Nura. He answered that he was busy settling his men in camp, and that he would come later. I wished also to communicate my new instructions to, and to come to a clear understanding with, him, as we were about to part. An hour or two having passed without his arrival, I sent again. He replied that he was tired, and had gone to bed. It was very obvious, therefore, that he wished to avoid a disagreeable explanation upon all that he had done. My instructions were therefore conveyed to him, and we continued our march; but scarcely had I left

San Donino when an *aide-de-camp* came up at full gallop to tell me that the division was attacked. We were not far away, and he begged me to suspend my movement, and even to come back to their help. General Vatrin, who was beside me, said:

'Nonsense! it is only a few *Cossacks*, like the other day.'

This speech was repeated to General Victor as coming from me, and contributed not a little to increase his ill-humour. A few minutes later I was told it was only a skirmish; a piquet had kept a bad lookout, and had been surprised by the enemy.

I therefore answered merely, 'General Victor has his instructions; let him keep to them,' and continued my route.

I have, forgotten to say that we were constantly followed by a large and ever-increasing number of waggons, which added to our difficulties, notwithstanding my repeated orders to do away with them. Those who drove them, guessing that prompt measures would probably be taken, hastened to unharness and unload, and even to burn them. Nearly all our wounded had been deposited at Piacenza, and, as usual, recommended to the enemy's kindness; some few had, however, followed us. I had ordered that each baggage-waggon and cart should take one or two, and this had at first been done, but the proprietors of these vehicles had left the poor fellows in the places where we stopped for the night. I was indignant at this.

Several of them were put under arrest, but nothing could be proved against them at the inquiry. They declared that the wounded could not bear the jolting of the waggons, and, unluckily, now it was too late to verify this statement. The burning of these carts freed us somewhat, and it was the real owners who suffered; but it was a necessary sacrifice, because of the trouble they caused us. We kept, however, a few for the transportation of our wounded as far as the nearest towns.

The army continued its movement, occupying the Apennines, or marching with the baggage along the highroads. We had to seize Reggio, and fight at Modena and Sassuolo. Had we not been compelled to obtain provisions to take us over the Apennines, I should have avoided every engagement at these last places; but as the Apennines offered no resources, I took up my position at Modena, after opening the road to Reggio. The enemy, who had at first displayed but few troops, attacked my entire line with a force superior to mine, and menaced the road to Pistoia, where General Calvin was. However, they made no stand, and retired into the mountains. My *aide de-camp*, Lacroix, followed them, and carried Sassuolo at the point of the bayonet, an affair which gained him much honour; he compelled 600 men to lay down their arms, took two flags and two pieces of cannon, and thus opened the communication for us who were engaged at Modena.

We also gained a victory there, and maintained our position. Meanwhile, we collected provisions, and levied a contribution (which brought in very little) to punish the town for a rising that had taken place, in which many soldiers had been assassinated and pillaged; some of them could thus be indemnified. The combat finished at nightfall. The enemy had passed the River Crossolo at three or four points, but had always been repulsed. We also made a few prisoners.

Before daybreak the army continued its march, leaving its positions to return to the Apennines. Montrichard's division, passing by Bologna, was to bring away the ammunition from Fort Urbino, and to leave there the artillery and military chests taken from the enemy. I do not remember what became of the prisoners; they were perhaps returned, to the number of 500 men, for on such a march they were a serious inconvenience, as they had to be watched and fed. (They were meant to have been exchanged later on for a similar number of our men.) We thus regained our former positions in the Apennines, without being molested, although we were followed. My headquarters were established at Pistoia while waiting for news of General Montrichard and the Army of Italy, whom I presumed to have made a movement towards Tortona, as they had not debouched on the side where I expected them.

We succeeded in reopening communications with Moreau and the Army of Italy. The latter had descended the Apennines by the Bocchetta, and had, at the foot of the mountains, a battle with one of the divisions of the great Allied Army on the very day upon which I retreated from the Trebbia. Had they come down sooner, it is probable that all the forces of Generals Souvorof and Mélas would not have attacked me, as they would have feared for their right flank, placed between two fires, as it would have been had the corps under General Bellegarde been forced.

General Moreau has never explained his conduct, although I have often pressed him to do so by word of mouth, by letter, officially, and by public summons. Why these delays? I am sure there was no ill-will on his part, but merely hesitation, which was part of his nature. I cannot say the same for his advisers. Among them was one man in particular[2] who had great influence, and was inspired by an unjust

---

2. General Gouvion Saint-Cyr.

animosity—it was more than unfriendliness—against me. It was this man, I have since been told, who principally contributed to augment this natural tendency to delay. What matters any detriment to the public weal, so long as private spite can be gratified! An explanation of this will come in good time, and I will not anticipate it. Moreau returned to the positions whence he had started, having been warned that Generals Souvorof and Mélas were retracing their steps with a portion of their forces in order to effect a junction with General Bellegarde.

While at Lucca I received a note from the commandant of the fortress of Mantua, informing me that he was blockaded, but not attacked; that he had a strong and courageous garrison, and that the place was sufficiently well provisioned to stand a long siege. I hastened to communicate this reassuring report upon the condition of a place so important to us. We continued our retreat in order to concentrate ourselves with the Army of Italy within the boundaries of Liguria. All our baggage was embarked at Lerici, on the Gulf of Spezzia; the infantry and cavalry passed over the Cornice road, and I went to Genoa, whither I had been summoned by Moreau to consult as to our future operations, although I was under his orders.

My health was at this time in a very bad state; my wounds were not yet healed, I spat blood, I had violent pains in my chest, and a sort of general inflammation, caused by the vexations and annoyances to which I had been abandoned, by long nights and excessive work, under most difficult circumstances; and I was worried by many different events which, with a little goodwill, loyalty, and honesty, could not have failed to be productive of the best results.

The concentration of the two armies in the neighbourhood of Genoa was decided upon. It was not without keen sorrow that we found it necessary to abandon to themselves the garrisons of the territories of Naples and Rome, to evacuate Elba, Tuscany and Lucca. Instead of sending us the reinforcements of which we stood so sadly in need, a fresh army was formed on the Var or at Chambéry, under the command of General Championnet. It was called, I believe, the Army of the Alps. I insisted more strongly than before upon the fusion of the two armies, and upon the necessity of leave of absence to recruit my health.

CHAPTER 11

Landing of Napoleon

During my first command in Rome I had begun a collection of objects of art, of curiosities and antiques, which I confided to the care of a faithful friend at the time of the invasion by the Neapolitan troops without any previous declaration of war. On my return to Rome, seventeen days later, I found it intact. It was considerably augmented by presents of pictures from the principal Romans, which I considered I might accept in return for important personal services that I was able to render them.

After the conquest of Naples, the French Government divided the objects of art among the generals who had taken part in it, after a commission of artists had selected objects wherewith to enrich our museum in Paris. I had succeeded General Championnet, and the commission was charged to set aside what should come to me. Some pictures, Etruscan vases, and ancient frescoes from the walls of Pompeii were given to me, valued at 800,000 *francs* (£32,000). I had them all packed and forwarded to Rome, with the treasures for the Government. In Rome I caused to be added to them all that I had acquired in that city, and the convoy continued its journey into Tuscany; its destination was Genoa, whence it was to go to Marseilles.

I thought no more about it; but on reaching Genoa I caused inquiries to be made, unfortunately too late, at the merchant's office to which they had been consigned. They had never arrived, and I discovered afterwards that the waggoners had not been able to pass beyond Pisa in consequence of the risings; that having waited there a long time, and spent all their money, they had deposited these precious things there and gone away. We had just evacuated Tuscany; I had passed through it, stopping at Pisa to review an army; the boxes were inscribed with my name, therefore the intention of stealing them was clear, as I was never told they were there. Had I been told, I might have sent them on board a ship at Leghorn or Lerici. They were rifled and sold. The following year we returned to Tuscany. I made every inquiry and a strict search, but the robbers and pillagers had taken flight, so that I lost one of the finest private collections of curiosities and objects of art then existing.

Among them was a complete imitation of a dessert, with all the fruit made of marble, and a magnificent silver epergne; also a valuable collection of ancient and modern marbles, carved lava from Vesuvius, etc. I had spent a good deal of my own money. There were also the presents that I had considered myself at liberty to accept, and the greater portion—of course the most valuable and rarest for a private individual—came from the distribution made by order of the French Government. My regret at my loss was the greater inasmuch as I was able to talk about it. I had no reason to blush for that or for anything else in my long military career.

While I was in command at Naples, I had caused searches to be made, on my own account, at Santa Maria di Gati for tombs containing Etruscan vases. Six were discovered, and were left closed until my arrival; they were not to be opened except in my presence. But events never permitted me to think of them again, and they, too, were thus lost to me.

The French Government at length appointed a new commander-in-chief, Joubert, for the Army of Italy, to replace Moreau. That of Naples was suppressed—united to the other; and I received the permission, so earnestly longed for, to return to France.

Moreau and I agreed to start together. I then learned by private means that Mantua, for the strength of which the commandant had so readily answered, had capitulated. The details of this event were so precise, the means through which I had received the information so trustworthy, that doubt was to my mind impossible. However, Generals Moreau and Joubert, and his chief of the staff, Suchet, declared that the news was false, and spread with a purpose, and that they had much more recent and trustworthy information. Of course, I wished to believe them; but, on the other hand, I could not doubt the honesty of my informant. This uncertainty was terrible, on account of the events which would soon come to pass; for if Mantua had really yielded, the besieging force would become an important and valuable reinforcement for the allies.

Their very inaction proved to me that they were waiting for the reduction of Mantua in order to recommence active operations. At length they marched. At the first intimation, Joubert collected his forces and started; I cautioned him to be circumspect, to beware how he advanced too far, and to assure himself of the truth of the intelligence, because, if Mantua had fallen, the forces would no longer be of equal strength.

Moreau and I had chartered some feluccas at Genoa; I had been waiting several days for him, when he sent me word that General Joubert had begged him to remain with him, so I started alone, hugging the shores of the Cornice towards Savona, Oneille, Nice, and Toulon, not without some uneasiness respecting the pirates who swarmed in those waters. I was, however, escorted by a small armed boat, which scoured all the creeks and small harbours. I was within two or three days of Genoa when I heard that Joubert had been killed,[1] the army routed, and the news of the fall of Mantua confirmed.

From Toulon I travelled by easy stages to Paris, where the somewhat cool reception given me by the Directory was made up for by public opinion. No Government ever weighs in the balance past services with a present check, and never takes circumstances, means, etc., into consideration. They must always have victories. No doubt the principle is a good one, but justice and equity demand that everyone should receive some share of the recognition due to him. Now and again newspaper articles would appear blaming my recent operations. I had a correspondence with Moreau upon the subject, as he and his staff seemed not altogether strangers to these articles. I was tired of his arguments and hesitation. He was now back in Paris. At one moment he advised me not to notice these diatribes; at another he undertook to refute them; then his papers, which ought to have come to him by road, had been mislaid. Losing patience, I at length told him that I would bring an action against him; and I did so, honestly and straightforwardly, but especially promptly. His defence was pitiable and confused; judgment was given in my favour, and that ended the matter.

I was not yet cured of my wounds, and fears were entertained respecting my chest. I was put upon a diet of milk and sago.

France was groaning under the weight of her arbitrary government. The Directory had neither credit nor consideration. It had made itself detested by the iniquitous 'Hostage Act,' and by its forced

---

1. General Joubert was killed at the Battle of Novi, July, 1799. His widow, *née* Mademoiselle de Montholon, became Marshal Macdonald's second wife. By this wife he had one daughter, afterwards Marquise de Roche-Dragon.—Translator.

loans. Intrigues were on foot to compass its downfall, and I was asked to put myself at the head of the movement; I declined. I believe, but am not sure, that a similar application was made to Moreau, who also refused.

All at once the news was spread of the unexpected arrival at Fréjus of General Bonaparte from Egypt; all eyes were turned to him, and from thenceforward he was regarded as an anchor of hope and salvation. He sought me out with considerable eagerness. I was on fairly intimate terms with his wife,[2] and some of his brothers and sisters. He desired precise information upon all that had passed in Italy. At a little dinner, at which Moreau was present, we gave him an account, and the opinion of my *amphitryon* was thenceforward settled in my favour.

The 18th *Brumaire* arrived. I took a considerable share in it. I was in command at Versailles, and my first care, on arriving, was to close a Jacobin club, which was never reopened. The great struggle was to take place at St. Cloud; it nearly failed. Had it done so, we should all have fallen victims to the party which, to the misery of France, would have been triumphant.

The question of reorganizing the armies now arose. Moreau was to have that of the Upper Rhine, and I that of the Lower; but he worked so skilfully behind my back that he succeeded in having them united in one, and the entire command placed in his hands. I was indignant at this double-dealing, and had a somewhat acrimonious conversation on the subject with the First Consul, who admitted having yielded to Moreau's pressure, but expressed his regrets to me. He added that he had believed that Moreau and I had agreed upon this together, and that Moreau had certainly given him to understand that such was the case.

'How could it have been so,' I asked, 'after all that passed between us in Italy, and after the explanation of these events that you yourself had from us at your own table?'

'That is true,' he replied, adding, 'Your health is not yet quite restored. Take care of yourself, and I will fulfil my promise presently.'

The first Army of Reserve was being then organized, and he kept for himself the command, having Berthier under him. He attempted and achieved the famous passage of the St. Bernard, and the victory of

---

2. Joséphine, daughter of Monsieur Tascher de la Pagerie, and widow of General Vicomte Alexandre de Beauharnais, married to Napoleon in 1796.—Translator.
(*Napoleon's Letters to Josephine* by Henry Foljambe Hall also published by Leonaur.)

Marengo crowned the bold and dashing enterprise.

Later on a second Army of Reserve was formed at Dijon, the command of which was given to me. It crossed Switzerland, and took the name of the Army of the Grisons,[3] which pointed pretty clearly to the mission with which it was charged. It was to act in the Rhetian Alps between the Armies of Italy and the Rhine, and to support them both.

A month's truce was arranged. I had orders, or authority, to concert operations with Moreau, who was very anxious for an interview; he was even desirous of coming to my headquarters at St. Gall; but it was difficult for him to leave his army, and I went to Augsburg, where he was established, and thence to Ratisbon, Landshut, and Munich, whence I returned to St. Gall. We settled our plan, and Moreau took it to Paris to explain and get it authorized.

I took with me on my journey General Mathieu Dumas, my chief of the staff, Pamphile Lacroix, and General Grouchy. I had been on distant terms with the latter since we had been in Holland; but flattered by, and grateful for, my reception, he related to me all the trickery and intrigue set in motion at Moreau's headquarters in Genoa to leave the Army of Naples unsupported and to get out of its difficulties as best it could. He told us that the chief promoter had been General Gouvion Saint-Cyr, who had not forgiven me for having replaced him in Rome, as if I had had anything to do with his quarrel with the Government Commissioners who recalled him. Moreau apparently failed to see the trap, and his hesitation, prolonged as it was, became tantamount to a desertion of me. You know the results and consequences of his proceedings.

Moreau's presence in Paris brought about a change in the commands. He was to take over that of Italy, and I to succeed him with the Army of the Rhine. I had orders to prepare for this change; but while I was doing so a courier informed me that the original plan was to be adhered to that Moreau was to return to his post, and I to remain at mine. At the same time, I received instructions to commence hostilities, and to begin operations upon the lines agreed upon with Moreau and the Army of Italy, to which they had been communicated.[4]

Situated thus between the Army of the Rhine on my left, and that of Italy on my right, communicating and acting as the centre for both, I had more natural difficulties to surmount than enemies to conquer.

---

3. 6 *Fructidor*, year viii. (August 24, 1800).
4. General Brune commanded the Army of Italy.

The latter were entrenched in all the passes of the Alps, which I had to cross in all their breadth as far as Trent on the Adige, especially the Splugen, Tonal, etc., which were covered with snow and ice. More than once discouragement nearly overcame my men. I went in person to all the most dangerous places, sounding the snow, trying the ice, and measuring the depth of the abysses that surrounded us. Avalanches had swallowed whole squadrons.

Finally, by dint of perseverance, boldness, or, I perhaps should say, rashness, we succeeded—more by good luck than good guidance, but not without great losses—in gaining the *plateau* of the Splugen where the monastery is situated, and eventually the right bank of the Adige. Whether I advanced or retreated the danger was equal. I therefore could not hesitate. This adventurous march forced the enemy to retreat precipitately before us, to evacuate that portion of the Alps from the Vorarlberg to the Tyrol, and helped the other two armies in their operations. The first thing done was to conclude armistices, to which I was a party, and the peace of Luneville crowned the campaign.[5]

I passed the remainder of the winter and the beginning of spring at Trent, whence I was ordered to bring my army back into Switzerland, across Italy. I raised my cantonments and started; on the road a courier brought me my nomination to the post of envoy extraordinary and minister plenipotentiary to the Court of Denmark,[6] with orders to return immediately to Paris. All my tastes were opposed to such a career; but the post was offered to me as a military operation covered by a diplomatic cloak.

---

5. Treaty between France and Austria, signed February 9, 1801.
6. Nomination dated *Germinal*, year ix. (March, 1801).

CHAPTER 12

Napoleon Elected Emperor

The kingdom of Denmark, especially its capital, was threatened by an English fleet: I was informed that the Government had asked for a French general to undertake the defence of the country, and that they had thought of me. I will not deny that I was flattered by the choice, and anxious to join my name to the events of which that country was to be the scene; but I had the firmest intention, which I kept, of quitting diplomacy as soon as the military part of it was concluded. I therefore started for Paris. I did not expect to get further than Nevers, for, while changing horses in that town, I heard of the disaster at Copenhagen abandoned by Sweden, Russia and Prussia, all of whom were bound by treaties to make common cause with Denmark. However, on reaching Paris, firmly convinced that my mission was at an end, the First Consul informed me that there was still hope of renewing the Quadruple Defensive Alliance, and desired me to start, *via* Berlin, promising that, if peace were the result of the events at Copenhagen, he would grant my request, and recall me immediately.

On reaching the capital of Prussia, I soon learned that Russia had broken away from the alliance by a treaty with England, leaving power to the three other countries to adhere to it. I immediately sent a special messenger to the First Consul with this news, and, foreseeing that the other Powers would adhere, asked leave to return; the answer I received was that, as I had got so far, I should go on and learn the intentions of the Danish Government, and that if peace were decided upon my expedition should be regarded as a mere journey, and I should be recalled at once. I thus went to replace your mother's father,[1] who was awaiting my arrival to go and take up the same posi-

---

1. Monsieur de Bourgoing, whose daughter became the Marshal's third wife.

tion at Stockholm. I had then no idea that I should ever be united to your lamented mother, who was then quite young, and whom I had hardly seen. That was in 1801, and it was not till more than twenty years later that the marriage took place, which so sadly terminated in less than four years.

Previous to my audience at Court, I was fully confirmed in my opinion that Denmark could never struggle unaided against so formidable a naval Power as England. The attack on the capital, the destruction of a large number of her ships, the successes of the bold and rash Admiral Nelson, who continued to fight in spite of the contrary orders of his chief, and notwithstanding a brave defence which merited a different fate, brought about an armistice which was existing when I arrived, watched by the English fleet as I passed through the Great Belt. My mission, therefore, brought about none of the anticipated results, arid my first despatch terminated by an urgent prayer to be recalled. I renewed this prayer for five months, but as peace was at that time-being negotiated with England, it was deemed advisable to retain foreign ministers at their respective posts.

The preliminaries having been signed,[2] and peace being momentarily given to all Europe, it was presumed that the motives I had put forward would no longer exist. I was therefore sounded with respect to the embassy in Russia, occupied by General Hédouville, who, like me, was earnestly seeking his recall. At last I obtained mine, and quitted Copenhagen in the depth of winter. On my journey I experienced every discomfort of the season, which was very severe in the North, and after a month of painful, fatiguing, and even dangerous travel I reached Paris, whence the First Consul had gone to attend the meetings at Lyons.

My stay in Denmark had not been without interest and pleasure. I was distinguished at Court, on good terms with the *corps diplomatique*, and well received in society. I studied the history of the country its laws and customs. There I found a people who, with unbounded love for, and confidence in one of its sovereigns, blindly abandoned its liberty, and submitted itself to their absolute power. So far they have had no cause to regret their action, but I doubt whether any of their powerful neighbours would ever employ the same generosity in order to guarantee their subjects from the abuses of violence or despotism.

To return to what concerns myself. I had a suspicion that Monsieur de Talleyrand had some motive, that I could not penetrate, for wish-

2. The treaty of Amiens, between France and England, was signed March 25, 1802.

ing to keep me at a distance. I had written him strong representations upon this point in private letters, but as he might have been prejudiced or biased against me, I called upon him. He received me with cold civility. I warmly pointed out to him, in presence of his wife and several other persons, how ill he had behaved, and abruptly quitted his house. Since then I have ceased to hold any communication with this personage, who afterwards degraded more and more his name and position. He has certainly from time to time made overtures to me, but in vain. I had estimated correctly the sincerity of his affection.

His ambition, however, had been amply satisfied at the Imperial Court as well as at that of the Bourbons; his supple mind, intrigues, and insinuations had secured this. When at last Talleyrand came to be better known and understood, all parties agreed to push him aside, and to let him extract what enjoyment he could out of a comparatively insignificant office,[3] and to live in regret, if not remorse. I admit having said too much about this individual, but it is because I know that he seriously injured me in the eyes of the First Consul by prejudicing him against me, and suggesting that I was opposed to his authority.

In 1804 the famous trial of Moreau commenced, and an attempt was made to implicate me in it by suggestions of an intimate friendship, which no longer existed. It seemed, however, to be recognised that my conscience was clear upon that point, and so I was merely watched, but left in peace.

Shortly after this trial the First Consul was elected Emperor, and the Government having thus become monarchical, was invested with the attributes of monarchy. In order to attain the dignity of Marshal, it was necessary to have had the command-in-chief of an army, and although this condition was not wanting in my case, I was not included in the first or in the subsequent lists of nominations. I therefore had to content myself with thinking that I had deserved to figure in them, and with the pride natural to me, added to the feeling that I was the victim of injustice, I took no steps to remove groundless prejudices. The time came when I congratulated myself upon having acted as I did, for circumstances so favoured me that I was able to win my baton at the point of my sword on the battlefield of Wagram.

In the year in which the Legion of Honour was founded, I was first made only Companion, together with all those who, like me, had received gifts of a sword of honour, but I was then promoted to be a Knight Companion (*Grand Officier*). My name must have passed un-

---

3. He was Grand Chamberlain.

noticed among others, for in the suspected position in which I then was living, its appearance there could only be regarded as a favour.

Like everyone else, I had signed the address of election to the Empire, but rather as a means of warding off anxieties and annoyances than with any hope of obtaining reward. I had no reason whatever for opposing it, still less for being jealous or desirous of it. My isolation chafed me on account of your elder sisters. They had received an excellent education at Madame Campan's, but the sight of their friends making brilliant marriages at the Imperial Court made me dread lest they should become enamoured of these exalted positions. But their own good sense, their judgment beyond their years, my advice, and the affection they bore me, convinced them that I was innocent of this disgrace, and they resigned themselves to whatever fortune might be in store for them.

I had just bought this property at Courcelles whence I write to you, and which I intend you to have some day; but notwithstanding the pleasures of a country life, and the delight of being at rest, my military ardour blazed up at the accounts of every fresh victory. However, this ardour quieted down when I remembered that my career was advancing, so much so that it was not without some alarm that I received orders to join the Army of Italy, after five years spent in retirement, to put myself at the disposal of Prince Eugène Beauharnais,[4] Viceroy and commander-in-chief. I was just about to return here with your sisters, who had finished their education, and whom I had removed from school. I was only spending a few months with them in Paris during the winter to perfect their accomplishments.

I think I received the order early in April, and at first I concealed the nature of it from them. The Minister could not tell me in what capacity I was to go, nor did he know much about it. He showed me the original of the Emperor's letter, which was remarkable for its brevity. It ran almost as follows:

> Monsieur le Duc De Feltre,
> Convey orders to General Macdonald to betake himself to Italy, where he will receive fresh orders from the Viceroy, and I shall be grateful to him for the services he will thus render.
> (Signed) Napoleon.[5]

---

4. Son of the Empress Josephine, by her first husband, and stepson of the Emperor.—Translator.
5. The ministerial order is dated March 28, 1809.

Having but a few days left to make my arrangements, it was natural that I should think first of all of your sisters. I asked and obtained from the Emperor admission for them into the educational establishment founded for daughters of members of the Legion of Honour at Écouen, and then under the control of Madame Campan, their former schoolmistress at St. Germain. Our separation, as you will easily believe, was very painful; they thought of nothing but the fresh dangers to which I was to be exposed.

Before proceeding, I must go back a little to mention a circumstance that I had omitted. Some friends, placed by their rank near the person of Joseph Bonaparte, King of Naples, who was in command of an army in that country, represented to him that I might be of great service, as I had fought there some years previously. He had on several occasions testified goodwill towards me, and it was suggested that he should ask the Emperor for my services. The latter, commanding the Grand Army in the North of Germany, had, I believe, established his headquarters at Osterode during the siege of Dantzic, which followed the bloody Battle of Eylau, where both sides claimed the victory, although the best and most impartial judges on our side considered it more than doubtful.

The Emperor consented, and caused orders to be sent me by General Count Dejean, who was temporarily holding the office of War Minister, to go at once to Naples, and place myself at the disposal of his brother.[6] This was not a military order; for, contrary to the usual forms, no letter of service was sent to me. It was therefore clear that King Joseph was at liberty to employ me as he pleased, either with the Neapolitan troops or as a civilian; for the Imperial Generals in the Army of Naples have alone the right of commanding French troops with their letters of service.

My blood boils even now, and my gorge rises, as I write these lines, to think of what a degree of abasement I should have sunk to had I been desired to command Neapolitan soldiers! I, who had fought and annihilated them at Civita-Castellana, at Otricoli—who had completely finished them at Calvi, although on all these occasions we were less than one against twelve or fifteen! I, who had been witness of their cowardice, their desertion, and their flight! I, who had invaded their territory but a few days later! I say no more, and return to my departure for the Army of Italy in 1809.

---

6. The ministerial authorization is dated February 28, 1807.

Chapter 13

Warnings and Defensive Measures

A few days after receiving my orders I was informed that the Emperor, while at the opera, had received intelligence that the Austrians had crossed the Inn on April 12th. It occurred to me as probable, and my idea was eventually verified, that on the same day they would most likely commence hostilities and operations in the North of Italy. I therefore started the day after the Emperor had received the news.

I only halted for a few hours at Turin to see General Caesar Berthier, who was employed there, I forget in what capacity. He informed me that hostilities had been recommenced, and told me of the first success of our troops five or six hundred prisoners taken, and two pieces of artillery. He had first transmitted the news to Paris in a telegraphic despatch, adding that the whole army was advancing. I was still so far away, that I feared I might not be able to come up with them before some Important engagement: and, in spite of the entreaties of the general and his wife that I would stay and rest at least four-and- twenty hours, I started again immediately.

When I reached Milan, I found that no one knew anything of the supposed victory that had been telegraphed[1] from Turin to Paris; even the whereabouts of the army was unknown. I was a stranger in the town, though I had spent a few weeks there in 1798, just before I was sent to take the command in Rome; I had then known a few French officers, but they were all absent now.

However, a certain Signor Bignami, a banker, having accidentally heard of my arrival, came to see me, and told me confidentially that he knew, from commercial sources, that the army had met with a check,[2] and was retreating, though few people had as yet been informed. I

---
1. By means of semaphore posts.
2. Battle of Sacilio, lost by Prince Eugène, April 16, 1809.

tried to prove to him that he was mistaken by quoting what General Berthier had said; but he shook his head, and his assurance began to make me think that there really was something in his commercial intelligence.

It was too late for me to present my respects to the Vice-Queen; but among other names that he mentioned to me as belonging to persons attached to her Court, he spoke of Comte Méjean, whom I knew a little, and offered to take me to the *palazzo* where he dwelt.

We learned that Monsieur Méjean was at the Council. I gave my name to the usher, desiring him to inform that personage that, as I was only passing through Milan on my way to the army, I should be much obliged if he could tell me where the headquarters were, and whether the Vice-Queen had any messages for her husband. On hearing my name, he quitted the Council, and hastened to me; he took me aside, and confided to me that a courier, the previous night, had brought intelligence even more disastrous than that of which Bignami had spoken. The letter brought by the courier was couched in more or less the following terms:

> Pressed by the enemy, and yielding to the cries of the inhabitants that I was abandoning them, and to the desire of the army, who wished to fight for their homes, I have given battle, and lost it!
>
> Eugène.'

Thereupon I said that I must at once have horses and start. He urged me to come and see the Vice-Queen, and offered to accompany me, assuring me that she would forego etiquette. But, as I was in travelling dress, I begged him to tell the Princess that I thought the best means of showing my devotion, and of being agreeable to her, would be to go direct to her husband's headquarters. Before leaving Méjean, he begged me to say nothing to Bignami, who would be sure to cross-question me. I limited my replies to saying that at Court they could add nothing to the news he had already received, and that no belief was placed in it. We separated, and I got into my carriage very downcast at this rebuff.

A battle in Italy, however serious it might be, could only be of secondary importance. The decisive point was Germany, where the Emperor was commanding in person. But it might have a bad effect upon the Italian mind, already prejudiced against us, kept under as they were, but not conquered; and upon that of the Germans and their armies, although they had been so often beaten, and their territory so often invaded by us. But they were like the teeth of Cadmus; no sooner was one army destroyed than another came to take its place. They seemed to rise out of the ground.

I had a high opinion of the military talents of the Emperor, who had so often performed miracles; I trusted him now, and I was right.

Between Brescia and Verona, at a place called Desenzano, on the Lake of Garcia, I met a colonel whose name I have forgotten. Still terrified at what he had witnessed and heard, and believing that the enemy were at his heels, he had just left headquarters, but was unable to tell me where they were situated. He was carrying orders to arm and provision all the forts in Piedmont—in short, to put them into a proper condition of defence. The disaster must have been considerable to necessitate such hasty orders! This colonel was in such a hurry, that I could obtain no details from him. Some leagues farther on I found the terror increasing, and it became worse as I drew nearer to the scene. I met a courier on his way from headquarters to the Emperor; not even he could tell me whence he had started, and all that I could extract from him was that he had been sent after this unfortunate battle.

At length I reached Verona. All was in confusion. The wounded were coming in in large numbers, as well as fugitives, riderless horses, carts, baggage-waggons, carriages, crossing each other, meeting, blocking the streets, and filling the squares; in short, all the horrors of a rout. The siege artillery stationed on the glacis had been promptly removed to Mantua. The authorities were without news, and crowded round me to ask for some. I could scarcely believe that I had come there in order to obtain information myself. Rumour said that the army was marching for Mantua, where it would rally; but it seemed to me impossible that, however great might have been the misfortune, they should abandon the high road to the Milanese capital.

Notwithstanding all the warnings I received upon the dangers I should meet along this road, I resolved to follow it, and was glad I had done so. Scarcely had I left the gates early next morning, when a courier appeared. He came from Vicenza, where he had left the Viceroy, who was just preparing to start for Verona. This courier was carrying orders to the siege-train to make for Mantua, an order which, as I have said, had been forestalled. I did not stop to interrogate this letter-carrier, as I was now within a few hours of headquarters.

I entered Vicenza, to the surprise of all who saw a carriage coming in the opposite direction to that followed by all the others, which would, moreover, have soon been followed by troops, had it not been for my unexpected appearance. News of my arrival soon spread, and the inn where I stopped was blocked with visitors and inquirers. The army was to a great extent formed of troops that I had had under my orders when I commanded in the Roman States and in Naples, so that I felt quite at home. Everyone gave me a different version of what had occurred, and, as usual, laid the blame upon the inexperience of their leader, the jealousy of the generals, and so on.

The Viceroy, who from his windows had seen a post-chaise pass, suspected that I might have come, and sent several *aides-de-camp* to find out and to desire me to come straight to him. He received me cordially, or, I might say, effusively. He was even more taken up with what the Emperor would say and write than with the affair itself.

'I have been beaten,' he said, 'at my first attempt in commanding, and in a bad place too. The Emperor will be furious; he knows his Italy so well!'

'What induced you to fight?' I asked. 'One can generally refuse a battle. And in such a position too, with that narrow gorge behind you, which made retreat so difficult in case of necessity! You are very lucky not to have had to do with a bold, enterprising enemy, otherwise every hope of safety for your army must have been abandoned.'

'That is true,' he answered. 'I yielded too easily to the prayers and complaints of the Emperor's subjects. I was surrounded, deafened by their cries that I was abandoning them without striking a blow. The army grumbled at having to retreat before a foe that they had so often vanquished before. I consulted and asked the advice and opinion of all the most experienced generals.'

It seems that all the latter had been satisfied with a laconic answer, to the effect that he was the chief, that he had only to give his orders, and they should be carried out; that the responsibility was too great for them. Which, being interpreted, meant, 'Get out of the difficulty as best you can.' These answers having roused his wrath, he only consulted his pluck, and without reflecting on possible consequences, gave battle and lost it.

'Never in future,' I said, 'give way to annoyance, or act precipitately. You see into what straits it has brought you. Where are you going now, and what do you mean to do?'

'Everyone is disheartened; no one speaks of anything but retreat. The orders are given and are being carried out at this moment.'

'Where is the enemy?'

'About three marches from here.' '

'Three marches, indeed! What would you do if they were on your heels? Is not this the home of trickery? Let me look at your maps and see if there is not some way out of the hole. If I remember rightly, a little river runs across here somewhere, with a canal and a number of brooks, which might easily be defended; dispute the Alpone on your rear, then Caldiero, through which I have just passed, but which would be a better position for the enemy, then the Adige, etc. Remember that the great issue will be fought out in Germany. You will learn the results, not from messengers, but from the movements of your adversary;[3] if they are rapid, it will mean that they have been victorious; if they are slow, as at this moment, it will mean that nothing is settled yet; if they are beaten, your adversary will retire, because he will not wish to abandon his communications with the capital, nor to be flanked and cut off by the victorious army that had just defeated him.'

To these reasons I added many others, not less powerful and convincing:

'If you retire without fighting from a position so easy to defend, the enemy will follow you. Where will you stop? On the rivers, or on the Alps? Now, if the Emperor is successful, and sends you orders to take the offensive again, you will have to try and force your way across these rivers. Shall you succeed with a discouraged army? It is doubtful. Do not let us therefore expose ourselves to such an accident, if we can avoid it; let us defend our ground foot by foot, and compromise nothing; finally, let us not risk a second battle, and do nothing unless we are sure.'

My arguments made an impression upon the mind of this really courageous and high-spirited young man. I continued:

'Summon the generals in whom you have most confidence, tell them your intentions, and hear what they have to say.'

'I know that already,' he answered. 'Look here; there goes one of them with his division. He took no part whatever in the action, and is now one of the first to be off, besides giving the worst advice.'

He thereupon gave orders for the unharnessing of his own carriages, which were preparing to start, and I returned to my lodgings to wait for the hour agreed upon for the meeting.

My arrival had produced a favourable impression in the army. I say it without vanity, ostentation, or pride. I was liked by my men, and

---
3. The Archduke John.

they had confidence in me; I had always taken a friendly interest in them. It was well known that my disgrace was the result of prejudice and injustice, and they thought better of me for agreeing to serve in a capacity inferior to those I had previously occupied. Hope began to revive even amid these sad circumstances.

At the meeting there was present a large number of generals and superior officers. The Viceroy explained the position of the army and the suggestions that I had made to him, and then desired me to lay before the meeting the extension that might be given to them, which I did very carefully, for fear of hurting the feelings of my audience. I was heard without interruption, but at the conclusion of my remarks General Grenier said, addressing himself to the Viceroy:

'Prince, no word has been said about the *morale* of the army, or about its present disorganized condition; I declare that it is such that I will not answer for my own division until it has had some days' rest behind the Adige at Verona.'

The others spoke on the same lines, and the Prince, promising to consider what had been put before him, broke up the meeting.

When we were alone, he asked me what I thought of General Grenier. I had had nothing to do with him, but we had met in the Army of the Sambre and Meuse, when I was leading thither from Holland fifteen or twenty thousand men from the Army of the North, just after his defeat in Germany and his retreat upon the Lahn and the Sieg. He had a good reputation as a general-of-division.

'As for *morale*,' I added, laughing, 'that of the gentlemen who have just left us seems to me no less shaken than that of their men. But you have some who took no part in the action; keep them here and let the others go. They will suffice for the time being, and you can recall the others in a few days.'

He fell in with my suggestion. As a matter of fact, we only needed a small number to guard the passes, and if the worst came to the worst, we were not far from the Alpone, a torrent between high banks, which would serve us in lieu of entrenchments. A portion of the troops, therefore, especially those belonging to General Grenier, were allowed to retire to Verona. General Pully's cavalry, which either had not been called up, or else had arrived too late to take part at Sacilio, received orders to reoccupy Padua, already evacuated in the general retreat that had been ordered when I arrived, and to which I had put an abrupt conclusion.

We had to consider the best provisional means of defence for ourselves in this land of surprises, and rode out to inspect them The Viceroy was good enough to make me a present of two horses, as I was without my equipment, which did not rejoin me, I think, until the month of August. I had, however, procured what was necessary for the time being.

The bridge of Vicenza could be easily defended by means of slight works; I suggested to the Viceroy what might be done, and asked him to order the Major of Engineers stationed there to carry them out. He called him and explained to him briefly what was wanted. I noticed that this officer did not understand a word of what was said to him, although he replied that he would carry out the instructions. I could not fail to observe it simply from noticing the face of the officer in command of this important post, and I communicated my idea to the Prince, who thought I was joking.

'Call him back then, your Highness,' said I, 'and ask him to repeat the orders you have just given him.'

The unlucky major stammered and shamefacedly admitted that he had not understood.

'Why did you not ask me to repeat my orders to you?' inquired the prince.

'I was wrong,' he replied, 'and I beg your Highness's pardon.'

A fresh explanation was given, and we rode away.

'See,' I said to the prince, 'how easily mistakes occur. You would have gone away in peace, thinking that your necessary orders would be carried out. You did not observe that, that officer, no doubt a very brave, good fellow, was not very bright; for if Heaven had endowed him with ever so small a share of wits, he would, on his own responsibility, have caused some temporary defences to be made at a point on which depended so much of the safety of his own men and of the army. Misunderstandings and blunders are often fatal, particularly in military matters; therefore, when I give a verbal order, I always have it repeated over to me, and have found it a good plan.'

I advised him to adopt it, which he did in the future with good results.

CHAPTER 14

An Incomplete Success

We held our position for three days, and the *morale* of the troops was already improved. While waiting for news of what was going on in the heart of Germany, the enemy made some feeble demonstrations; but as we were determined to risk nothing, we retired behind the Alpone, where the advance-guard was stationed. The rest of the army took up a position at Caldiero, having three bridges over the Adige in case of retreat, including that of Verona. We remained there quietly, and spent the time in a complete reorganization; losses were repaired by bringing up healthy men from the depots, and by drafting from hospital those cured of their wounds or sickness. It was considered advisable to skirmish a little, and to shoot every day, to familiarize the fresh men with fighting.

A feint I made with a portion of our troops succeeded at first, but unfortunately, our left met with a slight check, which decided the Viceroy to give counter-orders. I was unaware of this, as I was preparing to cross the Alpone, the defence of which had considerably given way before the energy of my onslaught; but the Viceroy came in person to the place to desire me to retire, and I had to obey. We returned to camp, regretting that we had not had liberty to reap the full benefit of our first advantages. Prince Eugène was still weighed down by the recollection of Sacilio, and this made him very nervous for long after, especially on two important occasions, of which I shall speak later.

We expected the Austrians to make a similar demonstration next day, and were prepared to give them a warm reception; but they stayed at home. This immobility was not altogether natural after their recent victory at Sacilio. I pointed this out to the Viceroy, and urged him to order a strong general reconnaissance. He did so. We followed with our reserves, when, through my telescope, I noticed a hurried movement of carriages and baggage-waggons.

'We have been victorious in Germany,' I said to the prince; 'the enemy are retiring.'

He also looked through his glass, saw the retreat, and gleefully stretched out his hand to me, thanking me for my foresight and for my advice, which events had so well justified. He sent orders to the camp to prepare to march, and himself rode up to the advance-guard, who were at the very moment sending back to tell him that the enemy were hastily retreating. When he left me to lead the march, I warned him to be prudent, and not to be over-excited by this adventure.

Some insignificant brushes between our advance guard and the enemy's rear-guard brought us to the brink of the Piave, the bridge over which had just been burned. It is a wide and very swift torrent, like all those in Italy; but they can all be forded except in case of heavy rain or melting snow. The decision to cross was taken, and carried out without difficulty; but all was nearly lost owing to precipitation. I was at the rear, and hastened my movement, so that I came up just in time to witness a check given to our troops, especially to a body of cavalry which had just possessed itself of, but had soon to abandon again, one of the enemy's batteries. The charge had been so impetuous that the gunners had had no time to fire; they were killed, and the artillery general taken prisoner. The Viceroy thought he was dealing merely with a rear-guard, but the captured general assured him on his word of honour that the entire Austrian army, commanded by the Archduke John, was there.

This news disconcerted the Viceroy. Only a quarter of our army had crossed the stream, and they were now forced back in the utmost disorder. Happily the enemy only attacked feebly, being entirely occupied in covering their retreat. My troops[1] began to come up. The Prince begged me to cross the river in person to stop the fugitives, and to take command of all on the left bank. Anxious in consequence of what he had heard from the Austrian General, he said to me:

'What are we to do?'

'The bottle is uncorked; we must drink the wine,' I replied. 'We were in too great a hurry, and our troops can hardly escape; but now that they are on the other side, we must support them as best we can.'

We settled that my men should cross as fast as they came up. I

---

1. General Macdonald commanded a corps formed out of Lamarque's and Broussier's divisions of infantry and a brigade of cavalry.

ordered that it should be in platoons, and that each man should hold his neighbour's arm. The torrent had increased considerably; stones slipped from under their feet and some of the privates were carried away by the current. It was a sad spectacle; but I was destined, only four years later, to see one still far more horrible.[2] When the fugitives began to arrive in disorder, they threw themselves into the water without observing the stepping-stones. I myself rushed in, sword in hand, to drive them back. After changing my clothes, I managed nearly to cross the swiftest part of the current by means of a small pontoon which happened to be there, and the shoulders of two men set me down dry foot on the other bank.

I assembled the generals, and announced to them that the army also was going to cross. In fact, the front column of my corps was a third of the way through the river. This movement, no doubt, stopped the enemy's attack, or, at any rate, slackened it. As the troops that had been pursued returned, they took up a position with their back to the left bank, so that a violent attack must either have precipitated them into the water, or compelled them to lay down their arms. My first care, after reassuring in a few words both officers and men, was to change this position for one perpendicular to the river, which thus flanked their left.

General Grenier[3] had just crossed considerably below me. He attacked and pursued the enemy by the same movement that I was making, so that we found ourselves placed perpendicularly to the river, as I have said. My own troops had been stopped and ordered to retreat by the Viceroy when they were already half-way across the river, because he had seen the rout of which I have spoken, and the pursuit of the enemy. He did not reflect that the best means of stopping it was to reinforce us. He observed to me afterwards, with some simplicity, that he regarded us as dead men, and saw no object in sacrificing more lives. I took the opportunity of addressing to him some remarks which he admitted were just, but by which, alas! he did not profit, such was the effect produced by the loss of the first battle at Sacilio.[4]

[He did not tell me what answer the Emperor had sent on being

---

2. In 1813, at the passage of the Elster, after the Battle of Leipsic.
3. He commanded a corps of two divisions.
4. The Viceroy at this time was very young. His after career vindicated him from any charge of personal want of courage. Indeed, after the rout of 1812-13, on the retreat from Russia, when even Murat deserted the army, it was the Viceroy of Italy who had the difficult task of reorganizing the army during Napoleon's absence in Paris.

informed of this defeat, but I learnt later that, after reading the despatch, the Emperor had sent for the courier who brought it, and asked whether he had met me, and if so, whereabouts.

'Near Verona,' answered the messenger.

'That is all right,' replied the Emperor.

I had not seen this courier, but was flattered by the reply, as it showed that the Emperor relied upon me to restore affairs in Italy.]

To return to the movement that I was executing. When my body of troops joined me the disorder was repaired. All who had crossed the Piave marched in splendid order and attacked the enemy, who now began to retreat. However, our extreme right, commanded by General Grenier, halted, although the fire was not very hot. I also halted, but for another reason. I perceived towards the middle of our front a mass of the enemy's infantry, covered by a sort of fortification that was nothing more nor less than an enclosure of sufficient extent to pen oxen during the night—a sort of back (*dossée*) of a trench. Some cavalry covered this infantry, who were firing at us. We had not any guns across as yet, I think. While our troops were halting, Colonel Vallin, of the Hussars, came and begged me to give him something to do. I told him not to stir without orders, and added that I would soon find work for him.

Thereupon I hastened off to the right, to get a better view of the enemy's central position, and to discover the reasons for General Grenier's inactivity. He told me that his troops needed rest. Just when they ought to have been pursuing vigorously! I gave orders to General Grouchy, who was in command of the cavalry at this point, and while he was conveying them to his men, I turned back to regain the centre. I saw Colonel Vallin and his squadron charging. I foresaw what must inevitably, and did, happen. The enemy's cavalry hurriedly withdrew, and allowed the squadron to advance, thus exposing them to the hot fire of the masked infantry, which I alone had perceived when I commanded the halt. My intention had been to outflank it on the right, and such were my orders to Grouchy. The enemy's cavalry, seeing Vallin's regiment hesitate, charged, and from where I was I could see that we were not getting the best of it in the melee that ensued. I spurred my horse, and came up with the unlucky leader, who was wounded in the hand, and fiercely reproached him for having disobeyed my positive orders. He replied that he had acted upon instructions from the Viceroy, who galloped up and said unreflectingly:

'Now then, *hussars!* let me see you charge those blackguards!'

Vallin had answered that he would have done so already, had not I forbidden him to stir.

'Never mind,' answered the Prince; 'charge all the same!' And he did so.

The Viceroy, who had been watching us from the other bank of the Piave, had made up his mind to cross, and had arrived just in time to order this grand mistake while I was away on the right. I rode up to him, and pointed out to him that he had most inconsiderately deranged my operation. He answered that he fancied there were only a few musketeers there.

'Do you suppose *they* would have stopped me?' I answered, and then proceeded to explain my plan, which might still be carried out.

He applauded it, and congratulated me upon all I had already done; in doing so, he was echoing the sentiments of the army, which was full of spirit and determination. In replying to the Prince's compliments, I asked to be allowed to carry out my own operation, adding that I would show him that I knew what I was about. [As I am writing only for you, my son, I need not put on airs of mock-modesty; I merely tell you the facts with the frankness that I am generally admitted to possess.]

'See!' I said to the Viceroy; 'the enemy's right wing is beating a hasty retreat! I am going to cut it off, and tonight I will make you a present of 10,000 prisoners.'

'I can see nothing,' he answered.

'Can you not see that immense cloud of dust gradually drawing away from us?'

'Yes.'

'Well, from that it is easy to divine that a general retreat is going on. Go to the left, make a feint as if to stop that movement, while I bring up the right, and order the centre to advance.'

We parted in a more amicable frame of mind; but it did not last long, for scarcely had he ordered the left to advance, when a few cannon-shot stopped him, and he sent orders to the centre and to the right, for which I was bound, to stop too. Amazed at such an order, I returned to the centre, which I found halted; and thus we lost our chance. I went in search of the Viceroy, whom I found at last. He told me that the enemy seemed inclined to defend themselves, and that he was unwilling to risk his army; that enough had been done, and that evening was advancing rapidly. Vainly did I point out to him that the firing was already slackening, and that its only object had been to cover the retreat of the right wing. He would pay no heed.

'In that case,' I said, 'I shall take no further responsibility. You are in command; give your orders, and I will carry them out.'

However, he left me the general command, and recrossed the river to spend the night upon the other side; while we remained in a huge meadow, or pasture-ground, without any shelter, and, what was worse still, without food for man or beast, as no baggage could come across until the bridge burned by the enemy had been rebuilt.

The Viceroy joined us early next morning, and General Grenier was ordered to follow him closely. The advance-guard belonged to me as the first corps, but for the present we formed the centre I accompanied the prince to the town of Conegliano. The principal officials of the place came out to greet him, and one of them said:

'Ah, your Highness! had you but pushed forward two squadrons, you could have cut off the entire right wing of the Austrians, numbering at least 10,000 men. They were fleeing pell-mell, in the most hopeless confusion of men, horses, baggage, and artillery. Their leaders could not make their voices heard, nor rally a platoon; and the confusion and stampede lasted all night.'

The prince looked at me regretfully; my only answer was a smile. Indeed, he had stopped my movement in a most untimely manner.

Nothing of importance occurred during the next few days: the enemy continued their hasty retreat, and we reached Udine. My corps was detached, so I could act independently. The rest of the army marched through Tarvis to Klagenfurt, and I was charged to raise the siege of Palmanuova; to cross the Isonzo; to take Goritz and Trieste; to do my best to facilitate the passage of General Marmont, Duke of Ragusa, who was under orders to evacuate Dalmatia and join us. Then I was to make for Laybach; to cross the Save, the Drave, and the Mühr; to take Gratz; and, finally, to effect a junction with the bulk of the Army of Italy, and to lead the whole body to join the Grand Army on the Sömmering. This was a large undertaking, and presented considerable difficulties; but I did not regard them as insurmountable. Besides, I had *carte blanche*.

The siege of Palmanuova was raised at my approach. The garrison and inhabitants received us as deliverers. I sent a strong detachment to Trieste, and the general who commanded it grumbled that I was 'sacrificing' him; but, as it turned out, he met with no resistance whatever. We crossed the Isonzo by main force, and took Goritz, where large magazines were established. We also found there some siege artillery from Palmanuova.

The heights of Prewald were fortified, and connected by earthworks and blockhouses: I battered down all that covered the approaches to them. Our first attacks having been wanting in vigour, I led them myself, and thus taught the generals that with more decision they would have lost fewer men. They combined together to hinder my operations, which I determined to head and carry out in person.

This line of forts was flanked on the left by precipices, and on the right by a range of lofty rocks. I sent some light infantry to escalade it, and from below they looked like pigmies: we even succeeded in hoisting up some field-guns. These demonstrations were made with no object but to deceive; however, we succeeded in investing the forts. The detachment from Trieste came up; its leader was charged to send emissaries to the Duke of Ragusa; none could pass, and we had no news of him.

During these operations, I sent to reconnoitre the passages leading to the quicksilver-mines of Idria, and from thence to the highroad between Trieste and Vienna; there were obstacles in the way of moving our baggage, but they might be overcome. Leaving troops, therefore, to observe the forts, I surveyed the base of the chain of rocks, and came out upon the highroad with the greater part of my forces. I sent reconnoitring parties out in every direction.

I marched upon Laybach, where a battalion of the advance-guard met an Austrian battalion in a bend of the road; both were very much in fault, as no skirmishers were out from either party. To see and to rush at each other with the bayonet was the work of a moment. Our men had the advantage of coming downhill, and the enemy were crushed; only a small handful of them remained to carry the news of their defeat to Laybach. So little did the enemy count upon the possibility of our march, that they had sent this battalion to reinforce the forts of Prewald and keep us in check.

An immense entrenched camp was intended to protect Laybach; but the insufficiency of their troops determined the enemy to disarm and abandon the side on our left, a well as the town, and to confine themselves to the defence of the fort and of the other side. I ordered a reconnaissance of the approaches , they were considered impracticable for a general attack; to besiege it we had no artillery, the bridge over the Save was in part destroyed, and we had neither time nor materials to restore it. I sent a summons, according to custom, to the commandant of the camp and forts, but he refused to surrender.

The capitulation of the forts of Prewald set a considerable part of my force at liberty, and the enemy were certain to have had intelligence of this. Their communications with Hungary and Croatia were still open; the liberation of my detachment made it easier for me to intercept them. The fort of Laybach, as well as the entrenched camp, was covered on our front by a marsh of considerable extent, and on another side by the Save. I could therefore only attack on the extreme right, as the left was unapproachable from the town. While, however, I was considering the best means of carrying the position, imperative orders reached me to leave only a detachment for purposes of observation, and to make for Klagenfurt with the rest of my army.

I could no longer cross the Save, and therefore could only start silently and by night in the direction indicated; in order to prepare for my march, I made active demonstrations against the fort and the entrenched camp. I had caused the marsh to be sounded, and had a road cut through it for the cavalry, who could thus come out upon the Croatian road. Orders were given that the troops who were to start for Klagenfurt were to be ready at nine o'clock that evening. Scarcely had we started, when a *parlementaire* was brought to me, charged with a proposal of capitulation.

'You are acting wisely,' I replied; 'I was just going to sound the attack.'

Having thus obtained every facility for temporarily rebuilding the bridge, I made my way direct by Marburg to Gratz, where I joined the Viceroy, who had preceded me.

The results I obtained from this operation, which I conducted alone, were the deliverance of Palmanuova, the forcing of the line of the Isonzo, the occupation of Goritz, Trieste, Laybach, the forts of Prewald, of that of Laybach, as well as its entrenched camp; ten or twelve thousand prisoners, a hundred guns, ammunition, weapons,' flags in proportion, and an immense quantity of provisions. The Emperor expressed his satisfaction to me through the Viceroy.

While we were in front of Laybach I was seized, as well as some of my men, with dysentery, which weakened me terribly, and which was increased by the work, and by the annoyances which were being secretly fostered against me by two of the principal generals. One of them was weak enough in mind and wits to allow himself to be influenced by the other,[5] who declared that the Emperor had only employed me in order to ruin me, that they would be dragged into

---

5. This was General Lamarque; the former was General Broussier.

my disgrace, that neither they nor the troops would obtain any favour or reward, etc. All this was repeated to me.

I had indeed noticed that some of my orders had been tardily executed when activity was necessary, and I should certainly have failed in some of my enterprises had I not directed them myself, which served only to increase the resentment of my antagonists, who found that they only obtained a small share in the success that crowned them. The situation, however, was becoming critical, and an opportunity presenting itself—two days before the capitulation of Laybach—I reprimanded one of them sharply, and threatened to put under arrest and send to the Emperor anyone who did not obey orders on the spot. This was in presence of a considerable number of officers and men, who loudly applauded my decision. Thenceforward my gentlemen did no more than mutter, but that did not trouble me.

CHAPTER 15

Advance to Raab

Shortly before my arrival at Gratz, I met a Russian officer, who told me of the sad results of the Battle of Essling. Our successes were such a poor compensation for such an unhappy event, that our joy was naturally turned into sorrowful regret. I found General Grouchy, who had preceded me by a few hours, at Gratz, whence he withdrew his troops to give place to mine.

The Archduke John, who had retired into Hungary, had not thought it necessary to defend the town, notwithstanding a well-bastioned rampart and the river Mühr, which was not easy to cross without pontoons. Grouchy had just concluded an agreement whereby the elevated fort that dominated Gratz was not to be attacked from the town, so as to preserve the latter from all harm. By this means, too, the bridge over the Mühr was given up. I therefore contented myself with investing the fort externally, and with preparing means to obtain possession of it either by a *coup-de-main* or by investment.

We were not even permitted to take the rest we all needed, after so much labour and so many forced marches.

I received orders to march into Hungary and to cause the fort to be observed, and even attacked if I saw fit. My route lay by Kermünd, the Lake of Neusiedel and Papa; we were then on the tracks of the Archduke's Austrian army, which was retreating to the camp at Raab. The Viceroy followed it. His cavalry had a sharp brush with the enemy, owing to their having too lightly engaged with an inferior force. One of our divisions lost its way and missed the rendezvous.

Although the Viceroy had sent me orders to take up my position at Papa, while awaiting fresh instructions, I did not think in his interest and in that of the army that I should obey. I was right, and he afterwards thanked me cordially, for he had much compromised the troops that he was leading to Raab by a serious and very imprudent engagement. I had started on my march, following the cavalry, who preceded us. The distance from Papa to the place where the engagement was being fought was, if I remember rightly, seven or eight leagues.[1] When I had advanced about two thirds of the distance, I met an officer from the Prince, bearing orders to raise my camp and join him. When the officer had left the Viceroy they were only skirmishing.

I made the utmost speed, but it was impossible to arrive in time to take part in the attack: but at least we should have been able to assist the retreat, if such had unfortunately been necessary. The commander-in-chief was actively engaged, and had already been repulsed several times when I came up; but as I turned the corner of a wood and of the heights, the battle-field was disclosed to my view. Several regiments were retreating in disorder; efforts were being made to rally them. I galloped up and presented myself to the Viceroy, who expressed delighted surprise at seeing me so speedily.

'I was very sorry,' he said, 'to leave you at Papa; you would have been very useful to me in this critical situation.'

'You have made a greater mistake than that,' I answered; 'that of giving and risking a battle with only a portion of your army, when you have that of the Archduke in front of you, in what seems to me a fairly strong position. But take comfort, here is my *corps d'armée*.'

'Where?' he asked quickly.

'Look behind you; here it is just debouching.'

'How grateful I am to you for your foresight!' said the prince, affectionately pressing my hand.

'Now then,' I said, 'one more attempt. Here is help; I am going to send up my troops.'

'No,' he replied; 'let them rest. We will call upon them later.'

General Grenier, who commanded the right, succeeded at length in routing the enemy and crowning the heights. We joined him. The sight of my men had revived the spirits of his. We ought to have taken advantage of this and pressed the enemy; but he refused, thinking that he had done enough, and saying that his men were too tired and needed rest. I tried to induce the Viceroy to give his orders, but recent events had made him very cautious. The enemy's infantry, however, were in disorder; we sent out some horse, unfortunately without any support, and the enemy were allowed to retreat quietly.

---

1. The French *lieue*, which I have rendered 'league,' is about $2^{3/16}$ miles in English measure.—Translator.

No notice was taken of my energetic protests, or of my saying that we should have to fight these same troops again next day, and perhaps at a disadvantage; that the Emperor's first question, on hearing of our victory, would be:

'Where are the results—the prisoners, guns, baggage?'

'You are too enterprising,' said the Viceroy.

'But,' I remonstrated, 'here, as at the Piave, you have only to stoop to pick up everything.'

He replied that he feared a sortie from the garrison at Raab if he followed in pursuit. I pointed out that if the sortie were going to take place it would have been during the action, and not when the troops were in full flight; that the very fact that no sortie had been made was a proof of the weakness of the garrison, which perhaps was doing its best with very inadequate forces, but which could not fail to be disheartened by what had just passed beneath their eyes. All was in vain, and the prince gave orders for the camp to be pitched.

He took me to supper with him, and on the way confirmed to me what he had already written more than once, the tokens of pleasure that the Emperor had given over my services and the rapid and surprising successes of my *corps d'armée*.

Next day I followed the enemy, who were much in advance of us. They were making for Komorn, a very strong place on the right bank of the Danube. We learned that the disorder into which they had been thrown at Raab had not yet been repaired. We spent some time in observation upon the river, vainly trying to break the bridge between the fortress and the left bank by floating down the stream against it some large boats laden with stones, which the enemy had not had time to sink. They had destroyed many others laden with grain of all kinds. There were nothing but water-mills there, and their destruction was a great injury to us: but the French soldier, always ingenious and industrious, found some smooth stones with which to grind his corn. Without this discovery there would have been no bread amid the abundance of grain.

The Grand Army at Vienna and the inhabitants suffered terribly from scarcity, chiefly of meat. Hungary, a country rich in crops, wine, cattle, etc., where also many horses are bred, offered us boundless resources. I immediately sent large convoys of wheat and oats, as well as 10,000 oxen, to the Emperor's headquarters. We also levied a large number of horses to remount our hussars and chasseurs, the breed being specially well adapted to light troops. Except the serfs, all the men wore hussar costume, and it is from them that it has been so universally copied. During the first days of our entrance into the kingdom we took them for irregular troops; happily we found them very peaceable.

CHAPTER 16

Battle of Wagram

After our fruitless attempt to destroy the bridge at Komorn, I received orders to advance towards Ofen, capital of Hungary; but shortly afterwards was recalled by forced marches to the chief headquarters at Ebersdorf, opposite the island of Lobau. It was clear that a great operation was being prepared. We were not the last to arrive, and by nine o'clock in the evening of July 4 we were at our posts on the Danube at the crossing-place that had been selected for the surprise of the enemy. We had marched sixty leagues in three days, and notwithstanding our excessive fatigue, and the heat of the season, we had but few laggards, so anxious were the men of the Army of Italy to take part in the great events that were preparing, and to fight in presence of their brothers-in-arms of the Grand Army, and under the very eyes of the Emperor.

That night an appalling storm burst upon us; rain and hail fell in torrents, driven by a raging north wind, the whistling of which mingled with the peals of thunder and the roar of cannon. This tempest was extremely favourable to our passage of the Danube upon bridges built on piles, at which they had been working since the fatal 22nd of the previous May;[1] they were masked by the thickly-wooded island of Lobau. I landed upon the island at about six o'clock in the morning: what we most wanted was a good fire to dry us, but the sun soon came out and warmed us with his kindly rays. Meanwhile, several corps of the Grand Army, which had roused the enemy from their security, were driving back their advance-guard, and this, being supported from behind, was slowly retreating towards the intrenched position of the camp.

---

1. The Battle of Essling had been fought on May 21 and 22.

I moved forward in my turn, and was momentarily placed in the second rank with the remainder of the Army of Italy. Scarcely had I deployed, being myself on the extreme right, when I heard cries of '*Vive l'Empereur!*' coming from the left.

The soldiers, as he approached, raised their *shakos* upon their bayonets in token of joy. He turned his horse towards the direction whence the cheering proceeded, and, recognising the Army of Italy, rode down the line; as he approached the right, I moved forward slightly. He spoke to no one, merely saluting with his hand. In spite of what the Viceroy had told me, that I should be pleased with my first interview, I was not more favoured than the rest. I do not know where Prince Eugène then was, but immediately on hearing that the Emperor had passed, he hastened up and said:

'Well, I hope you were satisfied. No doubt he confirmed by word of mouth all that I have written to you?'

'He did not address a single word to me.'

'What?'

'Not a word. He merely nodded, as if to say: "I can see through you, you rascal!"'

The amiable prince was miserable, fearing, of course wrongly, lest I should think that he had been a well-meaning but clumsy interpreter; and he gave me his word of honour, of which I had no need, so convinced was I of his friendly and honest truthfulness, that he had only written to me the Emperor's exact words.

It was already late. The troops of the Grand Army, tired with marching and fighting since the morning, formed into columns to let us pass. We thus had the honour of becoming the front rank and of pursuing the enemy, who only turned now and again in order to check our ardour. They eventually regained their positions, and we halted within short cannon-range. I was then in front of the position at Wagram; the village of that name was on the left, and that of Baumersdorf on the right. A violent cannonade continued along the whole line while we were forming.

The Emperor came up to speak to the Viceroy, with whom I was talking; I fell back some yards. He did not speak to me as yet, but I heard him say somewhat carelessly:

'Order General Macdonald to attack and carry the plateau. The enemy are retiring, and we must make some prisoners.'

Thereupon he went away. The prince, joining me, said:

'Do you know what the Emperor has just been saying to me?'

'Yes,' I replied; 'I heard his orders.'

'Well, what is your opinion?'

'I think the Emperor is mistaken; the enemy are not leaving, they are simply retiring to the intrenched position they have selected for the battle. Do you not see, the entire army is there, looking very brave? In order to carry through such an undertaking, although we have but an hour of daylight left, we should need to attack with the whole army. Lose no time—go, or else send these remarks of mine to the Emperor.'

But he was afraid of him, and answered: 'Not I! He ordered us to attack; let us do it.'

'So be it,' I answered; 'but you will see how we shall be beaten,' which of course happened, as it could not fail to do.

We started, well protected by artillery, but our leading columns soon stopped at the Russbach, a stream with steep banks, which covered the Austrian front. I sprang to the ground, made my staff do the same, and sword in hand we set the example of crossing it, and were followed by the men. This bold stroke drove the enemy back, and we obtained possession of the *plateau*. We were obliged to halt near their huts, and form into columns, in order to attack the enemy, drawn up not far off, and also to wait till General Grenier, who was crossing the stream with his troops, could come up to our support. We had passed the villages of Wagram and Baumersdorf, which other corps of the Grand Army had failed to take; they had even retreated. The enemy debouched in large numbers, and attacked one flank, while the columns that we had held in check advanced against us.

General Grenier's troops, amazed at this unexpected onslaught, threw themselves in disorder among my men, breaking their lines and scattering them. All my efforts to restrain them were vain, although, sword in hand, with the majority of the officers, I had drawn up a line to check the fugitives. A rout ensued, and we were carried away, crossing the stream in the utmost confusion.

The prince, who had remained on the other side, tried to stop the runaways. On coming close to him, I pointed out that he could not reform men under such a hot fire, as they were now panic-stricken, although a few minutes before they had displayed such resolution; that what he should do was to send some detachments of cavalry out of range, and that the fugitives would naturally stop on reaching them. Fortunately, the enemy was satisfied with having repulsed us, and dared not cross the stream in pursuit, although a few squadrons would have sufficed to disperse us, for night had come on, and we should have imagined ourselves charged by the entire Austrian army, and the result would not be difficult to imagine. The loss of my corps in killed, wounded, and prisoners was enormous, amounting to nearly two thousand men. General Grenier had his hand shattered by a bullet at the beginning of this 'brush,' as the Emperor called it.

I did not leave the Viceroy. We passed the night out in the open, as did all the army, keeping a sharp lookout while our officers tried to rally the fugitives.

'What will the Emperor think?' asked the prince anxiously.

'Nothing detrimental to you or me. He will realise now that it is too late, that his orders were hasty. Where I think you were wrong was in not taking or sending to him the observations that I had made to you before embarking upon this unlucky attempt,' the result of which was a foregone conclusion.'

At daybreak, on July 6, a violent cannonade began on our extreme right. We re-established our line, and formed up. The enemy in front of us remained motionless, but soon advanced some troops on the right; they slowly descended the heights as if to cross the stream in front of Bernadotte, who was posted on my left in front of the village of Wagram. On the right was Marshal Davoust,[2] who, marching against the enemy, was either warned, or else met them coming towards him. The firing was violent, and, as the marshal believed that he had the entire Austrian force against him, all our reserves were ordered up to support him and effect a diversion. The Emperor came to the spot where I was, and addressed himself directly to me, saying:

'Last night you carried the *plateau* of Wagram; you know the way up to it; carry it again. Marmont will at the same time attack the village of Baumersdorf; you and he seem to understand each other; I will send him to you.'

Marmont soon came, and we mutually agreed to support each other; and, in order not to expose ourselves to a repetition of the previous evening's occurrences, the general quite understood that the village should be carried before I commenced my attack upon the *plateau*; but while we were commencing operations, other events were taking place behind us on the left.

Masséna commanded at the real point of attack. The marshal could not make a stand against troops much superior to his own. He was driven back with great loss on to the *tête-de-pont*, by which

---

2. Duke of Auerstadt and Prince of Eckmühl.—Translator.

we had passed after crossing the Danube. The Austrians sent forward their right. Davoust was kept in check; Bernadotte, repulsed before Wagram, left me uncovered. The movements of the enemy on my left and rear were concealed from me by little hillocks and inequalities in the ground. I slowly advanced towards the plateau, because Marmont had met with considerable resistance at the village of Baumersdorf, when the Emperor came up and changed my destination.

The retreat of Masséna, which I then learned for the first time, and the retrograde movement made by Bernadotte, had left the centre of the army exposed. I therefore received orders to change my direction—to turn almost completely round, and go and take up my position near the hillocks. The Emperor betook himself to the highest of these in order to observe, and kept sending officers, one after another, to me to hasten my movements. The manoeuvre that I was carrying out, however, demanded some time, and, besides, I thought it would be imprudent to arrive disordered and straggling.

Vexed and anxious to know the reason for these reiterated orders, I galloped towards the Emperor, when I saw him leaving the hillock as fast as his horse could go, followed by his numerous staff. I continued, however, and gained the top of the hillock he had just quitted, when at once I saw what was the matter. The enemy, who were in great numbers at this point, were marching the more boldly that they encountered no resistance: I then understood (as the Emperor afterwards admitted) that his intention in thus hurrying me was to show that he was not in retreat there, as he was on the left. It was therefore necessary to risk something in order to carry this out with the utmost speed; but little did I think that this spot was to become shortly afterwards the principal point of attack, against which the numerous forces of the enemy would come to shatter themselves.

I therefore ordered four battalions, followed by four others which I deployed in two lines, to advance at the double; and while my artillery opened fire, and that of the Guard took up position (which the Emperor called the hundred gun battery), my two divisions formed themselves into attacking columns. The enemy, who were still advancing, halted; and redoubling their fire, caused us terrible loss. However, in proportion as my ranks became thinned, I drew them up closer together and made them dress up as at drill.

While I was doing this, I saw the enemy's cavalry preparing to charge, and had barely time to close my second line on the first one; they were flanked by the two divisions still in column, and the square was completed by a portion of General Nansouty's cavalry that had been put under my orders that morning. I ordered both ranks to open fire, my famous battery mowing down the cavalry. This hot fire broke them just as they were preparing to charge; many men and horses fell pierced by our bayonets. The smoke rising disclosed to me the enemy in the utmost disorder, which was increased by their attempt to retreat. I ordered an advance at the point of the bayonet, after previously commanding Nansouty to charge, at the same time desiring the cavalry officers whom I saw behind me to do likewise. Unfortunately, they were not under my orders, and the Emperor was not there to give any.

The enemy were in extreme disorder; but still their fire during their retreat did us much harm. I was in despair at the slowness of General Nansouty. Not far from us I saw a large number of abandoned pieces of cannon; the Austrian officers were bringing up men, by dint of blows with the flat of their swords, to remove them. At last Nansouty moved, but too late to profit by the gap that I had made in the Austrian centre. I halted to allow his division to pass; I was, moreover, so weakened that I dared not venture into the plain to pursue the enemy (the more so as Nansouty's cavalry was repulsed, but not followed) until the Emperor sent me reinforcements. Unfortunately, the favourable moment had been allowed to slip. The results would have been enormous had Nansouty charged immediately, supported by the cavalry which was in the rear.

I had no staff-officers round me—one of my *aides-de-camp* had been killed, as well as my orderlies; the others were either incapacitated or away on a mission. While I was thus awaiting reinforcements, a general officer in full uniform rode up to me. I did not know him. After the usual greetings, he paid me great compliments upon the action that had just occurred, and finished by inquiring my name, which I gave him.

'I knew you by reputation,' he said; 'and am happy to make your acquaintance on a field of battle so glorious for you.'

After replying to his compliment, I, in my turn, asked him his name: he was General Walther, of the Guard; I had never heard of him.

'Do you,' I asked, 'command that fine and large body of cavalry which I perceive in the rear?'

'I do.'

'Then why on earth did you not charge the enemy at the decisive moment, after I had thrown them into such disorder, and after I had begged you to several times? The Emperor ought to, and will, be very angry with his Guard for remaining motionless when so glorious a share was offered to them, which might have brought about such enormous and decisive results!'

'In the Guard,' replied he, 'we require orders direct from the Emperor himself, or from our chief, Marshal Bessières. Now, as the latter was wounded, there only remained the Emperor, and he sent us no orders.'

He added that at the Battle of Essling several generals had made use of regiments of Guards, and that they had suffered very much; wherefore, since then, Marshal Bessières had obtained instructions that they should only act altogether and under his orders, or under the direct command of the Emperor.

'But,' I retorted, 'there are circumstances in which such a rule cannot be considered as absolute—such a case as this, for example. The Emperor could not have failed to approve your action, as it would have secured the destruction of a considerable portion of the Austrian army. And, supposing that we had been repulsed instead of gaining a success, would you not have protected us? and would you have retired from the field without a blow because you had received no orders?'

These questions embarrassed him; he saluted, and returned to his troop. I afterwards learned that the Emperor had reprimanded him and the other generals of the Guard very severely; but the fault really lay with the Emperor himself. He should not have forgotten the restriction he had imposed, and should have remained in person at the principal centre of the action to direct everything. Later on, in talking over these occurrences with me, he was still very bitter against his Guard.

'Why did you not make them act?' he said. 'I put them under your orders!'

'I knew nothing about that,' I replied. 'I limited myself to repeated, but fruitless, requests. And how could I have made them charge, when I had endless trouble even to get General Nansouty to move? He wanted so much time to form his men!'

'That is true,' said the Emperor; 'he is rather slow.'

The reinforcement I had asked for came at last; it was composed of General Wrede's Bavarian division, and of General Guyot's brigade of light cavalry of the Guard. The enemy's retrograde movement had commenced, and I began mine to follow them. I thought the whole *corps d'armée* were doing the same.

Towards evening I caught up the rear-guard close by a village called Süssenbrünn, which was fortified with earthworks. I made a feint of attacking in front, while I made an oblique movement to outflank it; but the Austrian general, discovering my intentions, immediately beat a retreat. I called back the outflanking party, and warned General Guyot to hold himself in readiness to charge. He sent me back word that his Guards were always ready, a boast that he justified a moment later; for scarcely had I given orders to attack, than both his men and the Bavarians charged together. The two troops stormed the camp, and cut off the column, bringing me back 5,000 or 6,000 prisoners and ten guns. Scarcely were these prisoners removed, when a reserve, posted on a height commanding the village, assailed us with bullets, grapeshot, and a well-sustained musketry-fire. I saw General Wrede fall, and hastened to his assistance; his men raised him up, and he then said to me:

'Tell the Emperor that I die for him; I commend to him my wife and children.'

He was being supported, and, to reassure him, I said, laughing:

'I think that you will be able to make this recommendation to him yourself; and, what is more, that your wife will continue to have children by you.'

It proved to be merely a slight wound from a ball that had grazed his side. The wind of the ball had made him giddy.

The firing was then very severe, and the flames of the burning village helped to reveal our weakness, especially as night was coming on, and the enemy could see to shoot straighter. I became seriously uneasy on looking round and finding myself isolated; I had been so occupied in pursuing the enemy that I had failed to notice that the rest of the army was not following. I did not know what singular motive had stopped or suspended its movement, for at five o'clock they had taken up position, and I had received no orders countermanding my advance.

The Emperor, on the other hand, was much surprised to hear such persistent firing going on far off at one particular point of the battlefield. He sent several officers to discover the cause. I had no need to give explanations; our position spoke for itself. From these officers I learned that the whole army had been bivouacked since five o'clock.

Masséna also was a long way to the rear of my left. He too sent to know which was the adventurous corps engaged so far ahead.

Meanwhile, in the twilight, and by lying at full length on the ground, we could distinguish in the distance some bodies of cavalry coming towards us, or rather towards the fire, and this reassured me; but if the enemy had had any pluck, they could have surrounded me with superior force, seeing that all their reserves were collected on the heights. Fortunately, their sole idea was to cover the retreat and disorder of their wings.

The firing ceased on either side about eleven o'clock, but we remained under arms till daybreak. As I then perceived that the enemy had retired, I sent my cavalry in pursuit while waiting for orders. They kept on sending back numerous prisoners, including those taken the previous evening; these amounted in the aggregate to 10,000, and fifteen guns. At the Island of Lobau 20,000 prisoners had been made. I had therefore captured half the total, and the artillery I took was all that was captured.

A few hours later the Viceroy passed; he gave us great praise, and said that the Emperor was very pleased with me, that he had as yet given no orders as to our ulterior movements, that I was to wait, and that he would follow my cavalry. I then noticed for the first time that my horse had received a bullet in the neck, but which had remained between the skin and the flesh; he was taken away in order that it might be extracted. As for me, I went to one of the houses in the town, where I had passed a few hours the previous night, worn out, and suffering from a kick given me by my horse the day before.[3]

I soon fell asleep, but not for long, as I was awakened by cries of 'Long live the Emperor!' which redoubled when he entered my camp. I asked for my horse, but he had been taken away. I had no other, as the rest were far behind. As I could not walk, I remained on my straw, when I heard someone inquiring for me. It was an orderly officer, either M. Anatole de Montesquieu, or his brother, who was afterwards killed in Spain. He came by the Emperor's order to look for me. On my remarking that I had no horse and could not walk, he offered me his, which I accepted. I saw the Emperor surrounded by my troops, whom he was congratulating. He approached me, and embracing me cordially, said:

'Let us be friends henceforward.'

---

3. This is how it happened: I had my sword in my hand during the action; having dismounted while waiting for the reinforcements, I mounted again on their arrival. In doing so I pricked the animal's crupper with the point of my sword, which I still held, having lost my scabbard. Had I been farther away, I should have had my thigh broken, or it might have been even worse.—Marshal Macdonald.

'Yes,' I answered, 'till death.' And I have kept my word, not only up to the time of his abdication, but even beyond it. He added:

'You have behaved valiantly, and have rendered me the greatest services, as, indeed, throughout the entire campaign. On the battlefield of your glory, where I owe you so large a part of yesterday's success, I make you a MARSHAL OF FRANCE'[4] (he used this expression instead of 'of *the Empire*'). 'You have long deserved it.'

'Sire,' I answered, 'since you are satisfied with us, let the rewards and recompenses be apportioned and distributed among my army corps, beginning with Generals Lamarque, Broussier, and others, who so ably seconded me.'

'Anything you please,' he replied; 'I have nothing to refuse you.'

Thereupon he went away much moved, as I was also. Thus did I avenge myself for all the petty annoyances caused me by General Lamarque, who, although he had heard me mention his name first of all, still continued to worry me.

Scarcely had the Emperor turned his horse's head, when many exalted personages came to congratulate and compliment me. The one who showed me most affection was the Duke de Bassano, at that time Secretary of State, then Berthier, Prince of Neuchâtel, Major-General of the army. Both these men were in Napoleon's most intimate confidence.

'No doubt you knew what he intended to do?' I said to the latter.

'No,' he replied naively.

Then came embraces and handshakings that I thought would never end. Many would have passed me by had it not been for the Emperor's favour.

The Emperor caught up the Viceroy, and related to him with considerable emotion the scene which had just taken place and my elevation. The latter promptly despatched an *aide-de-camp* to congratulate me, to invite me to breakfast, and to beg me to bring my troops forward on the highroad between Vienna and Wolkersdorf. I found the prince in the hunting-lodge known as the Rendezvous; he was at table with the Artillery-Generals Lariboisière and Sorbier, the former of whom was killed at Königsberg, at the end of the campaign of 1812; the latter is still living in the neighbourhood of Nevers. As soon as I was announced, he hastened to meet me, and we embraced each other effusively.

---

4. Macdonald was the only Marshal created on a field of battle. Michaud, *Biographic Universelle*.—Translator.

'The good accounts that you have given of me have procured me this honour,' I said to him. 'I shall never forget it.'

'It is you, and you alone,' he replied, 'who have gained your *bâton*.'

The others joined in congratulating me; I only knew Lariboisière by reputation.

'I am sure,' I continued to the prince, 'that you knew what the Emperor had in contemplation, though you concealed it from me this morning.'

He answered frankly, 'No,' and added after a moment's thought, 'I remember now that while I was walking and talking with the Emperor in his tent early this morning we spoke of the battle. He regretted that so little had resulted from it, and. after a moment's silence said: "It is not Macdonald's fault, though, for he worked very hard." I see now,' added the prince, 'that he was then thinking of rewarding you, and was determined to give as much *éclat* as possible to your nomination.'

Such was the circumstance that raised me to the dignity of which, I am convinced, I had been deprived by intrigue when the first appointments were made. It was necessary to have had the command in chief of armies to obtain it, and I had had temporary command of that of the North, full command of those of Rome, Naples, and the Orisons, while several others had only commanded large divisions or wings. I think that I have already said that my intimacy with a person belonging to the Emperor's family weighed against me and also the Moreau trial, in which an attempt had been made to implicate me, but which attempt signally failed, as I was proved entirely innocent of any complicity, and finally intrigue and jealousy. One marshal the less, and especially a man who had every claim to the dignity, was a victory for the vain and the ambitious.

After breakfast the Viceroy proposed to me to accompany him to the Emperor's headquarters at Wolkersdorf, but I had no fresh horses, and, moreover, was suffering a good deal from the kick I had received.

'Here we are,' I observed, 'in hot pursuit of the Austrians. If the Archduke John, who is commanding their other army, and ought to be at Presburg, pursues us in turn, he may be able to seriously interrupt our communications. I suppose that the Emperor has taken steps to provide against this? Can you in any case question him so as to find out if he has any precise information as to the position and objective of this army. If really at Presburg, I fail to understand why it did not take part in yesterday's affair; but it is lucky for us that it did not.'

The prince departed, and on his return told me that he had submitted my observations, to which the Emperor had replied:

'What would the Archduke do on the rear of my army? He must know that the battle has been lost by his brother.'

'No doubt,' replied the prince; 'but if he meets with no opposition, nothing need prevent him from harassing you.'

'Well,' replied the Emperor, frowning, 'if he dares to do so I will wheel round and crush him!'

The prince had not recovered his stupefaction even when he related the answer to me.

Nevertheless, the Emperor thought over what I had said. Shortly afterwards he learnt that the Archduke John was making a movement to follow us. We immediately received orders to face about, and the whole Army of Italy went to meet the Austrian Prince, who in his turn retired as soon as he learnt that we had come to fight him and to join General Reynier's force. This general had replaced Marshal Bernadotte, who had been dismissed by the Emperor for publishing a general order, wherein he attributed the victory of the previous day to his Saxons, although they had vanished from the field and I had taken their place. That had been the object with which I was changing my direction, when the Emperor himself came to me to order it, and made me hasten so much by sending constant messages to be quick: speed was necessary, as I have related. The Emperor, very angry with Bernadotte, issued, to the marshals only, an order wherein he expressed his displeasure, and said that the praise given by the commander of the Saxon force belonged to me and to my troops.

As we were approaching the River March, a staff-officer from the Emperor's headquarters galloped up with a despatch from the major-general. 'What has happened?' I asked.

'Upon my word, I don't know. I hear some talk of an armistice, but I am not acquainted with the contents of the despatches I have brought you.'

It was indeed the armistice that was officially announced to me, with orders to halt.

'The armistice is signed,' I said to the officer. 'Quite likely,' he replied carelessly and indifferently. The next morning I received orders to recross the Danube, return into Styria, and take up my headquarters at Gratz.

The results of the battle had been so scanty that I could not conceive how it was that the Austrians were compelled to beg for an armistice; but I heard afterwards that their army was in such a state of disorganization that it was equivalent to a rout. Neither was it known then that the Emperor only granted the truce because he also needed opportunity to repair his enormous losses, and because we should infallibly have run short of ammunition. Rewards even were offered to those who collected the balls of either army. On our side we had fired close upon 100,000 rounds!

Annex to Chapter 16

We are indebted to the kindness of Mr. MacNab for an interesting letter written by Macdonald, then newly created Marshal, to his grandfather, only two days after the Battle of Wagram.

Stamersdorf,
July 8, 1809.

So highly do I value and cherish your esteem, sir, and so convinced am I of the interest you bear towards me, that I lose not an instant in informing you of an event which cannot fail to exercise a powerful influence upon my future and that of my children.

My misfortunes are over and done with. The Emperor, who condescended to notice my conduct at the two Battles of *Enzersdorf*[1] and *Wagram*, especially at the latter, to the success of which I was fortunately able to contribute, came next morning to my camp, publicly expressed to me in most flattering terms his appreciation of my conduct, restored to me his friendship and confidence, and, embracing me upon the battlefield, raised me to the dignity of Marshal of France.

Judge, sir, of my surprise and emotion, as I had no reason to anticipate so speedy and unhoped-for a return to the good graces of His Majesty. Therefore, with all my heart and soul, I have vowed to him unlimited devotion and attachment.

The crossing of the Danube was a masterpiece of prodigious genius, and it was reserved for the Emperor to conceive, create, and carry it out. It was performed in presence of an army of over 180,000 men. The enemy expected the attempt to be made at the same point as that of May 21.[2] They had prepared

---

1. The name given by Macdonald to the engagement of July 5.
2. First day of the Battle of Essling.

tremendous entrenchments, and had brought up a formidable body of artillery.; but, to their great surprise, they suddenly saw us attack their left flank and turn all the lines of their redoubts. We drove them back three leagues, and when, next day, they tried conclusions with us, they lost the game.

Never, sir, had two armies a mightier force of artillery, never was battle fought more obstinately. Picture to yourself 1,000 or 1,200 pieces of cannon vomiting forth death upon nearly 350,000 combatants, and you will have an idea of what this hotly-disputed field of battle was like. The enemy, posted upon the heights, entrenched to the teeth in all the villages, formed a sort of crescent, or horse-shoe. The Emperor did not hesitate to enter into the midst of them, and to take up a parallel position.

His Majesty did me the honour of giving me the command of a corps, with orders to break through the enemy's centre. I, fortunately, succeeded, notwithstanding the fire of a hundred guns, masses. of infantry, and charges of cavalry, led by the Archduke Charles in person. His infantry would never cross bayonets with mine, nor would his cavalry wait till mine came up; the *Uhlans* alone made a stand, and they were scattered.

I pursued the enemy closely with bayonet and cannon for about four leagues, and it was only at ten o'clock at night that, worn out and overwhelmed with fatigue, my men ceased their firing and their pursuit.

The same success attended us at all other points. His Majesty, who directed everything, amazed me by his coolness and by the precision of his orders. It was the first time I had fought under his eyes, and this opportunity gave me an even higher opinion than I already had of his great talents, as I was able to form my own judgment upon them.

The enemy's losses in killed, wounded, and taken prisoners are enormous. The Archduke Charles is himself wounded. My corps suffered more than any other. Out of three *aides-de-camp*, I have had one killed and another wounded; my chief of the staff and three out of my four staff-officers were wounded, and their horses killed. Out of two orderly officers, one was wounded, and the other's horse was killed; and, finally, my four dragoon orderlies were killed, together with their horses, close beside me. As for myself, I came through it in safety with Séguin, my *aide-de-camp*; I received nothing worse than a kick from a horse on the thigh, but it was a severe one. My horse received a charge of grapeshot in his neck, and my sword, which I carried in my hand, was broken by a ball.

There, sir, is my plain, unvarnished little story. You must send me many congratulations: first, upon the recovery of his Majesty's favour; secondly, upon my new rank; and thirdly, upon having escaped so miraculously from so many dangers.

I embrace you affectionately, and shall yet see you again, I trust, at Courcelles. I embrace Alexander, and would beg you to place me at the feet of Mdlle. MacNab.

Macdonald.

Chapter 17
Evacuation of Styria

As I passed near Vienna, on my way to Styria, I went into the capital, which I had not been able to visit as I came, and thence to Schönbrunn, the Emperor's headquarters, and hitherto the summer residence of the Emperor of Austria. Napoleon received me somewhat coldly, partly perhaps owing to some remnants of former recollections, and also partly because rumour said, both in the army and in Austria, that it was I who had gained the battle. There were plenty of people ready to repeat this most improper speech to the Emperor—a speech to which I was a stranger, as I only appropriated to myself that which had been really personal, and mine by right. The country and the people at Schönbrunn were alike new to me—I mean the Imperial Court, which greeted me very coldly: I limited myself to returning their courtesy.

However, the Emperor retained me to breakfast, together with Marshal Marmont, who had just arrived; Berthier, the major-general, was the third guest. Conversation at first turned upon the battle, and it was then that the Emperor made the remark to me that I have already quoted, respecting the Guards who did not act, and the slowness of Nansouty. Since then he had again visited the battlefield, and gone over the positions that I had successively occupied, deeply regretting the serious losses I had suffered. My squares, outlined by the dead bodies, were still in regular order.

During breakfast a despatch was brought to him from General Vandamme.

'Do you know what he tells me?' he said. 'Look, read for yourself!'

This general, who was in command of the Wurtemburg corps, and was preceding me on the road to Gratz in order to take possession of the town and castle according to the terms of the armistice, announced that on the way he had met the Austrian army from Croatia, led by General Gyulai, on the way to Vienna under orders from the Archduke John. Vandamme added that at a conference a temporary suspension of arms had been agreed upon, each army to retain its position pending fresh orders. We had risen from table, and while I was reading the letter the Emperor called in all the soldiers who had come to pay him their respects. When I returned him the letter he said quickly and aloud, so that all could hear:

'Where is your force today? Hasten its march—start in person; I put Vandamme under your orders. Such and such divisions will join you; take entire direction of everything. March against that army and crush it.'

However, while I was taking my leave, he drew me aside and whispered:

'Be prudent; try not to renew hostilities; we need rest in order to recover ourselves.'

General Vandamme, informed of the Emperor's arrangements, received me very coldly, although he had often before served under my orders, and instead of considering how to carry out the fresh ones he had just received, he began to declaim against the Marshals Oudinot and Marmont, who had been given that rank after me. He was quite ready to admit that I had earned it, but as for the others, no name was too bad for them. He was especially violent against the Emperor, who, at the beginning of the campaign, he said, had promised that within three months he would make him a Marshal and a Duke.

'He is a poltroon,' he went on—'a forger, a liar! and had it not been for *me*, Vandamme, he would still be keeping pigs in Corsica.'

This language was used in presence of thirty military men, most of them generals and superior officers of his own army corps, and Wurtemburgers! When he had cooled down, he told me that an Austrian general officer had come with a message, and was waiting to see me. It was General Zach, chief of General Gyulai's staff. I knew him personally, as he had been made prisoner at the Battle of Marengo, and taken to Paris, where I frequently saw him.

After exchanging greetings with him, I said:

'How comes this? Are we at war while our principal armies have agreed to an armistice?'

He replied that the Archduke, under whom his chief was serving, was independent of his brother, Prince Charles, notwithstanding the latter's title of *Generalissimo* of the Austrian armies, and that he would not recognise the truce.

'But,' I answered, 'the Emperor of Austria has sanctioned it.'

'I am not aware of it,' was his answer.

I put an end to the conversation, the only object of which clearly was to gain time.

'*Monsieur le Général*,' I said firmly, 'my orders are imperative to march upon Gratz. I shall move tomorrow morning at five o'clock, and shall attack you if I meet your troops; from that moment the suspension of arms is at an end.'

He calculated that there would not be time enough to communicate my determination to General Gyulai, and to transmit to me that general's answer. He begged for an extension of two hours, to which I agreed, convinced that by then the enemy would have decamped; and this proved to be the case. I had them followed, but after giving strict injunctions that no hostilities were to be attempted. Our troops soon caught up their rear-guard, and marched it in front of them without striking a blow, and thus we conducted the Archduke John's army into Croatia, while we ourselves went into Styria and Gratz.

The Archduke at length recognized the armistice, and evacuated the fort; his armament was composed of field-guns, which the Emperor ordered me to bring to his headquarters at Schönbrunn. My line of demarcation with the Austrians was the frontier of Hungary, and Croatia as far as Trieste. I improved the defences of the castle; after arming and provisioning it, I established my camp on the left bank of the Mühr, and my headquarters at the castle of Eckenberg.

Negotiations were carried on during the armistice, and during several months nothing occurred save alternations of peace and fresh outbreaks of hostilities. Peace was concluded at last; it was known as the Peace of Vienna.

On the Emperor's birthday (August 15) I received the 'grand cordon' of the Legion of Honour, the title of DUKE OF TARENTUM, and a present of 60,000 *francs* (£2,400). Previously to this, Generals Lamarque and Broussier had been promoted to the rank of Grand Officer of the Legion; but this did not prevent the former from carrying on petty intrigues it seems to have been his element. He displayed more talent in this direction than in military matters, although he believed himself the best general in the French service, as he modestly remarked to General Pully, who repeated it to me. Shortly afterwards I was able to get rid of him. At the time when I received the three favours that I have mentioned, the Emperor showered a large number upon my *corps d'armée*; but the recipients did not all seem equally satisfied, and some of them were certainly very small. I do not mention those who were dissatisfied at having received nothing.

While the armistice lasted, and even after the peace, fighting continued in the Tyrol against the insurgents in that country whom we had failed to reduce. My entire army corps was sent there except myself and my staff. I was very grieved to part with such brave troops, and they displayed great regret at quitting me for other leaders. General Grenier's corps replaced mine in Styria; that general was only half pleased at having me for a chief, and also complained that he had only received the 'grand cordon' for his wound.

After the ratification of peace, the Emperor returned to Paris, and the Viceroy to Milan; I had command of the Army of Italy. Shortly afterwards I heard of the Emperor's divorce, and rumours were current of a fresh marriage with a princess of Saxony or Russia. Indeed, negotiations were instituted with the latter Power, but the opposition of the Empress-mother caused them to be suddenly broken off.

The period for the evacuation of Austrian territory had been settled by a convention, but contingent upon the delimitation of the frontiers, the return of our prisoners, and the payment of a war indemnity. I was on the point of beginning my retrograde movement, when I received counter-orders through two couriers from Paris, who arrived within an hour of each other—one through Austria, the other through Italy.

The counter-order was based upon the idea that the Government at Vienna was not fulfilling the three conditions; but they were misinformed in Paris. I had already received the prisoners who were nearest at hand, and Austrian commissioners had long since arrived at Gratz to determine the frontier, which they could not do until the French arrived, and they tarried. As to the indemnity, it was to be paid at Vienna. I sent word of these facts to Paris; at the same time, Marshal Davoust, acting as commander of the Grand Army, stated, on his side, that the first payment had been made, and the other conditions performed—if not willingly, at any rate punctually.

This suspension of the evacuation might produce serious consequences, and an evilly-disposed person would have had no difficulty in bringing about a renewal of hostilities. The Austrians were to follow a day's march behind us, consequently they had to stop and put up with very bad quarters. My correspondence with them on this subject was not friendly. Finally, the orders for departure arrived. The States of Styria came to bid me farewell, and to offer me a present of considerable value for the care I had taken of their country, and the exemplary discipline I had maintained. I refused it, and, as they insisted, I said:

'Well, if you really think you owe me anything, I can tell you how to acquit your debt in a manner more agreeable to me. Look after the sick and wounded whom I am obliged to leave here for the time being, as well as the detachment and the medical officers of whom they have charge.' They promised. The weather was too severe to remove the sick; humanity forbade it at the risk of exposing the lives of these brave fellows.

The members of the States asked me if I knew anything of a piece of news that had reached Vienna through commercial channels—namely, the sudden arrival of Prince Schwarzenberg, Austrian ambassador in Paris, to ask the hand of one of the princesses for the Emperor. I replied that I was ignorant of it; but that such a step, contrary to diplomatic forms and customs, would only increase my doubt. I thought to myself that had there been any truth in it, the Emperor would have been more gallant and less suspicious, and would not have suspended our departure on the grounds I have mentioned; that, moreover, he would have sent a French ambassador to make a request which, in affairs of this kind, is purely a matter of form and ceremony, as everything has been agreed upon beforehand.

They replied that the earliest intelligence always came from commercial quarters, and that, doubtless, the next post would bring a confirmation of the story. They begged me to remain until its arrival; but, as my last troops were to leave next morning, I did not like to part from them, and I made these gentlemen promise to send an express to me at Marburg, where I intended to sleep. The express came; but the news was not confirmed, though there was some truth in it, as I shall show later. They had confounded the title of the ambassador with that of the First Secretary of the Austrian Legation, who had, as a matter of fact, been sent as a courier to Vienna.

I continued my movement of evacuation, and found at Laybach Marshal Marmont, Duke of Ragusa, and at Trieste General Count Louis of Narbonne, Governor of the town. They had both recently arrived from Paris, and told me that the negotiations for a marriage with a Russian Princess were talked about, and seemed impending; they treated my news from Gratz as apocryphal.

On returning into the kingdom of Italy, the army that I commanded was broken up. I sent troops into the garrisons assigned to them. I myself received orders to go to Milan, and on reaching there found fresh ones summoning me to Paris. The Viceroy, was not yet returned, but I met him between Cosne and Neuvy, and he told me that the agreement for the Emperor's marriage had been signed, but with an Austrian, and not a Russian, princess; it seems that the empress-mother had opposed and displayed objections to the marriage of her daughter, who afterwards married the Crown-Prince of the Netherlands, and that thereupon the Emperor had sent for him, Prince Eugène, and had despatched him to the Austrian Ambassador to discover whether he had power to treat; that, on receiving an affirmative answer from the Ambassador, the marriage-contract had been drawn up, the Prince of Neuchâtel sent to Vienna to make the official demand, and that he was on his way to Milan to fetch the Vice-Queen, who, with him, was to assist at the marriage-ceremony, which was already fixed for April 2.

When I reached Paris, I found the Court and town ringing with the news of the day; but I was anxious to fathom what I had heard at Gratz. At last, by dint of inquiring, I got the following explanation from the Duke of Bassano:[1]

The Austrian Ambassador, Prince Schwarzenberg, foreseeing that the negotiations with Russia would very likely fall through, and considering that this alliance would be of great value to his sovereign and country, asked for instructions in case application should be made to him. The answer was affirmative and eager. Monsieur de Florett, First Secretary of the Austrian Legation, carried the Ambassador's despatch, and brought back the plenary powers; his mission became bruited abroad, and thus the first news of it had reached Gratz. Fortified with the necessary authorization, Schwarzenberg, like a clever diplomat, let it be known secretly that he had plenary powers. The Emperor, who was always hasty, dissatisfied with the answers of Russia, which he regarded as evasive, seized the opportunity, broke with Russia, and treated with Austria.

The Emperor received me with the utmost kindness; he had had very satisfactory accounts of the behaviour and conduct of the troops that I had just taken back into Italy. I fancy also that he had heard something about my refusal to accept the present offered to me at Gratz, and of my recommendation for kind treatment of the sick whom the bad weather had compelled me to leave behind in the town. He made minute inquiries concerning my financial position,

---
1. General Maret.

said that I ought to have a hotel in Paris, that he knew I was not rich, that he had adopted me, and would treat me like the other marshals. Some had been given 1,000,000 *francs* (£40,000), others 600000 *francs* (£24,000), independently of their more or less high endowments. I discreetly waited, and the question was never mooted again.

About this time, however, I received a proposal for the hand of your sister in marriage; and the Emperor, hearing of this, and knowing that I could give her but a small portion, promised, of his own accord, a dowry of 200,000 *francs* (£8,000), which he afterwards converted into an endowment.

CHAPTER 18

Blockade and Surrender of Figueras

After the Emperor's marriage he appointed me Commander-in-chief of the Army of Catalonia and Governor-General of the Principality.[1] I had a very strong objection to the manner in which war was carried on in Spain; my objection had its root in the dishonesty—or what in high places is called policy—which caused the invasion of the country; however, the noble and courageous resistance of its inhabitants triumphed over our efforts and our arms. I obeyed, nevertheless, and started. I led a very active life, that was as odious as it was exhausting. The enemy were ubiquitous, and yet I could find them nowhere, though I travelled through the length and breadth of the province. The only important result of the campaign was the siege and capture of Tortosa by General Suchet, whose operations I covered.[2]

The next campaign, that of 1811, commenced with a fresh series of marches and provisioning of fortresses. I received orders to lay siege to Tarragona, but I had neither means nor sufficient force; the Army of Arragon had all. I therefore proposed to the Government that a portion of my troops should be provisionally handed over to General Suchet, so that he should experience no embarrassment, and that there should be unity of command. My plan was approved, and I returned to Barcelona to keep an eye upon everything.

I had scarcely arrived there, when I heard that the Spaniards had surprised and taken the castle of Figueras, a place almost impregnable. It was my arsenal; my artillery, ammunition, provisions, regimental baggage, everything was stored there. Want of supervision lost us the place. But the Spaniards had not time to remove as prisoners the garrison they had so strangely surprised. We collected hastily all our

1. The appointment is dated April 24, 1810.
2. General Suchet was made a Marshal in July, 1811.

scattered detachments, and invested the fortress. I wrote most pressing letters to General Suchet to restore to me the troops I had placed at his disposal, but only one messenger reached him, either at Lerida or Saragossa, although the distance from Barcelona was but slight.

This event caused a great sensation, and increased excitement in the Peninsula, especially in Catalonia, while it also stimulated the activity of our opponents, their efforts and their courage. The Spaniards tried to throw reinforcements into the castle and to secure the prisoners, but they were repulsed.

The Emperor ordered that I should be summoned from Barcelona. It was necessary to detach 5,000 or 6,000 men from the investing force to cross the country. At the first receipt of the news I had formed the plan of going to Figueras with an escort of fifty cavalry; but so much pressure was brought to bear upon me, and so much was said to dissuade me from so rash and dangerous an enterprise, that I yielded and waited for the detachment.

On arriving I found orders to push on the siege vigorously, but my guns and ammunition were all inside. I asked for others, but they could not be supplied. I had therefore to content myself with investing and surrounding the fortress with lines, armed with field-guns; not to attack it, but to prevent sorties or assistance. I remembered the famous siege of Alesia,[3] and I caused analogous works, allowing for the difference of locality, to be made. Each corps was ordered to cover itself, and I had excited their emulation by my constant presence and my encouragements I spared myself neither labour nor fatigue. We had already spent two months and a half round the place, which seemed quite decided not to surrender as long as the provisions held out, and there was any hope of succour.

We had now reached July 13; the date is well imprinted on my memory, as I then had my first attack of gout. It lasted a long time, but although horribly severe, my moral nature suffered more than my physical from this paralysis.

I had succeeded in surrounding the place so closely that nothing, not even a cat, could have passed. General Guillot, a prisoner in the place, although he was closely watched, found means to send me information by some Spaniards, whom he had seduced by promises of large rewards. I thus knew the strength of the garrison, the amount of provisions, and could calculate almost to a day when the surrender would be made.

---

3. Besieged by Caesar and defended by Vercingetorix.

Our troops kept a very sharp lookout, as we expected almost daily to be attacked from outside. The Spaniards made demonstrations, and announced the landing of English troops. More than once, in fact, we had observed a large number of transports at sea. The Spanish commandant, discovering General Guillot's communications, had his messenger shot, and tried and condemned to death the general and several other officers, but he dared not execute them. I was informed of what was going on, and threatened the Spanish general with reprisals.

Notwithstanding the limitation of the rations, the end was near. Out of regard for such of our prisoners as were sick, but who could be moved, he caused them all to be brought out and laid on the glacis. According to my information, the place could not hold out beyond August 15 or 20. I felt certain that the garrison would try to make a way for themselves through my lines; all my dispositions were made accordingly. It was the more necessary to redouble our vigilance, as we were already weakened by sickness.

I thought that the Spaniards would select August 15, the Emperor's birthday, for their sortie. We kept the day with great rejoicing, having prepared some grand fireworks, of which the crowning-piece was to be a general fusillade directed against the town, with shells and grape-shot!

Nothing stirred during the night, but next morning the fire from the fortress slackened. We observed considerable movement on the ramparts, which was continued the following day. As no messenger appeared, it remained evident that a vigorous sortie was contemplated, and we got ready to give it a warm reception.

It did take place eventually on a dark night, and in the profoundest silence; but the unevenness of the ground caused the head of the columns to waver, and made their weapons jingle, and this attracted the attention of our advanced outposts. They hastily fell back upon our lines, and, moreover, without lighting some little piles of sticks, as they had been told to do, in order to throw light upon the scene. It was to be presumed, and it eventually proved, that the Spaniards would attack with swords, as a single discharge, showing where they were, would have sufficed to attract all our forces to them. We awaited their approach, and as soon as they opened the attack we threw some hand-grenades amongst them; but the powder was damaged, and only gave out a thick, colourless smoke.[4]

---

[4] I had ordered some Bengal fire from Toulouse, but it only arrived after the place had surrendered.—Marshal Macdonald.

This attempted sortie was brave, and did honour to the general and his garrison; it was repulsed after several attempts on their part. They did not expect to meet so many obstacles; even the abattis stopped them. From the summit of the ramparts it was easy to misjudge them, they looked like so many little bushes. The Spaniards lost a large number of killed, wounded, and taken prisoners; on our side no one had a scratch.

Next day the enemy ran up the white flag, and sent a *parlementaire* to treat for the surrender. I accorded them the honours of war. The garrison laid down their arms and remained prisoners; out of respect for their bravery, the officers retained their swords.

I transferred my quarters to the town, where shortly afterwards my attack of gout was followed by one of fever. Being unable to continue to exercise my command, I asked for a successor, who was granted me. I returned to Paris, only just able to walk on crutches.

CHAPTER 19

Preparations for the Russian Campaign

When I reached Paris I found all prepared for the famous, albeit disastrous, Russian campaign[1]. Notwithstanding the state of my health, which, however, was improving, I was ordered to start during the month of April, 1812. I had left my armchair in the fortress at Figueras; I left one crutch in Paris and the other in Berlin.

I had command, on the left of the army, of the 10th corps, made up of the Prussian contingent, and of a division formed of three Polish regiments, one Bavarian, and one Westphalian; my staff was French. The King of Prussia[2] wrote to me begging my attention for his men.

We marched to the Niemen, where we took up our position, and on June 24 the entire army crossed it during the night, without the slightest opposition. The Russians retreated before us; I did not fire a shot till we came into Samogitia.[3] My route lay towards the Dwina; I was ordered to garrison the Baltic coasts and to lay siege to Dunaburg and Riga. The former of these fortresses existed only on plans, but it possessed a good *tête-de-pont*.

A reconnaissance made beyond the Dwina, between the two places, caused an alarm upon the right of the river, and determined the Russian generals to set fire to the suburbs of Riga, which might have aided our approach to the citadel, and to evacuate the *tête-de-pont* of Dunaburg, which I occupied.

---

1. *Napoleon's Invasion of Russia* by R. G. Burton and *Napoleon's Russian Campaign* by Philippe Paul de Segur also published by Leonaur.
2. Frederick William III.
3. Anciently a province of Poland, now comprised in the Russian Government of Wilma. Keith Johnston's *Geographical Dictionary*.

It was then that we discovered that the fortifications of this imaginary town only existed on paper, and not in reality. Here and there a little earth had been turned, but there was not even a hut, consequently no inhabitants, only an old Jesuit church in ruins.

I had orders to recall the siege-artillery from Magdeburg, where it had been recast at enormous expense. Another train had left Dantzic for Riga; it required no less than forty thousand horses to bring it. It was placed at Grafenthal while waiting for the troops and material necessary to convey it across the Dwina, and to invest Riga. I submitted several plans; but as the army was going farther away towards Moscow, I was left in uncertainty and indecision. During the interval a body of 10,000 Russians, coming from Finland, attempted to possess themselves of the whole siege-train, but it was valiantly defended by the Prussians. I had, in pursuance of orders, taken up my headquarters in a windowless and unfurnished castle not far from Dunaburg, on the extreme right of my line; I hastened up with some troops, but the affair had already terminated to our advantage. From the account ,I sent in of this incident it was realized that the season was too advanced, and this enormous and valuable material too exposed, and I received orders to send it back to Dantzic.

The evil genius that impelled the army to Moscow had planned out its misfortunes from the very opening of the campaign until it closed with the forced retreat. The Emperor, should he fail to make a passage for himself, had conceived the idea of making for my positions—an illusory idea, which was scarcely more practicable than that of preserving this ill-fated army. I was informed of the daily trials they had to meet with, and although I offered my services, together with those of my inactive, well-fed, and warmly-clad troops, I was left stationary.

I began, however, to draw in my posts, and to concentrate my forces gradually. The enemy, who watched my every movement, fancied that I was preparing to retreat, and attacked me at various points to harass me; I encouraged and laid a trap for them, into which they fell head foremost. I turned suddenly, attacked them vigorously, and broke their line. They fled, leaving a large number of prisoners in our hands. This affair would have produced much more important results had the Prussian General Yorck obeyed my reiterated orders to proceed rapidly from Mittau in the direction of Riga, in the rear of the Russians, as soon as I had broken their line. I had already observed in his letters a marked increase of coldness on the part of this general, which increased with the misfortunes of the Grand Army; but I was still far from suspecting the catastrophe that occurred shortly afterwards.

The Emperor, having succeeded in forcing the passage of the Beresina, and reopening communications with Wilna, started incognito for Paris, leaving the command to Murat, King of Naples. This was an additional misfortune, for this general, of the most distinguished bravery, was really only fit to lead a cavalry-charge, or to harass the enemy by his activity. He hoped to be able to rest and reorganize the debris of the army at Wilna, but the Russians dislodged him four-and-twenty hours after his arrival. The last remains of that immense army perished there.

On quitting Wilna, Murat at last ordered me to fall back upon Tilsit. This order was dated December 10. It was confided to a Prussian major, who, instead of coming direct to me as he might have done in thirty hours, followed the high road from Königsberg to Tilsit, Memel, and Mittau; he was thus nine days in reaching me. I received it during the day of the 18th, and as I had foreseen everything, and made all my preparations beforehand, all my columns moved the next day, December 19. I was already aware that the enemy's scouts were crossing Samogitia behind me. I fully expected to meet with every sort of obstacle, and resolved to overcome them all. The most serious matter was not the enemy, but the River Niemen. The bridge had been removed on account of the ice, and if the thaw began all my efforts would be vain.

I threw out parties on every side, so as to mislead the enemy as to my real destination. At a given point I sent off my advance-guard towards Taurogen; I led the centre by another route, and General Yorck had command of the rear-guard, and occupied each day the bivouacs I had the previous one.

We had to push forward, and the troops had but very few hours' rest out of the twenty-four; but to counterbalance that they were well clad, and did not want for provisions, in consequence of the precautions I had taken in July to establish depots everywhere. My experiences of the winter campaigns of 1794-95 in Holland, and more especially of that of 1800 in the Grisons, and when crossing the Alps, had made me requisition 30,000 sheepskin *pelisses* from the Polish and Russian peasants, giving them in exchange the skins of the sheep consumed by my troops. This wise precaution saved them from hunger and cold, which was so severe that, during a portion of my march, the thermometer went down to 27 or 28 degrees *Réaumur*. I lost only a few men, who, in spite of the penalty of death with which I had threatened both sellers and consumers of spirits, got drunk and perished, removed by the cold into eternal sleep.

The enemy had posted troops on either side of the Niemen to dispute my passage. They were vigorously attacked by the generals of my advance-guard, Grandjean and Bachelu, who did well in not waiting for me. I had made a detour in order to flank and turn the enemy. The affair had terminated, after great slaughter, to the glory of the two generals by the time I came up; they had made some thousands of prisoners, and taken several pieces of cannon.

I established myself at Tilsit, and opened communications with Königsberg. I informed General Yorck of the happy issue, and desired him to hasten his march; we had opened the way, and he might arrive the following day. The weather was milder, and the thaw had begun. My troops had a day's rest, of which they stood in some need. My intention was to continue the retreat as soon as my rear-guard joined me; but I waited in vain. I knew that the enemy, by forced marches, were crossing the Niemen above my position, and that their principal body were following the course of the Pregel in my rear. I was therefore exposed to be cut off a second time on the road to Königsberg.

I sent in all directions after General Yorck. Two days previously he ought to have arrived at Taurogen to support my advance-guard, which had quitted it in the morning; they had no news of him. At that time this general was preparing an act of treachery unparalleled in history.

Four days had already passed in uneasiness, impatience, and, I may almost say, anguish. The news brought in by my emissaries—the Prussian officers—was so uniform that it could only have been concerted; they had neither seen nor heard of General Yorck. I tried to keep back my suspicions, to crush them; I thought that a feeling of honour ought to prevent their existence; some obstacle, sudden panic, might have determined the general to retrace his steps, and to make for Memel with a view to re-entering Prussia—a direction that I meant to take myself if I failed to open a passage across the Niemen. The thaw might at any moment destroy the ice; the enemy were reinforcing themselves, manoeuvring, gaining upon me, and approaching the only communication that, to tell the truth, I was still keeping.

Had I been less confident in other people's honour, the attitude of the Prussians would have opened my eyes to what was going on around me. Far from being uneasy at the fate of the rear-guard, they seemed not to trouble about it, especially since the arrival of an officer of their nation, who had come post-haste from Berlin. He was, I believe, a Count von Brandenburg, a natural brother of the King. When they were in my presence they appeared to share my uneasiness. Various signs, and the opinion of my generals, coincided with my suspicions. I argued in this manner, which seemed to me common-sense, and to admit of no reply:

'If they have orders, or if they take upon themselves to abandon our cause, what hinders or prevents them? They are our principal force—17,000 or 18,000 men against 4,000 or 5,000; and, moreover, can I count upon the two Bavarian and Westphalian regiments forming a division with three Polish regiments? As to the latter, no doubt can exist about their fidelity; I was wrong to have conceived any about the others.'

I added:

'They will explain to us that the misfortunes threatening their country compel them to separate themselves from us; but they will not drive their cowardice to the extremity of giving us up. They would ask nothing better than to see us leave here, so that they might charge us with having abandoned the rear-guard,' as I was frequently begged to do.

I heard many stories, too, which were proofs of ill-will, and even of insubordination and disobedience.

I ended by declaring positively that until the end, which could not be long delayed, I would remain firm in my resolution; that my life and career should never have to bear upon them the blot of having abandoned, on account of fears which were perhaps imaginary, the troops committed to my care; and that, under any circumstances, I was determined to risk everything, even to recross the Niemen to go in search of the rear-guard, rather than voluntarily separate myself from them by quitting the banks of the river.

On the last day of the year 1812 the enemy made demonstrations all around me. During the night I feared an attack on the town of Tilsit, which was open on all sides. I ordered the troops to concentrate on all the roads, to send out patrols and reconnoitring parties, to keep a good look out, to barricade themselves well, and, finally, to be ready to take up arms at the first signal.

The weather was very bad. The troops commanded by General Bachelu, who was detached, refused to obey and to march; his decision of character carried the day; they formed up, but their disposition was far from reassuring. A Prussian battalion was on duty at headquarters.

'They will carry you off!' someone said to me. 'Let us go!'

'No,' I replied; 'I prefer to risk it.'

Between eleven o'clock and midnight, the commander of this battalion came and told me that he had received orders from General Massenbach, his chief, to get under arms.

'That must be a mistake,' I said; 'I only gave orders that the troops should be ready in case of an alarm. Go and say that to your general, and say, further, that I do not wish to fatigue or wet the men unnecessarily.'

He came back no more; probably he had been let into the secret.

Although they were on their own territory, the Prussians applied to me for money to satisfy their wants. I had no authority to dispose of the contributions levied in Courland; however, as they had power to take what I would have refused them, I caused a distribution of about half, or perhaps a third, of the sum demanded, leaving it to the Governments concerned to arrange about repayment.

The Prussians informed me with some haughtiness that they had a right to a share of the contributions; there was nothing for it but to put a good face on the matter and dissimulate. The same commander of the headquarters battalion came and told me that the money given for his troop was insufficient; that they were in want of shoes; that he had just discovered some hundreds of pairs in a shop, but that they would not let him have them on credit. He asked for 1,500 or 2,000 *francs* (£80) more.

'You are too late,' I answered; 'the treasury is shut.'

However, as he insisted, I gave him the money out of my own pocket, and never saw it again.

In great uneasiness about the thaw, I had the ice sounded night and morning. While, wrapped in my cloak; I was trying to get the sleep that had avoided me for four nights, Colonel Marion, of the Engineers, came to me at dawn, and said:

'I congratulate you, *Monsieur le Maréchal*, you have at last received news of General Yorck.'

'No,' I replied quickly.

'I fancied you had; for as, in accordance with your orders, I was testing the ice, I saw all the Prussians rapidly recrossing the Niemen. I thought you had sent them to meet the rear-guard. General Massenbach, as he passed by me, gave me these two letters for you.'

'Good heavens!' I exclaimed; 'we are betrayed—perhaps given up; but we will sell our lives dearly.'

I hastily glanced at the letters, caused the assembly to be sounded immediately, gathered our faithful Poles, Bavarians, and Westphalians at the back of the town, and commenced a forced march in order to gain the Forest of Bömwald, a sort of defile. I harangued the troops, not concealing our difficulties, and promised them a month's extra pay if, as I trusted we should, we succeeded in reaching Dantzic in safety.

The Prussians had displayed such haste in their desertion, that they had omitted to warn the detachment that acted as my escort. The officer commanding them came to me shortly after my orders had been issued, and, from his unconscious appearance and manner, it was easy to see that he suspected nothing of what had happened. He could not speak French, but I caused an account of what had passed to be related to him; he turned pale, and shed tears of indignation. He wished to remain with and follow us. I told him to call his men to horse; thanked his detachment for their zeal, fidelity, and attachment; gave them 600 *francs* from my own pocket, and the same to the officer for a horse; and, despite their entreaties, sent them to join their compatriots.

CHAPTER 20

A Terrible March

While our weak body of foreigners was assembling, the authorities of Tilsit, frightened and alarmed for the safety of their town, came to implore me to preserve it. They thought we were going to set alight to it out of revenge for the defection. I sent them back reassured, and we started in good order. The enemy's scouts pursued us; I had no cavalry now to keep them at a distance, and they were not worth powder and shot.

Two *parlementaires*—one Russian and the other Prussian—were brought, by mistake, to me in the midst of my column. The latter summoned me insolently to lay down my arms; I treated him with scorn, and dismissed him. I did not know until after the former had left me that he was a Frenchman, formerly *aide-de-camp* to General Moreau, and by name Rapatel. I did not recognise him; but, more prudent than his comrade, he asked me to come to an arrangement with his General, Prince Repnine, who proposed a suspension of arms until the peace, which he said was imminent, was concluded, and to give him an interview in the meantime.

The trap was too clumsily set to catch me. I told him that a suspension of arms could be brought about without a convention; that he could easily see that I was only marching in order to retire, and that they could very well stop following if they thought fit to do so; that, as to the interview, as I had no reason for refusing it, I would meet his prince at a certain spot at a given hour the next day, but that after that hour he need not trouble himself. He left, and I continued my march towards the forest.

We marched for twenty-two hours in rain, through water, and in pitchy darkness; many of my men fell out, wearied, but rejoined us next day. At length, at six in the morning, we reached this dense forest.

I had caused the entrance to it to be guarded by the troops, who, before and while I was waiting at Tilsit for the rear-guard, had escorted our baggage to Labiau.

The *aide-de-camp* who had accompanied the *parlementaire*, and who was to bring back the answer to my proposal, had not returned. The hour fixed for the interview struck; no sign of Prince Repnine. However, we thought we saw him riding up; but it was only an officer commissioned to apologize for the unpunctuality of his general. The prince, who had chanced to be away when my *aide-de-camp* came, asked for a delay of an hour or two.

'I quite understand,' I answered, 'that the prince may have business to see to; but so have I. Present my compliments to him, and express to him my regrets at missing this opportunity of making his personal acquaintance; he will esteem me the more for it. His *ruse* is too simple.' I added: Does he really suppose that I am to be taken in by such groundless, not to say absurd, pretexts? Return, and send me back my *aide-de-camp*.'

As he wished to protest that his general was acting in good faith, I made him remount his horse. Scarcely had he gone a few yards, when the cannon became audible. I called him back, and said:

'What is the meaning of that? Is it thus that your general exhibits his honesty? You deserve that I should retain you as a hostage, but I will give your prince a lesson in good faith. Return to him, and say that henceforward any communications between him and me must be carried on by cannon-balls.'

The firing ceased at the outposts; our commandant told me that he was under arms, when the enemy, meaning to drive him back, charged him. He had received and repulsed them with bayonets, and they had retired. My *aide-de-camp*, who was with the prince, begged to be sent back, observing that he was horribly afraid of French bullets.

'Go,' replied the prince. 'I have ordered the firing to cease, and my troops to retire. I meant to surprise your general, but he has been sharper than I.'

We reached Labiau, where I found orders to go straight to Königsberg, to confer with the King of Naples.

I left the command to General Grandjean, who had General Bachelu under him; during my absence they had a very sharp skirmish at Labiau. On the road I met counter-orders. The King, compelled, he said, to go to Elbing, and being unable to see me, begged me to send him a plan of operations, and my opinion upon what we ought to do in our present position.

I had no hesitation in recommending what I should have ordered myself had I been commander-in-chief—the evacuation of all places in Poland, the kingdom of Prussia, and on the Vistula, to concentrate upon the Oder with the troops arriving from Italy, and to await the fresh levies that were being made in France.[1]

My division came up with me, and I took under my direction that of General Heudelet, composed of freshly-joined conscripts.

We reached Königsberg, where I found Marshal Ney alone. He had committed the mistake of evacuating the town at the first manifestation of an insurrection, which might have broken out at sight of the enemy, who were close behind us. I suggested to the marshal to come away from it immediately with me; some hours later he required all his courage to carry him through several threatening groups. I had returned to my troops, occupied partly in keeping off the enemy, and partly in obtaining provisions, and it was to them that Marshal Ney[2] owed his safety.

At nightfall I continued my retreat towards Elbing. The King of Naples sent me orders not only to stop, but to return to Königsberg. I caused representations to be made to him concerning the obstacles in the way, warning him that the enemy had already advanced by another road upon Preussich-Eylau, and that he himself would be immediately surrounded, or that his communications would be cut off. He reiterated his orders, adding that I was misinformed, that he had numerous spies about the country, and that the enemy could not move a step without his being informed of it.

Judging better than he, I took no notice of his orders, and continued my retrograde movement, which made Murat furious. He soon changed his tone, however. The advance of the enemy upon his right flank and rear being confirmed, he applauded my foresight, and summoned me post-haste to Elbing to confer with him. I had kept along the Passarge as far as I could consistently with prudence.

I arrived during the morning, and found the King ready to mount his horse, and very impatient to get away. I pointed out to him that, as my troops could not arrive before the evening, his sudden withdrawal

---

1. The whole character of the campaign of 1813 would have been changed had this far-seeing step been taken. The invested fortresses may have detained a certain portion of the enemy's troops until their surrender, but they also locked up a large body of veteran French troops. See also chapter 24.—English original Editor.

2. *Ney: General of Cavalry—1769-1799*, Volume 1 and *Ney: Marshal of France—1799-1805* Volume 2 by Antoine Bulos published by Leonaur.

would be the signal for an insurrection, and for the pillaging of the magazines, the preservation of which was so necessary to my men. My representations were in vain, and his resolution was strengthened by the noise of cannon from my rear-guard, who were fighting as they retreated. He desired me to remain a few days at Elbing, and then to throw myself immediately into Dantzic, of which I was to take the command. I showed him the impossibility of holding Elbing with so few troops, that we were almost outflanked as it was, and that even next morning it would be too late to leave it. As to remaining in Dantzic, I observed that there was already a specially commissioned Governor in the town,[3] and that he would quite rightly refuse to yield his command to me. Thereupon he told me to send all my troops thither, and to go myself to his headquarters, the position of which was as yet undecided. I asked him if he had not carried out at least a portion of the plan I had submitted to him.

'No,' he replied; 'I have forwarded it to the Emperor, whose orders I shall receive in three days at latest.'

'What!' I exclaimed, 'you have forwarded it? It was sent to you in confidence. The Emperor, who probably is in complete ignorance as to all that has taken place, and is still occurring, will be furious, and rightly, too, if this plan has not been developed.'

'I limited myself to asking for his orders,' he answered coldly.

'And where shall we be in three days?' I added.

The Emperor ought to have been on the spot, and even then I should have doubted his determination, and yet the adoption of my plan was the only reasonable course. These garrisons, which were thus to be left to themselves, without appearance, and, I may add, without hope of speedy succour, were bound, with the exception of Dantzic, to fall for want of provisions, and by their own weakness. It was already too late for Pillau and the places in Poland, but not for Dantzic.

The Prussian Government appeared to ostensibly disavow the defection of its troops; I would have entrusted to it the care of this place, not because I had any faith in its honour, but in order to occupy a portion of its forces, which would have diminished the number of our enemies, by giving it an interest in keeping this important place from the greed of Russia. I demonstrated that by this means we could unite on the Oder all our fighting troops; that is to say, about 60,000 or 70,000 men. The Russians had also suffered severely. The Prussians

---

3. General Count Rapp. (*Rapp: the Last Victor* by Jean Rapp, also published by Leonaur.)

would need time for organization, and by taking up that position we should hold in check the greater portion of that monarchy. We could thus wait in safety the levy of 300,000 men that was being made in France.

Nothing could be urged against this reasoning, and Murat therefore did not attempt any answer. He was entirely occupied with his retreat, and his return to Naples, which he effected immediately, without any notification to the Emperor. He made over his command to Prince Eugène; it was a pity, both for it and for himself, that the Emperor did not give it to the Prince in the first place when he left the army.

Knowing the indifference of the King of Naples, of which he had just given me fresh proof in sending to Paris the plan I had prepared for him in confidence, and in announcing that he would within three days receive orders which he would not be able to execute even in part, I required of him, before we separated, that he should give me written instructions. He at first made difficulties, which proved his impatience to start, but at length gave way, and they were taken down by Count Daru, who was present at the interview. He then mounted his horse, and started amid the shouts of the populace, which were called forth rather by his extraordinary costume than by his person.

Orders had been given to all the troops in Elbing to follow him, but I retained a regiment of infantry to protect the magazines until the arrival of my own men; this, however did not prevent a large portion of them being pillaged. I gave my soldiers some hours' rest that night, and then we continued our retreat. We had great difficulty in crossing the Vistula on the ice, and in scaling the steep declivities of the left bank. The courage of my troops redoubled as we neared Dantzic, which was regarded as the goal of salvation, and the end of fatigues, privations, and sufferings.

Since leaving Courland we had fought every day and marched every night. This had weakened us, but we were now within a few days' march of our long-desired haven. After the passage of the Vistula, a suggestion was made to me to lay an ambuscade for the enemy. It succeeded perfectly, and at length we took up our position around the walls of Dantzic.

I immediately resigned the command of my troops to General Rapp, the Governor. I was grieved at parting from them. Generals, commissioned and non-commissioned officers, and privates, although they were all foreigners (with the exception of my staff), and only our allies, had rivalled each other in their zeal, devotion, courage, and efforts, during the long, painful, and dangerous retreat we made during that disastrous winter from the banks of the Dwina, with no rest save our forced halt at Tilsit. I received from all thanks for having saved them from the perils which daily environed us; their regret at our parting was not less than my own. I faithfully kept the promise I had made. Officers and men received a present of a month's pay, the superior officers and generals in proportion. The small French division[4] did not share in it, as it had only been under my orders for a very short time—since Königsberg; but, in justice to it, I am bound to say that it behaved very well, although formed of only conscripts.

The next morning the enemy attacked part of our lines. General Rapp had invited all the generals to a farewell breakfast, and we were then at table. Each one hurried to his post; and that evening I started, not knowing where the principal headquarters were established.

I took the road to Berlin; there I learned that they were at Posen. I asked for orders, and did not have to wait long for the answer. I was ordered to Paris to assist in the reorganization of some new army corps. The day before my departure I was robbed at the inn of the sum of 12,000 *francs* (£480), destined for the expenses of my journey. My carriages had rejoined me; I sent them into Westphalia, near Cassel, to rest my horses during my absence. I felt real sorrow on learning that two very pretty Russian guns, of small calibre, that my troops had taken by assault from a little fortified castle on the Dwina, and which they had presented to me, had been left, by the carelessness of one of my *aides-de-camp*, at Dantzic in one of my baggage-waggons that needed some repairs I had intended them to decorate Courcelles!

I reached Paris without adventure. I had very little reason to be satisfied with the Emperor's reception of me. He started on seeing me, and said not a word. No doubt he felt resentment against me because of my proposal to abandon all that we held beyond the Oder. He had also been deceived by untruthful accounts of my treatment of the Prussian troops, which was said to have contributed to their defection; however, to convince himself of the contrary, he had only to read the letters of Generals Yorck and Massenbach. I left his presence indignant that all my efforts and devotion should have met with so bad a reward, and went no more to Court.

A few days later, however, I was recalled. News had just arrived that not only did the King of Prussia approve the conduct of his troops, but that he had allied himself with Russia, and that all his subjects

---

4. See earlier part of this chapter.

were taking up arms against us. Then the Emperor acknowledged to me that he had been misled concerning me and the disingenuous policy of Prussia; that I had acted wisely; that he had been incorrectly informed as to the last disasters of Wilna and Kowno. He said that our misfortunes were great, but not irreparable; that he and I had begun the war at the same time, and must finish it together; that it would be the last campaign we should undertake, and that I must get ready for it. He added that he put implicit trust in his father-in-law, the Emperor of Austria.

'Beware!' I answered. 'Do not trust the clever policy of that Cabinet.'

The auxiliary Austrian force had acted very feebly during our disastrous campaign. With a little determination (or without secret orders not to risk his troops) Prince Schwarzenberg, who commanded them, and who unfortunately had under him General Reynier with the Saxon contingent, might have held in check Tchitchakof's army, and prevented it from harassing our rear at the Beresina.

Chapter 21

Disorderly Retreat

It was in the month of April, 1813, that I started for Saxony to take up the command of the 11th corps of the Grand Army.[1] The day following my arrival at the Emperor's headquarters, I had orders to attack Merseburg, which I carried, or rather stormed, after a stubborn resistance; as I knew that the place was defended by Prussian troops who had served under my orders during the preceding campaign, and that they were commanded by the same general, my onslaught was the more vehement.

We marched upon Lutzen and Leipsic. I was in position between these two points; the allies were in front of us on the left bank of the Elster. The name of that river, which a few months later was so nearly fatal to me, has remained engraven on my memory. The Emperor, believing that all the enemy's forces were collected at Leipsic, sent thither General Lauriston, who commanded the left. He came up to me, and gave me orders to support him if necessary; but at that moment he received intelligence that the allies, who had debouched from Pegau, were advancing towards us. The Emperor would not believe it, because he was firmly convinced that their main force was at Leipsic. Marshal Ney, who was with him, confirmed him in that idea, and declared he had noticed nothing unusual on the Elster.

However, firing began, and was directed against the very point occupied by the marshal's corps; it increased in violence, and approached rapidly; then the Emperor despatched the marshal, and shortly afterwards followed him.[2] Warnings came in apace; but, notwithstanding them, the Emperor left Lauriston in difficulties near Leipsic, and me

---
1. Macdonald's nomination as Commander-in-chief of the 11th corps was dated April 10, 1813.
2. Battle of Lutzen, May 2, 1813.

in position to support or protect him; but scarcely had he reached the central position, when he changed my destination, and ordered me to march straight ahead towards the Elster. I had not started, when a second order came, telling me to go more to the right; but, as the enemy continued to advance, a third order directed me to march straight on to their guns.

We went at the double, and it was full time, for the enemy's cavalry had already slipped in between me and Marshal Ney, who had lost much ground. The enemy, having realized my movement, turned to retreat; but I had had time to point thirty pieces of cannon, and they galloped rapidly through my grapeshot.

We continued to advance on their right flank, and forced them into a position covered by a little artificial canal used for floating wood. After crossing—not without loss—a little valley, we crowned the heights; the plain lay outstretched before us, but without cavalry it would have been unsafe to venture there.

Suddenly the fire ceased all along the front of the army, and was directed at us; the enemy sent forward their cavalry reserves, composed of the Guards of the sovereigns of Russia and Prussia. Thrice they attempted to break our squares, but in vain; each time they were driven back with loss, and the third time in such confusion as must have given great advantage to our cavalry had we possessed any. Only a few squadrons covered our left, commanded by the Marquis de Latour-Maubourg,[3] who wished nothing better than to charge. I sent to beg him to do so; but the Viceroy, under whose orders he was acting, refused, in spite of my entreaties, as he did not wish to risk the little body of brave men who were our only resource. The battle was gained by the infantry and the artillery. It took a second time the name of Lutzen.

The battlefield, our front especially, was strewn with dead and wounded, whom, for want of means, we had been unable to move. Early next morning the Emperor paid us a visit. He was very pleased. He praised us for our energy of the previous day, and for the vigour of our attack, which had stopped the victorious march of the enemy, and turned the scale in our favour.

During the day, after we had crossed the Elster, which the enemy

---

3. When this gallant officer lost a leg during this campaign his soldier servant was greatly concerned. 'Why, you stupid fellow,' said the general (who had only just undergone amputation), to encourage him, 'you will have one boot the less to polish every day.'

did not defend, the Emperor generously distributed rewards, promotions, decorations, pensions, titles, *majorats*, etc., to my army corps. My reward was the command of the advance guard.

The enemy did not long occupy Dresden; they blew up the bridge, and only defended the Elbe long enough to protect their retreat by the right bank. While means for rebuilding or mending the bridge were being sought, my infantry got across the breaches by means of ladders; as soon as it was sufficiently repaired, the artillery crossed.

The Emperor, who, on this occasion, had taken upon himself the functions of baggage-master, stopped all vehicles; but I obtained an exemption for some of those belonging to my corps, and that evening took up my position on the heights above Dresden.

Next day I followed the traces of the enemy, but we had no affair of importance till Bautzen. I thought that I was being followed by the remainder of the army; but it had been allowed to rest, and I found myself isolated in presence of that of the enemy. In order to impose upon them, I spread out my troops like a spider's web, and waited the arrival of the other corps. Successive summons made them hasten their advance. A single step backward on my part would have exposed us to certain destruction; I therefore preferred to run the risk of staying where I was, pretending to advance, and lighting at night fires scattered among the different lines, so as to make believe that the whole army was present.

I thus passed several days, until at length our supports came up. We attacked at Bautzen, crossed the Spree, and I took a considerable share in the Battle of Wurschen, which brought us into Silesia, after two sharp skirmishes, at Bischofswerda, and before reaching Löwenberg. The former of these towns caught fire during the engagement; I believe the fire was the act of marauders after we had occupied it. An armistice was concluded during the action at Jauer, and after the occupation of Breslau. We went into cantonments; I took the district of Löwenberg for my army corps.

We had done enough to retrieve the honour of our arms after the terrible misfortunes of the preceding campaign. France and the army earnestly longed for peace.

A Congress met at Prague, but it was obvious that none of the Powers were acting in good faith. Austria was the soul of the Congress; she had in reality remained neutral since the reopening of hostilities, but, as afterwards transpired, she had bound herself by treaty with Russia and Prussia as early as the previous February. A significant proof of this was given by the manner in which the enemy retired before the armistice; they grouped themselves at the foot of the mountains of Bohemia, instead of recrossing the Oder. Driven into the position they had taken up, they could have no choice but to lay down their arms, supposing always that Austria meant to make her pretended neutrality respected; that was apparent.

The negotiations fell through, and hostilities recommenced, the allies being reinforced by the Austrians, and soon afterwards by the defection of the Bavarians. Before the truce was broken off, I had orders to reconnoitre all the outlets from Bohemia, from the Saxon frontier as far as the Bober, which was the line of demarcation on my front, while my right extended to the mountains. At the same time the allies entered Bohemia. They moved thither their principal forces, and attacked me two or three days before the expiration of the armistice. They expected to take me unawares, but I was ready for them, as, instead of cantoning my troops. I had formed camps sufficiently near each other to be able to concentrate promptly on any threatened point.

The day after my return to Löwenberg I received news that the enemy were attacking. I went half-way to the point indicated, but could neither see nor hear anything. The enemy's movements were concealed by hillocks and other obstructions on the ground. As I received no further news, I concluded that the post attacked had been forced, and that the detachment which defended it had been unable to fall back upon Löwenberg according to their instructions.

In order to clear up this doubt, and while my breakfast was preparing, I took a picket of cavalry, and rode out slowly and carefully to the point whence news had reached me that the enemy were advancing. On reaching it I found all quiet, and learned that the enemy had advanced, but had immediately retired again. Information had been sent to me by an orderly; I never received it, as the man must have lost his way or got drunk.

I had ridden three leagues out to this point, and as many from Löwenberg, in my first reconnaissance; our horses needed rest as much as we did ourselves. I accepted a meagre breakfast, heartily offered, with alacrity.

Just as I was remounting my horse to return, an officer galloped up as fast as he could ride, to tell me that the enemy had crossed the Bober at the very point I had quitted, that the attack had been so sudden that there had not been time to harness my carriages, which were probably taken; he was not certain about this, because, as soon as the enemy appeared, he had hastened away in search of me. I concluded that it could be only a brush at the outposts, and decided to return; but ere I had ridden half a league, fresh information and fugitives confirmed what I had first heard. I was thus cut off from the principal point, and from almost all my forces.

I waited a few hours more for the return of the scouts whom I had sent out; their reports all tallied. At last I decided to make a great detour, and bring in my outposts; we marched all the rest of the day and through the night, and reached Löwenberg worn out with fatigue. There I learned what had occurred. Lauriston's corps, which had joined me the previous day, had attached itself, to my troops, and together they had driven the enemy back across the Bober. They had had some losses, and my carriages were gone.

In consequence of the account of this event that I sent to the Emperor, he hastened up with some reserves and the Guard. We had taken some prisoners, and learned that the principal attack of the allies was to be made on the left bank of the Elbe. The Emperor, nevertheless, thought that he would still have time to force the passage of the Bober; we did achieve it, took Buntzlau, and pushed on as far as Goldberg.

The Emperor returned to Dresden. On his way he heard that the Emperors of Austria and Russia had debouched from Bohemia, and were marching upon that town. As he descended the mountain overlooking it, he could see the position of the allies. He was just in time to beat them and force them to retire, but unfortunately they were not pursued with sufficient vigour. The Emperor only sent Vandamme with his corps against them, and he, believing himself supported, pushed on boldly, and entered the defile of Töplitz.

As one of the enemy's corps had become cut off, the allies returned and attacked Vandamme, who was soon attacked also from behind by this same corps, which was only seeking a way out. Thus taken between two fires, in this sort of funnel, Vandamme surrendered, was made prisoner, and nearly all his troops with him.[4] The Emperor, it

---

4. Battle of Kulm, August 30, 1813. The Battle of Dresden, won by the Emperor, had been fought three days previously, on August 27. 'Vandamme, surrounded by forces ten times his own, refused to surrender; and, placing himself at the head of his only two available battalions, charged into the midst of the enemy in the hope of finding his death there. His horse was killed, a strong body of Russians flung themselves upon him, and he was taken prisoner. On the enemy's side, generals, officers, and privates admired Vandamme's courage, and felt the greatest (continued next page)

was said, was unwell, and had returned to Dresden with his reserves and his Guard while this disastrous event was in progress. As usual, Vandamme got all the blame, but this time he had only been guilty of an excess of zeal.

After the Emperor had quitted me and returned to Dresden to fight the allies, as I have related, he sent for me; and after telling me that he had need of Marshal Ney, put under my orders Ney's own army corps, together with that of Lauriston and General Sebastiani's cavalry. Ney and Sebastiani were carrying on operations in the neighbourhood of Leignitz, and, I know not through what misunderstanding, had retreated. The Emperor spoke to me of the immediate necessity of a diversion, and told me that it was with this object that he was uniting these four army corps, including my own, under my orders. He instructed me to advance rapidly with them, and threaten Breslau and the outlets of Bohemia into Silesia.

I immediately returned to my corps, and we started without delay. We met some cavalry near Goldberg, and a brush that ensued was disadvantageous to us; notwithstanding the efforts of Generals Reiset and Audenarde, my horse gave way. I hastened to rally them, and put myself at their head to lead a charge. I started them, and believed myself followed, when the enemy's cavalry came to meet me; as I knew that my men had retreated, I could do nothing but retreat too.

My infantry debouched, and passed through a deep ravine. General Meunier was beginning to form a square, which at that moment bore a striking resemblance in shape to an egg. Seeing me pursued and hard pressed, he proposed that I should join him; I refused, and passed near him. The enemy did not expose themselves to his fire; they were only anxious to mask their own retreat. We followed them eagerly, but were

esteem for him; but, incredible as it may seem, the kind treatment ceased, and was replaced by insults when the prisoner was taken to Prague. The Emperor of Russia and his brother, the Grand Duke Constantine, addressed him in abusive language, and the Grand Duke actually even snatched away his sword. Vandamme indignantly exclaimed, "My sword is easy to take here: it would have been braver to have come to fetch it on the battlefield; but you seem to like your trophies cheap." Thereupon the Emperor Alexander in a rage ordered the arrest of Vandamme, calling him "plunderer" and "brigand." Vandamme retorted, looking Alexander defiantly in the face, "I am no plunderer or brigand; and, anyway, history will not reproach me with having murdered my own father." Alexander turned pale at this allusion to the assassination of Paul I., and the French general was taken to the frontiers of Siberia.'
Baron de Marbot's *Memoirs*, vol. 2.
5. Battle of the Katzbach, August 26, 1813, against the Army of Silesia, under the command of General Blücher.

obliged to draw rein to give General Souham, who was commanding Ney's corps, and General Sebastiani time to come up.

The former received orders to leave the point where he was and make for Jauer, and to turn the enemy's right, while I made a front attack upon them at the Katzbach; General Lauriston commanded my right.[5] General Sebastiani arrived, driving before him a strong detachment of cavalry, that had become placed between two fires. It escaped us, however, by a rapid flank movement.

It had been steadily raining ever since the previous day.

From the heights whence the enemy retired we thought we could make out the leading columns of General Souham's army; I ordered some squadrons and light artillery to make a reconnaissance, and meanwhile I went myself to the right of my line at some distance away, and told Lauriston to send some light troops across the Katzbach to feel the strength of the enemy upon his left. These orders were all clearly given, and yet not one of them was properly carried out. General Souham, for instance, who had received his early in the day, failed to execute the movement intended to turn the enemy's right. His corps marched behind Sebastiani's cavalry, which were still advancing to the heights, although I had simply ordered a few squadrons forward merely for reconnoitring purposes. It was on returning from my right wing that I learnt these counter-movements. The enemy, whose centre was rapidly retreating, but who were not uneasy for their right, retired, and I saw their artillery coming into position.

Among other movements, the great fault was committed on our side of taking a number of guns to the heights. The ground was already soaked, and they could only be moved with extreme difficulty. I ordered most of them to come down, but the road was encumbered with other guns, and with the cavalry who were going up. I instantly foresaw what would happen, and, as a precautionary measure, sent forward a division of infantry to protect the two bodies on the *plateau*. The rain still continued; the men could not use their muskets. I went down in person and freed the base of the hill. The road was not more than twelve or fifteen feet wide; it was impossible to turn, the only thing to be done was to let all those who had started gain the summit, turn there, and come down again; and that took time.

While we were in this dilemma, the enemy deployed a large body of cavalry, protected by the artillery, and the infantry followed in columns. I had no news of General Souham, I did not even know if he had received my orders; the movements of the enemy were proof positive that, if he had received them, he had done nothing to put them into execution. Without his corps I could do nothing, much less give battle, although the enemy were already calling this affair by that name. Meanwhile, Lauriston, yielding a little on his left, crossed the river with a portion of his troops, and made a charge with all his cavalry.

In the centre our guns, sunk in the mire up to the axles, could not be moved; the artillery soldiers and gunners unharnessed them, and brought back the horses; the enemy dared not descend. I have already said that the infantry could make no use of their weapons; posted on the slope of the hill, they were safe from the attacks of the cavalry. Then the front column of Souham's corps came up to make bad worse, and to still further encumber General Sebastiani's position. The latter was in despair at the loss of his guns. Souham stammered out some reasons why he had failed to operate upon the points I had indicated.

It was getting late; the rain fell unceasingly, the ground was soaked, the ravines were filling, the streams overflowing; in such a disheartening state of affairs I ordered a retreat to Goldberg. A night march under such circumstances occasioned great disorder; the rain never ceased. Lauriston was anxious to take the road by which he had crossed the mountains. I remarked that it would most likely be impracticable; he insisted and I yielded, the more readily that the continuity of our retreat would thereby be rendered easier. But what I had suspected proved to be the case; he found the roads flooded, and was compelled to retreat. One of his divisions flanked him, receiving orders to follow such a direction as would eventually bring about its junction with him and us; we had to protect Lauriston's line of communications. At one very bad place several carriages were driven off the road, and got into the fields, where they remained, mine among others. I came up at this moment; the ammunition waggons were unloaded so that they might be more easily moved, but nevertheless we lost some. We gained a fairly sheltered place, where we posted the cavalry.

Near there we expected to meet General Lauriston's covering division that had flanked his corps; it was not to be seen; inquiries and searches were instituted, but there was still no news of it. All the troops were marching in disarray, wet to the skin, and, as Lauriston's and my corps were retiring on Löwenberg, we learnt that the bridge over the Bober had been dismantled, as the river had overflowed, and thus that our means of passage was cut off. In consequence of the floods, which were out in all directions, I was unable to communicate with Souham or Sebastiani, who were retiring upon Bunzlau, where there was a wooden bridge already very rickety; the engineers did their utmost to preserve it.

I waited four-and-twenty hours for Lauriston's division; the cavalry sent me word that they could no longer hold the position where I had posted them, and their searches for the division had been fruitless. Meanwhile, although water covered .the road leading to Bunzlau, along which Souham and Sebastiani were marching, a rumour spread among the troops that the road was practicable, as there was only water on it up to the knees; thereupon, without orders, they started off in confusion, as it was impossible to restrain them. I therefore let them go. I was compelled to recall the cavalry, and to abandon the wandering division, convinced that it would find its own way out of the difficulty somehow; but I afterwards had the grief of learning that, owing to the slowness of the general[6] in command, it had been obliged to surrender.

The rain had ceased, and the sun reappeared; we made a forced march, and eventually reached Bunzlau, where I found Generals Souham and Sebastiani. A large portion of their corps had crossed the bridge, as the two others had done, and continued a disorderly march to Bautzen; I sent orders to them to rally there. I could not gauge our losses; with the exception of the artillery on the heights of Jauer, and the little division, they were inconsiderable.[7] Having rallied all the troops, I took up my position.

I had sent a report of all these circumstances to Dresden. The Emperor, to whom the loss naturally appeared great, imagined that it was greater even than it was; he expected to find the troops demoralized and in disorder, and was agreeably surprised at finding them reunited

---
6. Puthod.
7. 'Marshal Macdonald,' says General de Marbot (*Memoirs*, Eng. edit., vol. 2), 'whose miscalculation from a strategic point of view had brought about this disaster, though he had lost the confidence of the army, was able to preserve its esteem by the honest and straightforward way in which he admitted his mistake. On the following day he called a meeting of all the generals and colonels; and, after inviting us all to help to maintain order, said that every man and officer had done his duty; that the loss of the battle was due to one man only, and that was himself; because, when it came on to rain, he ought not to have left broken ground to go and attack in an open plain an enemy outnumbering him immensely in cavalry; nor should he have placed a river behind him in stormy weather. This noble confession disarmed criticism, and each man did his utmost to contribute to the safety of the army during its retreat to the Elbe.'

and in good spirits.

The enemy had followed us, but on seeing our position appeared unwilling to risk an attack. The Emperor gave them no alternative. Having arrived with his reserves and his Guard, and saying nothing to me except that my news to him had been bad, he ordered me to advance and attack. We were soon ready, and marched forward eagerly; the enemy were driven back by our cavalry, which had been placed for the time under the command of Murat; but they made a good stand on the mountain of Hochchellenberg.

While we were attacking them there, the Emperor, seeing General Sebastiani near me, came towards us, and addressed him in the most violent language; I was indignant, and showed it. His complaint against the General was not the loss of his artillery on the plateau at Jauer, but that of his last cannon. Sebastiani, as I then learned from the Emperor, had sent him, without informing me, a private report; he interrogated the *aide-de-camp* who brought this report, pressed him with questions, and was told by him that his general, who had only one gun left, which he feared to lose, had sent it on with the baggage waggons, which, by another misfortune, had fallen into the enemy's hands. The Emperor added that the loss of artillery was the fortune of war; but that what irritated him was the seizure of that particular piece, seeing that artillery was provided for the protection of the troops, and not to be defended by baggage waggons. I warmly and heartily stood up for Sebastiani. The Emperor departed, leaving the command to me, with orders to follow the enemy.

Sebastiani was furious, and with reason, for he had not been spared even in presence of his own men. He wished to blow his brains out, cause himself to be killed, or send in his resignation. With great trouble I succeeded in calming him.

The enemy rapidly retreated, and our pursuit did not tarry. They crossed the River Queiss, which I left between us; as fresh reinforcements reached them they tried to turn us. My orders were not to expose myself to any serious action; in my turn, therefore, I retired, but slowly; we thus continued alternately advancing and retreating. They also did not seem very anxious to attack, unless they could feel certain of getting the best of it; but as they displayed numerous forces, I fell back to within a few leagues of Dresden. We were very badly off for provisions. and forage. The detachments which I was compelled to send out to search the villages were often obliged to come to blows, and soldiers who went out singly generally fell into the hands of the enemy. We were thus being slowly undermined, but the moment was not far off at which decisive operations would put a limit to this state of things: the allies were preparing for it.

CHAPTER 22

Commencement of the Retreat

Dresden, where the Emperor stayed, was the pivot for the army astride on the two banks of the Elbe; we remained on the defensive; communications were intercepted with France, whence we had drawn no assistance since the fresh outbreak of hostilities. The Emperor one morning sent one of his orderly officers to me to ask my opinion upon our situation, and what we had better do.

We were now in October—without rations, except such as could be collected by main force; but the soldiers were allowed to dig for themselves as many potatoes as they could find in the fields where we encamped. I told the officer plainly that, unless the Emperor immediately took the offensive—that is, if he saw any chance of success, which, in my opinion, was improbable, as we had hitherto failed to force our entrance into Bohemia—he exposed us to serious catastrophes: the army was daily growing weaker by sickness and the ordinary losses of war; that an unsuccessful battle would weaken us still further, and use up our ammunition, which we could not replace; that the magazines were empty, the country ruined; that, under these circumstances, the prudent course would be to retire immediately to the Saale, leaving a strong garrison in Leipsic, and to evacuate those places on the Oder with which we could still communicate, and, above all, those on the Elbe. The officer hesitated for a moment at the idea of having to carry such proposals.

'Go!' I said; 'the Emperor will realize their importance, and will be pleased with me for my outspokenness.'

He came back in a few hours to tell me that he had fulfilled his mission; that the Emperor, being in his bath, had called him in, and, after hearing him attentively, had made but one objection—namely, that the Saale was not a defensive position; that there was nothing but the Rhine; and that, since I thought retreat was necessary, we would go to the Rhine.

'Go and tell the marshal that,' he added.

'Quite so,' I answered. 'The Saale was only provisional in my proposal; the denies leading thither are difficult, and we can hold the enemy longer in check there than on the Elbe.'

He departed; but scarcely had he left me, when another orderly officer came to bring me an order not to commence the preliminary execution of my plan, but to advance at once. My reconnaissances and forage parties were already out, and I was consequently very much weakened in force. I told the officer to point out to the Emperor that I could not start until they had returned, and to add that, as I was compelled to send out for provisions, I begged him to give me his orders twenty-four hours in advance. It was not long before he returned, saying that the Emperor desired me to set out immediately with what troops I had, that the absentees would join me later, and that he himself would come with his Guard and his reserves.

I therefore started, leaving behind my heavy ordnance, as well as my baggage. A wood separated us from the enemy. At sight of us they fell back upon the heights of Bischofswerda. We left on our right a feeble line of their cavalry, from which we were 'Separated by a deep ravine which formed a prolonged circuit, and also covered the hill where I had left my siege guns. While I was attacking the heights of Bischofswerda, the Emperor came up to this artillery; he sent for me, and I found him helping to place it in position, and pushing with all his might to help the gunners.

'What are you going to fire at, Sire?' I asked him.

'At that line of cavalry down there in front of us.'

'But it is out of range, your Majesty! I saw it as I came back! They are only scouts; and there is but one line of them!'

'Never mind,' he replied, and gave the word to fire.

We could not see where the shot fell, and the cavalry remained motionless; I could not understand his object. At the seventeenth shot he ordered, this useless fire to cease, remarking:

'It is costing us too much.'

The enemy were driven back from the heights, and we followed them. The Emperor called me aside, and said:

'You were surprised at my firing?'

'Yes,' I answered, 'because that handful of cavalry was not worth powder and shot, besides being out of range.'

It had, moreover, just retreated.

'You see,' continued the Emperor, 'that with every volley one hits something; it may be a man of mark. Look at Moreau!—he was killed by a spent shot at Dresden. Look at Duroc or Bessières!'

As a matter of fact, Moreau had both legs cut off by a shot which was far from spent.

The Emperor moved his headquarters to Harta, or Horta; he invited me to dinner, and, instead of talking of our circumstances, would think of nothing but a lawsuit, then in progress, against some former contractors. In answer to my request to hare his opinion on the issue of the case, he replied, laughing, that the whole lot of them—plaintiffs, defendants, and witnesses—deserved hanging. On quitting him, I asked for his orders; he answered that he must sleep on them, and would let me have them in the morning. He sent them; and I was to march, because he wished to come up with the enemy and give battle.

I sent orders to my advance guard, on the other side of Bischofswerda, to march. An orderly officer from the Emperor accompanied me in order to report to him the position of the enemy, who were not far off. On the way, an *aide-de-camp* came to warn me that they were in great force; the orderly officer wished to return immediately to inform the Emperor.

'No,' said I; 'follow me. We will reconnoitre for ourselves, and then you will be able to say to the Emperor, " I have seen."'

The enemy seemed to have a force of about 80,000 men, and to be quite ready to receive us, or to cut us off. I told this to the Emperor, who replied that his object was gained, and that I was to profit by the darkness to return to the positions I had quitted on the previous day. He returned to Dresden. I was only disturbed by some demonstrations, but the day seemed very long, isolated as I was since the Emperor had left me; fortunately, the enemy had been advised of his arrival, but not of his departure.

Two days later he summoned me to Dresden. I told him that we could now see nothing of the enemy except some scouts; that they were preparing some movement, and perhaps manoeuvring to turn our flank.

'It cannot be to attack the entrenched camp on the right bank,' he replied; 'they are too timid to attack that.'

That evening when I returned, I heard that the enemy had suddenly disappeared entirely from in front of us, and were making for my left. Some prisoners were brought to me who confirmed the departure of their troops, which were, they said, going to Mühlberg, to cross the Elbe there. I sent them to the Emperor with my report.

That same night I received orders to abandon my position, and to come and occupy the entrenched camp, which other troops had hastily left; and twenty-four hours later I was relieved in my turn, and told to go on to Wittenberg. The Emperor was anxious to cross the Elbe there; and my advance guard had already started, when he received intelligence that the allies had quitted Bohemia, and were advancing towards Leipsic; thereupon I received counter-orders to make for the Partha.

A portion of the allied forces was already in position at about two leagues from Leipsic.[1] It was October 16; I well remember the date. We attacked with more vigour than unison, and one of my divisions carried a position known as the Swedish Redoubt at the point of the bayonet. It was necessary to support them. The cavalry came up sharply, and did very well; but the *carabineers* behaved very badly. With my own eyes I saw a squadron of the enemy outwit them at only ten sabres' length. Each side remained in much the same position at the end of the combat.

Next day, the 17th, although we were facing one another, within range, not a shot was fired—not even from a musket; but we could see the reinforcements taking their places in the enemy's ranks, and could distinctly hear the cheers of the soldiers. The night was equally tranquil. On either side everything was preparing for a bloody battle.

Early next morning, the 18th, the Emperor closed up his ranks; the enemy were already advancing to attack us. I had orders only to retire very slowly, which I did, but not without great losses, among others that of General Aubry, commanding the artillery belonging to my corps. At length I reached the lines. The cannonade was so violent, so multiplied, so extreme, that it might have been compared to a fire from two ranks of infantry, and very well maintained, moreover. I again lost a large number of my men, many of my artillery horses; one gun was dismounted, my ammunition was consumed. I ordered my infantry to shelter in ravines, and behind little risings in the ground. I thus remained inactive for several hours, while the battle continued

---

1. During the night of October 15, if reliance is to be placed on the account given by Baron de Marbot, that officer nearly succeeded in making prisoners of the Emperor of Russia and the King of Prussia, who were at the outposts reconnoitring on the Kolmberg.

with a violence equal to that with which it had begun, exposed to the fire of the enemy, to which I could not reply.

The army was then forming a crescent before Leipsic, of which one extremity was flanked by the Elster. I implored the Emperor to replace my artillery; he at length sent me a battery of the Guard, which arrived most conveniently, for the enemy, noticing that from this point they obtained no answer to their fire, concluded that they had silenced mine, and as they could see no troops, they thought they might establish themselves upon the raised point that I occupied. I soon undeceived them. As they boldly advanced, my troops suddenly showed themselves, protected by the batteries that had come to me; they retired, and their firing recommenced, but less violently than before; either they were economizing their ammunition, or else some of their guns had been dismounted too.

I was walking about with Colonel Bongars, and we deplored the great number of victims stretched at our feet; preoccupied solely with what was going on under our eyes, and with the melancholy issue that I foresaw, I regretted that the cannon spared me while striking down so many brave men. While we were talking over these sad circumstances, I saw the enemy retreat on my left, and the corps of General Reynier, drawn up in two lines, advance. The leading line was composed of Saxons, the rear of French. I gave orders to advance to their support, when what was my horror at seeing the front rank stop at the point the enemy had just quitted, and, turning round, fire straight at the French behind them!

Never was such treachery known in history. In the preceding year, when the Prussians deserted, at least they had the decency not to turn and fire upon us at the moment. Amazed, surprised, the second line fled, and was immediately pursued by the front line, which an instant before had been fighting under our banner. That there had been connivance was clear from the fact that the enemy supported this movement, and it would have been decisive for them had not the Emperor himself hastened to the spot to stop them and rally the line.

It was growing late, and the firing slackened on either side, and finally ceased altogether. Everyone kept his own position—at least, on the side where I had been all day—but our left had been pushed back nearer to Leipsic. We passed the night in the utmost watchfulness, foreseeing a too tardy retreat, but in nowise prepared for the terrible nature of the next day's catastrophe.

An officer was sent from headquarters to bring me orders to retire to the suburb of Leipsic at the end of the high road to Dresden; but he lost his way, and only arrived at seven in the morning.[2] A thick fog fortunately obscured our position, and we were able, therefore, to fall back unperceived. The other army corps had done the same thing, and we thus formed a fresh line. As the parks of artillery could not be moved, they were blown up; nothing could have been devised more likely to put the enemy on the alert and announce a decided retreat, and they were not slow to profit by the signal, advancing to the heights which commanded my position.

The gardens of the suburb were enclosed by earthbanks, which might serve as a slight bulwark against infantry and cavalry, but were useless against cannon. We had barricaded all the issues, crenellated the walls, but that served us very little against a heavy cannonade, which dealt frightful execution in the houses and among the troops. The enemy advanced in close columns; we stopped them for a moment. The fire was very hot, when General Girardin, at that time *aide-de-camp* to the Prince of Neuchâtel, brought me orders to immediately send a division to the extreme right to the assistance of Marshal Augereau.

'See for yourself,' I answered, 'whether I can spare any troops; I rather stand in need of reinforcements myself. Go and tell the Emperor so.'

'I have executed my mission,' said he; 'you must do as you please;' and he left me.

I had not even troops enough to keep my front in every direction, but I reflected that if Marshal Augereau's corps, and consequently the intervening regiments between him and me, were forced, I, who held the outside wing, would be outflanked and cut off, and I consequently determined to send, not a division, but a brigade of the Hessian division.

During this time, although we were defending the ground inch by inch, and the suburb had been taken and retaken several times, we were pushed right back to the *boulevard* of the town. I was then informed that the Hessian brigade was on its way back, having found neither friends nor foes at the point to which they were ordered, and this caused me great surprise. As I was pressed in front, I desired Marshal Poniatowski to attempt a final charge with the small body of cavalry remaining to us, while the infantry fell back to the bridge in order to cross the Elster.

The Hessian division had in the meantime entered the town, and

---

2. October 19.

I presumed it was by orders of General Marchand, who was in command. But instead of marching to the Elster by the broad street that leads to the bridge, the division went up to the ramparts, and opened fire upon us. This fresh treachery effectually discouraged our troops. They retreated in wild confusion, notwithstanding my efforts to maintain order, and swept me with them. To complete our misfortunes, I learned that the bridge, our only means of communication, had been blown up!

This appalling news, which we vainly strove to conceal, spread universal consternation; upon every face horror, fury, despair, were painted, and I was not the least excited among them. Neither before, during, or since the battle, had any precaution been taken to secure the Elster or the road to Lindenau—albeit, it would have been easy to find many places at which men of different arms and of different corps could have crossed, owing to the narrowness of the river. Neither had any troop been posted on the left bank to protect the retreat on the chance of the bridge remaining intact, or of others being established. The principal headquarters and the Emperor himself were at Markranstadt. I do not yet know by what name to call this criminal indifference: whether incapability, cowardice, or absence of all feeling, of all regret at the sacrifice of so many lives.

The bridge had been blown up several hours previously, but the noise of the cannon, of the fusillade, and of the ammunition waggons that were being exploded, had prevented us from hearing the noise. An attempt was made to lay at the door of a superior engineer officer the responsibility for this act, and the neglect of preparations for crossing, but no one dared to take steps to bring him before a court-martial; for it was quite clear that he had received no orders, and that on the contrary he had suggested to the major-general the advisability of preparing points from which to cross, and that the answer given him had been that it would be time enough when the Emperor ordered it.

The most likely version of the catastrophe is that the bridge had been mined, and left in charge of an unlucky corporal and some artillerymen or sappers, with orders to blow it up if they perceived the enemy. These poor fellows saw, heard, knew that part of the army was still on the right bank, but they did not know that there were no other points from which they could cross: they saw a few of the enemy's skirmishers, and that was enough to make them carry out their orders.

It was said afterwards that, even had the bridge remained intact, we could not have made use of it, as it and the approaches to it were blocked by artillery and waggons. That may have been so, but at least the infantry might have attempted to cross, the cavalry would have abandoned their horses, and thus many lives might have been saved. The block arose from the fact that no supervision had been exercised, no orders given to keep this passage clear. Two strings of carriages were passing to the right and left of the *boulevards* of Leipsic, a third along the principal street of the town: all three met at the head of the bridge, and it was a struggle which should get across first; the carriages caught each other's wheels, blocked up the space, and our unhappy fate was decided.

I escaped, however, with a firm resolve not to fall alive into the hands of the enemy, preferring to shoot or drown myself. Dragged along, as I have said, by the crowd, I crossed two little arms of the Elster, the first on a little bridge, holding on to the hand-rail, for my feet did not touch the boards (I was lifted up, and ten times over was nearly upset); the other upon a horse, lent me by a quartermaster, whose name I am sorry to have forgotten, though I have since rendered him a service.

I found myself in an open field, still surrounded by the crowd; I wandered about, it still followed me, convinced that I must know a way out, though I could find none marked on my map. There was still the main arm of the river to cross. Lauriston, who had been with me before we crossed the streams, was separated from me.

Some of Prince Poniatowski's *aides-de-camp* came and told me he was drowned; I still thought he was behind me. I had begged him, as I have already said, to execute a charge to cover our withdrawal, and had not seen him since his return. The charge had not taken place; the cavalry, having heard of the disaster at the bridge, had not followed him, and had thought of nothing but their own safety. These *aides-de-camp* shed tears on telling me of the death[2] of their prince; he had thrown himself into the water with his horse, but had been unable to climb the opposite bank, which was very steep; the tired horse had fallen backwards upon him, and both had been carried away by the swift stream.

---

2. Prince Poniatowski had only been created a Marshal three days before his untimely end! Rather than be taken prisoner, he leapt his horse into the rapid stream, though exhausted by a severe wound. His body was recovered five days later by a peasant when fishing.

During this story one of my *aides-de-camp*, Beurnonville, seized my bridle and said:

'*Monsieur le Maréchal*, we cannot help that; the important thing is to save you.'

Thereupon he hurried me away at a gallop to free me from the unhappy crowd that still surrounded me, and told me that Colonel Marion, who commanded the engineers in my army corps, had succeeded in crossing to the other side. He had had two trees cut down and thrown across the river, joining them with doors, shutters, and planks. We hastened thither, but the place was blocked by troops. I was told that Marshals Augereau and Victor had crossed this frail structure on horseback, notwithstanding all the representations that were made to them; that as the extremities were not fastened, and the two trees had slipped apart, the flooring had given way. There remained nothing but the two trunks, and no one dared cross them.

It was my only chance; I made up my mind and risked it. I got off my horse with great difficulty, owing to the crowd, and there I was, one foot on either trunk, and the abyss below me. A high wind was blowing. I was wearing a large cloak with loose sleeves, and, fearing lest the wind should cause me to lose my balance, or lest someone should lay hold of it, I got rid of it. I had already made three-quarters of my way across, when some men determined to follow me; their unsteady feet caused the trunks to shake, and I fell into the water. I could fortunately touch the bottom, but the bank was steep, the soil loose and greasy; I vainly struggled to reach the shore. Some of the enemy's skirmishers came up, I know not whence. They fired at me point-blank, and missed me, and some of our men, who happened to be near, drove them off and helped me out.

I was wet from head to foot, besides being in a violent perspiration from my efforts, and out of breath. The Duke of Ragusa, who had got across early in the day, seeing me on the other bank, gave me a horse; I wanted dry clothes more, but they were not to be had.

One of my grooms, named Naudet, who had charge of my pocket-book, not daring to come across, confided it to a soldier, who undressed and swam with it. I had no money to give him. Marshal Marmont lent me his purse, and I gave it to the man. He accompanied us, naked as he was, for three leagues, and I was still dripping. While we were still near the Elster, some skirmishers of the enemy came up in large numbers; I took about thirty men who had been posted not far from there to protect a cannon, and charged and dispersed them.

On the other side of the Elster the firing continued; it suddenly ceased. Our unhappy troops were crowded together on the river-bank; whole companies plunged into the water and were carried away; cries of despair rose on all sides. The men perceived me. Despite the noise and the tumult, I distinctly heard these words:

'*Monsieur le Maréchal*, save your men! save your children!'

I could do nothing for them! Overcome by rage, indignation, fury, I wept! Unable to give any assistance to these poor fellows, I quitted the scene of desolation. Some of those who had seen me fall into the river believed me drowned; the rumour of my death spread rapidly, together with that of Prince Poniatowski, among the broken remains of the army which had succeeded in crossing the Elster, and at headquarters. Great joy was shown when I was found to be alive; all embraced me, wishing to know the details of the appalling disaster and of my marvellous escape. The Emperor desired to see me. I was so indignant with him that I refused to accompany his messengers. However, I was so earnestly begged and implored to go and give advice, in the interests of the army and of France, that, for fear of some new piece of folly, I at last yielded.

There were a number of people with the Emperor, among others Count Daru. He was seated at a table, a map spread before him, and his head on his hand. With tears I related all that had happened.

For a long time I was haunted by the terrible picture, and the cries of my men, 'Save your soldiers! Save your children!' still ring in my ears, and excite in my breast the deepest pity for the poor fellows whom I saw throwing themselves into the water, preferring certain death to the risk of being massacred or taken prisoners.

The Emperor listened without interrupting me; my audience were effected in various degrees, and all by their attitude displayed their grief. I ended by saying that the losses of the army in men and material were immense, and that not a moment should be lost in collecting the remains, and making for the Rhine. We were then at Markranstadt; I had walked three leagues, still wet, and very tired. The Emperor noticed it, and said coldly:

'Go and rest.'

I left him, indignant at his indifference, for he offered me neither refreshment nor help,[3] and yet I think I had said, in the course of my

---

3. It could hardly be expected that at a time when the Ruler of France and Head of the Army had vital matters to settle he should have time to also undertake the duties of an attentive host. Under the circumstances, his advice was not other than sensible.

narration, that I had lost everything, baggage and carriages. After I had been pulled out of the river, the Duke of Ragusa told me that he had seen my carriages in the block on the *boulevard* at Leipsic, going in an opposite direction to the one I was following, while I, all the time, believed them to be at headquarters.

The previous evening I had sent orders that they should start, while the roads were yet clear and open; but, by another fatality, the *aide-de-camp* who was in charge of them fell asleep, and when he awoke it was too late. They were thus lost, together with a bag containing from 12,000 to 15,000 *francs* in gold (£480 to £600), which he had orders to keep in his portmanteau. He explained to me later that the fear lest it should be stolen in camp had decided him to place this bag in my carriage, whence he had forgotten to rescue it when he was compelled to abandon everything, and flee with my attendants. I had also lost a great deal of silver money with my carriages. This circumstance having become known, everyone, as I left the Emperor's presence, cordially offered me all the things of which I stood in need—changes of clothes, and their purses; but when I opened my pocket-book, I found a good number of twenty-*franc* pieces inside, and therefore refused the latter.

Chapter 23

Discouragement

The next day, October 20, at dawn, we started on our march towards the Saale. About 800 or 900 men, the remains of my army corps, had been rallied, and with these I marched. As we were without artillery or carriages, while the roads were encumbered with them, we marched along very easily. We crossed the river by a covered bridge, and I encamped for the night on the opposite side. I met Marshal Augereau, and asked him for an explanation of the order brought to me from the Emperor by General Girardin to send a division to his support, while I was bearing the brunt of so severe a combat in the suburbs of Leipsic; and, further, why nobody had been found in the place named. He replied with an oath:

'That idiot does not know what he is about! Have you not already noticed that? Have you not observed that he has completely lost his head in these recent events, and in the catastrophe by which they have been followed? The coward! He abandoned and was prepared to sacrifice us all; but do you imagine that I am fool enough to let myself be killed or made prisoner for the sake of a Leipsic suburb? You should have done as I did, and have gone away!'[1]

That was all I could get out of him.

The next morning we started again; on the road we met the provision waggons belonging to the Imperial Guard. For myself I had not a morsel of bread. I asked for some. The inspector or commissary in charge of the waggons made difficulties.

'Your carriages are lost,' I said, 'and will fall a prey to the enemy. Distribute at once your food and provisions to the troops around you.'

---

1. Characteristic advice of the Marshal, who abandoned to the enemy the second City of the Empire (Lyons) in the succeeding year.

I at last obtained five or six loaves from him, which I divided among my officers.

We had to recross the Saale. A slender bridge had been thrown across for the infantry, who precipitated themselves on to it in crowds, and caused it to give way. Nobody took command. I spent at least two hours in trying to re-establish order, and at last crossed over myself without having succeeded. It was then between two and four o'clock in the afternoon; I was told that the principal headquarters were in a village hard by. I saw the Emperor in front of a house, reclining in a chair. He did not appear to see me. The Master of the Horse (Caulaincourt) beckoned me in, and gave me a loaf of bread, a chicken, and a bottle of wine. I had not broken my fast, and received these refreshments with avidity and gratitude.

The Prince Major-General told me that he had sent me orders to continue my march, and that a little farther on I should find a broken bridge, which was being repaired; I went thither. I was alone with a groom. My officers had crossed the Saale pell-mell when I betook myself to headquarters for further orders; they thought I was going to return. I found a company of pontonniers and sappers at work; men on foot and led horses could pass, but not carriages. These men had been eating some broth, and I asked if they had any left.

'Yes,' they replied, and brought me some. I dipped some bread into it, and ate it greedily.

After this light repast I examined the place, and saw that no precautions had been taken to cover the bridge under repair. It was visible from the slope of a range of mountains, at the summit of which the enemy could place artillery and blow it to pieces, and that of course happened.

I again crossed in order to see if I could discover their number, and some of our skirmishers were sent in their direction. At the first gunshot the Emperor crossed the frail little bridge used by the workmen, and I saw him going away at a rapid trot on the other side. A column of our troops came at last to cover the principal bridge; before their front rank reached it I crossed it once more, and went to headquarters.

I did not know what had become of my little troop and my officers. I therefore remounted my horse, and followed the marching troops. It was now quite dark, and, as the road was blocked, we gained a bank that ran near it at the risk of breaking our necks by falling into the ravines or ruts; at length we reached the place where the headquarters were established. As I passed the Emperor's house, Caulaincourt recognized me, and begged me to come in and dine with the staff—they were just going to sit down; I accepted.

The next morning a small advance-guard was collected for me; the enemy were scouring the country. Late that night we reached Erfurt. The town, occupied by our troops, possessed a strong castle; General d'Alton was in command; but the gates were shut, as disorder was feared from arrivals late at night, though they did not escape it even on the following day. Stores of all kinds had been formed there; to save time and formalities they were burst open and ransacked.

We had been there for some hours, when the Emperor sent for me. I went to the castle, and first saw the King of Naples, who cautioned me that the Emperor's intention was to order me to find a strong defensive position, where he could remain for five or six days.

'You had better find a weak one,' added Murat with an oath, 'or he will not rest till he has ruined himself and us too.:

'Never fear,' I replied. 'Even if the position be excellent, I will tell him my mind about our situation.'

I was ushered in. The Emperor gave me the commission of which Murat had warned me.

'It is out of the question to make a reconnaissance at this moment,' I said, 'because there is such a thick fog that it is impossible to see fifteen yards ahead. But, Sire, I continued, 'are you in earnest in talking of remaining here?'

'The men are tired,' said the Emperor, 'and the enemy pursuing slowly. We must give them a rest.'

'No doubt that would be advisable, or even necessary under other circumstances,' I replied; 'but in our present state of disorganization, or demoralization, as I may as well call things by their proper names, we shall gain nothing by it. We must get to the Rhine as fast as possible. The majority of the men are already in disorder, and making their way thither.'

'But yet I am told that a considerable number have been stopped, and fifteen battalions formed.'

'You are being flattered and deceived,' I said with firmness. 'Exactly the same thing happened after the death of Turenne and the rout of his army. The courtiers told Louis XIV. that the troops were coming back across the Rhine in such numbers that, counting them all, there were now more men than there had ever been in the army! Louis XIV. himself made this judicious remark. Our men are going away pell-mell; all our efforts to stop them have been vain—their instinct urges them towards the Rhine. No one amongst us is ignorant of the defection of the King of Bavaria, nor of his treaty with the allies, nor of the movement that General Wrede is making by forced marches to cut off our retreat between this and Frankfort; and that, clearly, is why they are pursuing so slowly—to retard our march, and give Wrede time to get in our rear. If he reaches Gelnhausen' (a place that I already knew), 'it is very doubtful that we shall be able to dislodge him—if he has had time to establish himself, that is; and he will have plenty if your Majesty remains here for two or three days. You can now only count upon the Guard, and have to beware lest they be carried away by the force of example, as in the last campaign.'

All these reflections were self-evident.

The Emperor's attitude was one of profound meditation. Three other persons were in his room, and they had ceased writing in order to listen—two of them were, I think, his private secretaries; the third, the Duke of Bassano,[2] placed his pen between his teeth, and folded his arms. He kept his eyes fixed upon me, and displayed astonishment at hearing, for the first time, his Majesty addressed 'with such freedom and outspokenness. I stopped to hear the Emperor's decision. He at length broke silence, saying that he recognized the justice of my observations, thanked me for my candour, and would reflect upon what I had said, but that, meanwhile, he wished me to make the reconnaissance.

I left, and returned some hours later to report that the fog had not lifted, which was true, and that consequently I had only been able to observe what was immediately before my eyes—namely, that the neighbourhood of the town was very steep and uneven. Thereupon he said:

'Very good; we will start tomorrow.'

'Even that will be too late,' I answered; 'we ought to start at once. The men are continually leaving laden with booty.'

Nobody had attempted to stop the pillage. We had no choice but to remain where we were till next day.

On reaching Gelnhausen, I found the position occupied, fortunately weakly, by about a thousand men. The Kintzig covered it, and the bridge had already been broken, but so hurriedly that the beams were still floating about. Some of the enemy's pickets came near us. Many isolated men had stopped; I formed them into companies, and

---

2. General Maret.

made up a battalion. The enemy had no cannon at this point, and with mine I drove them away from the river.

As soon as the bridge was sufficiently repaired, I ordered an attack. The position might have been ambushed. The enemy were so weak that they made no effort to keep us back; but if they had had time to establish themselves, I do not know if we should have managed to dislodge them. Later on they received reinforcements, principally of cavalry; we skirmished all day, continually advancing towards a village, which we reached as night was drawing on. There was a castle in the place, and the Emperor came thither to take up his quarters, although he had already fixed them in a little village in the rear. Everything, therefore, had to be repacked, and the waggons reloaded for the move. In the village just mentioned, there was only one uncomfortable house; while in the place where I was, and whither Napoleon came, there was a castle, uninhabited, but furnished.

I received information that the Bavarian army was posted at Hanau. Its strength was unknown; but it had begun to arrive the previous evening, and troops had been coming in that same day. There had only been just time, therefore, to send a detachment to Gelnhausen, and some troops of cavalry to other points from Hanau. I had this information from a person who had come thence that very day, and who had been an eye-witness of what he told me.

The Emperor then sent for me, and inquired whether he were in safety, as his Guard had not yet come up.

'I cannot answer for it,' I replied. 'We only arrived after dark, shortly before you; and I do not even know whether all my troops followed me.'

'Are we, then, with the outposts?'

'Yes.'

He kept me to dinner, and sent for the person who had arrived that evening from Hanau, and whose words I had repeated. He liked to ask questions for himself, but he learned no more than I had told him. He declared that the Bavarians would not stand up against him. The next day proved him mistaken.

At daybreak[3] I started on my march. A short distance away we met the Bavarian outposts, supported by a strong advance-guard. I had to stop and wait till our cavalry came up, and crossed sabres with the enemy. We pushed them back into the woods of Hanau, whither we followed them. A fusillade began which my handful of troops could

---

3. October 30.

not stand; I made them retire into shelter several times. I also ordered the cavalry to charge in order to support my infantry. This state of things had lasted for some hours, when, wishing to see what was taking place on the high-road, I ventured out with some of my staff. As soon as we appeared we were greeted by a hot fire of cannon and musketry which compelled us to withdraw hastily into the wood. I had, however, had time to glance at the enemy's position, and what I could see of it was not very encouraging, nor calculated to inspire my troops with confidence.

All my messages to the Emperor to warn him of the resistance we had met with, of the reduction of our small means (of which the enemy, fortunately, could not judge, as they were scattered about the wood), and of the urgent necessity for reinforcements, remained unnoticed. I was much impelled to go to him in person; but I feared that if I left the men would become discouraged—my presence kept them together.

As we were not more than a quarter of a league from headquarters, I at length made up my mind; and, in order to divert observation, ordered a fresh charge of cavalry into the wood, and then started off at full gallop. On reaching the Emperor, I spoke to him very energetically about the position of affairs.

'What can I do?' he said indifferently. 'I give orders, and no one heeds them. I wished to assemble all the waggons at one point under a cavalry escort. Well, nobody came to do it!'

'I can quite believe it,' I returned: 'these men have experience and instinct, and rightly presume that the road by which you wish them to communicate is closed to us. But consider that our situation is no ordinary one. You must force a passage, Sire, and send forward, without an instant's delay, all the troops at your disposal. Why have not the Guard come up? We shall be utterly done for if they don't come immediately.'

'I can't help it,' he answered dejectedly.

Formerly at a sign, a gesture, a word, all had trembled around him, or he would have known the reason why!

However, the Emperor summoned the major-general, who declared that he also had given orders. They were repeated, the assembly was sounded, and I went away with a promise that a portion of the Guard would come and place themselves under my orders. I announced this news, and it encouraged the soldiers a little. The firing and the short charges continued; the Guard did not arrive—impatience reappeared. At length the bearskins of the Old Guard came in view; I pointed them out, and said that this troop would take our places while we rested.

Four battalions of *chasseurs* arrived; the general in command of them asked for my orders; I caused half of them to be deployed as sharpshooters, flanked by companies, and the two others in line to support them. They advanced to the scene of action. The mere sight of these veterans made the enemy retire from the wood; but it was still difficult to get clear of it, or even to line the fringe. The enemy continued to fire volleys of grapeshot and shells. We kept our position; that was a great deal. The Emperor came up, followed by his Guard and some other troops; he asked for information, which I gave him, reckoning the enemy's force as at least 30,000 men.

'Can we reconnoitre their position without danger?' he asked.

'Not without danger; we must risk it; I have already done it once.'

'Very good; come along.'

And away we went. Just as we were starting a shell burst close to him without hurting anyone. Straightway he stopped, dismounted from his horse, and from that moment till the evening it was impossible to get him out of the wood. He ordered General Drouot to discover a position on the right of the road where he could post the artillery of the Guard. The personal danger was extreme, but this brave general, as modest as he was distinguished, never gave it a thought.[4] In order to cause a diversion at this point, the Emperor ordered his cavalry to debouch on to the high-road; the *grenadiers à cheval* were in front. They charged, but were brought back and protected by a regiment of 'guards of honour,' composed of young men of good family, who were making their debut, but who showed great courage. The *grenadiers* rallied behind this regiment, while the dragoons swept forward and repulsed the enemy with great success, gallantly breaking their squares.

General Drouot had succeeded, not without heavy loss, in establishing his batteries, and others were afterwards mounted at other points. We had also succeeded in reaching the fringe of the wood; the enemy were retreating in every direction, and recrossing the river; but they still maintained their defence of Hanau, and there was still on our right a strong battery, which we could not succeed in silencing, and which was doing us considerable damage. We might have obtained great advantages from the retreat of the Bavarians, but as the Emperor

---

4. See note upon General Drouot in chapter 41.

spent the whole day in the wood,[5] he could see nothing, and everyone acted as he pleased without any concert. There seemed to be an idea that we had done enough in reaching the river and driving back the enemy; and no one observed, apparently, that, situated as we were, it was most important for us to reach the other side, and that, until Hanau had been stormed, our communications with France must continue interrupted.

The day was drawing to an end, and the battery just mentioned caused us great inconvenience; the shooting was very straight, and was aimed at the point where the wood debouched into the high-road. I was there in person.[6]

Nansouty's cavalry came through the wood. I asked him to charge and carry the battery; he refused, alleging the fatigue of his men.

'If you will only make an effort, then,' I said but received only the same answer.

I was urging him with some considerable heat, when one of the Emperor's *aides-de-camp*, General Flahaut, chanced to pass. Seeing me very excited, he inquired what was the matter.

'Look here,' I said; 'a slight effort would secure us that battery. If the

---

5. In a review of the first edition of this work, on its appearance in 1892, the *Australasian* newspaper remarks: 'To skulk in the hour of danger was the last thing which Napoleon would have done. His belief in his star sustained him in the unwavering conviction that he bore a charmed life; and he exemplified this only a year afterwards, at the Battle of Arcis-sur-Aube, by a well-authenticated incident which Macdonald passes over in silence. A shell fell immediately in front of one of the battalions of the Guard. Napoleon, spurring his horse, rode straight up to the smoking fuse, in order to give the veterans a lesson in *sangfroid*. The shell burst, the horse was killed, and, when the smoke dispersed, the Emperor was seen, calm and unhurt. "Don't be alarmed, my friends," said he; "the bullet that will kill me has not yet been cast." And, calling for another horse, he mounted it, and placed himself at the head of his soldiers, who recognized his supreme indifference to danger with shouts of enthusiasm.'

6. There is an accidental glimpse of the Duke of Tarentum at the Battle of Hanau in General Marbot's *Memoirs* (Eng. edit, vol.2). 'I keenly regretted the loss of my trumpeter,' says Baron de Marbot, 'who was beloved by the entire regiment no less for his courage than for his general behaviour. He was the son of a professor at the College of Toulouse, had been through his course there, and took great pleasure in spouting Latin. An hour before his death, observing the majority of trees in the forest of Hanau—whose spreading branches formed a kind of roof—were beeches, he quoted the lines from Virgil commencing: '*Tityre, tu patulae recubans sub tegmine fagi.*' Marshal Macdonald, who happened to pass at the moment, laughed heartily, exclaiming, "There's a little chap whose memory isn't disturbed by his surroundings. It is surely the first time that anyone has recited Virgil under the fire of the enemy's guns!"'

Emperor were here, something would be done duty, at least, if nothing more! Situated as we are here, it is of vital consequence to sweep aside every obstacle and to force our way through.'

'Would you like to see the Emperor?' he said. 'I will bring him to you.'

'Do, if you can,' I answered.

It was now late, and instead of coming himself, he sent orders to Nansouty to act. The latter moved at last. As soon as the enemy saw him, they retreated, which would have been a boon to us a few hours earlier.

I had rallied the remains of my division on the outskirts of the wood. We were at a short distance from Hanau; a few troops advanced thither, but stopped just out of range of a hot fusillade.

We had been at ease for some time, when I saw a shapeless column, preceded by a lighted torch, issue from the wood and defile along the high-road. I was told that a report was spread, no one knew how, of the evacuation of Hanau; and as the Emperor was sure of good quarters there, he had started without any further information. The torch was borne before him. All that had been in the wood, troops, carriages, artillery, led horses, etc., were following him in disorder.

I called for my horse in order to head him and warn him of his mistake; but the mass that widened out as it issued from the wood prevented me from passing. I also had to ride carefully along the edge of a ditch by the roadside; however, a few yards farther on I was able to cross it, and hastened on for a moment, so as to come up with the head of the column.

Suddenly a few shots were heard; the column stopped, and I saw the torch take a pace to the right and describe a curve retiring into the wood, whence the shapeless and ever-increasing mass was still pouring and pressing on the head thus suddenly arrested. I found myself caught in the mob, unable to advance or retire, without having succeeded in joining the Emperor. I tried to recross the ditch and to regain the edge of the wood, feeling very sorry that I had ever quitted it. At length I lost my temper, and ordered my bodyguard to force a passage for me sword in hand. They at once obeyed, crying: 'Make way! Make way!'

One voice alone could be heard in the crowd asking: 'What guards are those creating such a disturbance?' It was Count Daru, commissary-general of the army. I did not feel called upon to answer, or to make myself known. I succeeded in making my way back to the place I had left, leaving the mass to disentangle itself as best it could. Had the enemy known what was going on, and made a sortie from Hanau, the disorder must have been even greater, and their losses immense; happily, their only idea was to retreat.

In the middle of the night the Emperor sent me orders to collect a battery of howitzers, and to fire on the town; the enemy did not reply, whence we concluded that they were unarmed. They moved out at break of day, and our troops occupied the town.

Scarcely had this news penetrated into the wood, when the disorderly mass once more made its way out with no less confusion than on the previous evening. The Emperor himself passed, and gave me orders to relieve the troops in the town, promising that I in turn should be relieved by General Bertrand. I had not perceived until then that all the soldiers remaining to me had left, and had joined themselves to the living torrent that was flowing towards Frankfort, whither the Emperor was going in person. I sent after them, and recovered about 150 men, whom I brought into Hanau to replace a troop not much larger, of which General Souham had command. I found him in a house in the suburbs; he left, and I entered the town. The enemy were not far off on the other side of the river. The place had an enclosure, but could not resist an attack.

Just as I was sitting down to breakfast, Tuilier, commanding the engineers, whom I had sent to the top of the steeple, came and whispered to me that the enemy were advancing.

'Go back again,' I said, 'and let me know when they are near the gates.'

'They are not far off now,' he replied; 'and you have barely time to retire.'

The fusillade commenced as he was speaking. I left my breakfast, therefore, and, calling the chief officer of my little group of men, told him to hold firm, and that he would be relieved immediately. As I was quitting the town I met General Bertrand, who had orders to relieve us; he asked how many troops he should take in with him.

'All you have will not be enough,' I replied, and continued my journey.

Chapter 24

The Enemy Cross the Rhine

It was only at Frankfort that I found the scattered remnants of my division; we were also rejoined by the detachment I had left at Hanau. I had orders to continue my march to Mayence, which I reached that night. The bridge of boats had been so severely tried by the constant succession of troops, waggons, and artillery, that two pontoons had nearly given way. It had therefore been necessary to stop it from being used, and to close the gates of the *tête-de-pont*. My chief of the staff, who had preceded me, had posted a notice on the gates that all who belonged to my corps were to betake themselves to ———[1] and go into cantonments there.

The Emperor sent for me next day, and kept me to dinner. He reviewed all the circumstances and events of the campaign, dealing at length with the bad faith of the allies, especially of Austria at Prague, during the negotiations of the Congress.

Caulaincourt, his Master of the Horse, and Count Narbonne, his *aide-de-camp*, had, however, told me that the entire settlement had been in his hands; that, in reality, he ought to have given up some conquests or combinations, but that he could have retained Italy, the Rhine as a boundary, and the Protectorate of the Helvetian Confederation. That Napoleon had been pressed to consent to this, and warned that, in case of refusal, Austria would make common cause with Russia and Prussia. She made no secret of the fact that she was bound by a treaty, which had been obvious for some months past, as the allies, beaten at the beginning of the campaign, had retired into Silesia, to the foot of the mountains of Bohemia, ready to enter if they were driven to it, and this they could not have done had Austria preserved her neutrality.

---

1. The name of the place is omitted in the original manuscript.

They would have taken good care not to risk having to surrender at the foot of those mountains, as all their communications would have been cut off if they had lost a decisive battle. Moreover, had they not been certain of Austria's co-operation, they would have recrossed the Oder, near Breslau, in their retreat from Jauer.

Prudence recommended a compromise, but the Emperor, blind, and relying upon his ascendancy at the Court of Vienna, which he believed was further, strengthened by his position as son-in-law of the Emperor Francis, had obstinately refused to consent to the cession of Holland and the Hanse Towns, and to renounce the Protectorate of the Confederation of the Rhine. As soon as the armistice was denounced, he authorized his plenipotentiaries to make these concessions; those of the allies, however, replied that it was now too late, and that the question must be settled by the sword.

'Why,' I inquired, 'did not your Majesty consent sooner? The army earnestly desired it; the honour of your arms was repaired; your principal leaders begged it of you, both in the name of the army and of France, so sorely distressed. I myself ventured to point out the dangers of the situation to you. I represented the difficulties France had had in fighting against the Emperor of Russia and the King of Prussia; what, then, would it be when Austria, Sweden, and other lesser States leagued themselves with them? Our losses, I admit, had been somewhat repaired, but how? By recruits who were little more than children, by young untrained horses, already worn out by long forced marches. The renewal of hostilities would once more interrupt our communications; any serious reverse must infallibly ruin us; we had neither provisions nor ammunition; and, above all, we had to avoid discouragement, to keep up the spirits of the men.'

This reasoning had produced no effect upon him at the time of the negotiations, but now he admitted it was just.

'I did not agree to these concessions,' he said, 'because I feared that the allies would become more exacting, and would demand still more!'

'But in that case, Sire,' I replied, 'why did you, when unfortunately too late, end by consenting? Had you done so earlier, you would have given proof of your desire for peace; France and the army would have been grateful to you, and perhaps would have made greater efforts to secure it. Moreover, all the preliminaries declared that, beyond these concessions, the Emperors .would ask for nothing. You might have done more; you might have freed yourself with honour from the canker which is destroying your old troops in Spain, and ruining your treasury, had you restored Spain to herself and her sovereign, and thereby displayed a moderation which must have struck France, your armies, and Europe.'

'Yes,' said he, 'that is true; but now I must retain that country as compensation.'

During this conversation the bulletin of the allies upon the events at Leipsic was handed to him. Perhaps there was some exaggeration in their account, but I had to admit that, on the whole, it was but too true; they were intoxicated with their success, and not without reason.

Our situation was to France and Europe a striking proof of our reverses, of the terrible misfortunes we had already endured, and of those which threatened and must inevitably overwhelm us if peace, which of course could only be purchased by fresh concessions, did not speedily come to save the army and France. To these observations he replied that he was going to try to reopen the negotiations, but that he wished to keep the line of the Rhine, wherein I entirely agreed with him.

He informed me that I was to start for Cologne, and to take command of the line from Mayence to Wesel.

'With what troops?' I asked. 'With what am I to defend a tract of such extent?'

'I will send you some. They are coming in from all sides, and we are raising 300,000 men. You shall have eighty battalions and sixty squadrons. The enemy, hitherto concentrated, will be obliged to spread out, and we shall be strong at all their vulnerable points.'

He thought that the allies would be wearied, and would go into winter-quarters on the right bank of the Rhine, thus leaving him time to reform and reinforce his armies; but in less than two months we were doomed to be disappointed.

Before we parted he asked me to tell him the amount of my personal losses during the campaign. I merely said that they were considerable, which was true; I had not even a clean shirt left. He said that he had no money at Mayence, but that he would send me an indemnity from Paris.

'I was rich,' he added, 'at the opening of the campaign in 1812. The armies were well provided, the men paid regularly, and I had left 400 000,000 *francs* [£16,000,000] in the cellars at the Tuileries, of which 300,000,000 [£12,000,000] came from the contributions levied in

Prussia. I drew out 340,000,000 [£13,600,000] to help France in reforming the army in 1813; I have only 60,000,000 [£2,400,000] left. It is very little, and I have so much to do with it!'

This was intended to convey to me that I should only get a very small share. In fact, he only sent me, while I was at Wesel, a draft upon Paris for 30,000 *francs* (£1,200). I had great difficulty afterwards in getting it cashed, but eventually Monsieur de la Bouillerie, manager of the Crown property, very kindly arranged it for me.

I wrote next day to your eldest sister to send me some linen to Cologne, whither I was going. Souham lent me his carriage, and I started that afternoon, finding my staff and my weak force at Bingen.

Night was drawing on. They made useless efforts to retain me, but I insisted on starting. The road was bad; masters, men, postilions, everyone was asleep. We upset coming round a sharp curve recently cut in the rock, and, on leaving the carriage, unhurt, found with terror that we were within two feet of the edge of the Rhine. Had the horses advanced one step more, we must have infallibly perished in the river, after braving so many dangers, and I, in particular, having escaped the Elster. I reached Cologne without further accident, and was thence ordered on to Wesel and Nimeguen.

My command, on the right of the line, ended at Coblentz, but on the left extended to Arnheim. All our troops had recrossed the Rhine, and gone from Mayence to Wesel. This last place was strongly garrisoned, and General Bourke, the Governor, had orders to place all his troops at my disposal, but only to support my operations, without compromising the security of the place This general behaved very well to me; we reconnoitred outside, and decided that it would be safer not to advance.

I went to Nimeguen, where I had been garrisoned, while serving under Maillebois, at the beginning of my career; I had had my quarters there after the siege during the winter of 1794-95. At that time we were victorious; at the period I am now describing we were only acting on a very feeble defensive.

I made certain that the enemy were gathering round Arnheirn, which we held with only a small force. The town was defended by a sort of entrenched camp, but there were no troops to occupy it. I decided upon evacuating the place, and upon recrossing the Leek and the Waal. I saw with my own eyes the enemy's preparations, and that we had not a moment to lose; orders were given, but very badly carried out. Instead of retiring during the night, they waited till the next day, and the enemy attacked at that very moment.

We had 400 or 500 men in the town, but neither collected together nor ready to leave. They were dispersed; the gate by which we were to quit was not even guarded, so much so that the gatekeeper, whether through bribery or treachery, locked it, disappeared with the keys, and ran away at the first gunshot The detachment, therefore, had to capitulate. The troops from without crossed the bridge without destroying it, not knowing the reason why the garrison did not evacuate the town. The enemy seized the opportunity, and followed, but hesitatingly, half-way across. The very fact of the garrison being shut up within the place stopped the enemy's chief forces, as they thought it was much stronger than it really was; had it not been for that, they might have made it difficult for us to cross the Waal.

At Nimeguen there were two little armed Dutch boats. Fearing that they might commit some fresh act of treachery, and prevent the return of our troops, I ordered them to move down the river at once, without giving them a chance of learning what had happened. I thus succeeded in bringing across, without impediment, all the detachments that were still on the right bank.

I had opened communications with General Molitor, who commanded in the Province of Utrecht. I recalled him, and he crossed to the island of Bommel, whence he joined me with some more skeleton regiments. As I foresaw that we should ere long be compelled to withdraw from Nimeguen, I asked permission to evacuate at the same time Bois-le-Duc, Wesel, Venloo, and Maestricht; but it was refused. While waiting for an answer to my despatch, I inquired of General Bourke how long he would require to undermine and blow up the fortifications of Wesel, and to withdraw his garrison, supposing his instructions authorized him to carry out such an order if given by me. The question was simple; but it caused him such terror that his only answer to me was a request for an interview, but the events which followed prevented me from complying with it.

In asking for an authorization to evacuate these places, I was carrying out the plan of concentration that I had twice proposed under similar circumstances at the end of 1812 and 1813; but, in spite of the correctness of my views, experience had taught no lesson, and the garrisons were compelled to capitulate one after another. However, as we could look for no immediate succour, this system served to reinforce our fighting troops, and to weaken the enemy, who were obliged to leave garrisons in the places we evacuated.

I am aware that the other system has certain advantages—for example, that of detaining a large number of hostile troops by sieges or blockades, and of preserving resources and communications for one's self, if one can succeed in beating the enemy in the open field. But to obtain these advantages an army is a necessity; and when one has none, or nothing but a few shattered remains, and it takes months to raise a fresh one, it is better to have recourse to evacuation. This is especially the case when the places are scattered—like Zamosc, Modlin, Pillau, and Dantzic—if one is driven back to this side of the Elbe, and like those on the Oder and the Elbe when one has to retire to the Rhine. In my opinion, it is much better to run the risk of being obliged to recommence sieges, and to have a movable army, than to be reduced to mere bundles (*paquets*) of men, which have to end by giving way, as happened to us at the end of each of our last campaigns.[2]

I was told to stand firm; but with such an extended area as I had under my command, and with such small means, I could only watch the Rhine, and not defend it. The enemy tried to cross at Düsseldorf, and surprised the little garrison of Neuss. I hastened thither, and on the way learnt that it was only a feint, and that the enemy had re-crossed the river. They tried the same thing at several other points. All this was insignificant; but it served to warn me to act with circumspection, so as not to run the risk of being cut off.

I received no further orders, and the events which crowded upon me obliged me to act with prudence. I withdrew slowly to the Meuse, reinforcing Wesel, Venloo, and Maestricht, when I learned that the en-

---

2. Besides the large force shut up in Hamburg under Marshal Davoût (and which held out so gallantly even after the capitulation of Paris), the French had considerably over a hundred thousand veterans and conscripts blockaded in fortresses, such as Dantzig, Zamosc, Modlin, Stettin, Pillau, Thorn, Glogau, Torgau, Cüstrin, Wittemburg, Magdeburg, Wurtzburg, Freibourg, Erfurt, with Marshal St. Cyr at Dresden, and in smaller garrisons in Austria, at Mayence or Coblentz possibly, at Strasbourg, Kehl, Colmar, Dijon, Besançon, Belfort, Luxembourg, Thionville, Metz, Phalsbourg, Saverne, Bitche, Toul, etc., St. Sebastian, Pampeluna, and in Catalonia. At Antwerp, also, in the hour of adversity for France, instead of 'emigrating,' the stern Republican Carnot placed his sword at the disposal of the Emperor whose career he so highly disapproved of (a pleasant contrast to the many Frenchmen who, like Moreau or Dumouriez, stabbed their country in the back when they found its enemies in readiness to support them). All these fortresses were taken or besieged; of course no reference is made here to the garrisons of the interior, or even to Lyons, which was threatened. (See, too, a note by Colonel Phipps in the English edition of Bourrienne's *Memoirs of Napoleon*, vol. iii. and also General Marbot's *Memoirs*, Eng. edit, vol. 2.)

emy had opened the campaign, and definitely crossed the Rhine. They were advancing very rapidly, as they met no obstacles to speak of; they might even reach Liège before me. I hastened thither, and thence to Huy, Namur, and Mezières.

CHAPTER 25

Campaign in France

The Emperor rejoined the army at the first announcement reaching him of the passage of the Rhine;[1] but of all the levies and reinforcements that had been announced with such a flourish, none ever reached me. On paper, I was supposed to be in command of a force numbering from 50,000 to 60,000 men, whereas actually, with Molitor's division, which I brought with me, I had not more than 3,000.

I was going to Verdun to join the Duke of Ragusa,[2] who was in command on the left of our line, when I received orders to come to Châlons, whence I was sent to Vitry-on-the-Marne. A hostile force, 30,000 strong, was already in the neighbourhood. I rallied my troops at the *Chaussée*, where I was attacked, but very feebly, next morning. During the day, however, the enemy made preparations to dislodge me. I held our position till night, when I withdrew to Châlons. The evacuation of this place had already begun, but it would take us at least twenty-four hours to finish emptying the magazines, which were so precious to us.

The enemy appeared at break of day, and deployed in turn all their forces, which I reckoned at 30,000 men. Prudence unquestionably compelled me not to fight on such unequal terms, or not to expose Châlons; but, despite our utmost activity, the emptying of the magazines could not be effected before the following night.

On the other hand, the general in command at Vitry, who had 2,000 or 2,500 men, sent me word that he was in a very critical position without victuals or means of defence; that he was already invested

---

1. The allies crossed the Rhine on January 1, 1814; the Emperor did not leave Paris till the 25th.
2. Marshal Marmont.

on the right bank of the Marne, and that if he did not receive immediate orders to retire, he would be constrained to surrender, and that we should lose the garrison almost without striking a blow. I determined to send him the orders he asked for, and to protect his march on the way to join us. This was an additional reason for defending Châlons. My troops covered the town, and did, in fact, defend it very courageously till nightfall, when the firing ceased on either side.

General Yorck, who commanded at this point, had made up his mind to occupy the place; he summoned me to yield or to evacuate it, otherwise he would set it on fire. That would have been easily done, for many parts of the town are old, and the houses built of wood.

Owing to some misunderstanding, his flag of truce was admitted (although, according to my custom, I had renewed my prohibition), and was brought to me. He was the Count of Brandenburg, a natural brother of the King of Prussia, who in 1812 had arrived at Tilsit from Berlin a day or two before the defection of the Prussian corps. This corps was the very one that I had been fighting all day, and commanded by the same leader. I had hitherto always treated this young man with consideration and politeness; he showed a decided want of both to me in delivering his message.

'I have more respect for your character than you have yourself,' I said, 'otherwise I would cause you to regret your impertinent manner. I will not expose Châlons to the disorder attendant upon a night-occupation, but I do not mind telling you that I shall evacuate it tomorrow morning. Your general knows me well enough to be convinced that I shall not allow myself to be intimidated by threats any more than by deeds. That is all I have to say to you. Go.'

'We shall set fire to the town,' he replied. 'As you please,' I answered, and dismissed him. On the previous day I had given orders that the bridge should be mined, as also a triumphal arch that either gratitude or flattery had raised to the Emperor at its extremity, on the left bank of the Marne. It was not to be blown up except in case the mines failed—which happened—so as to obstruct the bridge, at least for artillery.

The threat of shelling the town was quickly put into execution, and immediately spread consternation amongst the inhabitants. I had made every preparation to extinguish the fire in the most exposed quarters. A few houses were set alight, and I then witnessed a heartbreaking spectacle, the authorities imploring me to evacuate the town, and part of the population running hither and thither half clothed,

BLUCHER (North).   **NAPOLEON (Central).**   **SCHWARTZENBERG (South).**

DIAGRAM SHOWING THE MOVEMENTS OF THE VARIOUS ARMIES IN THE SPRING OF 1814.

Senay. Verdun. Ste. Menehould. Rethel. RHEIMS. CHÂLONS. VITRY sur Marne. ST. DIZIER. Vassy. Laon. SOISSONS. CHÂTEAU THIERRY. EPERNAY. Champaubert. Etoges. Vauchamps. Montmirail. Sézanne. Fère Champenoise. Arcis-sur-Aube. BRIENNE. La Rothière. Troyes. Doulaincourt. Méry. Gros. TROYES. Lesigny. Bar-sur-Aube. La Ferté Sous-Jouarre. NOGENT. Meaux. Trilport. Provins. Bray. Villeneuve-l'Archevêque. SENS.

PARIS.

Brie. Guignes. Nangis. MELUN. Montereau. Fontainebleau.

R. B.

Valley of the Marne.   Valley of the Seine and Aube.

uttering cries of despair, and cursing the author of a war which had brought such desolation upon France, and to whom, all the same, they had recently erected a triumphal arch.

I groaned at this pitiful sight; but my duty would not admit of my yielding nor of compromising my troops and the general operations of the army. The night was very severe; it was freezing hard, and the poor creatures were half dressed. The women, their hair streaming and with bare feet, carried about their babies in long clothes. I shall never forget it. The enemy, observing that their fire produced no result, or perhaps for want of ammunition, ceased it, and the inhabitants retired to their homes.

I evacuated the place in broad daylight, after ordering a light to be set to the mines under the bridge; but they were badly laid, and only shook it. I then exploded those under the triumphal arch, and, when it had fallen, it made a sufficient obstacle to prevent an immediate entrance. The enemy, seeing us prepared to oppose any attempt, refrained from making one all that day.

My orders were to communicate with the Duke of Ragusa, who was supposed to be at Arcis-sur-Aube. I sent my cavalry there, but on the way they met that of the enemy, and fell back upon Étoges. The garrison of Vitry, which had retired unhindered, was already there. A portion of my corps accompanied me thither, while the rest made for Jaâlons. I thus covered the two main roads between Châlons and Paris.

On reaching Champtrix, I learned from some prisoners and from the inhabitants that part of Blücher's army was advancing to Montmirail. As this communication, therefore, was closed to me, I went across country to Épernay, where all my troops reassembled; but as it was possible—nay, probable—that the enemy would reach La Ferté-sous-Jouarre before me, if I did not take rapid steps to prevent it, I made a forced march. I had halted and slept at Épernay, and, on continuing my route, left my rear-guard behind to impede the enemy when they quitted Châlons. The egress from Épernay is narrow, and may be defended for a considerable time.

I stopped at a village among the hills on the left of the road; but scarcely was I settled there when I was told that my rear-guard, which, however, had not been pressed, was retreating, and that the enemy's *vedettes* had already reached the village where I was breakfasting. I had but just time to throw myself across my horse and gallop through the vineyards to catch up my troops, who had marched on some distance.

Had it not been for the peasant's timely warning, I should have been taken while at table. I escaped with nothing worse than a fright.

The general in command of the rear-guard had been frightened by false reports. I slackened his march, and made him face about each time the enemy seemed to come too close to us. We took up our position and rested for a few hours at Dormans, whence we continued our march towards Château-Thierry, which had already been passed by my front column. The important thing was to reach La Ferté-sous-Jouarre, where the two roads meet, and to pass the night there.

I learned, on arrival, that the Russian General Sacken was at Bussière. Had I been a few hours later I should have had to retreat to Château-Thierry and make for Soissons, which would have separated me from the army and have left Meaux uncovered, and from thence the enemy would have met with no obstacle till they reached Paris. My rear-guard still followed me. They had orders to destroy the bridge at Château-Thierry, but it was only partially done. My advance-guard took up their position at La Ferté, on the heights above the road to Montmirail, where they were soon after attacked.

We skirmished all day upon a ground favourable to that kind of defence, which allowed time for my rear-guard to come up; they were somewhat pressed, and only passed through La Ferté. I did not know where the principal headquarters were, as I could obtain no answer to my frequent representations upon my situation. I lost ground towards the evening, and, fearing simultaneous attacks from the two corps that were debouching by the two roads, I recrossed the Marne next day at Trilport, where the bridge had been mined, in spite of the opposition attempted by the inhabitants.

I had strictly forbidden that the bridge should be blown up without my express orders, and, as I wished to be on the spot, I remained where I was and slept upon a heap of faggots piled up there to be embarked, instead of going on to Meaux.

Utterly fatigued and worn out, I had fallen asleep near a large fire, when I was suddenly startled by a violent detonation. Valazé, General of Engineers, who was beside me, ran to the scene of the explosion. It seemed as if we were predestined to misfortune. Owing to some misunderstanding, a match had been laid to the mines; some of them had not exploded, but the bridge was so broken and shaken as to scarcely hold together, and it would have been too dangerous not to complete the work of destruction, the more so as a simple picket would now suffice to guard it, and as there was another bridge intact at Meaux.

I kept the Emperor carefully informed of my march, and of the circumstances that had brought me to this point. I also sent word to the King of Spain, who was commanding in Paris.

The alarm there was very great, and naturally so, for we were now only eleven leagues distant, and the great allied army was marching upon Nogent, Bray, and Montereau. The Emperor, informed by my despatches, made a very bold flank march, and, falling unexpectedly upon Blücher at Champaubert and Château-Thierry, gained a great victory.

I had received orders to direct my cavalry so as to assist these attacks, and, although it had to make a long round by Meaux, it arrived in time to take part in the success; then it was that I bitterly regretted the bridge at Trilport. Unfortunately these victories had no result save that of prolonging our agony; they raised the spirits of the men, but they thinned and weakened our ranks daily.

While these events were in progress on the Marne, the main army of the enemy had seized the three places mentioned above on the Seine. It therefore became necessary to let go our hold, and hasten with all speed to cover Paris, reassemble our scattered remnants, and give battle.

My troops were sent to a point between Brie-Comte-Robert and Guignes. While they were marching I rushed to Paris to put some business matters in order, little thinking that within a short space the capital would fall into the hands of the allies. I promptly rejoined my troops. After the reassembly was made and the attack ordered I was sent to Bray, where I found the bridge destroyed: the contest was confined to a sharp cannonade.

We were more fortunate at Montereau. The enemy had taken up a position on the right bank, where they were speedily attacked. One of our corps, repulsed at the first onset, was quickly supported by others who threw themselves forward gallantly, broke the enemy's ranks, and put them to flight. They recrossed the Seine in the utmost disorder, and were eagerly pursued, and I was sent for.

The allies retired beyond the Aube. On the way thither they sent *parlementaires* to propose an armistice. Generals were appointed on either side to treat. This armistice, the enemy stated, should be the preliminary of the peace that was being so slowly negotiated at Châlons. I know not whether either side were of good faith in this congress, but assuredly the allies were not.

Lusigny, between Troyes and Vendoeuvre, had been decided upon for the settlement of the armistice. The allies have since declared that the territory between the Seine and the Aube had been neutralized while the articles of agreement were being drawn up; but, whether by a misunderstanding or bad faith, the Emperor ordered the Seine to be crossed at Troyes, and sent me to Châtillon.

The negotiators of the armistice, finding themselves surrounded by fire, broke up the conferences. The Congress at Châtillon was alarmed at my approach, and the Duke of Vicenza, the principal French representative at the Congress, sent to me imploring me not to advance; if I did, all the foreign ministers threatened to retire. I stopped, and the Emperor approved my compliance.

While we were marching towards Bar-sur-Aube, he was informed that Blücher's army, which he had beaten and routed at Champaubert and Château-Thierry, was retracing its steps. He started with all his reserves to fight them again, leaving orders with me, as the senior Marshal, to take command of the troops he left behind him (that is to say, those of the Marshal Duke of Reggio, and of General Gérard, which were as weakened as my own), to cross the Seine in person, and put myself in line with these two corps on the Aube. I did this immediately.

I marched through a very difficult country near Essoyes, and took La Ferté; but while I was seeking to communicate with Bar-sur-Aube, where the Duke of Reggio ought to have been, some detachments of the enemy showed themselves at a short distance off,' beyond the woods belonging to the ancient abbey at Clairvaux. I immediately concluded that the two corps had been compelled to retire from Bar, but yet I could hear no cannon which could force them to such a step. I hastily summoned the troops who had carried La Ferté, and, as my communications on the left with them were thus cut off, and knowing of no other place save Bar-sur-Seine at which I could cross the river, I made a forced march throughout the night. I only reached the place a quarter of an hour before the enemy's advance cavalry. I at once sent news to Troyes, whither had gone the staff of the two corps.

Marshal Oudinot explained to me the position of affairs, and the reasons for his retreat. He pressed me, as I had the general command of the troops, to come and take my place more in the centre. I therefore continued my movement down the left bank of the Seine, and two days later reached Troyes.

For several days previously I had been unwell. On my arrival I was obliged to go to bed. The Marshal and General Gérard came to see me, and we agreed upon our plan. The first thing to be done was to supply Troyes with the means of temporary defence, so as to give my corps time to come up. We .settled that one of Gérard's corps should make as long a stand as possible within and without the town, the other being kept in reserve, and that, the Marshal's corps should be posted on our side of the suburbs, where they should await the arrival of my troops, which were to come up early next day. Our anxiety was lest the enemy might cross the Seine at Méry, occupy the high-road to Nogent. seize Bray and Montereau, and thus separate us from the Emperor. In that case we should have no road but that by Villeneuve-l'Archevêque and Sens.

I had betaken myself into the environs, the infantry of the two corps were placed as I have described; I was to follow them with mine. I was breakfasting quietly, when General Gressot, chief of Marshal Oudinot's staff, came to tell me that the marshal's troops had just been placed in the position agreed upon. I had ordered a portion of the cavalry to follow the old route by Pavilion and Le Paraclet.

As we were starting to join the marshal's force, an officer brought me intelligence that the enemy were just leaving Troyes, and that I had not an instant to lose; we were in a road running into the highway. I replied that such a thing was impossible, as there was one division within and without the town, another in the rear, and the Marshal's force in reserve.

'They are all gone,' answered the officer.

All gone and I had never been told of it!

Ill as I was, I jumped on my horse, when I saw the enemy's advance-guard. I dashed at them with my *aides-de-camp* and my escort, and we drove them back towards the town. Meanwhile, my carriages started at full gallop, and reached the high-road. I rejoined General Gérard, who was continuing his retreat, by order, as he told me, of the marshal, who was far on ahead. He had not remained in position, although General Gressot told me that he had placed his troops according to our agreement. Ten minutes later my communications were cut off.

We marched all day, skirmishing as we went. The cavalry had one brush. We were so far ahead that the enemy could not engage us in a very unequal combat. That evening we made our quarters at Grez and Granges. At the latter place I found Marshal Oudinot, and inquired why he had quitted his post that morning. He replied that the Young Guard was not intended for a rear-guard.

'If that is so,' said I, 'I have no further orders for you. You must go to the Emperor for them.'

I continued retreating. Next day we reoccupied our positions on the Seine at Nogent, Bray, and Montereau, to defend those points where the river might be crossed. But the enemy passed it below our left wing, thus making it necessary to change our direction, and march perpendicularly to the river. They deployed in front of us, made a vehement attack on our left, which was formed of the corps of the Duke of Reggio, and drove us back upon Provins. We held firm all day, but not without loss, crossed the ravines, the narrow denies, and the town, and took up our position in the rear.

Our situation was very critical, and we had no news of the Emperor, though not because we had not sent him reports. The enemy made no attempt next day; this inactivity did not seem natural, and I ordered all my cavalry to be in readiness to make a general reconnaissance the following day. The enemy had only left some feeble detachments to observe us, and were beating a hasty retreat.

On hearing this I quitted the *Maison Rouge*, where I was quartered with the Duke of Reggio, in order to follow their tracks. It was clear that this retreat, with forces very superior to ours, could only have been occasioned by a flank movement made by the Emperor. In fact, while we were on the road, I received orders to march with my full force in the direction of Arcis-sur-Aube. The Duke of Reggio made a forced march to attain the point mentioned. I hastened in front of my troops to reach Arcis, but on the way I came upon a morass, of which the ford had been spoiled and rendered useless by the transit of some heavy material. I ordered a search to be made for another, which caused considerable delay. While continuing my journey, I perceived afar off, on the left of the Aube, all the enemy's forces drawn up in squares, motionless, and my troops drawing away towards Vitry-sur-Marne. Much surprised at this movement, I spurred on my horse to learn the reason; I found the Emperor in the public square at Arcis near a camp-fire.

'What is your motive, Sire,' I inquired, 'for withdrawing your troops from here?'

'The enemy are retreating rapidly,' he replied, 'and I am cutting off their communications. We have got them now, and they shall pay dearly for their temerity. I have summoned the heavy artillery to Sézanne to follow my movement to Vitry, and have issued orders to our detachments at Nogent, Bray, and Montereau, to proceed there by forced marches.'

These detachments were commanded by General Pacthod; the artillery and waggons of my army corps were protected by them.

'What!' I exclaimed, 'the enemy retreating? They are in position on the other side. I myself saw them in considerable force. They also can discern your retrograde movement, and if they attack you here, how will you resist them?'

'They would not dare to do so; their only idea is to get across the Rhine, and if they be still there it is simply in order to let all their baggage-waggons pass. Besides, I have sent the Duke of Reggio and the cavalry against them, with orders to mask my movement, and to prevent the enemy from observing it.'

'How is that possible?' I inquired. 'The town is in a hollow; the Aube runs between two hills; the enemy are on one, and your troops are climbing the other.'

'Never mind,' said he; 'when will your force arrive?'

'Very late tonight.'

'Very good. You will support the Duke of Reggio, who will continue to act under your orders.'

He told the Major General to draw up my instructions.

While the latter was dictating them, Marshal Ney, who had been to reconnoitre the enemy, entered.

'What are they doing?' asked the Emperor.

'They are not stirring from their position, and do not look at all as if they meant to attack.'

A short time afterwards, while we were still in conversation, Colonel Galbois, of the general staff, galloped up to us at the top of his speed, and in an excited manner informed us that the enemy were advancing towards us.

'That is impossible,' said the Emperor.

At the same moment we heard the guns.

'Duke of Tarentum,' said the Emperor, 'mount your horse, and go and reconnoitre.'

I found the Duke of Reggio very uneasy; his position was indeed most critical.

'Hasten to the Emperor, I beg you,' he said; 'he must come to my help, otherwise I am done for.'

'Do not expect any help,' I replied; 'all his troops are on the way to Vitry. He is convinced that the enemy are retreating.'

We were still concealed by a slope.

'Let us see,' said I, 'what is threatening us on the other side.'

The marshal's cavalry quickly descended; I thought they were too much exposed. They would have done better had they been posted on the slope towards Arcis, with *vedettes* on the edge. Had that been done, the enemy would not have been able to gauge their force.

On reaching the top we found ourselves face to face with the enemy's scouts. We hastily turned, but I had just time to glance at our foes and to see that the allies were resolutely marching towards us.

'Hasten,' said the Duke of Reggio—'hasten to Arcis.'

'When I have got past your troops,' I said, 'for the sight of me galloping to the rear might intimidate and perhaps scatter them. You have three bridges,' I added, 'one on each side of you, and one in the middle of the town; have them guarded at once.'

I quitted him, riding leisurely. As soon, however, as I had passed his lines, I set spurs to my horse and galloped to Arcis, but the Emperor was no longer there. He had mounted his horse and followed his troops to Vitry. An officer belonging to the general staff was waiting to obtain intelligence from me, and with orders for me to remain at Arcis until I received further instructions.

Chapter 26

On the Marne

The Duke of Reggio's troops, hard pressed, were retreating in disorder; the danger was that the enemy might take advantage of the confusion to cross the river; they were already on the bridge. The Marshal had a division in reserve: I pressed him to order it up. It was of the utmost importance to us to retake the bridge, which was severely contested. We reconquered it, and at length set to work to blow it up. Night had fallen. My troops had arrived; they were posted at every point, but still we were not without uneasiness as to the possibility of a nocturnal attack.

An officer came from headquarters to ask for news, and to bring me orders to hold firm for two or three days. The Emperor's illusion regarding the retreat of the allies was not yet dissipated.

When morning dawned, we saw the enemy quietly in their positions. They remained thus all day, but towards evening they began to move apparently in the direction of Vitry. I immediately sent forward a division to forestall them, stop their movement, and cover mine. All our troops had orders to follow, a portion only of my cavalry remaining behind to check for as long as possible any troops which might debouch from Arcis.

From the road that we followed we were able to observe the enemy's march; we hastened to get through a nasty-looking defile. The following day was spent in skirmishing; but, as I foresaw a serious attack towards the evening, I drew up my infantry in a favourable position, not far from the point where the enemy would cross the Marne. The artillery covered them; my cavalry, which formed the rear-guard, received orders to retire if the enemy showed any disposition to charge, and to come and draw up behind my line, so as not to mask their fire.

While making these arrangements I was very uneasy, for, behind my left, I saw the principal allied forces marching along the Marne, and I feared that they would reach the ford before the division I had sent there; that was my only communication with the Emperor. The latter still retained his opinion as to the enemy's retreat. All these demonstrations, he insisted, were merely feints to deceive us the more thoroughly as to their veritable intentions of gaining the Rhine. He therefore continued his movement towards Saint Dizier and Vassy. As to myself, I was closely followed, and, on the rear of my right wing, Vitry was occupied by the enemy.

The two sides came into collision near the ford over the river Marne. The allies were fortunately repulsed by the French division, and, as night was drawing on, they did not think well to hazard an engagement on their flank, and left us masters of a point the importance of which had perhaps escaped them.

Events occurred upon my front exactly as I had foreseen them. The enemy had been reinforced, and now charged my cavalry, which came at full gallop and very hotly pursued, to take up the place that had been assigned to them. Scarcely was my line unmasked when their adversaries received a volley of grapeshot and musketry which threw them into the utmost disorder, and drove them off for the night.

We spent that night in crossing the river upon a miserable raft that we afterwards destroyed. Next morning found us drawn up in battle array upon the right bank, without having been disturbed either by the garrison of Vitry, or by the troops that we had repulsed on the previous day. They deployed before us; the river ran between us, and they were out of range. If, on the previous day, the enemy, who were in strength, had pressed us vigorously, it would have been all over with us, or, at all events, with our communications with the Emperor. These were unfortunately cut off for all who had been left behind, and who were to have reunited at Sézanne. I had made sure that this convoy had not passed before us; I had even noticed, as I came along near the defile I had traversed the day before, guns and carriages abandoned, evident proofs that either a combat, a surprise, or an alarm had occurred there. Having no horses that could draw it, I was unable to move all this material, which could not belong to the heavy artillery; moreover, I did not know whether any fresh orders had been given since those for the junction at Sézanne.

While we were facing the enemy I noticed that they were sending troops on towards Vitry, where they would have no difficulty in crossing the Marne.

I received at this very moment orders to send my cavalry to Saint Dizier, and shortly afterwards fresh instructions to follow with all my troops. As the Emperor had started thence for Vassy, I received fresh orders to cross the Marne, which I did next day without having been disturbed since the morning of the preceding day. I was instructed to take up a position between the Marne and Vassy.

We had just established ourselves, when I received warning, and soon afterwards saw that the allied cavalry was debouching from various directions. I sent word to the Emperor, who ordered me to advance while he came up in person. He collected all the cavalry that was available, and, going before us, drew up on the other side of the Marne in the plains of Saint Dizier.

The enemy had but few infantry, but they had collected at this point about 10,000 cavalry, with a proportionate amount of light artillery. The question was whether this cavalry was covering the army, and if not, what had become of it. The conflict was long and severe. As my artillery was placed upon the heights below which flows the Marne, I commanded the battlefield. Never since the beginning of the war had I an opportunity of seeing so many cavalry engaged. At length the enemy were broken and put to flight, losing 3,000 horses with all their artillery, and were pursued for some distance.

We arrived before Vitry next day, and had melancholy proof that the main army of the allies was no longer there; what could have become of it? It was not difficult to guess, for as it had not followed us, and had left a strong garrison in the town, it was clear that it had faced about and was marching unopposed to Paris!

We had tramped through pouring rain, with hardly any intermission; the men were utterly exhausted, and the ground so soaked that we could move neither cavalry nor artillery. The Emperor said to me:

'Storm the town.'

'What!' I exclaimed, 'in the present condition of the troops? Do you not see how large the garrison is on the ramparts? I grant that they are only made of earth, but, still, they are strengthened with *fraises*[1] and palisaded, and the fosses are full of water; how are we to cross them?'

'Collect some bundles of straw and throw them in,' answered the Emperor.

'Where are we to get them? There is nothing in the neighbouring

---

1. Rows of stakes projecting horizontally from the escarp to prevent escalade. Palisades are upright.

villages. And, besides, can we make a solid bridge with a few bundles of straw? Moreover, can there be any hope of success if such a *coup de main* is attempted with men utterly worn out like mine are now?'

As he still insisted, I dryly said:

'Try it, Sire, with your own Guard if you will; my men are not in a fit condition now ;' and left him.

He sent out a reconnoitring party, and their reports convinced him of the impossibility of the enterprise.

A bulletin printed by the enemy was brought to me, giving a detailed account of the seizure of the great convoy of artillery that had been collected at Sézanne, and of all the escort, who had been made prisoners, after a brave defence, at Fère-Champenoise, where the encounter had taken place. It included the names of the generals, and of the commissioned and non-commissioned officers. I saw the names of all those belonging to my corps. I took this sheet to the major-general, and begged him to let the Emperor see it at once.

'That I will not,' replied he; 'the news is too bad. Take it to him yourself.'

'No,' said I; 'you are our proper intermediary; it is part of your business.'

We argued the point with considerable warmth; but as I reflected that the knowledge of these events could not fail to alter the Emperor's plans, and that there was no time to be lost, I took the bulletin to him myself.

He was alone near a camp fire.

'You look very much disturbed,' he said. 'What is the matter?'

'Read this,' I answered, handing him the paper.

He read it through and smiled.

'It is not true,' he said. 'That is what the allies always do.'

'Not true!' I cried; 'but all the circumstances are detailed. I recognize all the names and appointments; our heavy artillery ought to be just about Fère-Champenoise now.'

'What day of the month is this?'

'The twenty-seventh of March.'

(The battle had taken place the previous day.)

'Look here,' said the Emperor, 'this is dated the 29th, which will only be the day after tomorrow!' For an instant I was nonplussed; I had not noticed the date.

'That must be a mistake,' I said; 'this unfortunate affair must have taken place yesterday at the spot mentioned.'

I took up the printed sheet again, and returned to the major-general's bivouac, where I found his officers and the Emperor's *aides-de-camp*.

'Well, what did the Emperor say?'

'He does not believe this bulletin is authentic.'

'Will you allow me to look at it?' asked General Drouot, of the artillery. He examined it, and continued: 'I fear that you are only too correct, *Monsieur le Maréchal*. It must be a misprint; this is a 6 turned tail downwards.'

I went with this explanation to the Emperor, who made no remark but:

'The devil! That alters matters.'

He walked up and down for a few moments, and then said:

'So you don't think we can carry Vitry by main force?'

'I thought,' was my reply, 'that you were convinced of it.'

'Quite true,' he answered. 'Very well, let us go away!'

'Where will you go?'

'I don't know yet; but for the present to Saint Dizier. Remain here,' he added; 'act as the rear-guard; keep the enemy in check, and prevent them from leaving the town. I will send you further orders; I am sure to get news at Saint Dizier.'

'Whatever it may be,' I replied, 'Paris, left without defence, will have fallen before you can get there if you are going thither, that is—and however fast you may travel. Were I in your place, I would go into Lorraine and Alsace, collect the garrisons from there, and wage war to the knife upon the enemy's rear, cutting off their communications, intercepting their convoys and reinforcements. They would be compelled to retreat, and you would be supported by our strongholds.'

'I have already ordered General Durutte to collect 10,000 men round Metz,' he said; 'but before deciding upon anything I must have reports.'

He started. That night I received orders to retire to Saint Dizier, and there found fresh ones to follow the Emperor, who had gone in the direction of Vassy, Doulaincourt, and Troyes, so the plan of throwing himself into Alsace and Lorraine had clearly been abandoned.

Chapter 27
Abdication of the Emperor

I am now drawing to the close of this hopeless struggle. Our long political and military agony was to be finished by a thunderclap. A new order of things is now about to begin, under which you, my son, were born, and under which we are still living—the reign of the Bourbons.

This ancient dynasty, having been turned off the throne, its head having fallen a victim to the Revolution, its family having since then wandered abroad, tried by means of proclamations scattered broadcast to regain its lost ground. No soldier was seduced, but its partisans took heart, first at Nancy, whither the Comte d'Artois, now on the throne, had ventured to betake himself; then at Paris, where some displayed resolution—after the city had capitulated, however.

I followed the Emperor's steps. I had arrived somewhere between Troyes and Villeneuve-l'Archevêque, when an order reached me to halt wheresoever I might be. In a postscript I read these words:

'You are doubtless aware that the enemy are masters of Paris.'

Although we had expected this grievous catastrophe, it affected us the more as we thought that the enemy might take revenge for the burning of Moscow, which, however, had not been caused by us, notwithstanding the rumour that had been spread at the time, and which still gained credence. Paris contained all that I held dearest in the world children, relations, connections, family, friends, and what little I possessed, with the exception of this property where I am writing these lines.

The Emperor had preceded the remains of his army. When within a few leagues of Paris, where he contemplated making the last efforts to delay the enemy, where he intended to wait for us, and at least to succumb with honour within a few leagues of Paris, I say, he heard of its surrender.[1] I thought that he would have retreated with us, and have fallen back upon our strongholds; instead of that, he summoned us to join him by forced marches.

The news of the loss of the capital spread rapidly, and occasioned much discouragement. Many soldiers left their flag, and retired to their own homes. Although we were in our own country, we were destitute of everything; we lived upon what we could pick up by marauding.[2]

Discouragement seized some of our generals. One of them even refused to charge the enemy, who were harassing our rear-guard, and in the hearing of his troops cried:

'Damn it, let us have peace!'

(A year later he got himself into trouble, was arrested, and only saved by the events of March 20. General ——— was either banished

---

1. 'Meanwhile Napoleon, every hour more alarmed, was straining every nerve to reach the capital. On March 29 the Imperial Guard and equipages arrived late at night at Troyes, having marched above forty miles in that single day. After only a few hours' rest, he threw himself again into his travelling carriage, and, as the wearied *cuirassiers* could no longer keep pace with him, set out alone for Paris. Courier after courier was despatched before him to announce his immediate return to the authorities at the capital; but, as Napoleon approached it, the most disastrous intelligence reached him every time he changed horses. He learnt successively that the Empress and his son had quitted Paris—that the enemy were at its gate—that there was fighting on the heights.

'His impatience was now redoubled; he got into a little post *calèche* to accelerate his speed, and, although the horses were going at the gallop, he incessantly urged the postillions to get on faster. The steeds flew along, the wheels struck fire in dashing over the pavement, yet nothing could satisfy the Emperor. At length, by great exertions, he reached Fromenteau, near Juvisy, only five leagues from Paris, at ten at night. 'As his horses were there being hurriedly changed at a post-house, called Cour de France, some straggling soldiers, who were passing, announced (without knowing the Emperor) that Paris had capitulated! "These men are mad!" cried Napoleon; "the thing is impossible. Bring me an officer!" At the next moment General Belliard came up and gave the whole details of the catastrophe. Large drops of sweat stood on the Emperor's forehead. He turned to Caulaincourt, and said, "Do you hear that?" with a fixed gaze which made him shudder.

'At this moment only the Seine separated Napoleon from the enemy's advanced posts on the extreme allied left in the plain of Villeneuve; their innumerable watch-fires illuminated the whole north and east of the heavens, while the mighty Conqueror, in the darkness, only followed by two post-carriages and a few attendants, received the stroke of fate.' Alison's *History of Europe*, vol. x.

2. These difficulties were not confined to the French army alone. On March 17, 1814, Blücher wrote to Schwartzenberg: 'I am struggling with the greatest want of provisions; the soldiers have been for some days without even bread; and I am cut off from Nancy, so that I have no means of procuring any.'

or made his escape, and eventually died mad in a lunatic asylum.)

A rumour spread that the Emperor had summoned us to Paris, in order to try to reconquer the capital. I myself received very direct and confidential news of this. I was implored to go in person to headquarters, in order to try to induce the Emperor to make peace, not to compromise what remained of France and the army, even to abdicate in favour of his son; that would be the best means of making peace between France and the foreigners.

The Emperor could not help being aware of these feelings, any more than of the general discontent that he had raised. As he might have taken it amiss if I left my troops without orders, and might have suspected a plot, I refused to go, and reserved my explanation until we should reach our destination. We were in ignorance as to what had been passing in Paris since its occupation by the allies, and the Emperor was no better informed than we were. We talked over our position—that is to say, over the army and its future, the misfortunes that had befallen France through the obstinacy of a single man. The past overwhelmed, the present was not calculated to reassure us.

On the last day of our march, just as we were mounting our horses, General Gérard, accompanied by several others, came to me in the name of his troops. I cannot now remember whether the Marshal Duke of Reggio was with me. Gérard was spokesman; he pointed out to me the condition of affairs: that everyone was tired of it; that our misfortunes were heavy enough already, without an attempt being made to aggravate them by a foolhardy resistance, which would only expose Paris to the fate of Moscow if we attempted to drive out the enemy, as was currently reported; that he and his men were in nowise disposed to advance towards fresh disasters. I replied that I agreed with them, which was quite true, and that I would freely express my opinion to the Emperor.

'In that case,' they cried, 'count upon us. You are our chief; we will obey.'

We started and reached Fontainebleau. Great excitement reigned among the officers; they crowded 'into my quarters, begging me to go at once to the Emperor, to speak to him in the name of the army, and tell him that they had had enough of it, and that it must cease. I promised to do all in my power, and begged them to leave me for a few moments.

While I was still dressing an *aide-de-camp* came from the Duke of Ragusa,[3] bearing a letter from my intimate friend General Beurnonville. This letter was addressed to me, to the Duke of Ragusa, and to the other marshals. One of the officers read it aloud while I went on with my *toilette*. The seal had been broken by the Duke of Ragusa, who commanded our outposts.

Beurnonville was a member of the Provisional Government. He praised Marshals Mortier and Marmont, and their troops, who had fought bravely in defence of Paris; he spoke of the magnanimity of the allies, of the Emperor of Russia in particular, adding that they would no longer treat with Napoleon, that we were to have the English Constitution, that the Senate was going to set to work, etc.

As soon as I was ready I took the letter, and, with the Duke of Reggio[4] and several other generals, I went to the castle. In spite of our request, we were all followed by our respective staffs. They feared lest the Emperor, warned of our visit, should make up his mind to lay a trap for us.

'The times are changed,' I said; 'he would venture it the less now that the army is with us.'

The feeling among the Guard even was the same; they shared the discontent of the army at the disasters that the Emperor had brought upon France. However, our officers insisted upon following us to defend us if necessary. Many others, of all ranks, in the courtyard and within the apartments, shared the same feelings; all displayed impatience to have an end put to their anxiety. There certainly was a project to march upon Paris, but no one seemed disposed for it.

As soon as we were announced, the Duke of Reggio and I were shown into the study, where the Emperor was with the Dukes of Bassano (Maret) and Vicenza (Caulaincourt), the Prince of the Moskowa (Ney), the Prince of Neuchâtel (Berthier), Marshal Lefèbvre, and others, whom I have now forgotten. This was the beginning of the scene that changed so many destinies.

The Emperor approached me.

'Good-day, Duke of Tarentum; how are you?'

'Very sad,' I replied, 'after so many unfortunate events! a surrender without honour! no effort made to save Paris! We are all overwhelmed and humiliated!'

'Certainly it is a great misfortune; what do your troops say?'

'That you have summoned us to march upon the capital. They share our grief, and I come now to declare to you that they will not

---

3. Marmont.
4. Oudinot

expose Paris to the fate of Moscow. We think we have done enough, have given sufficient proof of our earnest desire to save France from the calamities that are now crowding upon her, without risking an attempt which would be more than unequal, and which can only end in losing everything. The troops are dying of hunger in the midst of their own country, reduced in number though they are by the disastrous events of the campaign, by privation, sickness, and, I must add, by discouragement. Since the occupation of the capital a large number of soldiers have retired to their own homes, and the remainder cannot find enough to live upon in the forest of Fontainebleau.

'If they advance they will find themselves in an open plain; our cavalry is weakened and exhausted; our horses can go no farther; we have not enough ammunition for one skirmish, and no means of procuring more. If we fail, moreover, as we most probably shall, what remains of us will be destroyed, and the whole of France will be at the mercy of the enemy. We can still impose upon them; let us retain our attitude. Our mind is made up; whatever decision may be arrived at, we are determined to have no more to do with it. For my own part, I declare to you that my sword shall never be drawn against Frenchmen, nor dyed with French blood. Whatever may be decided upon, we have had enough of this unlucky war without kindling civil war.'

'No one intends to march upon Paris,' said the Emperor.

I had expected him to burst into a violent rage, but his answer was given in a calm, mild voice. He repeated:

'The loss of Paris is a great misfortune.'

'Do you know,' said I, 'what is going on there?'

'They say that the allies will not treat with me.'

'Is that all you have heard?'

'Yes.'

'Will your Majesty read this?'

I handed him Beurnonville's letter, and continued:

'You will see from it exactly what measures are being taken, as it is written by one of the members of the Provisional Government.'

'Can I read it aloud?' asked the Emperor. .

'Certainly,' I answered; 'it has already been made public in my room. You will see from the address that it was not sent to me alone. The Duke of Ragusa forwarded it to me open by an *aide-de-camp*.'

The Emperor gave it to the Duke of Bassano, who read it aloud. When he had finished, the Emperor took it from him, and restored it to me, thanking me for the mark of confidence.

'You should never have had any doubt of it,' I answered.

'Quite true; I was wrong. You are a good and honourable man.'

'The important thing is to make up your mind, Sire; public opinion is taking form, and there is no time to be lost.'

He turned to all who were present, and said:

'Very good, gentlemen; since it must be so, I will abdicate. I have tried to bring happiness to France; I have not succeeded; events have been against me. I do not wish to increase our sufferings. But when I abdicate, what will you do? Will you accept the King of Rome as my successor, and the Empress as Regent?'

We all accepted unanimously.

'The first thing to be done,' he added, 'is to treat for a suspension of arms, and I shall send Commissioners to Paris. I nominate for this important mission the Marshals Prince of the Moskowa and Duke of Ragusa, and the Duke of Vicenza. Does this selection satisfy you?'

We replied in the affirmative.

He drew up the act of abdication, but changed the wording two or three times over. It is not, however, very clear in my memory whether this was done precisely at that moment; I think it was, but will not affirm it.

The allies having come to the determination not to treat further with the Emperor, the Commissioners, who had just been nominated and approved, became less his representatives than those of the army, and it was in the name of the latter that they were to act. The Emperor said:

'Gentlemen, you may now retire. I am going to give directions relative to the instructions for the Commissioners, but I forbid them to make stipulations respecting anything personal to me.'

Then suddenly throwing himself on a sofa, and striking his thigh with his hand, he continued:

'Nonsense, gentlemen! let us leave all that alone, and march tomorrow. We shall beat them!'

I repeated to him briefly all that I had just said concerning the position of the army.

'No,' we all added, 'we have had enough of it; and remember that every hour that passes tells against the success of the mission that the envoys have to carry out.'

He did not insist, and said: 'Be ready to start at four o'clock,' and then dismissed us.

It was clear that he was only yielding to necessity, that his idea in summoning us so precipitately to Fontainebleau had been to order an immediate advance against Paris, as rumour had stated, and that he had not abandoned it, as only a minute previously he had said:

'Nonsense, gentlemen! let us leave all that alone, and march tomorrow. We shall beat them .'

Those words were to us a warning to take measures. After leaving his presence, we agreed that all authority should be placed in the hands of the Commissioners, that no step should be taken except under their direction until the conclusion of a treaty, and that the command of the army should be given to the major-general, as the senior, but with a promise from him to carry out no orders of the Emperor, of whatever character, but only such as should be agreed upon by the Commissioners, and giving immediate notice thereof to the different corps. He accepted the command, and made the promise.

The news of what had just occurred spread rapidly, and caused great joy. Everyone was relieved of great anxiety, and breathed prayers for the success of the proposed mission.

Scarcely had we reached the gallery, on leaving the Emperor, when he sent the Duke of Vicenza to recall me. We stopped, and I returned to him.

I have changed my mind regarding Marshal Marmont,' said he; 'he is commanding the outposts, and may be of use at Essonne. I wish you to take his place as commissioner. Will you accept?'

'Yes,' I answered; 'and you may rely upon my doing all in my power.'

'I know it,' he said; 'you are a man of honour, and I trust in your loyalty.'

'But,' I continued, 'you must give the marshals notice of this change.'

He told Caulaincourt to do so. On our way to where we had left the others in the gallery the latter told me that scarcely had we left the Emperor's presence when he said:

'Why did not Marshal Macdonald send me Beurnonville's letter by a courier?'

'That is part of your distrust of him,' the Duke of Vicenza had answered; 'we all know that he had received it an instant before coming to you with the Duke of Reggio, and that it had been read aloud after being opened by the Duke of Ragusa.'

'That makes a difference,' the Emperor had answered, adding presently: 'It seems to me advisable for the Duke of Ragusa to remain at

Essonne; I wish Macdonald to replace him. Call him back.'

Thus it came about that I was summoned to play a part in this great drama of the fall of the Empire, and of the colossus that had for so long weighed upon Europe, which had at length armed herself to overthrow it!

On rejoining our comrades we informed them of the change that had taken place; they thought the Emperor had already made fresh plans. We insisted then more strongly than ever upon the obligation undertaken by the major-general, and agreed to, moreover, by the Emperor—to wit, that he should do nothing except on the initiative and by direction of the commissioners.

We returned once more to the castle for our instructions. The Emperor read them to us. He had had the clause inserted which forbade our making any stipulation concerning him personally; then he gave his deed of abdication to the Duke of Vicenza, and we started for Paris accompanied by the hearty wishes of the army for the success of our negotiations.

The Duke of Ragusa's *aide-de-camp* had already preceded us to Essonne; he had informed the marshal of what had passed at the castle, and of the immediate arrival of the commissioners, amongst whom he had at first been appointed. He did not know that I had been nominated in his place. We found him in great agitation, complaining that he had not been summoned to the meeting, an omission which we explained to him had been quite accidental. We asked him to send a messenger to ask for a safe conduct for us, that we might have an interview with the Emperor of Russia.

While we were awaiting the messenger's return, the Duke of Ragusa informed us that he had received overtures from the allies to dissociate himself from the Emperor's cause with his army corps, and that he had replied by counter-propositions. He feared lest every moment should bring him word that they were accepted. I regret to say that they had been already accepted, which was proved by later avowals and by events that shortly occurred. He had made them in concert with his principal generals.[5]

This story is very painful to me, because it appears to imply a serious charge against the Duke of Ragusa, with whom my relations have since been friendly. I only mention it here in order to explain the part I played in the mission in which I was employed. Moreover,

---

5. See also some account of these negotiations from another independent source in the *Memoirs of General Savary, Duke of Rovigo.*

it is only for you, my son, although all the circumstances have been made public, and have called down much animadversion upon the poor Duke, which, added to other domestic sorrows, has made him very unhappy.

Our surprise, on learning from Marshal Marmont how far he had gone in his private negotiations, may be imagined. We pointed out to him his extreme imprudence, and the grave consequences that might ensue for France and the army, which by such a step would be placed at the enemy's mercy. But 'first get me out of the difficulty, and lecture me afterwards.' Every representation or observation was now unnecessary. The first thing to be done was to prevent this breach, and retard as long as possible the effect of the proposals made by the Duke of Ragusa. These had been already accepted, and this last fact he concealed from us, or from me, at any rate, so upset and anxious was he about the whole matter.

One of us advised him to go to Fontainebleau, promising that we would detain the enemy's messenger by telling him that the marshal had been summoned suddenly by the Emperor, and that he had to obey. This would only appear natural. Then, as it was unlikely that the Emperor of Russia would refuse to receive us, and to treat for a suspension of arms first of all, we would secure the inclusion of his troops. He refused, however, fearing that the Emperor might receive news of his private negotiation, and order his arrest and trial.

The Duke of Vicenza thought of and proposed another plan, which was to take the Duke of Ragusa with us, remarking that if our deed of nomination were not asked for, he would be supposed to be one of us; and in the contrary event we would say that we had added him. This settled, the Duke ordered General Souham, to whom he made over the temporary command of the troops, not to stir, whatever news he received, until his own return, which would take place at an early hour next day.

We were now informed that we might pass the allied outposts. We entered our carriages, Marshal Ney with the Duke of Vicenza, and the Duke of Ragusa with me. On reaching the castle of Petit-Bourg he observed that we were being driven up the avenue; he started.

'What objection have you?' I asked.

'It is,' he replied, 'the headquarters of the allies' advance-guard, commanded by the Crown Prince of Wurtemberg.'

'Well, what of that?'

'It is with him that I made my bargain, and supposing he requires its execution?'

'If that be so, stay in the carriage; as soon as we stop I will tell the two other commissioners,' which I did.

The *generalissimo* Prince Schwartzenberg came to meet us, and led us to the Crown Prince, who received us very dryly, telling us bitterly that we had caused the misfortunes of all Europe, which was true enough; but the reproach was the more out of place in his mouth, as he, like his father, was one day to profit by these said misfortunes, which brought him the title of King and the aggrandisement of the Grand Duchy of Wurtemberg after it had been raised to a kingdom. Though we did not tell him this plainly, we let him see that we thought it. He quitted the room with every mark of temper and annoyance, and did not reappear.

CHAPTER 28

Decision of the Allies

We all knew the *generalissimo* personally; he had been ambassador from his Court to the Emperor, of whom he had formerly been the very humble servant and courtier. It was he who, in 1810, had taken the most pains to bring about the rupture of the marriage-negotiations with Russia, and to play the principal part in making the Emperor marry the Archduchess, by letting it be known secretly that he had plenary powers to accept proposals, which were eventually made.

Astonished at finding the *generalissimo* at the outposts, and concluding that he intended to attack us, I expressed my surprise at finding him there, adding that if his intentions were hostile, we trusted to his honour to tell us so, in order that we might break off our mission and return to our posts. He replied by protesting that he had merely come to Petit-Bourg to pay his respects to the Crown Prince. He added that he had but just arrived when our messenger came to ask for a safe conduct for us, and that he had taken upon himself to receive us at the headquarters of his advance-guard. We could not go on to Paris without permission from the Emperor of Russia, he said, but he had sent to let him know of our arrival, and was sure that his answer would arrive ere long.

He was very polite to us, and our conversation naturally turned upon passing events and the object of our mission. We expected to find in him a strong partisan for the right of the King of Rome to succeed his father, and for the regency of the Empress. We were soon undeceived by hearing the Prince pronounce himself warmly in favour of the general cause of the allies as against the private interests of the House of Austria. His language was certainly that held at his Court, but it was impossible to believe that the Emperor Francis would sacrifice his daughter in this catastrophe, and help in precipitating her from the throne that he had so eagerly assisted her to mount. It appeared to us the less likely, as it was said that this Archduchess was his favourite daughter.

During this conversation someone came and called the Prince; he left us, and returned a quarter of an hour later, accompanied by the Duke of Ragusa. As the latter observed our surprise, he came to me in an off-hand manner, smiling, and as though relieved of a great weight. He told us that, having, without making himself known, discovered who were in the castle, he had learned that the *generalissimo* had preceded us, and that the Crown Prince had just retired to his own apartments. It then occurred to him to ask for Prince Schwartzenberg, and he begged him to allow their convention to have no sequel, as we, his comrades, were come to treat for the whole army inclusively, but on avowable and very different bases. To this the *generalissimo* had consented without difficulty. Had all things passed in this manner our discretion would have thrown an impenetrable veil over this fault; the destiny of the Duke of Ragusa decided it otherwise.

The conversation, or, to express it better, the discussion, upon the subject of the rights of the King of Rome, recommenced with even more warmth, and with no less resistance on the part of the *generalissimo*. His servants rescued him from his difficulty by announcing that supper was ready; it was between ten and eleven o'clock at night, and he told us that he had not dined. He invited us to share his supper, but we took no part in this German meal, for the reason that we had dined at Essonne a few hours previously. Supper was silent and melancholy; everyone kept his eyes on his plate; we observed each other. On rising from table we were informed that the Emperor of Russia was expecting us in Paris. The *generalissimo* came to see us off, and we started.

The Emperor Alexander was staying in the house belonging to the Prince de Talleyrand. We were immediately ushered into his presence; but before allowing us to lay before him the object of our mission, he begged us first to hear what he had to say. Thereupon he expressed warmly, and in the most chivalrous manner, his admiration for the French armies, the great glory with which they had covered themselves, notwithstanding the reverses they had met with, which in nowise detracted from their valour. He admitted that they had only yielded compulsorily to superior force, of which he had had an example recently at Fère-Champenoise, where a mere detachment, consisting for the most part of raw recruits, in blouses and round hats, had immortalized itself by its courageous resistance to all the forces collected at that point; he told us that he was deeply distressed at the loss of so many brave men, and that, after making every effort to save them from certain death, he had at last succeeded in inducing them to surrender as prisoners of war.[1]

He said further that he was no longer an enemy of Napoleon, now that he was unfortunate; that he had previously been his greatest admirer, his friend and his ally; that, on his side, he had faithfully carried out their treaty against England, that was, against her commerce, even though the said treaty caused cruel suffering to his own subjects (whose only means of obtaining what was necessary for their wants and comfort was by means of exchange), although they murmured aloud, and there was some danger of a revolution in his States. It had, however, come to his certain knowledge, he said, that, contrary to the treaty of prohibition, his ally permitted licenses to be issued, and that, notwithstanding his representations, which passed unheeded, he continued to issue them. He had therefore been obliged to shut his eyes to some traffic which Napoleon insisted upon closing. Some curt diplomatic notes were exchanged, and seeing himself threatened with a fresh war, he still had preferred to await the effects in his own country rather than provoke it.

'You know the results, gentlemen,' he continued; 'my armies, and the climate of my country, avenged my subjects for the miseries they had undergone. You were but passive instruments. I only esteem you the more for having done your duty, and proved your attachment, your devotion, and your fidelity to your master, of which you are now giving him a fresh proof, instead of doing as many others have done, who have thrown themselves into our arms, and done their best to bring about his downfall, and that of the French Empire. We were willing to treat openly with him at Prague, at Frankfort, and at Châtillon-sur-Seine; he would not consent, and see whither his obstinacy has brought him. We have now declared that we will not treat any further with him, because we can place no reliance upon him; but we do not wish in the smallest degree to take any part in the government of France, nor to lay her under any contributions, nor to diminish her ancient territory. We will even increase it.'

He recommenced his praises of the French army, of its marshals,

---

1. This was the affair related in the printed bulletin dated March 26, of which the 6 turned upside down made 29, and to which the Emperor would attach no credence while we were before Vitry.—Note by Marshal Macdonald.

etc. We saw through it, and clearly distinguished how much flattery there was in this long speech, which we did not interrupt.

When he had finished, Marshal Ney began to speak, and said some good things and some useless ones. We tried to stop him, but he replied in an angry voice:

'Let me speak. You will have your turn.'

The Duke of Vicenza was boiling over; it would have been more suitable for him to reply, as he was much better acquainted with the proper forms, and was more moderate. The Emperor listened quietly. At last conversation became general. We praised the generosity of the allies when they had gained the right to avenge themselves upon us; but we referred that generosity to his personal magnanimity. We spoke of the glory and bravery of the Russian troops, and of his own in particular, and made use of the weapons that he had employed to return all that he had with so much liberality and chivalry accorded to us. He seemed much touched.

After these reciprocal compliments we profited by his favourable disposition to ask for his intervention and support in favour of the cause that we had come to submit to him, and the proposals that we had to make to him—that is to say, the abdication of Napoleon, which ought to satisfy the allies, the recognition of his son as his successor, and of the Empress as Regent.

'It is too late,' he said; 'opinion has made too great strides. We have not checked it, and it is growing momentarily. Why did you not come to an understanding with the Conservative Senate?'

'By what right did it act?' we exclaimed. 'It has belied its title; it had no mission; a crawling, creeping, complaisant slave, it depended for its existence on the constitutions of the Empire. They are now overturned; it therefore is nothing. It is usurping at this moment an authority which can only emanate from national opinion, and that opinion has everything to fear from the resentment of the Bourbons, the *émigrés*, and the Royalists. Will your Majesty permit us to speak plainly to this vile Senate? Every institution, everything that now exists, will be threatened; those who have acquired national property will be sought out; a frightful civil war will be the result.

'The nation has made too many sacrifices; she has paid too dearly for the little liberty she has secured, not to be ready to do anything to safeguard it. The army will not allow the glory wherewith it has covered itself to be trodden under foot. Unhappy by the fault of its chief, it will, either with or without him, spring again from its ashes, stronger, more ardent than ever for national liberties, institutions, and independence. Henceforward its one aim will be to consolidate these without thinking of conquering or harassing other nations.'

The Emperor of Russia, struck by these arguments, was shaken.

'Be our mediator, Sire; it is a fresh field of glory, and one worthy of the great soul of your Majesty. You have declared that you made war only against one man; he is vanquished; let your Majesty show that you are a generous conqueror. Earn the gratitude of the great national majority, as you have earned ours by your magnanimous moderation.

The Emperor seemed much moved by our confidence in him, and said:

'I have no reason to object to your seeing the Senate. I do not care about the Bourbons; I do not know them. I fear it will be impossible to obtain the Regency. Austria is most opposed to it. Were I alone, I would willingly consent; but I must act in concert with my allies. Since the Bourbons will not do, take a foreign Prince, or choose one of your marshals, as Sweden did Bernadotte; there are plenty of illustrious men in France. Finally, gentlemen, in order to prove the sincere esteem and great regard I entertain for you, I will make your proposals known to my allies, and will support them. I confess I am most anxious to have the matter settled, for there are risings still going on' in Lorraine and the Vosges, and they are increasing; people are shooting each other there every day; a column of my troops lost 3,000 men while crossing those departments, and that *without seeing a single French soldier*. Your outspokenness has encouraged mine, and I do not hesitate to tell you these things. Come back at nine o'clock—we will finish then.'

We withdrew; on entering the great drawing-room we found there the members of the so-called Provisional Government, with the provisional ministers and other persons. Anxiety and fear were depicted upon every countenance. A discussion had begun, when the members of this Government were summoned to the Emperor's presence. They were all in disgraceful undress, and we had found the *Czar* in full military uniform.

They remained with him some time. The discussion in the drawing-room increased in animation. At length they reappeared, and wished to take a high hand and authoritative manner with us, which we promptly resented, telling them that they were a set of factious, ambitious men, who were betraying their country, and forswearing the oaths they had sworn.

The Prince de Talleyrand took no part. As the discussion became very noisy, the Duke of Vicenza raised his voice, and said:

'Gentlemen, you forget that you are in the apartments of the Emperor of Russia.'

Silence ensued, and Monsieur de Talleyrand invited everyone to go down to his room, adding that there we might seek, and perhaps find, a means of agreement and conciliation. We answered that we did not recognize their authority, and departed.

On my own account I had overwhelmed with reproaches my friends Beurnonville, and Dupont, who had accepted the Ministry of War. The latter had good reason to complain of Napoleon, who had caused him to be tried by a commission of Ministers and Privy Councillors who were devoted to him, instead of sending him before his proper judges, either the High Court, or a court-martial, for his share in the memorable and unfortunate affair at Baylen.[2]

I have forgotten to say that as we were leaving the presence of the Emperor of Russia one of his generals began to speak to him in a low voice. I heard the words, *totum corpus*, to which at first I attached no importance, but which gained great significance a few moments later.

We were going to the house of Marshal Ney. We learned here that our arrival had struck terror into the hearts of all the supporters of the new state of things; more than 2,000 white cockades had been removed from as many hats, and the Senate was trembling.

While we were at breakfast the Duke of Ragusa was called away. He returned a moment later, pale and as if beside himself, and said to us:

'My whole corps went over to the enemy last night.'

He took his sword, disappeared, and we saw him no more.

We deplored this event, which destroyed our last remaining hope, and at the same time gave colour to the assumptions of our enemies. A vast field of conjecture was opened to us by the impression naturally produced by such a sad piece of news. What must it not have been in the army, at the headquarters at Fontainebleau, after such an occurrence? Would others follow his example? Would despair increase? On the one hand we had isolated cases of desertion, which were alarming enough; on the other, we had the audacity of those ambitious men who had put themselves at the head of the movement in Paris from

---

2. The surrender of Dupont and his forces to the Spanish General Castanos, July 19, 1808.—Translator.

motives of personal interest, while our mere presence in the capital had sufficed to cause the disappearance of more than three-fourths of the white cockades. Besides, would not the allies, who had at first shown themselves so pleasant and willing to receive us, and to treat with an army whose broken remains even they dreaded, profit by so unhoped-for a circumstance, which lent such weight to their claims? However, confident in the chivalrous honour of the Emperor Alexander, we waited, not without anxiety, till he should summon us to hear the result of his conference with his allies.

The message came at length, and we were introduced into his presence. The King of Prussia was with the Emperor, who received us with the kindly, simple manner that has been observed by all who approached him. His face showed symptoms of secret satisfaction—the cause was not far to seek; he knew what had happened at Essonne.

The King of Prussia spoke first, and told us that we were the authors of all the misfortunes of Europe. The Crown Prince of Wurtemberg had apostrophized us in the same strain the previous evening at Petit-Bourg. The *Czar*, fearing that this would create discussion, hastily intervened.

'My brother,' said he, 'this is not the time to argue about what is passed,' and immediately entered upon the subject-matter of the conference. He told us that the question had been decided in the negative.

Thus was extinguished the last feeble ray of hope that our first interview had lighted as to the establishment of a Regency, contingent upon the abdication of Napoleon in favour of his son.

Alexander added that opinion in Paris was against it, and that this opinion was being rapidly spread in the provinces; that wives were always wives—that is to say, weak—and that Napoleon, wherever he might be, and with his authority, would dictate to his; that it would be easy for him to repossess himself of power, and that the thirst for vengeance would drive him to shake anew the foundations of Europe; that every nation had need of peace and rest, especially France, after so many years of disturbance, so many sacrifices, and so much bloodshed, from all of which she had gained immense glory, and nothing else, and that that glory had been too dearly purchased. Nevertheless, her territory should be enlarged, as to secure the political balance and equilibrium of Europe it was necessary that she should be stronger and more powerful than under her kings.

Who, on hearing this high-flown language, would not have expected that an extension of her frontier on the Rhine would be granted? The net result of it all was Chambéry and its environs!

The Emperor of Russia added that, as a proof of their respect and admiration for the army, of their esteem and friendship for France, which would soon be sealed, no war indemnity would be imposed or exacted by the allies, except a sum of 30,000,000 *francs* (£1,200,000), which was intended, I believe, as a little present to the King of Prussia.

They kept their word. It is true that they obtained, not an equivalent, but a considerable, reparation by their seizure of the immense store of war material contained in the garrisoned towns which were not taken by them, but which were made over to them by the disgraceful treaty of April 29. This treaty was published in the *Moniteur*, without signature, and public opinion protested that it had not been concluded gratuitously.

As we could oppose no further objections to the determination of the allies, the question arose as to their intentions regarding the ultimate fate of Napoleon and his family. Caulaincourt cleverly introduced the question, and I added that Napoleon had expressly enjoined and commanded us neither to discuss nor to agree to anything personal to himself. The Duke of Vicenza's question, therefore, arose partly from curiosity and partly from foresight, as it might happen that Napoleon, forgetting his restrictions, might wish to know beforehand what fate was in store for him.

The Emperor of Russia appeared surprised and incredulous. I showed him my instructions. After reading them over, and convincing himself of the accuracy of my statement, his demeanour became more solemn, and he said:

'I esteem him the more highly for it. Henceforward I cease to be his enemy, and restore my friendship to him. I was formerly his greatest admirer; I allied myself with him, approved every variation in his policy, recognised all the sovereigns he created and established, and the alliances he formed. I adopted, and faithfully carried out, his. Continental system as long as the treaty lasted. He demanded its prolongation, but this treaty was causing the utmost suffering to my country; and while I was ruining my subjects by forbidding all commerce, he was enriching himself by selling licenses. He threatened me. I put myself in a state of defence.

'He advanced to attack me, invaded my dominions, and drove me back into the very heart of my empire. I will say no more about the calamities which have produced such terrible results for you and for France; they brought about the catastrophe in which we, in our turn, have to play a part the fall of Napoleon and his dynasty. But he is in trouble. Today I become once more his friend, and I will forget everything. He shall have the island of Elba as his sovereignty, or *something else;* he shall keep the title by which he is generally recognised; his family shall receive pensions and preserve their estates. Tell him, gentlemen, that if he will have none of this sovereignty, or in case he can find no other shelter, he is to come into my dominions. There he shall be received as a sovereign. He may trust Alexander's word.'

During this speech the King of Prussia had, I think, retired. The Emperor declined to give any explanation of the words *something else* when we asked him what they meant.[3] We then asked for a draft in writing of the proposal, or rather decision, of the allies; but he objected, saying that the matter was one that ought to be treated diplomatically, and through the usual ministerial channels, whereupon we called his attention to the fact that Napoleon might fear false interpretations, or misunderstandings, and we urgently pressed him to have merely written down, without date or signature, what he had condescended to say to us by word of mouth concerning the resolutions of the allies.

He at length consented, left the room, and returned shortly afterwards holding in his hands a minute in every respect corresponding with what he had declared to us.

He gave it to Caulaincourt, granted us an armistice of forty-eight hours, in order to allow us time to go and return, furnished in the name of the army with sufficient instructions to admit of our treating upon the basis agreed to, and dismissed us.

We were at least as anxious to return to headquarters as the Emperor Napoleon and the army were to learn the result of our negotiations. The defection of the Duke of Ragusa's corps had naturally caused great excitement there. It was supposed, and rightly, that this occurrence might hinder our mission, and in every respect render its success doubtful. Our return calmed for the moment the most excited as well as the most timorous spirits.

---

3. An important note, which has a bearing on this point, will be found in vol. 3 of the English edition of Bourrienne's *Memoirs of Napoleon,* edited by Colonel Phipps, and published in 1885.

CHAPTER 29

Attitude of Napoleon

Immediately upon our arrival we went to the castle. It was one o'clock in the morning. It was with the greatest difficulty that the Emperor was awakened and persuaded to get up; Caulaincourt himself had to go into his room and shake him somewhat roughly. The fact that he was able to sleep so soundly in such a. situation would seem to denote that he was either perfectly indifferent, or that he possessed a mind calm beyond that of ordinary men.

He appeared at length, and thanked us for the efforts we had made. He said that the defection of Marmont's corps must necessarily have had great influence upon the determination of the allies. In that he was not mistaken, for in the second interview the Emperor of Russia had spoken to us, upon all that concerned our mission, in a much more haughty and decided tone than in the first. In speaking of Napoleon personally, although, as I have said, his attitude was solemn, yet he made with much grace the offer of receiving him into his dominions.

When we came to this special point the Emperor asked how he and his family would be treated, and expressed a high opinion of the character of Alexander. He said that he knew him sufficiently well to feel certain that, had he not been worried and imposed upon by the allies, and above all by the influence of England, Alexander would have treated with him, and would have maintained his sovereignty and his dynasty in France. He added that the Empress had written to him from either Blois or Orleans to be of good courage; that she was sufficiently convinced of the affection her father bore her to be persuaded, as she also wished him to be, that the Emperor Francis would never give his consent or permission to the dethronement of his son-in-law; that she herself was determined to share his fate, be it what it might, that no human power should keep her from him, and that she was preparing to join him.

'You do not know the Empress,' he said; 'she is a Princess of strong character. If necessary, she would play the part over again of Maria Theresa when she exhibited her son to the Hungarians.'[1]

We, however, knew how much this feminine influence had been worth during the campaign of 1813, for during the armistice and the negotiations at Prague she had guaranteed, so the Emperor told me, the neutrality of her father. But Napoleon, as is universally known, liked to cherish illusions.

We tried to brush away the frivolous hopes with which the Empress encouraged him; the strongest proof that she was mistaken was to be found in the violent opposition to us that had been openly displayed by the *generalissimo* Prince Schwartzenberg, and certainly he would not have acted as he did without formal orders from the Emperor of Austria, who was at Dijon, and whom he represented in the councils of the allies.

Napoleon could not help admitting that our observations contained some truth, but, suddenly leaving aside politics, the destiny of France and of the army, and only thinking of what was personal to himself, he came back to the offer made by the allies, and inquired whether we had discovered what was meant by the 'island of Elba or something else.' We answered in the negative, and after a few moments' reflection he said:

'It is probably the island of Corsica, and they would not name it in order to avoid the pun.[2] Very good, I choose the island of Elba. Do any of you gentlemen know that island? Is there a palace, a castle, a suitable or even tolerable dwelling there?'

We had none of us ever been there.

'In that case, seek through the army for an artillery or engineer officer. There must be some who have served there.'

He gave immediate orders to that effect.

He again spoke of Marmont's defection.

'It is I,' he said, 'who am probably the cause of it. I wished to know whether you had passed the outposts of the allies without difficulty,

---
1. Napoleon's belief and reliance upon Maria Louisa was a pretty trait in his character. Unhappily the Empress was made of very different material to Maria Theresa, and was able to console herself very readily during the captivity of Napoleon at St. Helena. After his death she was frequently married. (*Marie-Louise and the Invasion of 1814* by Imbert de Saint-Amand, also published by Leonaur).
2. What pun? Is some allusion meant to the abusive nickname of Corsican Ogre?

and also to talk with the Duke of Ragusa. I sent several officers in succession to summon him to give me an account of your journey. He had gone with you. His generals, who knew everything, and had had a share in the treaty of desertion, became uneasy at my repeated messages. They supposed that I knew all, and, fearing arrest, they took away their troops without even sending warning to the surrounding regiments whom they thus compromised and almost demoralized. The news upon this subject is very bad; it kept arriving, and it would appear that even the officers and generals are not quite free. Unfortunately we could provide no remedy; however, I ordered the echelons to advance and occupy the lines of Essonne.'

He had guessed correctly. He spoke of Marmont with great moderation, and we explained to him that he had been at first led away by indirect overtures from persons attached to him by friendship and bound to him by gratitude. Unhappily, having listened to these overtures, he made the mistake of answering by some counter-propositions, which he did not think were of a nature to be accepted; they were, however, and already were when we reached Essonne. But the actual catastrophe in nowise depended upon his will, for when he came with us to Paris he left stringent orders with his generals that whatever happened they were to await his return, which would take place early next morning.

This event was the more annoying to him because he had arranged with Prince Schwartzenberg, at Petit-Bourg, that, notwithstanding their private agreement, his corps should not be sent into Normandy, should not be separated from the rest of the army, and should be included in any arrangement made by our negotiation. Fate, however, willed otherwise.

Under the particular circumstances the Duke of Ragusa could only be accused of culpable thoughtlessness; under others it would no doubt have been a crime of high-treason. But under existing circumstances what had he to hope for or to gain, raised as he was to the chief dignity in the army, to the most distinguished social title? Office? He practically held it already. The Emperor did not pursue the subject; he was only dissimulating, as was made evident by a proclamation issued the following year on the occasion of his fatal return from Elba.[3]

---

3. 'The French were never on the point of being more powerful, and the *élite* of the enemy's army was lost without resource, ft would have found a tomb in those vast plains which it had so mercilessly laid waste, when the treason of the Duke of Ragusa delivered up the capital and disorganized the Army.' Extract from Proclamation of March, 1815, by the Emperor.

We begged the Emperor to take immediate steps to have the necessary instructions regarding so much of the negotiations as was personal to him and his family drawn up. He promised to send them to us next day, and thanked me personally for my behaviour and services. We retired, after again begging him not to delay, as there was a chance that the events at Essonne might increase the downheartedness of the army, and set an example to others. It was also necessary not to allow the goodwill and interest that the Emperor of Russia had displayed towards him and his family to cool.

During the morning we saw some of our colleagues, the Marshals, and a number of generals and superior officers. There was much excitement abroad, and, as a consequence of the discouragement in the army, opinion seemed to lean towards a change of government. We therefore had reason to apprehend partial and private desertions, and they occurred, notwithstanding all our efforts to prevent them. We pointed out that our strength lay in our unity; that by preserving our attitude, which was still formidable to the allies, we should awe them and obtain better terms; that it would be cowardice to abandon Napoleon, who was still their chief, and to leave him at the mercy of his enemies at home and abroad. Some regret was also expressed that he did not take the desperate step of fomenting a rising, and dragging the remains of our army to certain destruction, or, to crown our misfortunes, to civil war!

I cannot quite remember whether it was now, or at our first starting for Paris, that we made over the command of the army to Marshal Berthier, Prince of Neuchâtel, vice-constable and major-general. The exact moment does not matter, for although we were the Emperor's envoys, we bore also the title of Commissioners of the Army, and it was only in the latter quality that the allies would receive us. We therefore agreed and instructed the Prince of Neuchâtel that he was to carry out no orders of Napoleon respecting movements of troops, and that he was to be guided entirely by the orders that we, the Commissioners, would give him to support our negotiations. This arrangement was concluded; all promised and bound themselves to conform to it; you will see shortly how that promise was kept. Nevertheless, we never ceased repeating that upon our unity, and the firm and imposing attitude of the army, depended the success of our mission.

I commanded five army corps, including that of the Duke of Reggio,[4] who was again under my orders. In my absence I delegated

---

4. Marshal Oudinot.

this command to the Duke, and gave to General Molitor that of the corps of which I was titular chief; but for the sake of unity I placed it also under the instructions of the marshal.

After this long conference, at which many unnecessary things were discussed, we went to the castle. The bases of the treaty were prepared, and, furnished with plenary powers, we took leave of Napoleon, who appeared more resigned to his ultimate fate. He desired us to hasten matters, and bring about a speedy termination. We reached Paris late at night, and sent to apprise the Emperor of Russia, who postponed the interview until eleven o'clock next morning.

When we arrived, Alexander already knew that Napoleon had accepted the sovereignty of the island of Elba.

We were very graciously received, but on the one hand there were personal considerations, on the other Alexander was secretly very glad to see the satisfactory conclusion of a struggle that the allies feared might still be prolonged. They would not now have had to fight the remnants of an army, but an armed population. A large number of the inhabitants of the Vosges and Lorraine had formed themselves into bodies of *francs-tireurs*, and were doing great mischief to the communications of the foreign troops. The Emperor Alexander had told me, and has since repeated to me, that in those departments alone they had lost 3,000 men without meeting a single French soldier!

The great majority in the capital was in favour of Napoleon, and the entire National Guard were on his side. The allies did not feel very safe there. The armies that had evacuated Spain, the frontiers of Italy and Piedmont, were still at liberty, and might unite with ours; the garrisons on the Rhine and on the Meuse might form a considerable force, and support insurrections which, from being partial at first, might come to be very serious general risings; the energy of Napoleon, although weakened by so many reverses, might reawaken, and give a great impulse to France. All that was realized, and was, no doubt, the mainspring which rendered the Sovereigns so obliging, and the Provisional Government so uncomfortable, so weak, and so obsequious.

The first point for consideration was that of an armistice for an indefinite length of time, and a line of demarcation. The Emperor of Russia said that, to give us a token of his esteem, he authorized us to fix it. We hesitated an instant; then I spoke, and asked for the left bank of the Seine. Alexander replied that he would willingly consent, but pointed out that Paris would thus be cut in half, that meetings between the troops, who must necessarily cross the river on business, or for their wants, or simply from curiosity, might produce results disagreeable to the capital, and that it would be better to avoid any contact between the troops on either side. Moreover, he thought that the allies would never consent to withdraw their advance-guards from the positions they occupied militarily .; that it would be better and preferable to leave the troops outside rather than to fill the town with them, where they would be a hindrance to the inhabitants and to business.

We admitted the justice of these arguments, and did not insist. Thereupon the Emperor Alexander offered me a pencil, which I begged to be allowed not to take; but he insisted with so much kindness upon my drawing the line that I at last gave way. It went round the outside of Paris, on both banks of the Seine, starting from the outposts of the foreigners, leaving to us on the left bank all the places not occupied that day by their troops. A map of France lay upon the table, and the outline was soon made. The armistice included all the armies and all the places which in France or abroad were still holding out. Officers from both sides were to be sent to all points to stop hostilities; but as it was impossible to regulate from Paris the distant demarcations, we agreed that each side should keep the positions they might be holding at the moment when the envoys, who were to travel with the utmost speed, should arrive.

The line of the Seine was the most important; it described, from the mouth of the river at Essonne, a semi-circle round the outposts of the allies to below Paris. The Emperor of Russia, after examining and approving this outline, gave orders to Prince Schwartzenberg to have copies made of it, and to send out instructions for the immediate cessation of hostilities. He then put us into communication with the ministers representing the allied Powers, to draw up the articles of the treaty, of which he undertook to secure the acceptance of the terms by the Provisional Government, in return for the receipt of the act of abdication.

The most urgent matter was the notification of the suspension of hostilities. As soon as we were informed that the Austrian staff had finished making a clean copy of the line of demarcation, we went to Prince Schwartzenberg to receive our copy, to read over our respective instructions to the officers bearing the notification of the armistice, to learn their names, and arrange for their departure.

While my colleagues were settling these matters, I thought that I would verify the copy of the line of demarcation, and it was a very fortunate idea of mine to do so, for, either by accident or design, our line, instead of beginning at the river at Essonne, had been pushed back to beyond Fontainebleau.[5] The result of this would have been that the Emperor Napoleon must have emitted the castle, and our troops have retired to Nemours, and that very precipitately, for the convention upon this point was to be carried out within twenty-four hours.

What made me think then, and keeps alive my suspicion now, that this was not merely done by mistake, was the obstinacy with which the Austrian staff and the Prince himself declared that the original had been exactly copied. I demanded to see it, so as to compare it with the copy; it could not be found. They declared it had been returned to the Emperor of Russia; we insisted upon their sending for it, but they made objections.

At last, taking up my hat, I announced that I was going to the Emperor. Seeing my determination, and that my colleagues intended to support me by going with me, the Austrians yielded, and sent, or did not send, for the original map; but at the end of an hour or two, without producing this map, Prince Schwartzenberg told us that the Emperor of Russia said that we were right upon every point, and the copies were accordingly rectified.

When these points were settled to our satisfaction, my colleagues thanked me for the precaution I had taken of comparing the line of demarcation, which we were to send immediately to Fontainebleau. What disappointment and annoyance would have been experienced at the French headquarters if we had received this map without examining it, as a start must have been made without delay! While writing these lines I still tremble to think of what the consequences might have been, for we should not have yielded. This was a fresh proof to us of the honour of the Emperor Alexander.

I must retrace my steps a little to mention a circumstance which had escaped me. On our return to Paris, while at dinner with Marshal Ney, one of his *aides-de-camp* entered in a state of great joy, and said to him:

'The Emperor of Russia was very pleased indeed with your letter, and here is the proof,' he continued, showing round his neck a decoration with which that Sovereign had just honoured him. He added that Monsieur de Talleyrand, President of the Provisional Gov-

---

5. A similar account of this transaction, based upon information given by the Marshal many years previously, will be found in Bourrienne's *Memoirs of Napoleon*.

ernment, thanked the marshal for the important news he had given him. We all showed our surprise, and asked what this meant. Ney, much embarrassed, stammered out that on leaving the conference we had had with Napoleon the previous night, and fearing lest, in spite of his acceptance of the conditions proposed, he might commit some folly, he, Marshal Ney, had considered it his duty to send an account of what had passed to the Emperor of Russia, so that the allies, being forewarned, might take their measures accordingly!

We observed that he had no business to take such a step without consulting us, as his position as commissioner lent great weight to his actions. To reassure us he said he would show us copies of his letters. He summoned his secretary, who at first said he could not find them, and then came back to say that the minutes had been scratched out and altered, so as to be illegible. At that moment we received notice from the Emperor of Russia that he would receive us at eleven o'clock next morning. We thought we were going to inform him of Napoleon's acceptance of Elba, but he already knew all that had passed from Marshal Ney's letter, of which I have never heard the details.

Even without the sudden arrival of the tell-tale *aide-de- camp*, we were destined to know of this incident, for, before we were announced to the Emperor of Russia, we met Monsieur de Nesselrode, his Foreign Secretary, who paid some compliments to Marshal Ney upon his letter, and shortly afterwards the Emperor thanked him for it affectionately. As for Monsieur de Talleyrand, he was malicious enough to cause the letter he had received to be printed in the *Moniteur*, but whether in part or in full I know not.

This explains why Marshal Ney gave his personal adhesion to the new order of things unknown to us, and while we were still actually negotiating; and why, later on, after the signature of the treaty, he quitted us, and would not accompany us back to Fontainebleau. No doubt the *Moniteur* would have found its way thither, and he thus avoided the direct reproaches that Napoleon would not have failed to heap upon him.

Caulaincourt told me that, after being appointed one of the commissioners, Ney had gone back to Napoleon, and told him that he had not sufficient money for the expenses of his mission. Napoleon had answered that he had only small funds remaining at Fontainebleau, that he had ordered the recall of the treasure that was with the Empress, but that meanwhile he promised him 15,000 *francs* (£600). Caulaincourt added that he had received this sum on our first return from

Paris, and probably after he had written the letters to the Emperor of Russia and to Talleyrand. However, we wanted for nothing; we were driven in Napoleon's carriages, and the Duke of Vicenza paid in his name the expenses of hiring post-horses. But I have always heard that it was a custom of the Marshal whenever he was sent upon a mission to object that he had no money, and that Napoleon supplied him.

In relating this episode I am not moved by any animosity against Marshal Ney, whose bravery I have admired more than other people, and I was one of those who helped to name him the 'Bravest of the brave.' Besides, I am only writing for you, my son; this episode will simply serve to let you know the truth of what may be published concerning the letters to the Emperor of Russia and Monsieur de Talleyrand, when you are old enough to hear about, and understand, the momentous events in which I have been an actor, and which I witnessed.

CHAPTER 30

Reported Flight of Napoleon

I will now return to our negotiations and our line of demarcation. The annoyances and delays we had had to put up with were but a prelude to one much more serious annoyance.

While we were busied about sending out the couriers to settle the demarcations that had been altered upon our instance, we received an urgent message from the Emperor of Russia, demanding our immediate attendance upon him.

On arriving we noticed his severe manner and threatening tone.

'I am indignant, gentlemen,' he said, 'at learning the part you are playing here. Was it to deceive my good faith that you came hither as negotiators? Was it in order that you might assist Napoleon's escape?'

From our dismayed manner he could see that we were not affecting surprise. Indeed, we were confounded by this improbable news.

'What!' I said, 'can your Majesty believe that? After your generosity has been made known to and realized by Napoleon, after his acceptance of your offers guaranteeing his safety, can you believe that he would expose himself to seizure by the allied troops, that he would risk being taken by a band of *Cossacks*, and spending the rest of his life in captivity, if not worse? No,' I continued with warmth, I that cannot be; it is not true. This piece of news is false, invented; someone has wickedly deceived your Majesty, in order to check your kindness towards Napoleon!'

'Here is the report,' he returned, 'addressed to me, and signed by—I think, Prince Repnine, who commands my forces at La Ferté-Aleps; and I am bound to believe him.'

'Someone has deceived or led him into error,' I replied.

The report was in Russian; the Emperor translated it. In it his general informed him that the French General D——, who was opposed to him, had sent him word that he had just received intelligence that Napoleon, with fifty mounted *chasseurs* of his Guard, had fled, no one knew whither; that not knowing to whom to apply, he begged him to obtain orders for him and his cavalry from the Provisional Government.

This may all have arisen from the ill-will, misunderstanding, and intrigues of this same Provisional Government, which had numerous agents at all the points occupied by the army, to deceive the leaders as to the course of affairs, to discourage and alienate the men, and instigate defections. This was done to a large extent.

I proposed to the Emperor to send one of his *aides-de-camp* with one of mine to Fontainebleau, to verify this news, and to assure themselves of Napoleon's presence there. He agreed, and the officers started; but while awaiting their return he suspended all negotiations, as well as the execution of the demarcation agreed upon at the armistice.

On reaching Marshal Ney's house we had proof positive of the falsity of the news, for a letter had arrived from the Emperor Napoleon, dated that very day (and he was said to have taken flight the day before), demanding the return of his act of abdication, and revoking our powers. We could not imagine what had induced him to go back upon his previous determination, and we, in our turn, indignant that he should think us capable of lending ourselves to such folly (I might use a much stronger word), refused point-blank.

This demand, however, had one advantage, inasmuch as it proved to us that Napoleon was still at Fontainebleau; but we vainly strove to find the answer to the riddle of the flight, as well as the motives that had induced him to re-demand his act of abdication.

The *aides-de-camp* returned, and confirmed our assertion that there was no truth in the report of the Emperor's flight. The suspension was removed; we hurried on the tracing of the lines of demarcation, with directions that they were to be carried out forthwith, for our troops were very badly off in their bivouacs, and crowded in their cantonments for supplies. Rations were very seldom distributed, and this augmented discontent and discouragement, and increased desertion, to the great satisfaction of the allies and the Provisional Government, so awed were they by these skeleton remains of troops who had shown their valour in so many battles and had more than once made Europe tremble!

I cannot say the same for their leaders. They vied with each other in displaying anxiety to submit themselves, in spite of all our entreaties and advice. Scarcely had each one made peace for himself in the name of his troops, who were ignorant of what was going on, than he abandoned them, and hurried to Paris, down to General Molitor even, whom I had left in charge of my titulary corps, and who, despite my injunctions, made terms for himself behind my back.

I may repeat here what I have already said, that the honour of the Emperor Alexander would not allow him to profit by these desertions and to make them a pretext for breaking off negotiations with us, for we now only represented a fictitious army. He kept all his promises, all his engagements to Napoleon, and always recognized us as Commissioners.

While the negotiations were in progress, I questioned my *aide-de-camp* who had accompanied the Emperor's to Fontainebleau. He had learned there that a certain General Allix, commanding at Sens, had seen an Austrian Major pass on his way to Paris from Dijon, where his Sovereign was. It appears that this major told him that his master, from whom he was bearing despatches to the Emperor of Russia, disapproved strongly of all that had been and was still being done in Paris; that he had taken up arms against Napoleon in order to put a check upon his ambition and reduce his power; that he was quite willing, as he had undertaken, to enclose him within the ancient limits of France; but that he did not, and never would, consent to the dethronement of his son-in-law, his daughter, and the proper arid direct heir to their crown.

According to this real or invented story, the general had immediately sent notice to Napoleon, whose hopes were raised for a moment, but were quickly dashed again, for he learned from a better and more trustworthy source that his father-in-law approved of his deposition and the recall of the Bourbons. It was by the light of this will-o'-the-wisp that he had written to demand the return of his act of abdication. I have never been able to get to the bottom of the story of his flight. I might have questioned the French general who told it to the Russian, but for the sake of his honour I would not ask him to enlighten me.

At length, on April 11, the last signature was affixed to the treaty between the Foreign Ministers and ourselves. That same evening we handed over the act of abdication to the Provisional Government in return for their guarantee that the clauses should be carried out as far as concerned them, and under the guarantee of the allied Powers. The exchange of ratifications was fixed for the 14th, at eleven o'clock in the morning, at the house of Prince Hardenberg. I was charged to hand in ours.

The members of the Provisional Government had wished to impart some solemnity to the reception of the act of abdication; they had summoned their ministers and the members of their party. After we had handed in this document, rightly regarded as the last and most important ever signed by a Sovereign once the most powerful in the world, Monsieur de Talleyrand advanced towards us and said:

'Now that all is concluded, we ask you, gentlemen, to give in your adhesion to the new order of things that has been established.'

Marshal Ney hastened to say that he had already done so.

'I do not address myself to you, but to the Dukes of Tarentum and Vicenza.'

I simply answered that I refused; Caulaincourt did likewise. Talleyrand could neither change colour nor turn paler, but his face swelled, as though he were bursting with rage. However, he contained himself, and merely said to me:

'But, *Monsieur le Maréchal*, your personal adhesion is of importance to us, for it cannot fail to exercise great influence upon the army and upon France. All your engagements are now terminated, and you are free.'

'No,' I replied, 'and no one ought to know better than yourself that as long as a treaty is not ratified it may be annulled; when that formality has been fulfilled, I shall know what to do.'

Talleyrand made no answer, stepped back several paces, and we withdrew.[1]

Ney informed us that, as his mission was now at an end, he should not return with us to Fontainebleau; and then, apparently addressing me, he said:

'I shall not go there in search of rewards.'

'I am not in the habit of receiving, still less of asking for them,' I answered; 'and' (with an allusion to the 15,000 *francs*) 'neither have I received any in advance. I am returning thither to perform a duty, to keep to the end my engagements and the promises I have made to the Emperor.'

Next day, April 12, Caulaincourt and I started together for Fon-

---

1. It was not until after Bonaparte had written and signed his formal abdication that Marshal Macdonald sent to the Provisional Government his recognition expressed in the following dignified and simple manner: 'Being released from my allegiance by the abdication of the Emperor Napoleon, I declare that I conform to the Acts of the Senate and the Provisional Government.—Bourrienne's *Memoirs of Napoleon*, standard edition of 1885, vol. 3.

tainebleau. The Count d'Artois entered Paris, I believe, at the same moment with the title of Lieutenant-General of the Kingdom.

We found Napoleon calm and tranquil, although he learned that all was concluded. He again thanked us affectionately for all that we had done for him and his family. Not seeing Marshal Ney, he merely asked, without further remark:

'Did not the marshal return with you?'

It was easy for him to interpret the silence with which we received this suggestive inquiry, because he had noticed plainly that he was not there. It was nearly six o'clock. He kept us to dinner, but postponed it for an hour, in order to draw up the ratifications.

Just as we were going in to dinner he sent us word to begin without him, as he felt unwell and was going to bed; food was, however, sent to him. He also settled nine o'clock in the morning as the hour at which we were to come to receive the ratifications.

An *aide-de-camp* arrived from the Emperor of Russia, I know not whether before, during, or after dinner. He was the bearer of the ratified treaty, sent by his master to Napoleon out of courtesy. This *aide-de-camp* was, I believe, Monsieur de Schuvaloff, one of Alexander's favourites. He was admitted, I believe, but I do not know what passed between him and Napoleon. If the Duke of Vicenza ever writes his Memoirs, no doubt he will mention the subject.

All those who had remained at Fontainebleau, and who were for the most part attached to the service of the house and person of the Emperor, were overjoyed at seeing the termination of this great drama. They had nothing further to hope for from him; decency had kept them at their posts, but they longed for the moment of dismissal.

Next morning, at nine o'clock, I was introduced into the Imperial presence. The Dukes of Bassano and Vicenza were with Napoleon. He was seated before the fire, clothed in a simple dimity dressing-gown, his legs bare, his feet in slippers, his neck uncovered, his head buried in his hands, and his elbows resting on his knees. He did not stir when I entered, although my name was announced in a loud voice. After some minutes of silent waiting the Duke of Vicenza said to him:

'Sire, the Marshal Duke of Tarentum has come in obedience to your orders; it is important that he should start again for Paris.'

The Emperor appeared to wake from a dream, and to be surprised at seeing me. He got up and "gave me his hand with an apology for not having heard me enter. As soon as he uncovered his face I was struck by his appearance; his complexion was yellow and greenish.

'Is your Majesty not well?' I asked.

'No,' answered Napoleon; 'I have been very ill all night.'[2]

Thereupon he seated himself again, dropped into his former attitude, and appeared once more plunged in his reveries. The two other spectators and I looked at each other without speaking. At last, after a somewhat lengthy pause, the Duke of Vicenza again said:

'Sire, the Duke of Tarentum is waiting. The deeds which he is to take with him ought to be delivered to him, seeing that the delay will expire in twenty-four hours, and that the exchange is to be made in Paris.'

The Emperor, rousing himself a second time from his meditations, got up more briskly, but his colour had not changed, and his face was melancholy.

'I feel rather better,' he said to us, and then added: 'Duke of Tarentum, I cannot tell you how touched by, and grateful for, your conduct and devotion I am. I did not know you well; I was prejudiced against you. I have done so much for, and loaded with favours, so many others, who have abandoned and neglected me; and you, who owed me nothing, have remained faithful to me! I appreciate your loyalty all too late, and I sincerely regret that I am no longer in a position to express my gratitude to you except by words. I know that your delicacy and disinterestedness have left you without fortune; and I am not unaware of the generous manner in which you refused to accept a present of considerable value at Gratz in 1809, which the States of the province offered you in token of their gratitude for the strict discipline and order you maintained among my troops, and where your impartial rule did justice to all. Formerly I was rich and powerful; now I am poor.'

'I flatter myself,' I answered, 'that your Majesty thinks too well of me to believe that I would accept any reward in your present position; my conduct, upon which you place too high a value, has been entirely disinterested.'

'I know it,' he said, pressing my hand; 'but, without hurting your delicacy, you can accept a present of another kind, the sword of Mourad-Bey which I wore at the battle of Mont-Thabor; keep it in remembrance of me and of my friendship for you.'

---

2. It is alleged that Napoleon took poison on the night of March 12. [See Baron Fain's *Memoirs*; also Bourrienne's *Memoirs of Napoleon*, Eng. edit., vol. 3.] It is probable, however, that the Emperor had taken an overdose of opium, with the intention of obtaining artificial sleep for his overtaxed system, exhausted physically by his recent rapid journey to Fontainebleau, and mentally by the strain and anxiety of the previous weeks.

He had it brought to him, and offered it to me. I thought I might accept this present. I thanked him very warmly; we threw ourselves into each other's arms, and embraced one another effusively. He begged me to come and see him in Elba if any chance took me into Italy; I promised. At length we separated. The documents that I was to carry were given to me. I made my preparations for departure, and since then I have never seen Napoleon again.

Chapter 31

Delivery of the Treaty

I reached Paris that evening, and fulfilled on the following day the mission with which I was charged—the delivery of the treaty ratified by Napoleon himself. There was no exchange, for, as I have said, the Emperor Alexander had sent his personal ratification direct and with great courtesy first. The Foreign Ministers, who were assembled at the hotel of Prince Hardenberg, received me with great demonstrations of politeness, and showed lively satisfaction at finding the united efforts of the allied Sovereigns crowned with a success so unexpected for their cause. Prince Hardenberg appeared to have forgotten the peremptory manner with which I had treated him in January, 1813, after the desertion of the Prussian corps under my orders. He confined himself to asking me for news of various persons whom he had known in the French army, and with speaking to me of his friend the Count de St. Marsan, whom he had had the pleasure of meeting.

The Count de St. Marsan had spent several years in Berlin, till 1813, as French minister. He had followed the King of Prussia into Silesia, when he suddenly quitted his residence at Potsdam on hearing of the final disasters accompanying our retreat, and of the desertion of his body of troops, for which he appeared to fear that he might be held responsible. It was afterwards said that Monsieur de St. Marsan was more devoted to Prussia than to France, and that long before the catastrophe he had made his peace with the allies. I have never taken any pains to verify this rumour.

General Dupont, at that time Minister for War, and a friend of mine of many years' standing,[1] having learned that I had delivered

---
1. We had made acquaintance in 1784, in Holland, when we were both serving in Maillebois' legion; since then we had seldom been long without news of each other.—Note by Marshal Macdonald.

the treaty, came to me, in the name of the Comte d'Artois, Lieutenant-General of the kingdom, to solicit my personal adherence to the changes that had taken place. I had executed my engagements; I was no longer bound by oath; in a word, I was free. I had no other objections to make that could carry any weight, and I acted honestly and honourably in putting my hand to the document that appeared next day in the *Moniteur*. You will observe, my son, that I afterwards faithfully carried out the fresh engagements I had just contracted; it is an example that I recommend you to follow.

It was some time ere I went to the Tuileries to pay my respects to *Monsieur*, at that time Lieutenant-General of the kingdom, now King Charles X. My friends urged me. I had no objection to going, but I thought it more fitting not to show too much anxiety, after executing a mission not very well calculated to please the Prince, and especially after having exhibited so much resistance and opposition.

At length I went thither. The drawing-rooms were furnished as they had been at the zenith of the fallen Sovereign. Somebody told his Royal Highness that I was there, for I noticed that he immediately glanced in my direction, and came straight through the crowd towards me. I bowed; his first and last words were:

'How are you, *Monsieur le Maréchal?* I have not seen you before.'

Fancying that there was a reproach implied in his words, I raised my head, and said:

'No, *Monseigneur*, I had obligations and duties to perform. I will carry them out equally faithfully hence-forward.'

At these words, *Monsieur* turned his back upon me, which at first confirmed my surmise; but a few days later chance gave me an opportunity of discovering that his Royal Highness had unintentionally addressed me as he did.

The Emperor of Russia invited all the marshals then in Paris, together with the Minister for War and the Duke of Vicenza, to dinner. No stranger, not even of his own nation, was present. His Imperial Majesty no doubt wished to avoid arguments, discussions, and differences of opinion which might have bad results. Questions of politics and of party are like questions of religion. Everyone keeps to his own belief, the only difference being that soldiers argue more hotly.

The Emperor wished to talk freely to us and put us quite at our ease. The events of the war naturally furnished the chief topic. His Majesty never ceased praising the virtues of our soldiers: their obedience, devotion, knowledge, talent, heroic bravery, nay, rashness, their keenness in battle, their humanity after victory. He returned again to the subject of the feat of arms at Fère-Champenoise, and the splendid resistance offered by that handful of conscripts to the forces that surrounded them. 'I saved their lives in spite of themselves!' he said.

What astonished him above all was the manner in which both officers and men endured, without a murmur, such long and frequent privations, regarding all their fatigues as nothing. His Majesty spoke kindly of Napoleon, pitying his fallen enemy for the necessity he had forced upon him (Alexander) of taking the lead in the coalition.

Someone audaciously asked him whether the cavalier manner in which Napoleon had broken off, almost as soon as they were set on foot, the negotiations for the hand of the Grand-Duchess, his sister, had not contributed to cool his former admiration, and to decide him to approach England. He replied that such was not the case, and that, notwithstanding the absolute authority with which the *Czars* are invested, they have none whatever over the daughters, who in all matrimonial matters are exclusively dependent upon their mothers.

He added that he had promised to use his influence with his mother, but that Napoleon, knowing what strong resistance would be offered by the Empress Dowager, and her hatred of him, and wishing to contract immediately, and at any cost, an alliance which should legitimize his sovereignty, had drawn back and ordered his Ambassador at Petersburg to proceed no further with his proposition. He had then given ear to the underhand insinuations that, if he would turn towards Austria, there was no doubt that the Ambassador representing that Power had authority to treat for a marriage. The Emperor Alexander had already had wind of this when Caulaincourt came to him charged with the painful duty of announcing Napoleon's renunciation of his suit.

'I might,' he added, 'have considered this rupture as an insult, and have been offended by it, the more so as I said at the time, and the Duke of Vicenza can bear me out: "For my own part, I consider this alliance suitable, but my sister is not yet of a marriageable age, and I fear that my mother will oppose it strongly. However,' I will try to change her opinion, and in time, which is necessary, moreover, to my sister's development, we shall perhaps succeed in overcoming her objections." Napoleon took these remarks as a refusal, and we heard no more about it, as it was purely a family question, and not one of government or of politics that touched my dominions.'

Such were the explanations given to us by this Sovereign regarding a circumstance which had, at the time, been very much discussed privately, and of which very different views were taken. I am satisfied of the correctness of the story, for it was afterwards corroborated to me by the Duke of Vicenza, who told me further how extremely difficult his position had been.

The Emperor then turned the conversation to our official and private correspondence, which had been intercepted and deciphered so that he could read it.

'*Monsieur le Maréchal*,' he said, turning to me, 'some of your reports that we have seen have been very remarkable, as also your letters to your children, and their answers. They appear to be very fond of you.'

I begged the Emperor to have the goodness to cause them to be restored to me. He replied that they were in the hands of his sister, the Crown Princess of Wurtemberg, who had been charmed with them, but that he would ask her for them. I know not whether he forgot his promise, but the fact remains that they have never been given back to me. ,

Returning to the subject of the official correspondence, I said with a smile:

'It is not surprising that your Majesty was able to decipher it. Your Majesty had been given the key.'

He looked very grave, laid one hand on his heart, and extended the other.

'I give you my word of honour,' he said, 'that that is not the case.'

I alluded to the desertion of General Jomini[2], chief of Marshal Ney's staff, who had gone over to the enemy, carrying with him all the papers and documents relative to the situation, after the denunciation of the armistice in August, 1813.

Monsieur, Lieutenant-General of the kingdom, gave, in his turn, a dinner to the marshals and a few generals. We were not yet accustomed to seeing the Tuileries inhabited by a new master, who had so easily obtained possession of it, and who a few months previously had certainly had no idea of being there. He must, at times, have felt as much surprised as we were.

The prince received me with his well-known grace, which entirely dissipated the idea that he was prejudiced against me on account of my last visit.

---

2. *The Campaign of Waterloo, 1815* and *The Art of War* by Antoine Henri Jomini, also published by Leonaur.

The dinner was served with Napoleon's plate, glass, and linen; the imperial monogram did not seem to hurt the eyes of the newcomer then; his susceptibilities grew more delicate later. *Monsieur* was in very good spirits, did the honours courteously and kindly, and ate a good dinner. At dessert he proposed the health of the King. We bowed, and responded by the customary cry of '*Vivat!*'

Conversation turned upon various circumstances of the war, but so as to wound no feelings. *Monsieur* ended by praising loudly the virtues of the King his brother, his profound and extensive knowledge, his wit, and, above all, his prodigious memory, which was true enough; but what was less true, was the assurance that he gave us of his admiration for the deeds of arms, and the great talents of the French generals during two-and-twenty years, filled with celebrated and surprising warlike achievements.

In this connection the prince gave a word of praise to each of us. In short, we were much pleased with the attentions and politeness of *Monsieur*.

All they who, like me, have had opportunities of talking to King Louis XVIII., have been able to convince themselves of his indifference to military matters. I was one of the commanders of the Royal Guard, and he never put a question to me concerning my regiment.

The King was expected at Calais on April 24. It was intimated to us that His Majesty would have pleasure in receiving his marshals at Compiègne; and we went thither accordingly. The Duke of Ragusa and the Prince of the Moskowa preceded us, the former as bearer of a mission from the Provisional Government; the latter as having a mission of his own, namely that of congratulating the King in the name of the army and its leaders. They were both in advance, and met the King a league beyond Compiègne.

We awaited His Majesty's arrival, and entered the castle behind him. The Prince of Neuchâtel, who was at our head, made a speech, in which, with better right, he expressed himself as the real mouthpiece of the army.

The King interrupted him, in order to declare his appreciation of the step we had taken, and the pleasure he felt at seeing us, adding that he regarded us as the firmest pillars of the State, and that it would always be a satisfaction to him to lean upon us. He rose from his chair at these, words, and emphasized his meaning by placing one hand on my shoulder and the other upon that of one of my colleagues. We replied suitably.

The King presented us to the Duchesse d'Angoulême,[3] to the Prince de Condé, and to the Duc de Bourbon. The princess, whom I observed attentively, was dressed with the utmost simplicity; her demeanour and features were cold, thoughtful, and stamped with melancholy. I could not help identifying myself with her sad recollections, which were rendered still more poignant when, some days later, she went to the Tuileries and occupied the apartments of her unhappy mother. She herself told me this recently, when I returned to take up my abode in the Palace of the Legion of Honour, where both you and I, my son, experienced so terrible a domestic loss.

The two Princes murmured a few words, which neither my comrades nor I could hear.

The King invited us to dinner with him. Scarcely were we seated at table than, raising his voice, he said:

'*Messieurs les Maréchaux*, I send you some vermouth, and drink to your health and that of the Army.'

Fearing to neglect the proper etiquette, we rose and bowed to express our thanks. We ought to have replied by the cry of '*Vivat!*' which was formerly customary; but we were not men of former days, nor brought up at Court. However, we told the Prince de Poix, Captain of the Guards, that we had been in a difficulty, and that the fear of doing something incorrect had alone prevented us from drinking the King's health. He replied that it would have sufficed to ask His Majesty's permission to do so, but promised to tell him of our intentions, and of the praise worthy motives of our discretion. On our return to the drawing-room the King was most agreeable and gracious to all of us. After giving the orders, he saluted us, and we retired, delighted with the reception given to us by His Majesty.

Next day, at the hour of Mass, we returned to the castle. The King sent for us one by one, and addressed to each some complimentary words: then, making conversation general, he told us that he knew the army needed reorganization, and that, in order to carry it out, he begged for our opinions. I imagine that it was because I was right in front of the King, and most immediately under his eyes; but whatever the reason, he said to me:

'*Monsieur le Maréchal*, what is yours?'

---

3. The daughter of Louis XVI. and Marie Antoinette. She was the only child of her parents who survived the Revolution, and helped her husband, the Duke d'Angoulême, in resisting Napoleon on his return from Elba. Napoleon said of her that 'she was the only man of her family.'—Translator.

'Sire,' I replied, 'if your Majesty wishes for a plain opinion, deign to create a Council of War, taking the presidency thereof into your own hands. Every plan will be prepared in a sectional committee for each branch of the service, discussed and decided upon by the Council, and remitted to the Minister for execution. As to appointments, a triple list will be drawn up by each section, discussed and decided upon at a general meeting of the sections, and transmitted to the Minister. From these lists he should select names for the approval of the King. This Council should of necessity be composed of the heads of the army. Their experience in affairs, the knowledge they possess of the capacity and talents of their subordinates, will be a guarantee for good selections, and for justice and due regard to all. The Council, however, should only have a consultative vote, so as to prevent a possibility of the recurrence of the difficulties experienced by that of 1787, which impeded ministerial action. However, much good resulted from that Council, among other things the exercises and manoeuvres, which are still employed, and which only need to be modified and improved. The groundwork is so good that nothing better will ever be produced, although there are plenty of people quite ready to try.'

The other marshals having said that that was also their opinion, the matter dropped.

The King then said that, if we were staying at Compiègne, he hoped to see us at dinner. We expressed our thanks, but answered that we were anxious to return to Paris, in order to make his warm reception of us known to the Army, as well as his kind inclinations towards it, and so we took our leave. We were absolutely enchanted. We communicated to the generals and chief officers who had been under our command our hopes and the spirit with which we were animated.

On May 2 the King came from Compiègne to St. Ouen, where he slept, in order to make his entry into the capital. The inhabitants of Paris were ready to receive him with sincere and joyful demonstrations after reading a royal declaration dated from that place. We were invited thither, but remained forgotten during the reception of the foreign monarchs, deputations, etc. At length the King sent for us, and excused himself by saying that he had not been informed of our arrival, and that, had he known of it, he certainly would not have kept us waiting. It would have been impossible to make a better reparation to us for the carelessness of his court officials.

CHAPTER 32

First Steps towards Unpopularity

The declaration of St. Ouen had a wonderful effect upon the king's entry, which took place on May 4. A great majority of the population, even from the environs, crowded into the capital and greeted him with hearty acclamations. The marshals had been summoned to join the procession. We surrounded the royal carriage, containing the Duchesse d'Angoulême on the left of the King, and the Prince de Condé and the Duc de Bourbon facing him. His Majesty bowed graciously, and from time to time pointed out the duchess to the longing eyes of the crowd, as though to say:

'See this unfortunate princess; here she is, the only one who escaped the revolutionary axe!'

I saw some ladies at windows in the Rue St. Honoré so moved that they either fainted, or else pretended to.

The procession went to the cathedral, where the King was present at the solemnization of a '*Te Deum*' to return thanks, and then to the palace of the Tuileries. What memories must have recurred to the royal family at sight of those walls, which still bore traces of the fury of August 10!

There was a grand parade of troops in the courtyard, and among them were the remains of the Old Guard, who had been brought by a forced march, and, I believe, in one journey, from Fontainebleau. They had first been drawn up in line at the Porte St. Denis, without being allowed time to shave or wash themselves, and thence they had been brought at the double into the courtyard. It was believed that the King would pass through their ranks, but, whether from fatigue or indifference, he would pay no attention to this troop, although much pressed to do so.

It was a great mistake, and sowed the first seeds of that discontent of which, ten months later, the fatal consequences were felt. This famous regiment was not even permitted to take the duty at the Tuileries, although one of their battalions had given every satisfaction at Compiègne, and had been on duty all the time the King remained there.

Such neglect was deeply felt by these brave fellows, who had formerly had alone the privilege of guarding Napoleon and the *Château*.[1] By another fatality, which was not without its influence upon their discontent, no lodgings or quarters had been provided for them; and when at length they succeeded in obtaining private billets, every door was shut. There was no ill-will in this; the fact was that everyone had gone out to see the king's entry, and had taken advantage of the fine weather to remain out-of-doors.

I was informed by a lady of my acquaintance, possessed both of good sense and courage, that on her return from a visit to her parents she found several grenadiers disputing with the porter, who refused to admit them, notwithstanding that their billets were in perfect order, because his masters had not come home. They merely asked leave to rest in his lodge until their return. In refusing this the inflexible Cerberus had apparently made use of some contemptuous expressions, for the soldiers had laid hands on him, and he would have had a very disagreeable experience had not, luckily for him, my friend appeared. On learning the reason of the dispute she scolded the porter, threatened to have him dismissed, and, turning to the soldiers, said:

'My friends, it is a shame that you should be treated thus! Come in. You need refreshment, but everything is shut up. Porter, hasten to the baker, the pork-butcher, and the wine-merchant, and see that these gallant fellows have everything they require immediately!'

Her presence and consideration disarmed the anger of these veterans of the Guard, but she could not get them to cry, 'Long live the King!'

I suppose that many incidents of a similar nature occurred that day in Paris, and were not forgotten; and consequently, at the first news of Napoleon's landing, these soldiers remounted the tricoloured cockades and flocked to him. Much mistrust and many mistakes and follies contributed to increase the discontent.

The Dukes of Berry and Angoulême arrived soon after. The first, like his father, had had the good sense to put on the uniform of the

---

1. The Tuileries palace was commonly known as the *Château* during the period of the Restoration.

National Guard; the second, on the other hand, was dressed in an English uniform! The marshals had been commanded to go and meet him. The sight of his impolitic costume displeased us no less than his cold reception of us. He scarcely saluted us, and roughly asked his brother, at the same time pointing at us in ,turn:

'Who is this? What is that man's name?' and so on.

He was also very coldly greeted himself, although there were many people in the streets; but they went rather out of curiosity, and the warmest feelings were frozen by the sight of the uniform of our bitterest enemies. This was perhaps increased by a rumour which had gained wide circulation, that he ill-treated, and even beat, the Princess.

I repeat this statement, or rather this gossip, for what it is worth, because those who have the best opportunities of observing, remark on the contrary that this couple seem very fond of each other, full of sympathy and thought for each other; and this is especially noticeable in the princess, for whom my respect, attachment and devotion are very deep.

A Council of War had just been created, I know not whether by the will of the King or whether his minister, having heard of the conversation at Compiègne, and fearing that one might be forced upon him, took the initiative. I incline towards the latter belief, simply on account of the various selections made among the lower grades, whereas it had been stated at Compiègne that it should only necessarily include the heads of the army, the marshals, principal Controllers of Ordnance and Supplies, and some generals who had commanded army-corps.

A few days later I went to the *Château*. The King was on his throne, but not in state; some few persons were in the hall, amongst others the Duke of Wellington. His Majesty, seated, wearing his hat and playing with his walking-stick, desired me to approach, and, after introducing the duke to me, with whom I exchanged a few polite words, said:

'Well, you ought to be satisfied. I have formed a Council of War; what do you think of it?'

'Your Majesty's object has not been attained,' I answered. 'The minister has composed it of soldiers dependent on him who are in want of employment or promotion, and who on that very account, will be his very humble servants, docile to the opinions and wishes of his Excellency, so that your Majesty will never know anything except what it pleases the minister to show.'

'You are right,' replied the king; 'I will change and correct that.'

The modification consisted in the addition of three marshals, and I afterwards learned that the King insisted upon my being one of them. Dupont[2] had long known my independence, and our intimacy enabled me to superintend everything and say what I pleased. He would no doubt have been glad to avoid this alteration, which later on would have been of great service to him; but he could not keep me out after the formal expression of the king's wishes.

At length we met. The minister entered, holding a sort of provisional plan, the nature of which we could not learn, for he said that His Majesty demanded the immediate attendance of the Council.

'You want to play us a trick, my friend,' said I; 'but take care, I will speak out before the King.'

On reaching the *Château* our meeting began, under the presidency of the King, who had beside him *Monsieur* and his sons. Dupont sent to beg me to make no objection. He read his report, after which His Majesty asked for our opinions. When my turn came, I remarked that the report had been read too quickly for me to form any opinion, and asked that it might be printed, which was granted.

The Council of War was summoned to the *Château* for the second and last time. The printed copies of the report had been circulated just as we were starting for the Tuileries. Matters had been carefully arranged so that there should be no discussion.

In opening the meeting the King said that the breaking up of the armies had become so important that, since our first meeting, he had been obliged to order it, and to partition the regiments among the garrisons; that consequently our meeting became objectless for the moment; that he begged us to study the plan of organization; and, finally, that he would let us know his intentions later. We were never summoned again.

Thus vanished this dream of a Council of War, which, over and above the advantage of bringing together valuable opinions and experience, would have assured to the army that unity which is always so desirable—uniform instruction, precision, good fellowship, and, above all, the best choice of officers. Instead of this, preference was given to favouritism, decorations and promotion were lavished upon the incapable and careless, while merit languished and vegetated in subordinate ranks; the old *noblesse* invaded everything, and deep-seated

---

2. It seems strange that such a man should have been put over the greatest marshals and generals of France! *Vide infra*, chapter 28 note 2.—Translator.

discontent began to ferment. The princes also dispossessed, without any compensation, those who held the post of chief inspectors of the different Arms of the Service, and who ranked immediately after the marshals.

The Legion of Honour, instituted as a reward for merit of every kind, was thrown open to everybody, and it became evident that the intention was to discredit and deprive it of any value. But I must say that the Order of St. Louis was distributed with equal prodigality. The royal Government behaved like an invalid, who allows everything to take its chance without any supervision.

I have anticipated events, however, and travelled far from my Council of War. The sitting was occupied with narratives of military events, and parallels drawn between opposing generals. The King took considerable interest in the conversation, and after some hours declared the sitting closed.

During the brief existence of the Council of War, another political body was deliberating upon and discussing the constitutional Charter, based upon the declarations of St. Ouen. The Legislative Body of the Empire had been temporarily preserved. The ancient peerage, re-established but enlarged, formed, as in England, the Upper Chamber; the other one took the name of Chamber of Departmental Deputies.

I was created a peer, and at the royal sitting of June 4 took the oath; at the first business meeting of the Upper Chamber, I was elected one of the *Sécretaires du bureau*. The drawback to this distinction is that one must be very assiduous, and that one is very much tied, and I soon became so tired of it that, notwithstanding many requests, I have always since declined the honour.

The military divisions were erected into governorships. I had the twenty-first, of which the principal town was Bourges. I had been given my choice, and had taken that, as it brought me near my property. At the same time all the marshals were appointed Knights of St. Louis, and successively Commanders and Grand-Crosses of this military Order, which was revived, as were the other ancient Orders, without abrogation of the law abolishing them: such was the tendency to absolutism.

The object of the first Bill brought before the Chamber of Peers was to correct the abuses of the press. I fancied I discovered in it a violation of Article 8 of the Charter. I spoke and voted against it, and my little speech was considered very military. Notwithstanding strong opposition, the Bill passed by a majority of one, the numbers being fifty-six for and fifty-five against! This happened merely because one of my intimate friends, who had promised to vote with us against it, wrote 'yes' on his voting-paper. I saw him do it, and tried to seize the paper, but he had just time to drop it into the ballot-box. We should have had the majority on our side but for that. By what little threads do the destinies of Bills hang!

It is one of the functions of the *Sécretaires du bureau* to lay before the King the Bills that have passed. On receiving us, and after a few words addressed to one or two amongst us, Louis XVIII. spoke to me in a severe tone, fixing upon me his eyes, which were penetrating as those of a lynx.

'*Monsieur le Maréchal*, I am surprised at your having spoken and voted against this measure. When I take the trouble to draft a Bill, I have good reasons for wishing it to pass.'

'Sire,' I replied, 'your Majesty did not take me into confidence with regard to your Bills. They ought all to pass if they are drawn up by your Majesty. If the initiative is to belong to your Majesty alone, they might as well simply be registered, and we might remain dumb like the former Legislative Body. If, however, I have correctly understood the intentions of the Charter, it gives to every individual freedom of opinion and vote. I fancied that in this Bill I discovered a violation of Article 8, and I employed that liberty conscientiously, as I shall always do.'

The King made no answer, bowed to us, and we retired. Scarcely had we left the presence, when the Chancellor said to me:

'*Monsieur le Maréchal*, was that the proper way to address the king?'

'What do you mean?' I retorted; 'did I fail in respect to His Majesty?'

'No, not exactly; but you should have been more reserved, less blunt.'

'By which you mean that I should either have concealed the truth or displayed regret. I have never learned to twist myself, and I pity the King if what he ought to know be kept from him. I shall always speak to him honestly, and serve him in the same manner.'

The King showed me his resentment for some time, but afterwards treated me with the same politeness as heretofore, and, when he came to know me better, was not displeased with my bluntness, although he was King. I have been told of his saying on several occasions:

'His outspokenness tells me such and such a thing.'

The Court was daily losing ground in public opinion. It seemed as though the ministry and their agents were vying with each other as to which should give proof of the greatest folly, and the surroundings of the King as to which should exhibit the greatest haughtiness and conceit.

At this time the office of the Legion of Honour was presided over by a priest, the Abbé de Pradt, formerly chaplain of the god Mars. He suppressed the orphanages, which are now branches of the royal house at St. Denis. The relations of the pupils, their friends, and the members of the Order complained aloud, and numerous petitions were presented to the Chambers. I was a member of the committee of my Chamber, and was ordered to report upon those which put forward just complaints.

I conferred with the representative chosen by the other Chamber to report,[3] and we proceeded to make inquiries—first at the Legion of Honour itself. The Chancellor of the Order informed us that economy alone had prompted the King to take this step. The reason was a weak one, as educational establishments had as much right to public money as the members of the Order. Had they been treated with the barest justice, the subscriptions to them should only have been reduced by half; but more consideration should have been shown to widows and their children, because, in losing their husbands and fathers, they had lost their only means of support. We said that we should state to the proper quarter our reasons for advising the repeal of this impolitic order of suppression. The *abbé* admitted that there was some truth in what we said; but he thought that the order was too recent to allow of its revocation by the King, and begged us to let a short time elapse before bringing it about.

'No doubt,' I said ironically, 'and meanwhile the children will be sent away, the furniture sold, and later on it will be said that the funds are so low that they will not admit of the re-establishment of these houses! *Monsieur l'Abbé*,' I continued, 'you are concealing your real motives from us; we have a duty to perform; how we perform it must largely depend upon the amount of confidence you place in us. Speak frankly.'

He again protested that there were no reasons save that of economy; but from his hesitating manner we saw that he was deceiving us.

As we could get nothing more out of him, we went to the *superioress* of the Orphanage. She had as good grounds for complaint

---
3. Baron Lefèbvre.

against the Chancellor as Madame Campan,[4] whose establishment at Écouen had been suppressed, but most of the pupils in her house had been, at any rate, transferred to that of St. Denis. The suppression of the house at Écouen had been hurried on, in order that the property might be given to the Prince de Condé, although it had been given in perpetuity to the Legion of Honour by the sinking-fund (*caisse d'amortissement*), which had. I believed, purchased it from the State.

The *superioress* had had difficulties with the Chancellor, and attributed the suppressions to the personal dislike of the *abbé*. She told us that, having gone one day to the Grand Almoner to ask his protection for her community and pupils, the Chancellor had come in, and had been very angry with her for giving any information or details without his knowledge. She felt certain that the *abbé's* action arose from motives of personal animosity and a desire to avenge himself. She also complained of his correspondence, saying that she was thwarted in every attempt she made to improve the position of her pupils. It was quite likely that some of her complaints were tinctured by feminine bitterness; we took heed of nothing, except what could help us to discover the real reasons for this suppression.

We went next to the Grand Almoner, who told us that the Chancellor had been very much irritated at the visit paid to him by the *superioress*, and at her prayers for support and protection, but added that the *abbé* had always told him that the pecuniary position of the Legion required this economical step.

We agreed to take no notice of the complaints of the *superioress*, seeing that they were personal, and perhaps exaggerated, and to take as the basis of our respective reports the arbitrary manner in which the suppression had been effected, for, as I have already said, the educational houses had the same privileges as the members of the Order, having been created at the same time. Moreover, a few years later public money had been specially devoted to them, independently of their general funds. This annual contribution still exists, but other needs and circumstances appear to have interfered with its application.

The feelings of the members of the Order and of all the soldiers were clearly expressed; a portion of the public echoed them, not only in connection with this administrative action, but with many other causes of complaint What was the use of nourishing this discontent?

---

4. Whose *Memoirs of the Court and private life of Marie Antoinette* have been published both in France and England. (*Marie Antoinette and the Downfall of the French Monarchy* by Imbert de Saint-Amand, published by Leonaur).

It seemed to me that the important thing for us was to obtain the repeal of the order. Would speeches help us? They would probably only increase the opposition. The idea then recurred to me of negotiating the matter with the Minister responsible for the Legion of Honour. I suggested this to my colleague. He was a warm partisan of the opposition, a good fellow at heart, with excellent qualities; I had known him a long time. At the first mention of my proposal, he shook his head, but I soon brought him round, and without very much difficulty, adding that, if our negotiation failed, our hands would be strengthened. We agreed, therefore, to draw up our reports as though they were to be laid before our respective Chambers, and to seek an audience with the minister of the King's Household.

Monsieur de Blacas received us immediately, and seemed surprised, because he believed, as he told us, that the measure had been taken in the interests of the Order; he had not really investigated the matter, and had confined himself to laying before the King the report and proposed ordinance that the Chancellor had sent him. He opened a drawer and showed us the original report, and also the budget of the Order, which had not required him to make any profound calculations, for the proposal to reduce the salaries by half could be carried out by a stroke of the pen. We asked him to lay our reports before the King, and to let us know His Majesty's intentions with regard to our request for the repeal of the ordinance.

Some hours later the King sent for us, but the deputy of the other Chamber was nowhere to be found. As punctuality was necessary at the audience, I went alone. Monsieur de Blacas was with the King, and no one else. When I entered His Majesty rose, gave me his hand, and said:

'My dear Marshal, I thank you for the delicate manner in which you have set to work to enlighten and inform me of the truth. I only approved the measure because I was assured that it was in the interests of the Order; the true reasons, which you have put in so clear a light, were not placed before me. Therefore, it is with the greatest pleasure and alacrity that I revoke my ordinance.'

I thanked the King in the name of the Order and of the families interested, and added:

'Had your Majesty been better informed, you would, I feel sure, have maintained, or even created, these establishments, had they not been already in existence.'

'Certainly I would,' said the king; 'and in order to give you, my dear Marshal, a token of my satisfaction and confidence, I charge you with the task of drawing up the ordinance and re-establishing the orphanages.'

I withdrew highly pleased. On reaching home, I found my colleague, Baron Lefèbvre, formerly *intendant*-general of the army, and at that time occupying the same post in the Parisian National Guard. When he heard my story and the success of our joint inquiry, he lost his temper because he had thus missed his opportunity of declaiming against the arbitrary abuse of power, and had had nothing for his pains but the trouble of drawing up his report.

When my work was done, I took it to the Minister, who said:

'The Abbé de Pradt knows all that has been going on, and is very uneasy. He has asked the King for temporary leave of absence, and His Majesty is much inclined to comply with his request, only with an extension to perpetuity.'

The ordinance was published in the next day's *Moniteur*, and produced great delight, especially among those interested; but this triumph cost the Legion a large sum of money. Most of the pupils had been sent, with all their outfit, to their relations, who did not care to bring them back to school, and preferred to enjoy, until their twenty-first year, the modest pension of 250 *francs* (£10) which was allowed them to continue their education. It was, therefore, necessary to nominate fresh pupils, and provide each with an outfit.

Shortly afterwards a golden bridge was built for the Abbé de Pradt to bring about his resignation. He was granted a pension of 10,000 *francs* (£400) and the *grand cordon*, and this produced a very bad effect, which was heightened by the appointment of his successor, a general officer, a former *émigré* attached to the Court, and the favourite, it was said, of the heir to the Crown.

CHAPTER 33

Indifference of the Government

Heated debates in the Chambers, violent party spirit, a widespread distrust of the Court, regiments infested with *émigrés*, privileged bodies, in which the best places were prostituted to boys who had scarcely left school, while mature and excellent officers, bending under the weight of years, and scarred by honourable wounds, were vegetating on half-pay, ignored and almost despised by the newcomers—such was the general condition of affairs. The State could no longer profit by the revolutionary confiscations, for a simple ordinance had replaced the members of the royal family in possession of the lands not already sold.

Although the principle of the measure was just, the form in which it was introduced was wrong. An entire repeal of all the laws of the Revolution respecting national property should have been proposed. The ordinance of restitution, therefore, excited great discontent and much alarm. The former possessors worried and threatened the purchasers, amongst whom the most timid consented to friendly arrangements, transactions and indemnities, but they were not even then quite reassured. The majority kept possession, and threatened in return. The clergy, who since the Consulate had only been salaried, now wished to recover their property; but there was a great difference: they only had the usufruct of it, and so they were allowed to complain notwithstanding the insults and attacks that were uttered from every pulpit, the threats of eternal perdition made in every confessional to the weak or the dying, if they did not restore their lands and bequeath them to the Church.

On the other hand, the soldiers murmured at having lost their extra pay for service abroad, and saw with jealousy their more favoured comrades who retained theirs on the canals Of course, those in the highest places made the loudest outcry. All positions are relative; like them, I had lost the endowments that had been given me in Naples and Poland, but I had had the good sense to treat this increase of my means as merely temporary, and I regretted it the less therefore.

The Government seemed utterly indifferent to this state of things, and did nothing to remedy it. It only appeared to be carrying on constant petty underhand intrigues on behalf of its supporters, and more avowed ones on behalf of its members. One of the boldest among them insulted France and the national army with its 'right line,' in the Chamber; another, weak, wily, and ambitious, issued a police order which covered him with ridicule; an ex-minister of the Empire, so servilely, so abjectly devoted to his master, but not less ambitious than the other, ventured, in the Chamber of Peers, to pronounce these words, so agreeable to absolute ears:

'What the King wills, the Law wills.' ('*Si veut le Roi! si veut la Loi!*')[1]

Amid these various conflicts and discontents, and this feeling of discomfort, moderate men of sensible and conciliatory dispositions united, and sought means to calm the effervescence. The best plan, it was thought, to restore confidence and tranquillity, to revive security, and provide a guarantee for purchasers, and to improve the positions of *donees*, would consist in an equitable indemnity for all goods sold, the restitution of unalienated goods, and the division of the indemnities among the *donees*, beginning with the most needy. The State had profited by the confiscations, therefore the State owed the indemnities; nothing could be more rigorously just.

I felt this, and perhaps expressed it more strongly than others, and was consequently requested to make a proposal to the Chamber of Peers, where it was thought that my voice would be better heard, that, my words being listened to more favourably, would produce more effect, rally more supporters round the proposal, and do much to ensure its success. I fought against the proposal for a long time, but yielded at last to the consideration that I might be able to render a real service to the public and to the unfortunate soldiers.

A Director of Customs had the kindness to furnish me with an important memorandum, showing how the lands had been valued to the prejudice of the *émigrés*, those condemned to death or transported. Several of the people—M. Ouvrard among the number—gave me excellent suggestions, which were of value to me for the develop-

---

1. The Duc de Feltre. See chapter 40.

ment of the proposal. Everyone contributed his utmost. Sémonville and Monsieur de Castellane gave me the benefit of their experience and opinions, as did also the Duc de Lévis, who was my colleague in the Chamber. He and I had several interviews upon the subject; the duke, being hard pressed by his creditors, was personally interested in the success of the proposal.

It has been since said that Sémonville took the principal part in this matter, and there is some truth in the statement, as it was he who first mentioned the idea of indemnities to me. But other persons were interested in it, and it was in consequence of their union and their common support that I undertook to introduce the subject, as reporter of the commission which commanded the opinion of the majority.

After hearing the proposal, hope rose in many breasts, but several people were much disappointed. People who had cherished the idea 'that the Restoration would mean absolute restitution with interest came to me, the Duke of Fitz-James among others. He said:

'All or nothing!'

'Very good, Duke,' I replied; 'then it will be nothing.'

Then the soldiers, especially Marshal Ney, complained that I had restricted the indemnities to the humblest classes, whereas, they said, the rich had equal rights.

'I have thrown down a plank,' I answered; 'everyone will get across in turn. Had I done otherwise people would have been afraid. Besides, observe the difference: they who have been dispossessed by confiscation demand justice, while they who have been endowed have lost through the fortune of war, which also brought them their wealth. Their fortune was simply an act of favour, whereas the others had everything torn from them by the Revolution, with its blood, its horrors, its persecutions, its injustice, and its iniquities. It rests with you to bring up amendments and support them; I shall make no opposition.'

My proposition was afterwards referred to a committee, of which I was naturally one of the members; but after a few meetings it was found impossible to come to any conclusion, for the torrent of claims for indemnification opened such a chasm that Europe itself would have been inadequate to fill it. The final result was the law of December 5, 1814, allowing restitution for unsold property; the rest was adjourned.

During the session I had taken more or less part in political discussions. The following one was no less fertile in important debates, into which I was naturally drawn by my position.

Secret discontent was increasing, especially in the army. The Congress of Vienna '*dansait et n'avançait pas,*' as the Prince de Ligne wittily remarked. Austria showed herself haughty, vain, ambitious, and pretentious. Monsieur de Talleyrand, the French plenipotentiary, recommended his Government quietly to make some military dispositions, to send some troops to the frontiers under pretext of change of garrisons.

The princes of the Royal Family made various journeys through the departments, the object of which was to attract supporters to the royal cause. But wherever they went they failed by their own fault, in spite of the prodigality of their promises and the prostitution of decorations, especially of the Legion of Honour, which grievously hurt old soldiers who received none. They were all given to intriguers, and to partisans of the moment. To such an extent was the abuse carried, as well as the indifference to every good feeling, that they were distributed by dozens to prefects and sub-prefects, who decorated their friends, their flatterers, and their creditors with them! The princes were only surrounded by men of their own party, saw none but men of the old regime, and displayed the barest politeness to those authorities who had not been removed merely for want of men to replace them. Thus their Highnesses learned nothing, saw nothing, since they viewed everything only through the eyes of people who were passionately attached to the old order of things; hence arose violent murmurs and discontent.

The Duke and Duchess of Angoulême were sent to Bordeaux, and had to pass through the departments belonging to my government. I went to the chief town in order to do the honours to them, on their journey. I received their Royal Highnesses at the frontier of the department of Cher on February 28, 1815, and accompanied them to the boundaries of that of Dordogne. I was very kindly received by them, especially by the duchess. The recollection of her misfortunes bound me strongly to this princess, and I vowed to her a devotion which has never faltered for an instant; until now I have always had cause to be gratified by her constant marks of kindness. There were perhaps rather fewer decorations than usual during this journey, and some of them, owing to my intervention, were well placed.

CHAPTER 34

Landing of Napoleon

I returned to Bourges on March 5, intending to pass my time between that place and Courcelles, which was only twenty leagues off; but twenty-four hours after my arrival, during the night of the 6th, a courier brought me urgent orders to betake myself immediately to Nimes, to receive further instructions from the Duke of Angoulême, whom I had just quitted, and, as a preliminary measure, to march all the troops in my government to Villefranche, in the department of the Rhone. The ministerial despatch gave no reasons either for this precipitate movement or for my departure. The same courier was bearer of a packet for the Duke of Angoulême addressed to Bourges, though his itinerary ought to have made it clear that by that time—the evening of the 5th—the prince should be at Libourne.

I racked my brains to discover what extraordinary events could have happened, and naturally concluded that it was the result of the Prince de Talleyrand's requests from Vienna for decided demonstrations on the frontiers, and I thought that the massing of troops at Villefranche and Nimes was intended to show that France had means at command to support her demands against Austria. I imagined that similar gatherings were taking place in the departments on the Rhine and on the northern frontiers, but I was very far out in my reckoning.

During the night of March 7, a report from General du Coëtlosquet, Commandant of Nevers, to Lieutenant-General Lepic, his direct superior at Bourges, and which was at once communicated to me, announced

The Landing of Napoleon

and the arrival of *Monsieur*, brother of the King, on his way to Lyons. All my former conjectures tumbled to pieces I was thunderstruck by this intelligence, and then predicted the misfortunes which have since befallen France.

I started a few hours later. Had I received the minister's packet when near Limoges, I should have gone direct from there to Nimes by the Toulouse road; but I had come back to Bourges, and the road by Lyons was more direct.

On reaching La Charité, I learned that the Duke of Orleans had just changed horses there, hastening on his way to join *Monsieur*, who had a start of twenty-four hours. I was anxious to catch up this prince, whom I had known in the first campaign of the Revolution, when he was serving with the army of Dumouriez, to whom I was acting as *aide-de-camp*. Fortunately, he stopped to have luncheon at Pougues, otherwise I could not have caught him, as I had had great difficulty in procuring horses at La Charité, because the prince travelled with three carriages.

He told me all that had been known in Paris before his departure, from the landing of Napoleon and his rapid march upon Grenoble, the garrison of which it was believed would resist him.[1]

---

[1] 'To show you the confidence that I had in the disposition of the army,' said the Emperor, 'I need only recall to you an event perpetuated in history. Five or six days after my landing at Cannes in 1815, the advanced guard of my little army met the advance of a division marching from Grenoble against me. Cambronne, who commanded my troops, wanted to address them, but they would not listen to him. They also refused to receive Raoul, whom I sent afterwards. When I was informed of this, I went to them myself, with a few of my Guard, with their arms reversed, and called out, "The first soldier who pleases may come forward and kill his Emperor." It operated like an electric shock, and "*Vive l'Empereur!*" resounded through the ranks; the division and my Guards fraternized, all joined me, and advanced together to Grenoble. Near Grenoble the brave Labédoyère, a young man, disgusted by the conduct of the *misérables* against whom France had fought and bled for so many years, joined me with his regiment. At Grenoble I found the regiment, in which, twenty-five years before, I had been captain, and some others, drawn up on the ramparts to oppose me. No sooner did they see me than enthusiastic cries of "*Vive l'Empereur!*" were heard, not only from them, but from the whole of the National Guard and the townspeople: the gates were pulled down, and I entered in triumph. What is singular, and strikingly shows the sentiments of the troops, is that almost in a moment the six thousand men by whom I was thus joined mounted the old tricoloured cockades, which they had kept as treasures when the army had been obliged to adopt the Bourbon anti-national flag. I advanced to Lyons, where I was joined by the very troops charged to defend it against me, and the Comte d'Artois was happy to escape, escorted by a single dragoon, from the city he had commanded a few hours before. To all his entreaties, offers, and prayers, "*Vive l'Empereur!*" was the sole response.' O'Meara's *Napoleon at St. Helena* (edition of 1888), vol. 2.

'At any rate,' I said, 'we can count upon General Marchand,[2] as he hates Napoleon personally, and is his declared enemy. Therefore you may count upon his fidelity, as well as upon his endeavours to resist and avenge himself.'

I travelled with the prince as far as Moulins; there we had to part company for want of horses, and I was obliged to wait for the return of his, so that he had a start of several hours.

At the last stage, while the horses were being changed, I received a letter from *Monsieur*, who had just learned from the Duke of Orleans that I was following him, in which he begged me to lose no time in reaching Lyons. He sent me also a confidential letter, written by the Captain of his Guards, Count des Cars, to say that his position was very precarious, that Napoleon had advanced so rapidly as to be within one day's march of Lyons, and that the garrison showed such bad feeling that he could not trust it to defend the passage of the Rhone.

I entered the postmaster's house in order to read and answer this letter. So well had the secret of its contents been kept, that, on coming out of the house to give my letter to the courier, I found a large gathering of engineers collected, and to them the courier was relating all that was known at Lyons concerning the march of events and the spirit of the garrison! This was confirmed by the postilion, and was practically the contents of my letter from Count des Cars.

I started at last and very rapidly, but just outside the town an axle of my carriage broke, and it upset. I was none the worse for my fall, but the accident occasioned a further loss of time, as I was obliged to walk the rest of the way. On reaching the hotel where I was in the habit of stopping, I found two officers waiting to conduct me to the house of the Governor, where *Monsieur* had dined; a third came up immediately afterwards to bring me to the presence of his Royal Highness.

It was between nine and ten o'clock on the night of the 9th of March. The authorities of the town, as well as the generals and colonels, were with *Monsieur*. He knew from the Duke of Orleans that I was on the way to Nimes.

'The roads are intercepted,' he said to me, 'and you can no longer pass. Remain with us, take the command; I give you plenary powers.'

The prince then told me that no reliance could be placed upon the troops, and that he had given orders to evacuate the town early next morning. My surprise was extreme.

'Abandon Lyons!' I exclaimed; 'where, then, will you stop after

---
2. This General was in command of the 7th Military Division.

quitting the barrier of the Rhone?'

'We have neither ammunition nor guns,' he replied; 'the troops have declared plainly that they will offer no resistance, and the majority of the population is with them and against us.'

The situation beyond a doubt was very serious and critical.

'Let us try something before giving up,' I said; 'let us suspend our retreat; we can always come back to that if necessary, for, if Napoleon is within a march of the town, let him make as much speed as he likes, he cannot arrive until between one and two o'clock in the day, as he' has to lead wearied soldiers. Let us assemble our men at six in the morning, see them, speak to them; we may gain something by it. We will try to change their opinion by attacking them on the subject of their honour, always a delicate point with a Frenchman. We will explain to them the misfortunes that must result from a civil war, and the danger to France, no less great, of seeing all Europe raised in arms against her for the second time.'

My advice was unanimously agreed to, and orders were given to countermand the evacuation, and to summon all the garrison to meet next morning in the Place Bellecour. Having accepted the command, I ordered that all communication between the two banks of the Rhone should cease; that all boats should be brought over to our side and moored there; that strong outposts should be placed on the right bank and along the roads; that the Morand and De la Guillotière bridges should be barricaded and put into the best state of defence that time would permit; and, finally, that a succession of patrols and reconnoitring parties should be sent out so as to give us the promptest information. In a word, I made all the dispositions that can be made in a campaign when troops are in front of the enemy. Particular commands were assigned; each officer had a certain number of troops and posts to establish and watch. These points settled, I finished by ordering a ration of brandy to be served out before the review, and we separated.

On reaching my hotel, accompanied by the generals in command, I asked them to speak to their chief officers and to do their best to induce the men to give Monsieur a good reception at the review. I spent the night in giving orders and obtaining information.

Between three and four in the morning General Brayer, who had command of one of the territorial subdivisions, came to me; he had served with me through part of the campaign of 1813 and that of 1814. He came to tell me that the men refused to be reviewed by the

Princes, but that they would be delighted to see me, their old General. I was thunderstruck at this news.

'Who can have put that idea into their heads?' I asked. 'Are we on the eve of a fresh revolution? Is every bond of discipline relaxed?'

'No,' he answered; 'they have been excited by some public-house speeches; the officers are not less excited. So many follies have already been committed! So little interest has been taken in the soldiers, and so many injustices done in order to make places for *émigrés*, *chouans*, and Vendeans, upon whom rank, honours, and distinctions have been showered!'

'From your manner,' I said, 'I gather that you share these opinions.'

'I do,' he replied; 'I agree with them; but I will do my duty to the end.'

(You will very shortly see, my son, how that duty was performed.)

'It is getting late,' continued Brayer: 'it is more than time to warn *Monsieur* not to appear before the troops, to prevent him from being insulted and received without respect.'

I rapidly considered all the consequences that this might produce; but how could I undertake to make such a communication to His Royal Highness? What would happen if he attempted to brave this warning, as he very likely would? A brilliant idea occurred to me, and I promptly set about carrying it into effect.

On entering *Monsieur's* apartments I found his officers standing about waiting till he awoke. I remarked that the communication I had to make to him would brook no delay; Count des Cars entered his bedroom and announced me. I told his Royal Highness that the reports I had received during the night regarding the state of mind of the men were no better, and that I had thought that his presence might be a constraint upon them; that perhaps it would be better if I saw them alone, being accustomed to war and soldiers, and being one of themselves—to use an expression in vogue at that time; that they could express their opinions more freely, and that I would send to let him know at the earliest favourable opportunity. From this the prince could guess or penetrate my real motive; he learned it later, but not from me. I returned to my rooms to wait till the troops were drawn up in the Place Bellecour.

I was vexed that the weather was wet, but I was still more annoyed on learning that no rations had been served out, that it had been impossible to find during the night either the commissary-general to sign the orders for the regiments, or the storekeeper to give out the brandy.

At the time fixed for the review, General Brayer came to fetch me; he had brought me a horse, and we started in pouring rain. As we reached the Place, on the right of the troops, acclamations broke out, and were repeated as I rode down the lines. Many inquisitive people mingled their voices with those of the men, but no other name or titles except my own were distinguishable.

This beginning seemed to me a good omen; I was deceived by it, and soon found out the fact. I ordered a square to be formed, and rode into the middle of it, so as to be the better heard by everyone.

I began by thanking them for their reception of me, flattering myself that it arose from a recollection of the care that, from duty as well as from attachment to my men, I had always taken of their comfort; this has been the constant preoccupation of my long military career. I continued by saying that I highly recognized their loyal services, their devotion in good and bad fortune; that though we had succumbed at last, it had at any rate been with honour, and that it had required all the armies of Europe, as well as some great blunders on our own side, which could not be imputed to us, to bring about results that could not have been prevented. I added that they all knew that I had been the last to submit, and that thus we had fulfilled our obligations, but that, released by the will of the nation, we had contracted others, not less sacred, to which the Royal Government would find us equally loyal; that the invasion that had collected us at Lyons would let loose upon our fatherland misfortunes even greater than those of the previous year, since then ancient France had remained intact; but this time the allies would make us pay dearly for a fresh appeal to arms. I cannot remember what more I said to stir these men; they heard me in silence.

I was very excited. I finished my speech by saying that I had too good an opinion of their fidelity and patriotic feelings to think that they would refuse to do as I did, who had never deceived them, and that they would follow me along the path of honour and duty; the only guarantee that I asked of them was to join with me in crying: 'Long live the King!' I shouted this several times at the top of my voice. Not one single voice joined me. They all maintained a stony silence; I admit that I was disconcerted.

My attempts on the other squares were equally fruitless. The word seemed to have been given to all the troops.

While making similar attempts on the cavalry, I sent for *Monsieur*, hoping that, notwithstanding what had been reported to me during the night, he would be received respectfully, if not cordially, as I had at first been. I also wished that the prince should be a witness of my endeavours, and that our common efforts might succeed in overcoming this obstinate and dreary silence; but we failed a second time. We had come to the last regiment, the 14th Dragoons, if I remember rightly. The prince went up to an old and decorated trooper, spoke to him kindly, and praised him for his courage, of which he bore the proofs on his breast. The dragoon—I can see him now—stood motionless, impassive, with staring eyes and open mouth. His colonel and several officers, who were shouting '*Vive le Roi!*' with us, addressed him by name, exhorted and pressed him, but he remained unshaken. *Monsieur* was crimson with anger, but had the good sense not to show it.

We did not let the troops march past, but sent them straight to their respective positions and quarters, arranging for the defence of the bridges and fords over the Rhone as though in presence of an enemy. I then told *Monsieur* that we might perhaps be more successful if we made another attempt upon the officers by themselves. They also had displayed coldness, but they might have felt some awkwardness in presence of their men.

I therefore gave orders that they should all assemble in my rooms, from the general down to the youngest sub-lieutenant. I begged His Royal Highness meanwhile to visit all the bridges, so as to make sure that the defence works agreed upon the previous evening had been carried out. The prince liked the idea, and started for the Rhone, while I went to the meeting.

CHAPTER 35

Retreat

There was such a large muster that my rooms could not contain all who were present; the staircases were crowded. I entered upon my subject by saying all I could think of best calculated to stir their loyalty, no longer foreshadowing, but proving to absolute certainty, all the dire misfortunes that would come upon France and themselves. I saw that they were very animated, excited and eager. The bitterest and most stinging reproaches were heaped, often disrespectfully, not only upon the Government, but upon the King and Royal Family. Loud were the complaints made of prodigality, unfair distribution of promotions and decorations, neglect, and contempt of former services. I, of course, tried to lay these faults at the door of the ignorance and intrigue by which the throne was surrounded;[1] further,

I said that the King, whose intentions were good and pure, would, when he was better informed, apply a prompt remedy to these grounds of complaint, which I undertook to communicate to him, and for which we would find redress, but at this moment our country was to be served and saved.

Vainly did I exhaust myself for two hours, holding my ground against all these men, who, without personal rudeness to me, spoke their minds very freely. It was easy to see why the troops had remained so silent; they took their cue from their officers. There were several

---

1. In 1814, when Masséna was presented at Court, or when he went to take leave of the King on departing for his command at Marseilles, the great personages by whom His Majesty was surrounded cleared but very narrow space for him to pass through. He had no sooner delivered a few words than he found himself without the circle. Masséna frequently alluded to the clever way in which they cut him off and separated him from the King. 'When I was on the field of battle,' said he, 'I did not employ so much dexterity in making my prisoners.'—Madame Campan's *Memoirs* (edition of 1883), vol. 1.

grounds of complaint referred to *ad nauseam,* and one of these was the formation of the King's Household, a corps of officers taken exclusively, and most unwisely, from the ranks of the old aristocracy, with the exception of one or two representatives of the new nobility. What was called a 'trooper' ranked as an officer, nay, as a superior officer; a sub-lieutenant of the household was a lieutenant-colonel, and so on. Complaints upon this subject were, unfortunately, too well founded; and their anger at seeing a lot of beardless boys dressed in uniforms resplendent with gold lace, and nearly all decorated with ribands, and with the epaulettes of superior officers, was excusable.

I repeat that all they said upon this subject, allowing for some exaggeration, had foundation in fact; but I could not succeed in making them understand that, in our critical position and difficult circumstances, the destiny of the country depended absolutely and entirely upon them. They had made up their minds to take their chance of that. They were determined not to fire upon the Grenoble troops that had deserted. I succeeded in extracting from them a promise to hold their positions and to retaliate if they were attacked, but this promise seemed to me weak, and was given with a very bad grace. There was nothing more to be gained, and I was worn out with the long and profitless discussion, so I dismissed the officers, and only kept back a few generals who thought with me. We went together to *Monsieur*; from our sad and downcast looks he guessed that our attempts had failed. In giving him an account of what had passed, I told him that we could not reckon upon any defence being made, that discontent and bitterness had taken possession of every heart, and that, as His Royal Highness's presence was no longer necessary, I begged him to depart at once.

'And what will you do?' he asked.

'I shall stay where I am; I have nothing to fear from the soldiers, but I fear there may be danger for you.'

'No,' he answered; 'I shall stay, if you will not come with me. After the proofs of devotion you have given, I will not leave you alone exposed to the turn of events.'

'I repeat, *Monseigneur,* that I am running no risk; you have given me the command, I will exercise it to the last moment. Some incident may arise favourable to your cause; I will seize and turn it to advantage. But in Heaven's name start; time is flying.'

He seemed inclined to remain, and, I appealed to the officers to support me. The Duke of Orleans, who was present, also declared his intention of remaining, with or without *Monsieur*. The latter eventually yielded, but required the Duke of Orleans to accompany him, an order which he had regretfully to obey. At length *Monsieur* decided to get into his carriage. He charged me to send counter-orders to the troops on the road to Lyons, so as not to bring them into contact with the garrison. Their dispositions were supposed to be better, but an electric spark seemed to have produced the same feelings all through the army.

Monsieur told me that he had passed along the quays and bridges of the Rhone, that no defensive preparations whatever had been made, that he had distributed money in order to hasten the work, and that he had received a promise that it should be begun at once.

At last, to my great relief, I saw him start, escorted by some mounted National Guards,[2] some *gendarmes*, and a detachment of the 14th Dragoons. His departure took a great weight off me, for the presence of the princes had become very embarrassing. If they had been taken by Napoleon or arrested by the garrison, they would have been held as hostages for his personal safety; and had such an event occurred, royalist public opinion would have made me responsible. It would have gone even further, and accused me of giving them up!

No doubt there would have been plenty of witnesses to justify me, including the princes themselves, but the idea would have spread rapidly. It would have been impossible to refute it at first, and then one would have had to write volumes to destroy it; for once the name of treason is pronounced, however innocent the accused or suspected person may be, headstrong men will refuse to be convinced, and will always believe that it had foundation in fact.

I could quote many instances; I will give but one, the execrable assassination of the Duc de Berry.[3] All the evidence went to show that the crime had been conceived and carried out by the scoundrel who committed it, and by no one else. Even now there are plenty of these violent men who believe that this crime was the result of a conspiracy. The only satisfactory point in this terrible misfortune was the imme-

---

2. 'The mounted National Guard (who were known Royalists) deserted the Duc d'Artois at this crisis, and in his flight only one of them chose to follow him. Bonaparte refused their services when offered to him, and, with a chivalrous feeling worthy of being recorded, sent the decoration of the Legion of Honour to the single volunteer who had thus shown his fidelity by following the Duke.'—Bourrienne's *Memoirs of Napoleon* (edition of 1885), vol. 2.

3. Second son of the Comte d'Artois (Charles X.), assassinated by Louvel, February 13, 1820.—Translator.

diate arrest of the detestable murderer; had he not been taken, suspicion and distrust would have lain upon all the 'constitutional party,'[4] without exception. There are still a considerable number of people, on the opposite side, who believe it; but the opinion is losing ground, and remains only in a few of the densest heads. In spite of party differences and political animosity, there was but one voice throughout the land, and that was raised to call down the vengeance of the law for the punishment of this abominable crime.

Although I was somewhat calmed by the departure of the princes, I was far from being easy. The minds of the men, of the officers, and, I must even add, of the generals of the 19th military division, seemed to become more excited as the decisive moment drew nearer. I sent for the *prefect* and the mayor, and while waiting for them telegraphed[5] a short message about the state of affairs to the Minister for War, of which he only received the heading:

'Marshal Macdonald to the Minister for War.'[6]

Monsieur had desired me to send it, and to announce his departure for Paris with the Duke of Orleans. I had also carried out the prince's orders about halting and retiring the troops that were marching towards Lyons. I shortly afterwards learned that the *prefect* had quitted the town; the mayor alone arrived.

At the meeting of the officers they had promised me that if attacked they would fire in retaliation, but that they would not take the initiative. From that moment I resolved to bring the combat to close quarters; but as I was warned that our soldiers would not fire first, I thought that among so large a population as that of Lyons it would be easy to find twenty or thirty devoted men, or men who would be won over by the promise of gain and reward. It would only be necessary to dress them in the uniform of the National Guard; my plan was to place them at the advance posts, in front of the troops, to put myself at

---

4. The term 'constitutional' (*constitutionnel*) is applied to all those who followed the Revolutionary movement while detesting its horrors, and who openly rallied themselves under the protecting shield of the Charter; the others are the inveterate adherents of the old regime and of absolute power.—Note by Marshal Macdonald.
5. The semaphore telegraph had been brought to great perfection during the reign of Napoleon.
6. This message was no doubt intentionally curtailed. Three years previously London had been thrown into dismay by the accident of a sudden fog coming on during the transmission of the semaphore signals from Plymouth, and for some hours a message remained incomplete, beginning, 'Wellington defeated at Salamanca . . .' [the French under Marmont on July 22].

their head, and fire the first shot. This stratagem might be successful, if the engagement became general, and our soldiers decided to imitate our shooters. I know from experience how very slight a matter will suffice to change men's opinions.

Hitherto Napoleon had met with no opposition.[7] A few battalions and squadrons only had joined him, but an unexpected resistance, although so far in the centre of France, at the entrance of a town of such importance, with the Rhone as a barrier, ought to make him reflect, and recall to his mind the courageous defence made by the town against the Republican army.[8] The troops he brought back with him, wearied and disgusted with their sojourn in the island of Elba, must have before their eyes the fear of being sent back thither, and the dread of an even severer punishment. Finally the garrisons of Grenoble and Vienne, seduced and led away as they had been, might recognize that they had made a mistake, and repent of it.

Such were my illusions; but, weak as was my hope, what would happen to Napoleon if my dream came even partially true? What proves that my reasoning was not entirely without some foundation is, that when I was at Bourges, after the submission of the army, I heard from the grenadiers who had been in Elba, and who were garrisoned there, that they had been delighted to return to France, but if they had met with the slightest resistance, the smallest obstacle, or even a single shot, they would have thrown down their arms and sued for mercy. This I heard from all ranks, men, officers, even the commander himself.[9]

When the mayor entered my room, I told him of my intention. He was the only civil official who had remained at his post. I was surprised at hearing him answer that he would not be able to find a single man to do what I wanted.

'It is impossible,' I cried, 'that a town which defended itself so valiantly in 1793 in support of the Royal cause should not now contain one single veteran of that date burning with the same zeal?'

---

7. The subjoined skit of the year 1815 may serve to show how the landing of Napoleon was regarded:

'*What news? Ma foi! The Tiger has broken out of his den. The Monster was three days at sea. The Wretch has landed at Frejus. The Brigand has arrived at Antibes. The Invader has reached Grenoble. The General has entered Lyons. Napoleon slept last night at Fontainebleau. The Emperor proceeds to the Tuileries today. His Imperial Majesty will address his loyal subjects tomorrow.*

8. In 1793.

9. See chapter 42.

The mayor shook his head. I dismissed him.

After having arranged an appearance of defence, and even offence, if I could only succeed in bringing my troops back to their duty, I rode in the company of the Governor, Viscount Digeon, Count Jules de Polignac (*Monsieur's aide-de- camp*, whom he had left at my disposal), some other generals and staff-officers, to visit the posts, and to see for myself what obstacles had been prepared to stop the advance of Napoleon. I was not surprised to find that little or nothing had been done; the money that *Monsieur* had distributed had been quietly pocketed. The communications between the banks had not been interrupted; the order to bring the boats across and moor them on our side and to guard certain fords had riot been carried out. The same remark applied to the reconnoitring parties, which should have been sent out to announce the approach of Napoleon's scouts. This piece of neglect made me particularly angry, and I severely scolded the general officer charged with this duty. I sent out myself some patriots in echelon, and after making a few more arrangements, I went from the Guillotière to the Morand bridge.

The disaffection that I met everywhere gave me good grounds for fearing a complete desertion and a catastrophe; I therefore gave private orders to have the horses put to my carriage and to have it taken to the outskirts of the suburb of Vaise, at the junction of the roads towards the Bourbonnais and Burgundy respectively, so that I could follow either one or the other according to circumstances if I were compelled to retreat. At the Morand bridge no barricade had been made. It was guarded by an iron gate; nobody knew where the keys were. I gave a man ten *louis* (£8) to go and buy some chains and a padlock. My money went the same way as that of *Monsieur*.

As I quitted this bridge on my way back to the other, I noticed the bustle caused by the return of a reconnoitring party. It could not have gone very far, and had no doubt seen or met what we must call the enemy. What had happened? My anxiety was great, but it was ended by the arrival of a staff-officer, who galloped up to me and said:

'A reconnoitring party has just returned.'

'What has it seen?'

'Napoleon's advance-guard.'

'Far away?'

'Just coming into the suburb of the Guillotière.'

'What happened?'

'The two parties drank together.'

'Hasten to the Place Bellecour, bring up the two battalions in reserve there; place one on each side of the bridge.'

The quays were crowded; boats were coming and going, transporting to the left bank the inquisitive people who could not cross the bridge occupied by our troops. The latter were ready to advance—to do their duty, or to betray us? As I reached the bridge-gates, cries of '*Vive l'Empereur!*' burst from the other side of the river. On the quays the crowd took up the shout, and echoed it in a deafening manner.

I instantly put into execution the design I had formed of making some show of resistance. I intended to gain the head of the bridge with my staff, stop the first men who appeared, seize their weapons, and fire. The bridge was blocked by troops in columns.

'Come along, gentlemen!' I cried; 'we must get down.'

We jumped off our horses and hurried along on foot as rapidly as we could, but scarcely had we reached a quarter of the distance when the 4th Hussars, Napoleon's advance-guard, appeared at the other end of the bridge. At this sight officers and soldiers mingled their cheers with the shouts of the populace; *shakos* were waved on bayonets in token of delight; the feeble barricades were thrown down; everyone pressed forward to welcome the new arrivals to the town.

From that instant all was lost. We made our way back, and remounted our horses; there was no time to lose, for I rightly imagined that the 4th Hussars would meet no resistance at the Morand bridge, and they might reach the suburb of Vaise before us by following the quays, which is what eventually happened.

General Brayer, who was still with me, on hearing me give orders for the immediate evacuation of Lyons, took off his mask, and said:

'It is useless, *Monsieur le Maréchal*; all measures have been taken to prevent your departure.'

'Surely, sir, you know me too well,' I answered, 'to suppose that I can be easily stopped. I shall know how to make myself respected, and to make a way for myself with my sword.'

He moved towards his men without replying. But another obstacle presented itself. The crowd had become so compact that it would have been vain for me to attempt to pass through it, had it not been for the arrival of two battalions of reserves which I had summoned with the intention of posting them on the right and left sides of the bridge. The mass had to give way to admit of the passage of the troops. I took advantage of it to march with the column, making gestures to them as if to indicate where they should go. There was such a noise that it would have been impossible to make one's self heard. Having at length reached the rear of the column, I went along the quay. Colonel Dard, of the dragoons, whose regiment was not far away, came and asked me for orders; without stopping, I said:

'Get your horse and follow me.'

'Whither?'

'To the Bourbonnais high-road.'

I think his regiment refused to obey him, but am not certain, and have never been able to discover positively.

As we crossed the Place Bellecour, Comte Roger de Damas, governor of the 19th division, which was drawn up in the square, wished to stop. He was very confident, and had taken no precautions. I pointed out that it was now too late, and that the slightest delay would cause his arrest. He ran great risks, and had everything to fear, as a former *émigré*; but he would not be convinced, and went to his lodgings, while we started at full gallop. He had the good fortune to make his escape in disguise.

A little farther on I met *Monsieur's* escort returning. As we passed I gave orders to the officer in command to follow me with his detachment, adding that the regiment was behind us, and we pursued our road with the same speed, when, in the middle of the suburb, we met a brigadier and four hussars from Napoleon's troops, who had come by the Morand bridge and the Quai de Saône, and who barred the way; they were all drunk.

The brigadier advanced to seize my bridle, crying:

'General, surrender yourself!'

He had scarcely uttered the words when, with a blow of my fist on his ear, I knocked him into the gutter, whence he had sprung. A *hussar* threw himself upon General Viscount Digeon, who said:

'What! You scoundrel, would you dare to arrest your General?'

'Oh, is it you, General Digeon? You must join us.'

The General imitated my method of disposing of his man, as did also Viscount de Polignac and the others who were behind us.

I was wrapped in my cloak, and was only distinguishable by the white plume in my hat. The appearance of the hussars had been so sudden and unexpected that we had had no time to draw our swords. On looking round to see if we were being followed, I saw that the detachment of dragoons had passed the *hussars* without taking them prisoners, whence I concluded that they were in league with them, and that they would arrest us if they could catch us; we therefore pressed on faster.

On the way General Digeon kept repeating to me that he knew a short cut to the Bourbonnais high-road, but while we were seeking about for it we reached the extreme end of the suburb. At the moment of the catastrophe, I had sent my courier on ahead with orders to send my carriage forward. It had been standing there for several hours, with my *aides-de-camp* and my secretary. The postilions had got off their horses, and were probably in some public-house they could not be found. I threw a sad glance at my carriage, which contained a considerable sum in gold. One of my *aides-de-camp* handed me a pocket-book through the window, but we passed so swiftly that none of us could seize it.

Poor General Digeon, somewhat upset at having missed his short cut, did his utmost to induce me to take the Burgundy road instead of the Bourbonnais, which I knew very well. He had mistaken the two. As we galloped on he said:

'We are on the Burgundy road; there is a very bad feeling abroad there. You will be taken.'

I could neither calm him nor convince him that we were on the right road. A short distance ahead I perceived two *gendarmes*' horses tethered to a post without their riders. We might, by signal or otherwise, have them unfastened and brought after us, for ours were so tired that they could scarcely move. I gave orders that the *gendarmes*' horses should be untied. We were still pursued by what we believed to be enemies; they had even gained upon us somewhat, but at last they slackened their speed, and we were compelled to do the same, as our exhausted horses had of their own accord dropped into a walk.

About a mile from the Tour de Salvagny, the first stage on quitting Lyons, I saw a general officer coming towards us. It was Simmer, who had been through the campaign of 1813 with me, and had served with great distinction. I had met him the previous day coming from Clermont with two battalions. He had received my orders to halt, and was on his way to Lyons for fresh instructions. Surprised at finding me on the road when he thought me still in the town, he asked what had happened. My only answer was:

'Have you any fresh horses to lend me?'

'Yes.'

'Then go and have them saddled and bridled.'

He started at a gallop. I did not lose sight of the detachment that was pursuing us; we had drawn away from it somewhat. At last we reached the post-house. The two battalions were under arms, and received me with proper honours. Some of my party thought they noticed some national cockades among them; I did not myself. The horses were soon ready, and we changed immediately, and taking General Simmer aside, I told him in a few words what had happened, and said:

'Order your troop to retreat.'

'They would not obey.'

'Then leave them, and follow me.'

With these words I started again, and the general remained behind.

Poor Digeon, preoccupied with the fear of being taken, suddenly perceived the white plume in my hat, and implored me to remove it. I hesitated, but at length, in order to pacify him, I pulled it out and tore it to pieces as we were galloping along, and notwithstanding the inconvenience of the wind and the rain. Just then his horse stumbled and fell; fortunately he was only scratched, and soon was in the saddle again, though we had to go rather more slowly. I noticed that our companions were a long way behind. They had probably found no horses at the post- house, and I was much afraid they would be taken; but I could not have saved them, and should only have been arrested as well. I presumed they would have presence of mind to strike into the cross-roads and into the open country.

In this state of doubt we galloped on, when we saw in front of us some horses being led. General Digeon, who expected to meet his along this road, concluded that they had passed the night at Tarare, and that those would be his horses. As his sight was very bad, he did not recognise them until we came close up to them. This was a piece of luck. We instantly jumped down and saddled and bridled them ourselves. Those we had left were very hot; they either smelt or saw the water of a little stream which ran near there, and we let them go. As we were remounting we perceived some horsemen far behind us, without being able to discover whether they were our companions or our pursuers. Away we went again.

As we passed through Tarare, a man leaning against a door, with a cotton cap on his head, greeted us with a feeble shout of '*Vive l'Empereur!*' On reaching the foot of the mountain, where carriages stop to have extra horses harnessed to them, I felt too faint to go any farther without having some food. I had not dined the previous evening, and had eaten nothing all day. It was then between four and five in the afternoon. We were told that *Monsieur* was about half-way up the hill, which is very long. We were very anxious to catch him up to tell him what had happened, and I, especially, to get a lift in his carriage, for I could scarcely sit my horse any longer; my skin was already broken.

Poor General Digeon, who had not yet got over our meeting with the hussars in the suburbs of Lyons, wished to push on; but I needed time to breathe; my horse's action was so uncomfortable that it had produced a violent pain in my side; his trot would have been much worse. There were only two of us, and without quitting my saddle, I asked him to keep watch while I was brought some bread and cheese and a glass of wine. I ate very little of this frugal repast, only just enough to satisfy my immediate needs. The general ate in his turn while I kept a lookout. I do not think our halt lasted more than eight or ten minutes. We started off again at a gallop, notwithstanding the hill, and indifferent to the fate of our horses; what was important to us was to catch up the carriages, which we should otherwise have missed.

We came up with them just as they were at the top of the hill. On seeing us, *Monsieur* guessed what had happened, and offered us places in his carriage. I accepted; but as I was dismounting, Digeon said to me in a low voice:

'Don't get in; we shall be taken; they will go very slowly and will want to stop.'

'All the more reason,' I returned; 'we will hurry on, or share the same fate.'

Possessed with his idea, he continued on horseback, but did not, however, get beyond the next stage, where he was very glad to find a place in the carriage containing *Monsieur's* staff. His Royal Highness gave me a seat beside himself, that, I believe, of the Duke of Fitz-James Count des Cars, Captain of the Guards, and the Duc de Polignac, Equerry, completed the party.

CHAPTER 36

Ney's Desertion

It would take too long to report our conversation during the journey. It first turned upon the chief event of the day and its causes; the discontent which was universal, but especially rife in the army; the choice of ministers, their incapacity for governing, their untimely opinions, their uselessness, and that of their agents. I must do *Monsieur* and his officers the justice to say that they seemed thoroughly alive to the mistakes that had been made. Were they in good faith? I think so; fear had worked wonders. *Monsieur* said that he would enlighten the King, and ask him to improve matters.

'It is too late,' I said; 'the impetus is given. But I cannot hide from myself all the misfortunes that are about to assail France at once—the smallest, which, at another time, and under different circumstances, would be the greatest, will be civil war in the departments of the West You yourself, *Monseigneur*, what have you learned of public opinion in the journeys undertaken by you or your sons? Nothing, except the opinions held by your partisans, who are blinded by their momentary grasp of power. You despised the men who could have advised and assisted you to good purpose. They understand matters, and to them the Restoration ought to have gone for its strength, or, at any rate, for a better direction. You should have attracted the army, received it well, identified yourself with it, noticed your officers; they would have fraternized together. Confidence once established, intimacy would soon have followed. They would have become the links in a great chain, and more openness and loyalty, if not attachment, could not fail to have resulted.'

All these remarks were considered true and sensible. My hearers answered:

'True, quite true.'

Monsieur added:

'Well, I myself have often thought of taking general officers as *aides-de-camp*; forty or fifty offered me their services, but the fear of hurting the feelings of the majority of them induced me to postpone my decision.'

'It would have been better,' I replied, 'to run the risk of offending a few people. You would have been compensated by the advantages accruing from the establishment of friendly relations, which would have been valuable to you on your rounds of inspection, by bringing into stronger relief the good qualities of the Royal Family.'

This conversation bore fruit, for, on his arrival in Paris, *Monsieur* took as his *aides-de-camp* Viscount Digeon and Count Bordesoulle.

We stopped to dine at Roanne, at the house of a certain Flandre, the post-master. I only cite this fact, as he afterwards fell a victim to a lying denunciation, which the authorities never took the trouble to verify. At that time—I am now speaking of the Second Restoration—sentences of dismissal were very common. Flandre was accused of having refused to supply *Monsieur* with horses, whereas, on rising from dinner, we found the carriages harnessed, and were able to start at once. I know not what were the political opinions of Flandre, but he was so overjoyed at having received *Monsieur* under his roof that, while the prince was entering the carriage, he offered us a glass of some most delicious home-made liqueur, which *Monsieur* regretted having missed.

He was deprived of his appointment by the *prefect* of the department, either from motives of personal vengeance of his own or of someone else, or upon false reports that might easily have been verified, as the majority of the inhabitants witnessed the arrival and departure. What made me so angry was that all my efforts, all my attempts to bring about the revocation of this unjust sentence, were useless. At the moment of writing, my indignation is as great as it ever was.

Can anyone be surprised that people at length became embittered by so much injustice? I do not know whether application was made for the intervention of *Monsieur* or his officers; this, however, I do know, that 500 other post-masters simultaneously suffered the same fate.

We continued our journey without hearing any more of our pursuers. *Monsieur* reviewed a regiment of dragoons that was on its way to Lyons, and made it turn back. We only made a short halt at Moulins, to give us time to eat a very scanty breakfast, the *prefect* having been taken by surprise, and we being in a hurry. We reached Nevers that evening, and there the prince dined, and remained several hours consulting with the authorities as to the best means of defending the Loire. A very boastful General, Du Coëtlosquet, was in command of this subdivision of my government. He told His Royal Highness, and repeated it to me, that he was thoroughly in touch with the country; that, if he were provided with funds, he could immediately raise 4,000 men, and put the bridge in a proper condition of defence; in short, that he would answer for the future.

Monsieur asked my opinion. I shook my head; but noticing that His Royal Highness seemed to fancy this project, or rather this assistance, as a drowning man will clutch at anything, I replied that if in reality the general had as much influence as he said, we would not hesitate, although I considered the expense useless, seeing that in all probability Napoleon would take the direction of Burgundy, where he was more sure of finding public opinion in his favour and that is what happened.

Even supposing he had followed our road, he would not have met the obstacles that Du Coëtlosquet said he could put in his way, for a few days later we learned that either the very evening of, or the evening after, our departure a small boat containing a light, and apparently prepared for fishing purposes, had come near the bridge; that the news had spread that the general was going to set fire to it—the bridge was at that time on piles—and that thereupon a great riot had taken place. Du Coëtlosquet only escaped popular fury by hastening across country to Bourges without stopping. So this man, who had the effrontery to boast that he could dispose of the population, could not find a shelter in the whole length and breadth of his command.

After settling everything at Nevers, we reached Briare. It was Sunday. The prince wishing to hear Mass, I sent a request to the priest to celebrate a Low one. We went to church, but as it was the hour of High Mass, it was hopeless to persuade the priest, and not only had we to assist at High Mass, preceded by the sprinkling with holy water, but also at the sermon, with all the notices, etc. The priest was old, and very slow. *Monsieur*, pious and devout as he was, was much annoyed at it all; he displayed great impatience, and was red with anger, but, nevertheless, he very kindly received the priest afterwards while he was at breakfast. At length we started, and reached Paris next morning at five o'clock. The King was not awakened.

Monsieur de Blacas, minister of the King's Household, was waiting in *Monsieur's* apartments for his arrival. He said that the excitement was great; that the evacuation of Lyons was differently interpreted, as no details had as yet come to hand, and that there was much anxiety among the soldiers. He asked me what I thought about it. I replied that in all probability the story would increase like a snowball, and that, just as at Lyons, the troops would not attack one another, but that, all the same, measures should be taken, as a favourable opportunity might occur.

Monsieur begged me to go and rest. I went home, in truth sadly in want of it. I was in considerable pain from the chafing occasioned by bad saddles and indifferent horses. I had not taken off my clothes since March 8, and it was now the 13th. I went to bed, but was unable to sleep, for, notwithstanding the care I had taken to forbid my door, it was forced open, and many people came, rather from curiosity than interest.

Next day, to my great astonishment, my carriage, which I thought had been taken at Lyons and lost, was restored to me; it was a very pleasant surprise. Everything was intact, and my *aides-de-camp* told me they had met with no difficulties whatever. I had taken a considerable sum in gold with me, as I thought that I was going to keep house for some time at Bourges, and later at Nimes, for which place I was bound when events stopped me at Lyons, and compelled me to retreat.

In the course of the day I went to pay a visit to *Monsieur*. His Royal Highness asked whether I had seen the King. I answered that I had not.

'Go to him; he will be delighted to see you; he is very pleased with your conduct. Here,' he added, 'is a paper which His Majesty desired me to give you.'

'What does it contain?' I asked in astonishment.

'The King,' he said, 'has learned that you have lost your carriage, with all your effects and money. He does not wish that you should suffer for your devotion and good services.'

I replied that I was profoundly touched by His Majesty's kindness, but that, as I had lost nothing, my pride would not allow me to accept it.

'Take it, all the same,' said *Monsieur*; 'the King will be very vexed if you refuse.'

I stood out, and told His Royal Highness that my carriage had been restored to me without the slightest loss.

I then went to the King. His Majesty rose and gave me his hand, praised and thanked me for my zeal. I, in my turn, thanked him, and spoke to him of the conversation I had just had with *Monsieur*. The King pressed me to accept his offer, but ceased insisting when I told him that my devotion needed no encouragement, and that I did not consider I deserved a reward for having done my duty.

The King then told me he was organizing a corps of which he intended to give the command to the Duc de Berry; that I was to be his first lieutenant, and that a council of war was to be established.

'That is quite right,' I said; 'but as we have good reason to fear that our troops may desert, whither will your Majesty retire in case of being compelled to momentarily abandon your capital?'

The King exhibited great surprise, as though this idea had never crossed his mind.

'But,' said he, 'surely we have not come to that?'

'No,' I replied; 'but we may come to it in five or six days. Your Majesty must know what Napoleon's activity is. It will not take him longer than that to reach Paris. Unless he be stopped on the road, he will push forward rapidly, and there is no reason to believe, after what occurred at Lyons, that any regiment will show resistance.'

'I have great confidence in Marshal Ney,' said the king; 'he has promised to seize and bring him to me in an iron cage.'

'I believe,' I answered, 'that he will do his utmost to carry out his promise—he is a man of his word; but his troops may desert. Bad example is catching, and, unfortunately, the contagion is spreading.'

'I will think it over,' said the King, as he dismissed me. 'My Ministers are coming; I will speak to them upon the subject.'

They were absolutely incapable of giving any sensible advice, as they were panic-stricken.

At this council a royal sitting of the Senate was decided upon for the next day. I was summoned to take part in the procession, and the King, as he passed me, pointed to the medal of the Legion of Honour that he had been advised to wear. Nobody was likely to remark or be pleased by it. This Order, which was the reward of all services, and during the last years of the Empire almost exclusively of military services, held a high place in public opinion; it was consecrated by an article in the Charter; but after the Restoration the intention seemed to have been to debase it by the prodigality with which it was distributed.

The King was received with acclamation; he made a very touching speech. *Monsieur* and his sons threw themselves into his arms, swearing fidelity to the Charter. This scene electrified the Senate and the public. The King had declared that he would die upon his throne, and four days later he abandoned it. It must be said in fairness that he could not count upon any resistance being made to Napoleon.

The first council of war was much too numerously attended; there was too much discussion and too little action. I agreed with nobody; they all seemed to me too timid, as usually happens at meetings of this kind. Everything was afterwards concealed from me, although I was second in command; and the poor Duc de Berry, who was inexperienced, was bullied in order to induce him to do what was for the interest of individuals without regard for that of the public. .

I desired to give him some private information. I went to him on March 18; I criticised several measures, and spoke also about the steps that had been taken to keep me aloof, as people feared my vigilant eye, my honesty, and uprightness. The prince, already entangled, received my remarks and plain observations very badly. An excited discussion followed, which ended in my resignation, which I sent to the King with an explanation of my reasons for the step. The King was grieved, and would not accept it; but I was absolutely determined to take no further part whatever beyond loyally carrying out what I had sworn.

I begged His Majesty to tell me to which department he intended to withdraw in case of necessity. This time he was less reticent, and replied:

'To La Vendée.'

'All will be lost,' I said, 'if your Majesty goes thither. No doubt you have more partisans there than elsewhere, but the majority will take no active part, being tired and worn out with civil war. You will be pursued, the coast will be seized, and your retreat will become impossible. Go rather to Flanders. Feeling in the northern departments and in the Pas-de-Calais is better than anywhere else. Lille or Dunkirk offer you absolute security. You have exits by land and sea, close to the frontier, whence you can easily gain a foreign country in case you are threatened with a siege. Raise some battalions of royal volunteers; garrison the towns with them, if you can count upon none of the regular troops. One or other of these places will serve as a rallying-point for your adherents, and you can establish your government there for the time being.'

The King reflected, and said:

'The plan is not bad; we will wait for further news.'

The courtiers, who were not long in learning what had passed between the Duc de Berry and me, were sorry, especially for my resignation. I had become to them a sort of guarantee for my principles, since I had recently given proofs of them at Lyons.

In the evening of the same day the Duc de Berry sent for me; I was somewhat surprised at the message. On entering his room he offered me his hand, embraced me, and said:

'Let us forget all that passed this morning. The King has ordered me to put into your hands the management of military matters. We will work together. Henceforward you are in charge of everything.'

'It cannot be done so quickly as that,' I answered. 'Put on the orders that tomorrow, at ten o'clock, I will take over the command, and that all correspondence is to be addressed to me.'

At seven o'clock next morning the prince summoned me to come at once. I found him much agitated. His first words were:

'We are betrayed by Marshal Ney.'

'Impossible!' I exclaimed; 'the marshal is a man of honour. His troops have perhaps abandoned him, and taken him with them by force.'

'No, it is he who took them over to Bonaparte.'

'What proof have you?'

'Generals Lecourbe, Bourmont, and Clouet, the marshal's *aides-de-camp*, who have quitted him, have just arrived, and are gone to convey the news to the King. And my regiment too! Galbois has taken it over as well, and only yesterday he was swearing and protesting on his soul and body that he was loyal! I had treated them so well! They have deceived me abominably! But what are we to do now?'

'Come to a speedy resolution,' I answered; 'we must first send all the troops out of Paris to Essonne or Corbeil, on the two roads to Fontainebleau. All resistance is now out of the question. We must save the King and the Royal Family, and not expose them to be kept by force in Paris as hostages for Napoleon, for I feel confident that they would suffer no personal injury.'

While orders were being sent out, I was informed of the treasonable remarks that were being made in barracks. Just then *Monsieur* entered, and said that the King wanted me. I followed the prince to his presence.

His Majesty was calm; he gave me his hand, and said:

'Well, you know what has happened. What is to be done now?'

'Sire, you must go to Lille. I advise that the troops should be ordered to quit Paris with the view of favouring your departure. Assemble your military Household on the Champ de Mars, and announce your intention of reviewing your troops at Essonne. Once in the military school, you will be in safety.'

Several Ministers were present. The Minister of War had ordered the garrisons of the North to advance, and had assembled them at Péronne under the command of the Duke of Orleans; the Duke of Bourbon was sent into the West. The other ministers had taken no steps and made no preparations, such, for instance, as the emptying of the Treasury, for funds were very necessary, whether to raise a large number of royal volunteers, to attract the partisans of the king's cause, or to establish the Government at Lille. It was discovered later that a great deal, on the other hand, had been distributed to the generals, officers, and soldiers, the latter of whom were employing it in toasting Napoleon in the public-houses with loud shouts of '*Vive l'Empereur!*' There was good ground for fearing a mutiny. I sent word to the generals and officers that I should hold them responsible if the marching orders were not executed. I also recommended that, after the review, the King should return to the Tuileries, if the population of Paris remained calm, as his presence would restore confidence, and give time to make further arrangements; the proposal was approved.

The generals who had quitted Ney had reported to the King that he had said in announcing his determination, 'All the marshals are of my opinion.'[1]

They exhibited doubt and surprise, and one of them answered:

'Surely you do not include the Duke of Tarentum, for he has just shown at Lyons that his loyalty can be depended upon.'

'Oh, as for him,' answered Ney, 'we do not count him; and, what is more, we do not want him!'

As the King had told this story in presence of the princes, some of the ministers and myself, I fancied that his intention was to flatter me, and answered that I was delighted that the marshal was so well informed as to the sentiments governing my conduct; that certainly he had had a proof of them the preceding year, during the negotiations relative to the abdication, and that while he had deserted his

---

1. In 1815 the attitude of the marshals was as follows: Macdonald, Oudinot, St. Cyr, Victor, Marmont, Kellermann and Pérignon were on the side of the Bourbons—Augereau and Berthier were in retreat; and rather more than half and the ablest of the marshals were on the side of Napoleon, *viz*., Davoût, Soult, Ney, Suchet, Grouchy; and less actively, Murat, Mortier, Masséna, Moncey, Jourdan, Lefèbvre, Brune, and Sérurier. Bernadotte was on the throne of Sweden, and Lannes, Bessières, and Prince Poniatowski were dead.

master I had remained faithful to him until the last moment. I had many preparations to make and orders to give, so I asked the king's permission to retire.

CHAPTER 37

Plan of Escape

In the course of the day the King sent for me just as I was on my way to the *Château*, to inform him of the departure of the troops, who had obeyed their orders, but grumbling and with very discouraging remarks. On reaching the Tuileries I perceived the Royal carriages harnessed, an enormous crowd collected, greedy for news, officers hurrying hither and thither, pack-horses laden with portmanteaux. Everything looked prepared for departure, though the carriages were harnessed as though for an ordinary drive.

The King had desired me to come in civil dress, so as not to be observed or remarked. He told me he intended to go to the Champ de Mars, and that, according to the report I sent him of what passed, he would decide what to do.

After his departure I mingled with the crowd, and approached different groups. I heard no disloyal language, but various expressions of opinion upon the state of affairs, upon the effect likely to be produced on the troops by the King's presence, upon the absurdity of fifty old men armed with guns and halberds, most of them in the uniform of general officers and wearing various orders outside their coats, who were marching two and two towards the Tuileries to offer their services. I must admit that they did not look martial, and gave reasonable ground for amusement to the crowd that always finds something to laugh at even in the gravest circumstances.

The King had been gone scarcely half an hour when I saw him come back. Surprised at so speedy a return, I went to the *Château*. The crowd was increasing every moment, and made the kng anxious; I told him that from what I had been able to see and hear it meant nothing out very natural curiosity; that it was, moreover, a Sunday, and that the day was sufficiently fine to attract a large number of people to the Tuileries gardens. The carriages for the King and his suite were still standing in the courtyard. I begged him to send them away, because then the larger number of the inquisitive crowd would depart, and when the palace returned to its ordinary quietude the remainder would disperse at dinner-time, and my words proved correct.

The King had returned owing to a misunderstanding. He had met his military household marching towards St. Denis, a warning that they were, in case of necessity, to advance in that direction having been transformed into an order for immediate execution. The King had commanded it to retire, and, after marching past him, it had returned to the military school.

It was known that Napoleon would reach Fontainebleau that very day; he might travel post, cause himself to be recognized by the troops along the road, and bring them up with him; but not having positive information as to their feelings towards him, and not knowing how he would be received in Paris, although he had plenty of supporters there, he might naturally conclude that, as the King was still there, some measures of defence would have been taken.

These reasons, when I put them forward, were appreciated, and had the effect of tranquillizing the Royal Family for the moment. I then proposed to clothe a Swiss regiment in French uniform, to place it in advance of the troops at Essonne with orders to march upon Fontainebleau, as though to join itself to Bonaparte. The disguise would have deceived every eye, and had it succeeded in seizing his person or even in crossing swords, how many calamities would have been thereby spared to France! The Duc de Berry rejected the idea; the King said that if this regiment failed it would be very seriously exposed; I replied, crossly, that that would be better than compromising the monarchy.

Not only was the plan given up, but the King added:

'I see that all is now over. Do not, therefore, let us engage in useless resistance. I am determined to start. Try to bring our supporters into Flanders, and to get the regiments that went out this morning to follow us. No fighting, *Monsieur le Maréchal!* Recall to St. Denis all the troops that wish to return.'

'Allow me to point out, Sire,' I replied, 'that this determination is premature. The troops have barely reached the places to which they were ordered; we must let them rest. I will go to the headquarters at Villejuif, whither a courier can be sent to me with orders to hold myself ready to march. No one will know whether it is to be an advance or a retreat. An hour later, another express might bring me an order to follow you. I alone shall know the direction you have taken. Meanwhile, your Majesty will have prepared everything for your departure, and will enter your carriage between eleven o'clock and midnight.'

'But,' said the Duc de Berry, 'what if the sentinels of the National Guard, who are on duty at the palace, prevent our departure, as they did at the beginning of the Revolution to the unfortunate Louis XVI., when he wished to go to St. Cloud? What are we to do then? Are we to scatter them with the bodyguard?'

'No, nephew,' said the King hastily; 'we must not alienate the inhabitants of Paris.'

'I do not think,' said I, 'that the sentinels will oppose any resistance or put any obstacles in the way of the King wishing to review the troops at Essonne. But I have a scheme whereby every pretext for insubordination can be avoided. The King can place absolute reliance upon his household and servants. Very good. Let the gates and doors be shut at ten or eleven o'clock. The carriages can draw up at some distance off, or, if necessary, outside Paris. The King, on leaving his apartments, will gain the Pavilion Marsan through the palace; thence he will be carried in a sedan-chair to a hackney-coach, which will take him to his own carriage.'

The Duc de Berry suddenly interrupted me by saying:

'Pray, sir, where do you suppose we can find a chair large enough to contain, or two men strong enough to carry, His Majesty?'

This unexpected outburst made even the King laugh. He said that he would think it over, and commanded me to come that evening to receive the password which would be given as usual.

On leaving his room, the Duc de Berry asked me if I should start for Villejuif after the password was given. Upon my answering affirmatively, he said he should go thither also, and we separated.

As the inquisitive crowd noticed no further preparations at the *Château*, it dispersed, as I had foreseen, about six o'clock. When I returned to the palace at half-past eight, I found the usual quiet reigning in the courtyards, but the interior presented a very different spectacle. It was with great difficulty that I could pass through the drawing-rooms to reach the king's study; they were full of courtiers, some devoted, some curious, but all entitled to the *entrée*. The King came in, talked for a few minutes, gave the password, and withdrew, beckoning me to follow him. The princes were assembled in his study. On entering it the King said:

'My departure is fixed for eleven o'clock; I will carry it out according to your advice.'

'In that case, Sire,' I answered, 'I will take leave of your Majesty. As soon as I reach Villejuif I will give orders to the troops to hold themselves in readiness to march, but I will not move them until I receive instructions from your Majesty.'

'I am going there too,' said the Duc de Berry.

'*Monseigneur*,' I answered, 'I have been thinking that it is unnecessary for you to disturb yourself, as the troops are to come back. Your Royal Highness may follow the King to St. Denis, where I expect the troops to arrive between seven and eight tomorrow morning—if they will obey orders, that is. In any case, I shall be there at that hour with the staff.'

The King said that I was right. The prince replied that there was no reason why he should wait at St. Denis, as the troops were to continue their march, and that he would accompany *Monsieur* to place himself at the head of the King's Household, who were to start from the Champ de Mars. As I was about to withdraw, the King warmly pressed my hand, and said:

'*Au revoir*, my dear marshal; I shall never forget your zeal and devotion.'

The drawing-rooms were not yet empty. A general who had formerly emigrated, and who was worthy of respect by reason of his great age and services—Monsieur de Viomésnil asked me for advice. He afterwards became a Marshal of France, but at that time my acquaintance with him was very slight. His honesty pleased me. He had been given the command of a sort of battalion collected at Vincennes, composed of 700 or 800 half-pay officers of all ranks. The plan was to enrol them among the Royal volunteers who were being raised, or at least so it was believed, in Normandy.

'These officers,' said he to me, 'are very excited, and I can do nothing with them. I have written three letters, and paid the same number of visits to the Minister for War, and can neither see him nor get any answer. What had I better do? Give me some instructions.'

'You are a good man,' I answered. 'Don't give another thought to your battalion of officers; pack up your things and leave Paris tonight.'

'What!' he exclaimed in surprise; 'is the King going?'

'I cannot tell you more than that. You ask me for orders; I give you advice. Say nothing about it, I count upon your discretion;' and so saying, I left him for Villejuif.

I did not find the staff there, but only Generals Ruty, of the artillery, and Haxo, of the engineers. General Maison,[1] Governor of Paris, and commandant of one of the divisions, wrote to me that, as he had learned from the Duc de Berry that the troops were to return, he would join his division at St. Denis.

I issued the warnings and orders agreed upon, and as soon as I was certain they would be executed, and being warned that the head of a column was approaching Villejuif, I quitted it with the two Generals just named. The staff was not to be found at St. Denis any more than at Villejuif, but all the members of it, without exception, had received the largesse paid at the commencement of a campaign, and promises of handsome presents according to their future services.

I waited in vain till one o'clock for the arrival of the troops. An *aide-de-camp* from General Rapp, who commanded a division, came up, just as I was starting, to ask for orders. I gave him some for his general and for the other divisions, and they were simply to continue their march next day.

This battalion of officers, which the day before had been at Vincennes, now appeared, I know not how, at St. Denis. General St. Sulpice, who commanded it, told me that they were much excited and in a state of ferment, and as this condition of mind might have momentous results, I ordered him to direct them towards Rouen, so as to avoid any contact with the troops that were supposed to be arriving. He warned me that they would refuse to obey. I told him to try. He did so, but in vain.

Just as a detachment of artillery from La Fère entered the town, I was informed that it was approaching. I sent General Ruty to order it to retreat, but the half-pay officers, beside themselves, joined with the artillery, and Ruty, in trying to compel obedience to my orders, nearly fell a victim to them. I learned at the same time that General Maison was being pursued, 1 do not know why, and had been obliged to flee

Shortly afterwards another similar scene presented itself to my eyes. The carriages belonging to the Duc de Berry passed through St. Denis on their way from Villejuif. The mutineers seized them, compelled the postilions by threats of violence to dismount, mounted the horses in their place, and I felt ashamed to see French officers in uniform, epaulettes on their shoulders and forage-caps on their heads, behave as they did. They were mostly drunk and excited; and if there is any excuse

---

1. Made a Marshal after the fall of Napoleon.

for their conduct, it is to be found in that fact. I still blush for them!

Tired of waiting vainly at St. Denis, I started at one o'clock for Beaumont, where 1 established my headquarters for the time being. A large number of half-pay officers were assembled in front of the inn where I was staying, the first on the left beyond the square, I anticipated some opposition from them, but was absolutely determined not to allow myself to be insulted with impunity, even though I should get into difficulties; but they remained quiet, and were polite, even respectful.

At Beaumont I found the rear-rank of the King's Household, dismounted body-guards, some leading their horses by the bridle, others lying down in carts, others on foot, their knapsacks under their arms. It all looked like a rout after a defeat; and, as I did not stop at Beaumont, I found the road similarly garnished as far as Noailles. I left at Beaumont the same orders as at St. Denis, and hired post-horses to rejoin the princes at the head of the King's Household.

About half-way I had the pleasure of meeting your sister, De Massa,[2] and her children. Her husband was *prefect* of Beauvais. Fearing what might happen, he was sending all he held dearest to Paris; but as the party might run some risk, either on the road or at St. Denis, or even in the capital itself, I took them back with me, convinced that they would be safer at Beauvais.

The princes intended to pass the night at Noailles; I arrived just as they were about to sit down to table. They invited me to join them. After giving them an account of what I had seen and heard, I said that they must not trust to the troops, and strongly urged them to continue their march, in spite 'of the disorder among the King's Household On learning that my daughter was in the village, they had the kindness to send some dinner to her. When the repast was finished, I asked where the King was. *Monsieur* knew that he had started for Lille, but did not know whether, on leaving Beauvais, he had taken the road to Abbeville. I asked for orders, and he desired me to try and rejoin the King, to whom I might be of great service.

I took leave of their Royal Highnesses and, with your sister, started for Beauvais, which we reached between eleven o'clock and midnight. Your brother-in-law was much surprised at the return of his wife, but, after hearing my explanations, was delighted to see her. He told me that the King had taken the Abbeville road. I was sorry to hear it, as

---

2. The Duchesse de Massa, one of the marshal's daughters by his first wife, Mademoiselle Jacob.—Translator.

his enemies might believe and spread the report that he intended to withdraw into England, and thus cause discouragement among his supporters.

After remaining a few hours at Beauvais, and leaving fresh orders for the troops (as though they were likely to reach there), I was just about to depart, when an *aide-de-camp* from General Grundler, permanent Secretary at the War Office, entered and handed me a letter, informing me that the minister[3] had not appeared since the previous day, stating that they did not know what to do, and begging for my orders. I told the messenger that by the time my orders reached General Grundler he would no longer require them. As a matter of fact, he had left the War Office by the time his *aide-de-camp* reached Paris!

Nobody along the road could tell me whether the King had halted, or whether he was still moving forward, and in this state of uncertainty I entered Abbeville. Nothing indicated the presence of his Majesty; no guards at the gate; no life in the streets.

On my way to the inn I passed and recognized the Comte de Jaucourt. I stopped and called to him. He was one of the king's ministers, and, if I remember rightly, had charge of the Foreign Office in the absence of Monsieur de Talleyrand. He informed me that the King had been in the town since the previous day, and that he had received no news since he left the capital. He also begged me to go straight to him. I said I must first go to the inn to change my clothes and have some breakfast. I had not undressed for several days. While I was dressing, Monsieur de Jaucourt went to announce me, and summonses came in rapid succession.

I found the King as calm as when tranquilly reigning in the Tuileries. He received me with the utmost kindness, and questioned me concerning all that had occurred. No means of communication, either by courier or *estafettes*, had been established; but they had omitted to destroy the telegraphic communication, a circumstance likely to be made use of in Paris. I then asked the King what he was doing in Abbeville.

'I am waiting here,' he answered, 'for my brother and my Household, who ought to arrive this morning.'

'Your Majesty,' I replied, 'does not know that your Household will only reach Beauvais today (March 22). It will require two days more to arrive here, and will then probably be in the same disorderly condition as it was when I saw it yesterday.'

---

3. The heroic Dupont of Baylen celebrity.

I implored the King to start, because he would not be in safety until he reached Lille, and to take the shortest road by Hesdin and Béthune. His Majesty displayed great objection to that road, preferring the longer one by Boulogne, Calais, and Dunkirk. I pointed out that this road, running as it did by the sea, would give colour to the rumour that he was about to leave his kingdom and embark; that orders might be sent from Paris to forbid his admission into those towns, whereas the road to Béthune was still clear, and that to Péronne covered by the Duke of Orleans, who had collected there all the garrisons of the neighbouring towns, even that of Lille. I added that he had not a moment to lose.

The King yielded at last, but insisted upon dining first, and the utmost that I could manage was that dinner was ordered for an hour earlier. He desired me to precede him, with full powers to prepare the way for him, and to order horses. He had no courier, only two footmen on the box of the carriage in the liveries they wore at the Tuileries. I started.

The post-house of St. Pol was some distance away, outside the town. It took some time to procure horses, and meanwhile, towards one in the morning, I ordered some food. Scarcely had I seated myself at table when the King was announced. The news of his arrival having suddenly spread abroad, a large portion of the population collected and rushed into the room of a poor woman, whither he had been conducted to rest. The worthy soul had torn down some old bed-hangings to serve as a carpet for the feet of her guest. The homage of the inhabitants was so noisy and inconvenient that, to save the King from being stifled, the Prince de Neuchâtel and Monsieur de Blacas, Minister of the Household, were obliged to stand guard over the door with their drawn swords. The latter looked exceedingly comic in that attitude.

The same devotion was displayed at Béthune. I waited there for the King in order to receive his final orders, as that was the last stage before Lille. His Majesty alighted in the public square while the horses were being changed. It was five o'clock in the morning. The whole population turned out, men and women in very slight costumes. The sub-*prefect* himself stood by the carriage-door, one leg half bare, his feet in slippers, his coat under his arm, his waistcoat and shirt unbuttoned, and his hat on his head! He could not take it off, as his hands were fully occupied in trying to keep his sword in place and to fasten his necktie!

CHAPTER 38

An Inconvenient Loss

On reaching the barrier of Lille I saw that it was shut, and the drawbridge raised. It was nine o'clock. I inquired the reason of the gatekeeper, who could give me no information except that, as a large number of troops had arrived the previous day, only one gate, I forget which, had been left open. I had no one on horseback to send there. I grew nervous lest a rising should have occurred in favour of Napoleon. I already pictured the King in difficulties, and reproached myself for having prevailed upon him to take that road. However, if the troops had taken possession of the town, there was no reason why they should have closed the gates, and they would have had cavalry posted outside to give them intelligence of all that passed.

As I could not succeed, either by cries or signs, in making myself understood by the sentinel on the rampart, I obtained a scrap of paper from the gatekeeper, and wrote to the commandant, whoever he might be, a few words, stating my name and announcing the speedy arrival of the King. I wrapped this note round a stone, and, having passed the barrier, threw it over the ditch. It fortunately fell upon the rampart; the sentry picked it up, and called the officer on duty. I waited for some time, and, being still uneasy, sent back to stop the king's carriages, so that they might retreat if we found ourselves on hostile ground.

At last the drawbridge was lowered, and an officer advanced. It was your uncle, Paul de Bourgoing,[1] at that time *aide-de-camp* to the

---

1. Brother of the marshal's third wife, Mademoiselle de Bourgoing, who was the mother of the son Alexander, afterwards Duke of Tarentum, for whom these *Recollections* were written. The marshal's second wife was Mlle de Montholon, widow of General Joubert, who was killed at the Battle of Novi, July, 1799. By her the marshal had one daughter, who married the Marquis de Roche-Dragon.—Translator.

Marshal Duke of Treviso. He looked so surprised, so bewildered, so embarrassed, that I suspected some trickery, although he told me that all was quiet, that the Duke of Orleans and his commanding officer, Marshal Mortier, had returned the day before from Valenciennes, that they were much surprised at the sudden approach of the King, and that he knew no more.

In order to obtain clearer information I sent the chief of my staff, General Hulot, into the town, and questioned the officer during his absence. He expressed surprise at my incredulity, and repeated to me, upon his honour, all that he had just stated. This tranquillized me, and I was made still easier by the return of General Hulot, who told me that the Duke of Orleans and the marshal were following him with an escort, and were going out to meet the King. I then sent my *aide-de-camp* to inform the carriages they might advance. They soon appeared; the procession going out to meet them reached the barrier at the same moment as they did.

The King at length entered Lille. I accompanied him on horseback. It was market-day. The King was received with acclamation by the inhabitants and country folk, but coldly by the troops, especially by a battalion of light infantry drawn up just inside the gate. We discovered during the morning, on reviewing the garrison, and from the reports of their leaders, that the same feeling prevailed throughout the troops.

The King caused it to be announced that he would visit each corps. This step was not expected, but I was one of the first to recommend it. The return of these troops was a serious annoyance. We had no reason to hope that they would quit the town if ordered to do so, and the Royal volunteers were already several days on the road to Paris, whither they had been summoned by the minister. I have already said that nothing had been attended to, foreseen or ordered. The Duke of Orleans, even, had been left without notice of the King's march, so that on suddenly learning his departure, but not the direction he had taken nor his future plans, the Duke had thought he was doing right in raising the camp at Péronne and dismissing the regiments to their respective garrisons.

During the evening the King held a private council, at which I was present, with the Duke of Orleans, Monsieur de Blacas, and the Marshals Berthier and Mortier.[2] His Majesty first caused a letter from *Monsieur* to be read to us. I have a clear recollection of its substance, as

---

2. Prince of Neuchâtel and Duke of Treviso respectively.—Translator.

it was read four or five times, and discussed quite as often.

On reaching Beauvais, the day after I had left it, *Monsieur* had been informed that the larger portion of the King's Household could not march together, that they would infallibly be overtaken, that they were not in a state to defend themselves, and that the liberty of the Princes would be seriously endangered; that, consequently and owing to their ignorance of the King's whereabouts, it had been decided to disband the Household; and, further, that as the princes dared no longer risk remaining in France, amid so many hostile garrisons, they would start immediately, take ship either at Tréport or Dieppe, and rejoin His Majesty as speedily as possible in England or on the Continent.

Such was the tenor of this letter. At the very moment when its text was being discussed by the Princes, the news arrived that Napoleon was to enter Paris that very day. This had the effect of hastening their decision, which they immediately communicated to the King. The messenger, however, who carried the letter had not succeeded in coming up with him before he reached Lille.

On leaving Abbeville, the King had announced to *Monsieur* his determination to make for Lille, and had sent him orders to bring the Household thither by the most direct road from Beauvais. The two despatches had crossed one another, and the King therefore did not know whether, after what his brother had told him of the state of the Household, he had been able to execute the orders sent to him or not.

This was the subject of our discussion. I maintained that it was impossible that *Monsieur* should not have deferred to the King's orders, and marched with all the Household that was available. My opinion was shared, and we discovered, after calculating dates, that Monsieur ought to reach Arras or Béthune either that very day or early the following morning. The King then displayed some reluctance to waiting at Lille amid troops whose dispositions were so clearly unfavourable to him. The Duke of Orleans and the Marshal Duke of Treviso hastened to reassure him, and said that they would answer for their submission at any rate for some days. This pledge, however, did not satisfy him, and he announced his intention of starting that night for Dunkirk on the plea of visiting the frontier.

I pointed out that after giving out that he intended to establish the seat of his Government provisionally at Lille, where he had been so loyally received by the population, it would not be worthy of the King to leave it secretly, that it would be more honourable to keep the promise made of reviewing the garrison next morning, and that he could then announce his intention of going to see Dunkirk and returning thence to Lille. The King, however, possessed by a dread of being prevented from executing his plan next day, expressed his firm intention to start that same night.

I resumed my arguments as to the dignity of a King of France, the inconvenience attending a plan which might seriously endanger the Princes and the Household, who were advancing in all security to Lille; the greater nobility of risking everything rather than hurt the feelings of a town which, on its awakening, would learn the news of a departure that might be very justly stigmatized as a flight. For a moment I thought my arguments had prevailed, but the King's mind was made up, and I had to yield. It was arranged that he should start at midnight, that I should precede him with full powers to act as I thought best, and the sitting terminated.

The Prince de Condé had arrived during the day. We were all surprised, and with difficulty suppressed our laughter, out of respect for his age and the presence of the King, when we heard him gravely ask whether, as the next day was Maundy Thursday, His Majesty would perform the usual ceremony of the washing of feet.[3] The moment was well chosen! Even the King could scarcely control his laughter.

The King had quitted Paris in such haste that there had only been time to pack one portmanteau for his use, and this had been stolen on the road. His Majesty felt the loss the more as this portmanteau contained ail his clean linen—six shirts, a dressing-gown, and pair of slippers to which he was specially attached. On telling me of the theft, he said:

'They have taken my shirts; I had not too many of them.' And then he added in a melancholy voice: 'But I regret my slippers even more. You will realize some day, my dear Marshal, the value of a pair of slippers that have taken the exact shape of your foot!'

Little did the King think that a few hours later he was going to lose his entire kingdom!

At eleven o'clock, just as I was about to start, the Comte de Blacas was announced. He said in a determined voice:

'*Monsieur le Maréchal*, I have thought over what you just now vainly pointed out to His Majesty, namely, that it was unworthy of a King of France to seem to flee by a clandestine departure at night, thereby

---

3. A Catholic ceremony performed on Thursday in Passion Week, when a certain number of poor men have their feet washed in church.—Translator.

displeasing his supporters and exposing himself to the sarcasms of his enemies. If you are still of the same mind, postpone your departure for a short time. I will go and renew your observations to His Majesty. He is in safety here, at least until tomorrow, for I have taken the precaution to have all the gates of the town shut, and nothing can enter without my authorization. I shall be warned if any couriers or travellers of importance arrive.'

Thereupon he left me, and came back half an hour later to tell me that the King consented to remain until ten o'clock next morning, that he had found him in his shirt-sleeves shaving, and that at the first word he had laid down the razor, flown into a violent passion, and exclaimed with an oath:

'Why do they keep changing their plans every minute, and prevent me from starting or from going to bed?'

'It was,' added Monsieur de Blacas, the most ridiculous scene—his attitude, his shirt-cuffs turned back, his face one half red with anger, and the other white with soap. At last the King calmed down, finished shaving, and went to bed.'

I did the same, being worn out with fatigue.

I was still fast asleep when, at seven o'clock the following morning, Monsieur de Blacas came to me again on behalf of the King.

'What has happened now?' I asked.

'Not one of my orders was carried out,' he replied. 'The gates of the town were left open; travellers, couriers, stagecoaches passed through freely. The mail has arrived. The *Moniteur* contains a full account of Napoleon's new Government. I have ordered every copy to be seized.'

Poor Blacas had forgotten that there were many other papers being widely circulated, each containing the same news.

I dressed hastily, and went to the King's apartments. I found there the Duke of Orleans and the Marshals Berthier and Mortier. We were ushered into his Majesty's study.

'Dunkirk is out of the question now,' he said. 'I have just been informed that the troops are taking off the white cockade and substituting the so-called national cockade for it. After what has happened in Paris, which will probably occur everywhere else, I am no longer in safety here.'

I tried to reassure the King, but this time he was absolutely decided. He ordered horses, meaning to start across the frontier at once.

'Sire,' I said, 'he who throws up the game acknowledges himself beaten. This state of things assuredly cannot last long; but, since your mind is made up, permit me to stay behind.'

The King displayed surprise; he frowned, and became pensive. I continued:

'I have loyally done all in my power to maintain the authority of your Majesty and to keep you in possession of your dominions. You wish to abandon them. I will conduct you in safety to the frontier, but I will go no farther. I should only be in your way, a charge, an encumbrance to you. I will remain unalterably attached and devoted to your Majesty, and faithful to my oath. Some event may occur in the interior of the kingdom during your absence (which can only last a few months), and I may be able to serve you better in France than elsewhere.'

The resolution of the Congress of Vienna, taken on March 13, had reached the King either the previous evening or during the night. It declared the intention of all Europe to arm against Napoleon. This intelligence had just been printed and advertised without producing much effect. Its authenticity even was doubted in the town.

It was clear that France divided could make no stand against such a mass of forces; she had already succumbed once when she was not divided, and when a strong hand held the reins of State. My prediction that the King would be back in a few months was not baseless therefore. I terminated my speech by offering my marshal's baton as a proof of my sincerity. The King had recovered his usual serenity. He praised my honesty, and, as a token of his confidence, acceded to my request. Marshal Mortier asked the same favour, which was also granted to him.

Poor Prince de Neuchâtel was biting his nails with vexation. He was one of the captains of the Body-Guard, and on duty; he could not, therefore, ask for the same permission. On leaving the presence he followed me in great distress, and told me that he would resign as soon as they reached Ghent, that he would then go to Bamberg to fetch the princess and his children, with whom he would return to France, He begged me to inform his family and friends of his determination, even by means of the newspapers. I promised to do so, and kept my word. He feared lest he should be taken for an *émigré*.

Before entering his carriage, the King desired to compensate Monsieur de Brigode, mayor of the town, at whose house he had stayed. He gave him the rank of Commander of the Legion of Honour, and on his return conferred a peerage upon him. As soon as all was ready he started, escorted by a detachment of the National Guard, some *gendarmes* and *cuirassiers*. The Duke of Orleans and Marshal Mortier accompanied him as far as the barrier, at which point I begged the King to order them to return to the town to restrain the garrison.

I sent General Hulot to Menin,[4] to warn the commandant of that foreign town of the King's arrival, in order that there should be no mistake, for without this precaution they might have opened fire upon the carriages and the escort. He also had orders to engage horses, to advise the Custom House officials, and to point out exactly where the frontier was, because I was personally determined not to cross it, lest the publication of the fact that I had done so with the King should cause alarm to your sisters and my family. A very touching spectacle was presented to us along the road, the entire population on their knees in the mud, their hands raised to heaven, imploring the King not to abandon them. Later on His Majesty liked to recall these scenes of devoted attachment, which moved him very much.

On reaching the frontier I stopped the carriages. General Hulot had brought a superior English officer, who was commanding the troops at Menin. I begged him to show all the respect due to the King. He seemed to understand me, though he could not speak a word of French nor I of English. The King thanked the escort, and ordered them a considerable largesse.

My farewell with His Majesty was very painful. He addressed me most affectionately; I was much touched. The King presented me with a handsome snuff-box, bearing his portrait set in diamonds. I refused it, saying that the image impressed upon my memory would suffice. The King insisted, and said kindly:

'It is only a souvenir. Goodbye, my dear Marshal; I am grateful for your devotion.'

'Goodbye, Sire,' said I in reply; '*au revoir* in three months' time.'

Not a year had passed since the King had returned to his country when he quitted it for the second time. His restoration had produced acclamations and transports of joy; it seemed to promise happy days to France after thirty years of disorder produced by the results of a revolution which shook the world, and which finished by coming round again to its starting-point. France, however, had conquered the Charter and constitutional privileges; the Charter was to have been the palladium of our liberties, it had been solemnly sworn to, and the first legislative act of the Government was to violate it. History will

---

4. A town just across the Belgian frontier.—Translator.

teach you, my son, by what a series of faults, acknowledged by the King in his proclamation at Cambrai at the time of his second return, his ministers displeased the nation. That is why Napoleon, on landing, found a large majority favourably disposed towards him, as unfortunately for France it was, but the country paid dearly for this sad and painful episode.

CHAPTER 39

The News of Waterloo

To return to my story. After seeing the King cross the Lys and enter Menin, I returned with the escort along the road we had come. At about one-third of our journey I called a halt, to give the horses time to breathe, and then galloped back to Lille. I was summoned to the Duke of Orleans, where I found all the authorities, generals, and commanding officers. I was surrounded by people wishing for details as to the King's journey, which I gave.

During the night the Duke of Orleans and his excellent and lovable sister started for Tournai; they embraced us warmly. Marshal Mortier invited me to stay with him next day; I had need of rest, and accepted his invitation, and after dinner went to bed.

I have omitted to say that before the departure of the Duke of Orleans I asked him if he knew whether the King had informed *Monsieur* of his determination to leave Lille. The prince said he had probably not done so. I begged him to write to *Monsieur*, but he preferred that I should undertake it, as, from my not having quitted the King, I was in a better position to give a detailed account. The Duke of Orleans read and approved my letter, so I wrote a second copy, and sent one by each road, namely, by Arras and Béthune. We charged the commissary-general of the King's Household, who had brought *Monsieur's* despatch, dated from Beauvais, with one of the letters, another person who had arrived at the same time was entrusted with the other, and both were strongly urged to lose no time in acquitting themselves of so important a mission, which concerned the safety of the princes and the Military Household.

I awoke very late next morning, and sent my apologies to the Marshal Duke of Treviso for not being able to come to breakfast. I promised, however, to dine with him, and meanwhile begged him to let me know the news, and to send me the paper. I never was so amazed in my life as when I received a message from him that he could not entertain me at dinner, as he had received orders to leave for Paris immediately, and to make over his command to Count d'Erlon. On receiving this extraordinary intelligence I hardly knew whether I was awake or dreaming, so surprised was I. Nevertheless, I went straight to the Marshal, who confirmed the message he had sent, and told me that he had already made over his command. I blamed him for his precipitation, as I feared for the Princes who were bringing up the King's Household to Lille. The garrison had already adopted the tricoloured cockade, whether by order or spontaneously I know not.

General d'Erlon, who, I believe, commanded the division before the arrival of Marshal Mortier, had taken part with Napoleon, and had even made some attempt in his favour previous to the announcement of his landing. As this act of hostility to the Royal Government had failed, he had hidden himself, but was now quite ready to take over the command. Seeing that the marshal was determined to start in a few hours, I returned home, sent for a passport and some horses, entered my carriage, and drove off on the way to Béthune, so as to avoid the delays which would be occasioned along the direct road followed by Marshal Mortier.

The gates were closed, or at any rate that leading to Béthune was, the staff in Lille having forgotten to give orders that it should be opened for me. An officer on duty there obstinately refused to allow me to pass, notwithstanding my rank and my passport, which I showed him. I reprimanded him very severely, and threatened him with the future weight of my resentment, but at the second Restoration I voluntarily forgot all about the matter. A good many of the privates, however, took up my cause, while I sent notice to the commandant. At length another officer arrived and opened the gate.

On reaching the post-house at La Bassée I found no horses. I wished to push on with those I had, but they were dead-beat, and I had to give .them a rest. While waiting in the inn I heard my name pronounced in a neighbouring room. Nobody knew who I was, but as I wished to find out what was the matter I walked in and made myself known. A tall young man said he had two letters of mine they were franked with my name. He showed them to me, and I recognised them as those I had written the previous evening to *Monsieur*.

'By what accident,' I inquired, 'did those letters fall into your hands?'

He answered that the commissary-general, to whom I had given them, and who was a great friend of his, had asked him to follow one or other of the two roads on the chance of meeting *Monsieur*, while he went off to visit a friend in the neighbourhood. It was evident that he cared very little for what might happen to his Royal Highness. I took possession of the letters, and, my horses being ready, pursued my journey.

It was eight or nine o'clock at night when I reached Béthune. The gates were closed, and I had great difficulty in getting them opened. A portion of the King's Household was on the watch there, as a detachment of the garrison of Arras, apparently hostile, had presented themselves, and demanded admittance. The Duc de Berry, perhaps imprudently, had gone out and forced them to retreat; but there was reason to fear that they might come back at night in larger numbers.

Monsieur had learned, I know not how, that the King had quitted Lille the previous morning. He determined to go and join him by the shortest road with all the available troops. Notwithstanding advice to the contrary, they took abominable cross-country roads, where many carriages and guns remained fast in the mud, instead of following the high-road to La Bassée, whence, by another good road, they could have reached Bailleul; but they were frightened by the sight of the Arras detachment, and dreading lest they should meet another from the garrison at Lille, they prepared to go across country. I heard that, before starting, *Monsieur* had decided to disband the remainder of the Household.

As soon as my arrival in the town became known, a large number of generals and superior officers came to me for advice. As they were not in a position to defend themselves, I told them to put into execution the orders they had, to send notice to Lille and Arras so as to prevent hostilities, lay down their arms, distribute the funds remaining to each company, or give up a few months' pay, in order that everyone might be enabled to procure plain clothes; for in uniform, and travelling singly, they ran the risk of being attacked at every step.

General Dessole was also at Béthune; he was in command of the National Guard at Paris, but, as he was also Secretary of State, he had started to rejoin the King at Lille. On hearing of his departure, he would neither follow him abroad nor return to Paris; he begged me to accompany him to Amiens, and we travelled together. The town of Doullens was crowded with cavalry, at the head of whom was General Excelmans, hastening after the King's Household. I had stopped to breakfast, and he came to see me, looking rather uneasy. He had had cause of complaint against the Royal Government, and had consequently warmly embraced Napoleon's cause.

'What!' I exclaimed, 'do you mean to say that you would have the heart to fall, sword in hand, upon a few brave men who have remained true to their oaths? Why don't you arrest me? for I tell you I have kept mine, too, and will never serve the cause you have embraced. Think what you are doing. Sooner or later you must certainly be entangled in the meshes of the vengeance that cannot fail to overtake you. All the great Powers are marching towards our frontiers; tremble at the results of a reaction!'

These observations had little effect upon General Excelmans, because he was excited and embittered. He was an excellent man at heart, very brave, but excitable; he would have done his duty well had he been employed. He promised me, however, that he would slacken his speed and respect the liberty of individuals.

At the next stage an advance-courier met mine. He belonged to Marshal Ney, and there was, consequently, no hope of avoiding him. We were then serving very different sides. Just as our carriages were passing, he ordered his to stop.

'You are going to Paris?' he cried. 'You will be well received. The Emperor will welcome you.'

'I will spare him that trouble,' I replied. 'I shall not see him, neither shall I join his party.'

With these words we parted. My determination was fixed only to stop in Paris just long enough to attend to some business, to see no one, and to start again immediately for Courcelles. A few days were sufficient for me.

General Dessole would not remain in Amiens; he could not remember the name of a single friend in the town, and did not consider himself in safety there. He preferred to push on to the neighbourhood of Paris, and only enter it after nightfall. I stopped at Écouen. I underwent a close examination at the barrier, but my passport was in order, and we were allowed to enter. Poor Dessole's memory again completely deserted him. He was much disturbed, and very anxious as to what might happen to him. Napoleon did not like him. I told him that at the end of the Rue de Clichy I should leave my carriage, and go in search of news. He fancied that we were followed; I did not care if we were. We separated, he still in doubt as to what he would do or where he would go, and not daring to return home.

I went to the house of your sister De Massa, but found no one at home, and had no better success at the houses of several other friends. I then decided to go home. Madame de Sémonville, who knew that my return was expected, was waiting for me, and I was much surprised at finding General Dessole with her. He told me that, when we separated, he had observed that our carriages were watched; he had therefore jumped into mine, and on entering my courtyard had found the same spies there. In answer to my porter, who asked what they wanted, they replied that they had orders to be there, but they had eventually taken their departure. I do not know whither Dessole had sent his carriage. I offered him a bed, which he refused, though he did not know where to betake himself, and was in terror of being arrested. For my own part, I feared nothing personally; I was guaranteed by the services I had rendered to Napoleon at the time of his abdication at Fontainebleau. I had also heard from General Ricard, who had come from Vienna to Lille, bearing to the King the resolution passed by the Congress on March 13, that he had read a little pamphlet upon a visit to Elba, in which Napoleon had spoken of me in laudatory terms. General Ricard promised to give me this little publication, but I never received it.

In order to induce General Dessole to do something, I suggested to Madame de Sémonville that she should take him in her carriage and drive very fast through different quarters of the town, so as to put any spies off the scent. The advice was followed, they started, and I heard next day that Dessole had safely reached the country.

I gave my porter the strictest orders to admit no one but my family or a few friends whose names I mentioned to him. I sent my carriages to Courcelles, intending to follow them very shortly, and hastened to settle my business, when, at the moment that I least expected it, the porter announced Marshal Davoût, the Minister of War. He had been foolish enough to believe that my orders could not be applicable to so important a personage. In order to avoid the unpleasantness of this interview, I told him to say that I was unwell, and not able to see him. While I was uttering the words, the marshal, who overheard them, entered.

'Too late!' said Davoût; 'I have to speak to you on very important matters.'

I had no choice but to listen. When we were alone, the Prince of Echmühl began with some ordinary remarks; then, coming to Napoleon, he said that he was sent by him to reiterate to me the expression of his gratitude for the course I had pursued during the last agony of the Empire; that he wished to thank me himself, and that he offered me an interview, which should be either private or public, as I wished.

I had no hesitation in refusing. I answered that I had been faithful to his cause and his person until the last moment; that I had now undertaken other engagements, which I should carry out with the same fidelity; that I felt sure that Napoleon knew me too well to imagine that I could be seduced by temptation of fortune, title, or brilliant employment; that my determination was firm, and my mind made up, and that insistence was useless. I added, in a decided voice, that a continuance of this conversation, painful as it was to both of us, would be an outrage upon my honour, my feelings, and my pride.

'You appear, Macdonald,' said the minister, 'to have tried and condemned us all very summarily! Speaking for myself, I entered into no engagement whatever with the Bourbons. I was in command at Hamburg when Napoleon fell;[1] they permitted me to be attacked in scurrilous pamphlets, to which I replied. I have never even seen the King, nor have I received anything at his hands. I am, therefore, free, and I embrace the cause of liberty, which I have long defended.'

'No doubt,' I answered, 'liberty and Napoleon are synonymous terms. These liberties will end by putting chains on our necks. We shall see Europe raised against us, drunk with revenge and resentment, from which, hitherto, France has been preserved merely by the *Czar's* authority. Did not the Charter ensure us all the liberty and independence we could desire? The institutions would have secured to us these two great bases of the social edifice. No doubt the Royal Government has committed grave errors; but consider the immensity of the peril into which we are about to be dragged, and judge for yourself whether these errors were of such a nature as to render a complete overturn necessary, and to call for an inquiry. I am wrong,' I added warmly; 'there will be no inquiry. Can France, divided as she is to-day, resist a coalition of foreigners and their armies?'

'But,' he argued, 'the Emperor assures us that Austria is on our side.'

'Either he deceives himself or he is deceiving you. Have you seen

---

1. Hamburg, it should be remembered, held out gallantly, even after the fall of Paris, in 1814. The campaign in Belgium in 1815 might have been greatly altered in character had this able general been free to have taken part in it in place of Ney or Grouchy.

the declaration of the Congress of Vienna?'

'No.'

'Read it.'

'Is this an authentic copy?'

'It was sent to the King by Monsieur de Talleyrand. General Ricard brought it to Lille, where it was immediately printed, published, and advertised. I am surprised that it did not reach you by courier.'

'The deuce! This alters the case. May I take it with me?'

'You may; I have several copies.' He retired. Although it was clear to me that he was shaken, he continued in the occupation of his post, and eventually had reason to repent of having done so. I was then able to render him considerable service.

I reiterated my orders to my porter, which were thenceforward carried out rigorously. General Mathieu Dumas, who had been chief of my staff when I commanded the Army of the Grisons, came to see me. He was refused admission. He was intimate with Marshal Davoût, whom he had recently served in the same capacity as he had me. I suspected that he was charged by Napoleon and the marshal with a mission of the same nature; nor was I mistaken, for, finding that he could not see me, he wrote to me upon the subject, and added that he begged me to consent to an interview or else to go to the Tuileries. I answered so strongly, and giving such reasons for my refusal, as at length to secure my being left in peace. I was on very good terms with Mathieu Dumas. I was sorry not to see him; but, in our respective positions, I should have been wrong to receive him.

During my work at Lille, and since my return, I experienced every now and then a difficulty in breathing, which occasioned me some inconvenience. It was a premonitory symptom of an attack of gout, which laid me up on the very day preceding that fixed for my departure. The attack was very severe. I should have been choked had they not succeeded in drawing it down to my feet. It caused me tortures, and lasted three months, so I was compelled to postpone my departure.

As soon as I was well enough I started, but stopped at a distance of six leagues from Paris to rest for a day. While there I heard of the disaster at WATERLOO. As this catastrophe put the finishing stroke to Napoleon's political career, I renounced my intention of continuing my journey, thinking that I might assist in hastening the return of the King—our one hope of preventing anarchy.

CHAPTER 40

Mission to Paris

Events succeeded each other rapidly in 1815. The remains of the army were collected around Paris, Napoleon was once more compelled to abdicate, and a temporary Government established. This Government, wishing to gauge the opinions of the generals, called a meeting, to which I was invited. I refused to attend it, as I had resigned my command to the King, and felt that, if I accepted the invitation, I should appear to be associating myself with recent events and recognizing an order of things which my opinions would not allow me to support

One of the first proceedings of this Government had been to raise new levies and organize battalions of federates, who soon adopted a bullying, threatening manner towards all who were not in agreement with them—that is to say, the partisans of Royal Government. I decided to return secretly to Paris, so as to be on the spot and better able to profit by chance events. I entered it at night, and took shelter with one of my *aides-de-camp*. So well hidden was I that next day everyone knew where I was! This discovery did me no harm; on the contrary, it brought about an interview with Monsieur Hyde de Neuville, who brought me (better late than never) a note from the Duchesse d'Angoulême, then in London, and unlimited powers from the King, with a nomination to a membership in a secret Government, which was to restore proper authority as soon as possible. Monsieur Hyde de Neuville, who had quitted Ghent a month previously, had been to London in the hope of finding means of returning to France. They were fighting on the frontier, so it would have been imprudent to attempt to enter there.

Several private meetings were held in my house, of which I had openly retaken possession. We had many supporters in the capital, and it was proposed to risk a Royalist movement. I was opposed to it, as I did not see how we were to struggle against the temporary Government with Fouché at its head, and also because the army was still too exasperated to abandon the cause into which it had been dragged.

Our party consisted of Marshal Oudinot (Duke of Reggio), of Messieurs de Sémonville, D'André, Du Bouchage, and Baron Pasquier, with one or two others whose names I have forgotten. Baron Pasquier entered while we were discussing the advantages of, and objections to, attempting a rising. He brought Monsieur de Vitrolles with him; both had just come from Fouché. They declared that the movement was unnecessary; that the Duke of Otranto (Fouché) was in the interests of the King; that he had received from him plenary powers later than ours; that our intentions were known, our every step watched, and that we should infallibly fail. Baron Pasquier added that in a few days we should have by force things that we might vainly attempt to obtain by other means.

Monsieur de Vitrolles confirmed what he said, and they added that they enjoyed the full confidence of the Duke of Otranto, who did nothing without asking and taking their opinion. Monsieur de Vitrolles was an ultra-Royalist, and was therefore above suspicion.

We decided to do nothing, but thought it would be only proper to inform the King of the reason why we took no steps. One of us was to be deputed to go to His Majesty, and I was asked to undertake the mission; I agreed. Fouché was informed of this next day; he wished to see me. I at first felt very strong disinclination to such an interview, but was persuaded to agree to it, as I was informed that I should be told of many things for the King which could not be entrusted to paper. The capitulation of Paris and an armistice had just been arranged; the French army was retiring across the Loire.

At the appointed hour I went to the Tuileries, where the temporary Government held its sittings. I expected to be received privately, but I found the Duke of Otranto and some of his colleagues amid a number of generals and others. Several came to greet me. A heated discussion ensued. I treated them very severely, reproaching them for the misfortunes under which France was groaning, and accusing them of having provoked the strangers, who in two days would be masters of Paris. They all talked at once, and such nonsense that at last Fouché took me aside, and said:

'Never mind them; they are a set of fools.'

One of his colleagues called to me, in a loud voice:

'*Monsieur le Maréchal*, you are going to see the King. Tell him that what we want is independence, the tricoloured cockade and—'

I did not hear the remainder, contenting myself with a shrug of my shoulders. The days of the temporary Government were numbered.

Fouché confirmed all that Pasquier and De Vitrolles had told me the previous evening at our meeting—he was working on behalf of the King. He begged me to assure His Majesty of his devotion and fidelity—to say that, if he had played a part in recent events, it was only in order to serve him better! He urged me to impress upon him the advisability of coming quickly, and of preceding the foreigners, if possible, so as to check any movement by his presence. He added that, if the King wished to give an agreeable surprise to the nation, and thus attract the army to himself, he should wear the tricoloured cockade, which he ought to mind the less as he had worn it before the emigration. He ended by asking me to go and see Davoût, commander-in-chief and Minister for War, who was expecting me, and would give me my passport. I took leave of Fouché, and went to the War Office.

Marshal Davoût received me warmly. He told me that the effective force of the army that was going to the other side of the Loire amounted to 150,000 men and 30,000 horses, with 750 pieces of ordnance; that he would place this imposing force at the King's service if he would leave them the tricoloured cockade and wear it himself; that the great majority of people in France were deeply attached to these colours, under which they had so often fought victoriously; that that would be the best means of regaining the affection of all citizens worthy of the name; and that his Majesty might then give the army a chief of his own choice, if it did not please him to leave him (Davoût) at its head.

I promised, as I had done to Fouché, to relate faithfully to the King all that I had heard; but I added that I doubted his accepting the conditions laid down.

As a matter of policy, I am still convinced that the adoption of these colours, on the occasion of the first Restoration, would have saved France from the calamities that weighed so heavily upon her; but at such a moment, in presence of the allies, could the King honourably decide upon such a course? Although policy excuses everything, even the greatest mistakes, one had been committed at the first Restoration, and perhaps, also, at the second, because this was not clearly understood. It cannot be said that the mistake was committed a second time owing to want of good advice. The King was inclined to give way when I saw him, but the counsellors he brought from Ghent dissuaded him.

I started with Monsieur Hyde de Neuville; although we were serving the same cause, I was far from sharing his extreme opinions. A staff-officer passed us through the outposts, and it was with a feeling of sorrow that I found myself among those of the foreigners.

It was believed that the King was at Cambrai; but that very day he had come to sleep at Arnouville, a few leagues from Paris. His Ministers preceded him; I met them rather on this side of Louvres. They halted on learning who I was. They had no news from Paris, and that which I brought appeared to them so important as to make them anxious that the King should stop at Gonesse, whither we went to wait for him.

His Majesty embraced me very cordially, praising the fidelity I had maintained towards him. He gave me a private interview, which lasted for a full hour. The King could not get over his surprise at finding the importance that was attached to so apparently trivial a thing as the cockade—'a plaything' he called it.

'But, your Majesty,' said I, 'were you only playing when you once adopted and wore these colours?'

'The circumstances were very different,' he replied. 'At that time I had to master the Revolution.'

'And to make use of it,' I hastily remarked, 'on your first return. The circumstances are the same now. Moreover, were not these in former days the colours of the Royal Family, and did not the Dutch receive them from Henry IV.?'

'Yes,' answered the King; 'but they were the livery colours of his house.'

'No doubt your Majesty will also remember that at the gates of the capital the same monarch remarked that " Paris was well worth a Mass"?'

'Certainly; but it was not a very Catholic speech.'

Finally the King said he would consult his Ministers and allies, and took me on with him to Arnouville.

After dinner, *Monsieur*, the Duc de Berry, the principal officers, and some of the ministers came in. The King said:

'My brother, my nephew, here is our friend the marshal; embrace him.'

Monsieur did it with very good grace, but his son displayed some embarrassment and reluctance. I do not know whether he thought the favour too great, or whether he remembered the discussion we had had before the departure of the King. Conversation turned naturally upon existing circumstances and the causes that had produced them. Everybody indiscriminately, but especially the army, was accused of having joined a colossal plot to upset the Royal Government and restore Napoleon.

I, on the other hand, maintained that the faults of which I could speak boldly, since they had been avowed boldly in the proclamation of Cambrai—prodigality, injustice, abuses, favours distributed without discernment, violation of the Charter, haughtiness, contempt—had contributed to embitter the army and a portion of the nation; that even had Napoleon not appeared, there would have been risings, as they had been foreshadowed by unmistakable portents. I declared, with the same boldness, that certain Generals had not followed a straight line, to use the expression of Count Ferrand; that when they found their influence spreading, the appearance of their old leader had sufficed to turn all their heads, as a spark might create a conflagration; that, on the whole, the officers were not guilty; and that, in acting as they had done, they simply followed the regimental money-chests. A proof, an unanswerable proof, that there had been no plot was contained in the fact that during the Hundred Days no individuals had boasted of having had anything to do with it. Had it been otherwise, men would have been proud of it, and publicly solicited rewards. Surely those who had done wrong would not have been kept from self-glorification by vanity or indifference.

'There is much truth, my brother, in what the marshal says,' remarked the King; but the audience did not appear convinced. The King dismissed us.

Next day I saw several of the ministers privately; they appeared uncertain what to advise, but to me it seemed clear that they had already resolved to reject the proposals I had brought the previous day to Gonesse. Monsieur de Talleyrand, who had been sent to Neuilly to the allied generals, had returned to give an account of his mission. A council had been held immediately upon his arrival, and after a short deliberation he started again for Neuilly, no doubt in order to announce the result to his allies. I learned that Fouché had gone there also, more probably to treat for his own private interests than for those of France.

I tackled the ministers immediately upon the subject of the colours. They somewhat awkwardly admitted that the presence and opposite opinion of the allies had placed an invincible obstacle in the way. It became obvious that, if we could no longer impose acts of government, we must submit to accepting those of the conqueror. Several of them, Baron Louis, the Marquis de Jaucourt, and others, invited me to a conference in the open air, and I learned that they were charged to reconstruct the Ministry, and to offer me the Secretaryship for War. The Duc de Feltre[1] was standing not far from us. I pointed him out, and said:

'There is the man with the best right to it.'

'No,' said Baron Louis; 'we will not have as a colleague a man who, in a speech in the Chamber of Peers, under a representative Government, dared to proclaim that "What the King wills, the Law wills."

I had myself heard these remarkable words; and this resuscitation of a superannuated maxim, dating from the time of absolute monarchs, had produced considerable murmurings against, and some abuse of, their author.

I at first pleaded my incapacity, the condition of France and of the army. I declared plainly that, foreseeing as I did acts of severity, I would not consent to be made the instrument for applying them to men who were unfortunate rather than guilty; that, in short, I had neither strength, courage, nor capacity to support such a burden. They pressed me, but to no purpose; they then exhibited great regret, which I had no reason for not believing sincere, and begged me to name somebody. There were few generals who had taken no part in this Revolution. I named them, and left the choice to my auditors Mortier, Oudinot, Gouvion St. Cyr, Dessole, and some others whom I do not now recollect. They desired my opinion upon the subject of the two last. I had no connection with nor any feeling for or against either.

'Is St. Cyr fond of work?' they asked. 'Many people say he is lazy.'

'I am not aware of it. He is a man of great military capacity, firm, honest, jealous of other people's merit. In the army he is regarded as what is vulgarly called a "bad bed-fellow." In the coldest manner imaginable he allowed his neighbours to be beaten without attempting to assist them, and then criticised them afterwards. But this opinion, not uncommon among soldiers, is perhaps exaggerated, and he is admitted to have wits, calmness, and great capabilities.'

He justified this opinion both in the army and at the War Office.

Dessole seemed, at the moment, to be more in favour with my interlocutors. His character was gentler, more trusting than the oth-

---

1. General Clarke, War Minister under Napoleon.

er's; he also possessed greater administrative qualities, having generally occupied the post of chief of the general staff. But under existing circumstances, and after so great an alarm, it was indispensable to select a man who combined firmness and conciliation. The former of these qualities should predominate, and it was just that one in which Dessole was lacking. He had recently given proof of this in my presence when I brought him back from Béthune to Paris—hesitating, undecided, not knowing what to do. However, he afterwards became President of the Council and Foreign Secretary.

Loud were the railings against France and the army, as I have mentioned in my account of the conversation the foregoing evening; those who were about the Princes and who had emigrated vowed vengeance, though I must add that their vengeance was to be brought about by means of the allied armies. For the sake of truth I must add that the ministers with whom I conferred displayed great moderation, and lamented with me the disaster of Waterloo, and the yoke that the foreigners were preparing for the shoulders of our country.

During our conversation, from which this digression has carried me away, we were struck by a sudden uproar rising from the courtyard of the castle. We hastened up, and saw General Lagrange, who had only one arm, struggling with some guards of the blue and red corps. They were abusing him for not having followed to Ghent a company of *mousquetaires*, of which he was commander, and were tearing off the emblems of his rank. We ran to his assistance, but the Duc de Feltre, who was close at hand, had already delivered him from the hands of these madmen.

I expressed in round terms my indignation and my opinion of their cowardice in attacking a one-armed officer; I told them that they should exhibit their bravery in presence of and against the enemy, and not against a man who had given proof of his on many battlefields. As soon as the King was informed of the occurrence he sent down an expression of his indignation, and his intention of inflicting punishment; at the same time he sent for me. This incident naturally broke off our conference.[2]

The King began by thanking me for the firmness I had displayed

---

2. A very different incident occurred in one of the Peninsular battles. As Colonel Felton Harvey was leading his squadrons to an attack, his sword arm disabled and hanging down, he was on the point of being cut down by the colonel at the head of the French cavalry opposed to him, when the latter, observing his defenceless condition, suddenly brought his sword at the critical instant to a salute, and passed on.

towards his guards, but I stopped him by saying that it was the Duc de Feltre who had put an end to the outrage to which General Lagrange had fallen a victim, that I had come up too late, but soon enough, however, to lecture his guards as they deserved. He then said that he had ordered an inquiry, and would punish the guilty severely.

'But,' he continued, 'I had another motive in sending for you. You told me that Monsieur Fouché[3] would make over the government to me if I would agree to the conditions you were charged to submit to me. I cannot speak very decidedly just now, because I must deliberate with my allies; but you understand that my dignity will not suffer me to take the reins from *his* hands. Return, therefore, to Paris, tell him to make over his powers to you, and that I will not fail to requite the services he has recently done me.'

I knew that the Duke of Otranto was at Neuilly in conference with the allied generals and the Prince of Benevento (Talleyrand). I had the intelligence from Beurnonville. Apparently the King was ignorant of the fact, for he started, but soon recovered, and said:

'Very good; if he be away you will see his colleagues, and notify my intentions to them.'

'But, Sire, they will do nothing in the absence of their leader, and they are sure not to be all of the same opinion.'

'Go, all the same. If you do not see them, remain in Paris; in the contrary event, come back as soon as possible and inform me of what has happened."

I bowed, and was about to start upon this mission, when he stopped me, and said:

'My dear marshal, there is yet another service which I am going to ask of your zeal;' and, giving me a folded paper that was lying on his writing-table, he continued:

'This is your nomination as Arch-Chancellor of the Legion of Honour. It was presented to me by Monsieur de Talleyrand, and I signed it at Roye.'

I refused this office for the same reasons as those I had previously given in refusing the Ministry of War. At the word 'Ministry' the King seemed surprised, but said with great kindness that he considered me equally worthy of either, and insisted so much that I ended by giving way. He largely increased the dignity of the office by restoring to it the title of a Secretaryship of State, and permitting it to have direct communication with the Sovereign. These privileges had existed under

---
3. One of the regicides.

the Empire, but had been suppressed at the Restoration; the title had been reduced to that of Chancellor only, and the officer could only communicate with the King through the Minister of the Household. I was to be dependent upon the President of the Council, inasmuch as his counter-signature was necessary.[4] When this matter was settled I started for Paris to carry out the mission with which the King had charged me.

On the way I reflected upon what had happened during the morning. Why, on the one hand, were the ministers I have quoted so anxious to secure my services, while, on the other, the King pressed me so earnestly to accept the Arch-Chancellorship? He, clearly, was but the echo of Monsieur de Talleyrand, who was interested in keeping me out of the Government, where I should have been too much in his way; but as the King, apparently, wished that I should hold some office, the Prince of Benevento suggested the Legion of Honour for me. It was clear that some intrigue, of which his colleagues were kept in ignorance, was concealed under this business. The matter had been arranged between the King and the Minister, who in his haste had forgotten to countersign the appointment. I did not think well to have this informality put right. It was now useless, as I was already in office. The document has remained in the same state ever since.

On the road I had to endure the painful spectacle of, and to pass through, an enemy's camp. I also passed General Dessole, wearing the uniform of the Commander of the Parisian National Guard. He was going to pay his respects at Arnouville, and was uneasy as to what reception he might find; we exchanged a few words, and I was able to reassure him. As a matter of fact, he was retained in his post, and next time I saw him he was in good spirits, and had recovered his courage.

According to my anticipations, I found neither the Duke of Otranto (Fouché)—who was at Neuilly—nor his colleagues in the temporary Government. They had met that morning for the last time. Since my mission had no longer an object, I remained quiet.

---

4. I think I have already referred to the question of orphanages founded for the daughters of members of the Order. I have not leisure to read over again what I have written on this subject, from a bad habit I long since contracted. I write a great deal and very rapidly; I should discover many mistakes, but in order to correct them I should have to erase them or recommence my work, and I should never have time enough, although I rise very early. (The secret is that I know the value of time, and never waste it.) However, do not imitate my bad habits; write less and more correctly. But, after all, these historical notes are for you alone, and you will make allowances for your father.—Note by Marshal Macdonald.

CHAPTER 41

Marshal Macdonald takes the Command

Early the next morning a courier brought me an order to be at St. Denis at mid-day. I started in uniform, followed by a saddle-horse, when, at the turning from the Chemin de la Révolte, opposite the castle of St. Ouen, I perceived the royal carriages and escort, coming out of St. Denis, and following the direct road. I mounted my horse and rode across country, catching up the procession just as it was entering the village of La Chapelle. The King waved his hand to me in a friendly manner, and so did Monsieur. Marshal St. Cyr and some generals surrounded the carriage. I joined them.

The reception by the Parisians was less demonstrative than at the first entry. On the *boulevards* they were even colder than in the suburbs and the Rue St. Denis. At that point Marshal Moncey joined the procession. The King turned away his head from his salute, and *Monsieur* withdrew his hand indignantly when the marshal advanced respectfully to take it. He was in disgrace for having continued in office during the Hundred Days.[1]

On reaching the Tuileries I was much surprised, and no doubt others were also, at seeing close by the door of the throne-room the Duke of Otranto, to whom the King gave his hand as he passed! I was not less surprised at learning that on the previous evening he had been appointed Minister of Police.

I had heard on the road that St. Cyr was to have the War Office. It was a very good choice, but from the state of mind in which I had left the ministers after our interview in the park at Arnouville, I rather ex-

---

1. It is greatly to the honour of Marshal Moncey that he boldly refused to take part in the trial of Marshal Ney.

pected it to have been given to Dessole, towards whom they seemed then inclined. These events happened on July 8.

A few days later I was installed as Arch-Chancellor of the Legion of Honour, and entered upon my functions. I did not, however, take possession of the palace, as it was in the hands of the allies.

The army had retired to the other side of the Loire, and took its name from the river. Its commander, Marshal Davoût, Prince of Eckmühl, had made it take the oath and put on the white cockade. He then resigned. Eyes seemed turned to me to take his place; the King sent for and proposed it to me. I realized all the weight attaching to so thorny and difficult a command, for now there was no longer any question of fighting an enemy, but of fighting opinions, and to induce the army to submit to disbandment, which was being openly discussed, only, it was said, this disbandment was to take the shape of a formation of soldiers and officers into new corps, to be called legions.

I pointed out to His Majesty how inconvenient to myself personally, and how little in the interests of the State, such an appointment would be. My objections were anticipated. The King did his utmost to remove them, but it was not an easy task. I had always borne a strong affection for this army, notwithstanding its errors, and perhaps because it realized them, and I had to expect opposition to the proposed measures, and excitement secretly kept up by the allies, who were anxious to re-open hostilities, so as to have an excuse for crossing the Loire and wasting a new country; and last, there was a feeling against me, because I had taken no part in the unhappy conflict of the Hundred Days. I have since had proofs that I was mistaken as to this last point; the army appreciated my character, my honesty, and my friendly feeling towards it, and respected my opinions and conduct. It remembered that a year previously I had worked hard for the interests of the Emperor and his family, and that I had been the last to acknowledge the new order of things. I owed Napoleon nothing; he had long neglected me, and left me under the burden of a sort of disgrace; but he was in trouble, and I forgot everything.

The King insisted so strongly, so obstinately, upon the personal service he begged me to do him—those are his own words—that he overcame my scruples. I consented, but upon two solemn conditions. Firstly, that I should have absolute freedom of action; secondly, that I should never be called upon to act as the instrument in any steps that might be taken against individuals, still less that I should be charged with their execution. After these two essential points were settled, the

King sent me to the War Office for my instructions.

After expressing great satisfaction at hearing that I had yielded to the King's wishes, Marshal St. Cyr told me that he could not conceal the importance of this command, of which the Prince of Eckmühl could endure no more; that his entreaties to be relieved became more and more pressing by every courier, and that he begged me to hasten my preparations and go to Bourges as soon as possible. The impolitic ordinances of July 25, whereby several generals and other persons who had taken an active part in the Hundred Days were banished or brought up for trial, had been published, and, will it be believed? these sentences had been pronounced upon a report from Fouché, Duke of Otranto, Minister of Police from him who before and during the period had so largely participated in the events with which they were filled! I was very anxious as to the effect these. measures would have on the army. A consolation, however, was awaiting me at Bourges—Massa, your sister's husband, had, much against his will, been sent there as Prefect; his wife had accompanied him, and I went to stay in their house.

My arrival created great excitement and general uneasiness, which I dissipated next day when I received a visit from the corps, headed by the Marshal Prince of Eckmühl, whom I had informed of all that had passed The generals feared that my despatch-box was filled with orders of arrest or deprivation. I undeceived them by saying that I had too high an opinion of them to believe that any among them could injure me by thinking me capable of deceiving them. They assured me that it had never entered the head of one of them.

'Let those,' I continued, 'who are unfortunate enough to appear on these fatal ordinances take measures for their safety; they have not a moment to lose. At any minute orders may arrive of which I shall be powerless to prevent the execution; the only thing I can do is to give them this warning and facilitate their means of escape.'

Several of them were present, and profited by my advice. Amongst others were Generals Laborde and Brayer, the latter of whom had commanded at Lyons on the occasion of the catastrophe of March 10. It was he who had told me, at the decisive moment, that all measures had been taken to prevent my departure. He was now much ashamed, and stammered out his excuses.

'Fly!' was my answer.

General Drouot not only disdained to flee, but insisted upon forestalling his arrest by going and surrendering himself at the Abbaye prison. All arguments were unavailing to turn him from this determination, which he put into immediate execution. As it fell out, he acted wisely, for at his trial he was acquitted. He was the most upright and modest man I have ever known—well educated, brave, devoted, simple in manners. His character was lofty and of rare probity.[2]

However, in the case of political crimes, for so they are called by those who triumph, the wisest plan is to flee from immediate vengeance. One can explain afterwards. Time (which allays passions and party-spirit) and intervening events co-operate in producing indulgence and forgetfulness.

This was exemplified in the case of many of those who were aimed at by the ordinances. It would have been the case with the unhappy Marshal Ney, had he profited immediately by the passports procured by his wife from the leaders of the foreign army. She implored him on her knees to lose no time in making his escape, but he answered curtly:

'Upon my word, madam, you are in a great hurry to get rid of me!'

The unfortunate widow herself told me this characteristic story. Louis XVIII. told me and many other people that when Ney took leave of him, he promised that if he could seize Napoleon he would send him back to the King in an iron cage. He was an intrepid commander, but very changeable in his mind and disposition. I quite be-

---

2. An interesting picture of the gallant General Drouot (not to be confounded with General Drouet, Count D'Erlon, recently referred to in these pages) is given in Odeleben's *Campaign of 1813*:

'Drouot, the well-known Commander of the Artillery of the Guard, was a very remarkable man.... He always had a small Bible with him to read, which constituted his chief delight; and he avowed it openly to the persons in the Imperial suite—a peculiarity not a little remarkable in that staff, and the admission of which required no small degree of moral courage. He was not without a certain shade of superstition, for, as Napoleon usually brought him forward at the most hazardous moment, and he was always exposed at the head of his troops, his situation was full of peril; and he was careful on such occasions to array himself in his old uniform of General of Artillery, as he had long worn it, and never received any injury. When near the enemy he always dismounted from horseback, and advanced on foot in the middle of his guns, and by a most extraordinary chance neither himself nor his horse was ever wounded. His modesty was equal to his knowledge, his fidelity to his courage, and he gave a shining proof of the latter quality by accompanying Napoleon to Elba amidst the general defection by which the more exalted objects of the Emperor's bounty were disgraced.' (Quoted by Sir A. Alison in his *History of Europe*, vol. ix.)

This was the man inscribed by the Bourbons for possible massacre like Marshal Ney.

lieve that he made this remark, but am convinced that he would never have sullied his reputation by putting it into execution. He was too confident, and it cost him his life.[3]

Speaking of General Drouot recalls to my memory an anecdote which he did not know, and which I related to him in 1820, when he came to see me at Contrexéville.

A few days before the fatal Battle of Leipsic I was dining at Dresden with the Emperor in the company of Murat and Berthier. As we were rising from table the Duke of Bassano arrived. Murat took the Emperor aside, and they talked excitedly for a few moments, when the Emperor, turning towards me, said:

'Ask the Duke of Tarentum; he knows how infamously he behaved.'

They were talking about the Italian General Lecchi, who was accused of having caused the jeweller Caron to be shot at Barcelona, in order to seize his property; and, further, of having caused all those to be shot who took part in the assassination, so as to conceal every trace of the crime. This had occurred under my predecessor in Catalonia. An

---

3. A painfully vivid account of this dark page in French history is given in the Comte de Rochechouart's *Memoirs*, from which the following is abridged:
'On the morning of December 7 I took upon myself,' says Rochechouart, 'without consulting the prisoner, to order up a carriage. The Marshal saluted us. I felt a great relief when I saw him in a blue overcoat, with a white neck-handkerchief, short black breeches, black stockings, and no decorations. I was afraid that he might have been in uniform, and that, consequently, it would be necessary to have it "disgraced," and to have torn off the buttons, epaulettes, and decorations. On seeing the bad weather, he said, smiling, "Here is a nasty day." Then turning round to the cure, who was drawing back to allow him to get into the carriage, "Get in, *Monsieur le Curé;* presently I shall precede you." The two officers of *gendarmerie* also got into the carriage, placing themselves on the front seat. At a few hundred paces from the railings of the Luxembourg, in the Avenue of the Observatory, the procession halted. Seeing the door opened, the Marshal, who expected to go to Grenelle, advised perhaps that a manifestation would be made in his favour, said, "What! already arrived?" He naturally refused to kneel down and to let his eyes be bandaged; he only asked Commandant Saint-Bras to point out to him where he should stand. He faced the firing-party, who held their muskets in the position "Ready!" and there, in an attitude which I shall never forget so noble, so calm, so dignified and without the least bravado, he took off his hat, and, taking advantage of the short space of time left him by the Adjutant in moving to one side, and giving the signal to fire, he pronounced these few words, which I heard very distinctly: "*Frenchmen! I protest against my condemnation, my honour....*" At these last words, as he placed his hand on his heart, the reports of the muskets were heard; he fell dead. A roll of the drums and the cries of "Long live the King!" which arose from the troops formed in a square, terminated this dismal ceremony. The Hero of the Beresina was no more.'

inquiry had been instituted; it was closed, and the documents relating to the case were taken to the central police-office at Barcelona.

I had just arrived to take up the command and Governor-generalship of the principality, when I received orders to forward all these documents to the Chief Justice. I then heard the story; so horrible was it that I could not credit it, and I said so to the Emperor.

'Indeed!' he exclaimed; 'it is only too true. The Chief Justice studied carefully all the evidence, and reported thereupon to me. The proof was complete, and had the scoundrel been brought to judgment, as I ought to have ordered him to be, he would have been sentenced to death. I refrained out of consideration for his family, which had rendered me several services during my Italian campaigns.' Then, turning to Murat, he said: 'You insisted upon his being let off because of your intimacy with this monster's sister. But rid me of him; I forbid you positively ever to employ him.'

Just then General Drouot was announced. He was *aide-de-camp* to the Emperor, and had been sent to Pirna to superintend the preparation of a bridge to be thrown across the Elbe, and had orders not to return until it was completed. The Duke of Piacenza (Le Bran), another *aide-de-camp*, was at Meissen upon similar business.

'Sire,' said General Drouot, 'I come to inform your Majesty that the bridge will be finished in an hour.'

The Emperor, still excited by his discussion with the King of Naples, did not allow him to finish his sentence.

'What do I see!' he exclaimed in a passion, 'a general officer who has the honour of serving as my *aide-de-camp* setting the bad example of not entirely carrying out my orders! You deserve to be dismissed! Go, sir! Return to Pirna, and do not let me see you again until the bridge is finished!'

The unlucky general saluted, and retired without a word. The Emperor seemed to have forgotten that he was not alone, for when he turned round he showed surprise, and immediately changed his tone.

'That is a good man,' he said; 'he is very distinguished, full of merit, modest, a first-rate mathematician. He will be a Member of the Institute at the first vacancy.'

Just as he was concluding this prognostication, of which after-events prevented the realization, the Duke of Piacenza arrived.

'Is the bridge ready?' asked the Emperor in a hard, imperious voice.

'It will be in two hours, Sire,' was the reply.

Napoleon scarcely allowed him time to finish his answer. He was not angry now, but quite beside himself with rage. He sent Le Brun back to Meissen, but on rejoining us said nothing about a vacancy in the Institute!

CHAPTER 42

Mission to Lyons

At my interview I carefully avoided everything that could resemble personal reproach, but represented to my hearers the situation of France, the loads which were already weighing her down, the necessity of not adding to them, and of not aggravating their own position.

They were moved by my frank and well-intended words; they promised me their help, and kept their word. The most difficult task was to settle differences between themselves. They reproached themselves with having mutually seduced and tempted each other. I intervened, in order to prevent this leaven of discord being introduced among the men, and added:

'As the faults and errors that have been committed are common to all, it is useless to debate the question; the chief thing is to wipe out the recollection of them.'

There was already enough discontent among the troops, without adding fuel to the flames. The interview had lasted a long time; I saluted them, and they withdrew, all more or less satisfied.

I augured well from it; the first step had been difficult, and the result surpassed my hopes. Conversations at dinner and private audiences did the rest, and thenceforward we worked very well together.

At the end of the day some body-guards in disguise arrived, armed with orders to the heads of the *gendarmerie* to assist the bearers in arresting the persons named in the ordinances. They showed me their instructions and authority.

'You must on no account show yourselves,' I said; 'for in the present state of the army I cannot answer for your personal safety. Let me quiet them down; I have already made a good beginning. Remain hidden here. I will order you some food, and will have mattresses prepared in a room for you. Tomorrow we will see what to do.'

They were far from suspecting my intentions; for greater safety, I had their door locked. I knew not where to find the threatened men, to warn them. The Prince of Eckmühl had just left me; he was to start next morning for the country, but I did not know where, to await the turn of events. I went straight to him. and gave him warning.

'Send word at once,' I said, 'to all those whose names are on the lists. Send couriers into the cantonments: this will give them a start of eight or nine hours.'

I do not know how they managed it, but they all got clear away— even General de Laborde, who was laid up with gout at the time.

The next day I set the officers of the Body-Guards at liberty.

'Now, gentlemen,' I said, 'you can execute your mission.'

They withdrew, but discovered, somehow, I know not by what means, the warnings that had been given, and returned a few days later to reproach me with their imprisonment, which had brought about the failure of their mission. They would report it, they said.

'Do so,' I answered with a laugh; 'but you owe me some thanks, for I saved you from the certain fate which awaited you had your disguise been penetrated.'

'We would have risked it,' said one of them.

'Then pray why did you disguise yourselves?' I retorted.

This stinging answer disconcerted them.

'Since your mission has now lost its object,' I continued firmly, 'in your own interests, quit the neighbourhood of the army at once. Go and make your report.'

They withdrew without another word. I never heard what report they presented; the Government maintained silence upon the point, but the late Duc de Berry, who still bore me a grudge for our discussions, wrote to me very bitterly. He ended by saying that, were he commanding in my place, he would have all the recalcitrants thrown out of window; to which I replied that one would not have time to do it, to say nothing of the risk of having to lead the way one's self.

All my care was now given to soothing down irritation. I was laden with work, overwhelmed with complaints from the authorities respecting persons under them. Events had marched so fast that the departments situated beyond the line of the armistice and the junction of the Loire and the Rhone had not been warned; they had no stores, and were living from hand to mouth without any security for the next day's provisions. I rearranged the cantonments and enlarged them, but without gaining any substantial relief. Things had not simply been eaten, they had been wasted, and this is always sure to happen when there is no regular distribution of rations. However, I should never end if I once began entering into all these details. I will go on with my story.

The decision concerning the disbandment came at last. Submission was fairly general. I softened the bitterness of it as far as lay in my power—consoling some, encouraging others. My whole correspondence with the Government is a standing proof of my efforts, and of the interest I took in each individual case; and when the men who had sided with the army were oppressed and abused by the reactionary party, I warmly defended them in the Chamber of Peers[1]—all that is in print. I also had to defend myself personally against strenuous opponents in the matter of that unlucky disbandment question. The successful party wished to reward me with the post of *Grand Veneur*, or by the gift of a fine house or property. They insisted; I sternly refused. My pride rebelled at such a proposal. The idea of accepting a reward, when I was helping to deprive so many brave men of their active pay, that is to say, of part of their livelihood![2]

---

1. See my speeches on the Recruiting Bill, of which I was reporter, on the Bill dealing with the interests of absentees, and especially my opinion expressed in the discussion on the Bill concerning electoral colleges.—Note by Marshal Macdonald.
2. About this time I learned a fact which will create no surprise, as it affords another proof of the chivalrous disinterestedness of Macdonald's character. When in 1815 several marshals claimed from the allied powers their endowments in foreign countries, Madame Moreau (to whom the King had given the honorary title of *Madame la Maréchale*, and who was the friend of the Duke of Tarentum), wrote, without Macdonald's knowledge, to M. de Blacas, our ambassador at Naples, begging him to endeavour to preserve for the Marshal the endowment which had been given him in the kingdom of Naples. As soon as Macdonald was informed of this circumstance he waited upon Madame Moreau, thanked her for her kind intentions, but at the same time informed her that he should disavow all knowledge of her letter, as the request it contained was entirely averse to his principles. The marshal did, in fact, write the following letter to M. de Blacas: 'I hasten to inform you, sir, that it was not with my consent that Madame Moreau wrote to you, and I beg you will take no step that might expose me to a refusal. The King of Naples owes me no recompense for having beaten his army, revolutionized his kingdom, and forced him to retire to Sicily.' Such conduct was well worthy of the man who was the last to forsake Napoleon in 1814. M. de Blacas, who was himself much surprised at Macdonald's letter, communicated it to the King of Naples, whose answer deserves to be recorded. It was as follows: 'If I had not imposed a law upon myself to acknowledge none of the French endowments, the conduct of Marshal Macdonald would have induced me to make an exception in his favour.' It is gratifying to see princes such scrupulous observers of the laws they make for themselves!—Bourrienne's *Memoirs of Napoleon Bonaparte* edition of 1885, vol. 3.

The Royal Guard had just been created. I was one of the four major-generals. Officers had been sent out to recruit among the former Imperial Guard, which consisted of the *élite* of the army. A large number joined the new regiment to finish their term of service and secure their pensions. They were models of steadiness and good conduct.

The battalion which had been formed the previous year, to serve as a guard to the Emperor at Elba, was much distrusted, but was eventually admitted like the others. I had ordered it to come to Bourges, where I had opportunities of talking to many officers, non-commissioned officers, and privates. They all assured me (as I have already mentioned in an earlier chapter) that, believing themselves exiled eternally, they sighed for a chance of returning to France. They were therefore delighted at learning, after their embarkation, that they were about to make a descent upon our Mediterranean coast. As the Emperor was warmly received everywhere, and as they met with no obstacle, they were happy to tread once more the soil of their country.

'But,' I asked them, 'if you had met with resistance, if you had been repulsed, would you have embarked again if possible?'

'Oh no!' they replied. 'The opportunity of quitting that island was too good to be missed.'

'But if you had met with opposition, would you have attacked, fired?'

'No, no! We would have committed no acts of hostility; that would have ruined our cause. We would have laid down our arms and asked leave to retire to our families.'

'And have abandoned the Emperor?'

'We had given him sufficient proof of our devotion. Everyone for himself. Besides, he caused his own misfortunes and ours, and we were not called upon to continue his victims.'

'But it was of your own choice and of your own free will that you sided with him.'

'No doubt; but at that time we thought it was a garrison, and that we should be relieved. When we reached the island, and learned that it was to last for life, and as we were miserable there, we were seized with discouragement and home-sickness. We therefore embarked gladly, not knowing whither we were bound; but at any rate we were changing our place!'

With the exception of the majority of the officers, who, from affection or gratitude, had attached themselves to the fortunes, good or bad, of the Emperor, and who would have been delighted to accompany him to St. Helena, all were overjoyed to find themselves at home again. Such were the constant expressions of these soldiers, whom I frequently questioned until they left me.

The disbandment was carried out nearly everywhere without difficulty; but some regiments of the ex-Guard mutinied, as did the *Chasseurs à cheval* and the Grenadiers at Aubusson. Their pretext, whether true or false, was the settlement of their pay, which no doubt was much in arrear, and the Government resources were slender. Power had been given, at my request, to a financial agent to advance a portion of the money. I tried to borrow the remainder, and offered security to the inhabitants of Bourges; but despite the respect and esteem in which they held me, I could not raise more than 60,000 *francs* (£2,400).

Order and submission were re-established in the regiment of *Chasseurs* by dint of some arrests and a display of authority made by the lieutenant-general commanding the 20th Military Division at Périgueux. With the exception of a few men led astray by a subaltern officer, who, with them, was made prisoner a few days later, the Grenadiers returned to duty of their own accord when they discovered that they were being dragged into a criminal enterprise. The officer paid for his mistake with his life.

The disbandment came to an end at last. It was not without a cruel pang that I witnessed the disappearance of this valiant and unfortunate army, so long triumphant. No trace now remained of it. An ill-wind had blown and dispersed it like dust; we were now at the mercy of the foreigners! The loss in rank and file was but temporary. Departmental legions were to be created. The loss in material was immense, incalculable, including as it did arms, harness, saddlery, cavalry and draught horses, that were handed over to farmers who had not the wherewithal to feed those they already possessed. They were taken into the meadows and woods, and abandoned there. Saddles and harness were heaped pell-mell in convents and damp sheds. Eighty-two thousand infantry were disbanded; only thirty thousand muskets found their way back into the depots; sabres, pistols, *musketoons*, shoulder-belts, all vanished in the same proportion. I had before pointed out what would happen; the Government turned a deaf ear.

I had now been six months at Bourges; all was finished, and I begged leave to resign. I was kept waiting another two months, as it was considered that my presence served as a moral force in the absence of any physical. At length I returned to Paris, and once more took up the duties of Arch-Chancellor of the Legion of Honour.

There is no personal circumstance connected with my military or political career that deserves mention after this period (February, 1816), except that I believe a suggestion was made of offering me the Ministry of War, thinking that the man who had so well succeeded in reconciling feelings and duty during the important operation of disbandment could alone create anew a good army. Some interviews took place, but resulted in nothing.

In 1819 or 1820 I was sent to preside over the electoral district of Lyons, as I had previously done over Bourges. I went thither against the grain, and not without considerable reluctance. It was considered important. I know not why. The King's intervention was even required, and I yielded.

When the Duc de Richelieu quitted the Ministry, he proposed to the King that I should succeed him in the Presidency of the Council, and take at the same time the Foreign Office. Monsieur Roy, at that time Minister of Finance, who retired with the Duc de Richelieu, confided this to me, but the Duke himself never mentioned it. I would certainly not have accepted the position; my devotion would not have carried me to those lengths.

I remember a conversation that I had on one occasion at St. Cloud with *Monsieur*, by whom I was sitting at the table of Louis XVIII. During his reign the chief officers, as well as those in waiting, were admitted, by right, 'to have luncheon with him. *Monsieur* said to me:

'Before the Revolution, you served in the Irish Brigade?'

'Yes, *Monseigneur*.'

'Nearly all the officers emigrated?'

'Yes, *Monseigneur*.'

'Why did you not do the same? What kept you in France?'

'I was in love, *Monseigneur*.'

'Ha! ha!' he said, laughing; 'so you were in love, sir?'

In the same tone, and with an expressive glance, I replied:

'Yes, like other people; I was married, I was about to become a father; and, besides, your Royal Highness knows that people emigrated for many reasons. They were not in all cases compelled by public feeling to leave the country, especially the young officers, like myself at that time, who cared very little about politics. They sometimes went for very bad reasons, debts, etc.,' and I continued in the same tone: 'I must make a confession to your Royal Highness.'

'What is it?'

'It is that I love the Revolution.'

Monsieur started, and changed colour; I hastened to add:

'I detest its men and its crimes. The army took no part in it. It never looked behind, but always ahead at the enemy, and deplored the excesses that were being committed. How could I fail to love the Revolution? It was that which raised and made me what I am; without it, should I now enjoy the honour of sitting at the King's table next to your Royal Highness?'

Monsieur, who had recovered himself and his good temper, clapped me on the shoulder, exclaiming:

'You are quite right; I like your honesty.'

May, 1826.

Coventry, le 6. 7 Juin 1850

J'avais le projet en quittant Paris, en
chemy ventant de vous trouver le bon par
un prospère mais ne serait ment douté
de savoir s'avoir à Halbes to the prince
trouvés être s'vul permit. J'ai eu
a montage mg, me voi ma arrêté ici, j
un homme par Deganneau, l'aîné comme
pour vous Sablon en moments un lettre
différence été ctre avec d'hiver tre c

Monsieur Servant m'apporta ce soir
vos Instructions. Temps si pressant de
Sortir.

Je [surveyerai?] [illegible] bien [Carafa?]
aujourd'hui (tous les [illegible]) [illegible] de bien
armer de vos [illegible], dans [le?] [illegible] [illegible]
[illegible]. Le Dauguerry, de [illegible] [illegible]
[illegible] [Chabanne?], et à vous [pour?])
[illegible] Johan.

Agréez mon cher [illegible], [illegible]
[illegible] et [illegible]

[signature]

Appendix

TRANSLATION OF THE FOREGOING FACSIMILE LETTER

Courcelles-le-Roi,
September 6, 1833.

It was my intention, my dear neighbour, when I quitted Paris to come and give you greeting as I passed, but an event, at the thought of which I still tremble, has been almost fatal to me. My son has been all but drowned at Montargis, where I stopped to breakfast with a friend. He was rescued by a boatman just as he was about to disappear. This circumstance delayed me considerably, and I was only able to make my bow as I passed St. Brisson, and since then the bad weather has prevented me from going out.

In sending to fetch [next words illegible], . . . I beg for news of you. of your husband and children, of D'Argant, of his mother, and of Madame de Chabans, and I pray you to send me some.

Receive, my dear neighbour, my homage, respects, and attachment.

Macdonald.

Note:—The words in the facsimile difficult to decipher are, "*en envoyant chercher une carrossée à Gien (tous les Saint Mars)*," etc.

THE MARSHALS OF NAPOLEON[1]

Augereau,
Pierre François Charles, born at Paris October 21, 1757. Fought in Italy, at Jena, Eylau, and Leipsic. Marshal in 1804, Duke of Castiglione in 1808. Died a natural death June 12, 1816.

Bernadotte,
Jean Baptiste Jules, born at Pau June 26, 1763. Fought on the Rhine, in Italy, at Wagram, and at Walcheren. Elected Crown Prince of Sweden 1810. Fought against Napoleon at Leipsic, and Marshals Ney and Oudinot previously. Marshal in 1804, Prince of Ponte Corvo in 1805. Marshalate annulled. Became King of Sweden 1818. Died a natural death March 8, 1844.

Berthier,
Alexandre, born at Versailles November 20, 1753. Fought in Italy, and acted as Major-General and Chief of the Staff to Napoleon in most of his campaigns. Marshal in 1804 Duke of Valengin and Prince of Neufchatel in 1806, Chief Ranger and Vice-Constable of the Empire 1807, Prince of Wagram 1809. Fell out of a window at Bamberg and was killed June 1, 1815.

Bessierès,
Jean Baptiste, born at Proissac August 6, 1768. Fought in Italy, Egypt, Spain, at Jena, Friedland, Eylau, Wagram, and in Russia. Marshal in 1804, Duke of Istria in 1809. Killed near Poserna, in Bohemia, May 1, 1813.

---

1. *Napoleon's Marshals* by R. P. Dunn-Pattison published by Leonaur.

Brune,
Guillaume Marie Anne, born at Brives-la-Gaillarde March 13, 1763. Fought in Switzerland, in Italy, and in Holland. Marshal in 1804, afterwards Count. Murdered by his own countrymen at Avignon August 2, 1815.

Davoût,
Louis Nicolas, born at Annaux May 10, 1770. Fought at Perpignan, on the Rhine and Moselle, in Egypt, at Marengo, Ulm, Austerlitz, Auerstadt, Golymin, Eylau, Friedland, Eckmühl, Aspern, Wagram, constantly in the Russian campaign, and in the memorable defence of Hamburg. Marshal in 1804, Duke of Auerstadt in 1808, and Prince of Eckmühl in 1809. The most successful and one of the ablest of Napoleon's Generals. Died a natural death June 1, 1823.

Grouchy,
Emanuel (Marquis de), born at Paris October 23, 1766. Fought under Hoche and Moreau, and in La Vendée. Sailed for Ireland. Engaged in the campaigns of 1805-6-7 against Austria and Prussia, at Madrid, against Austria in 1809, and in the campaigns of 1812, 1813, 1814, and at Ligny and Wavres in 1815. Count in 1809, and Marshal in 1815. Marshalate annulled. Died a natural death May 29, 1847.

Jourdan,
Jean Baptiste, born at Limoges April 29, 1 762. Present in the American War 1778-1783. Fought under Dumourier, and at Wattignies and Fleurus, and in Italy, on the Rhine, and in Spain. Marshal in 1804, and Count in 1814. Marshalate annulled. Died a natural death November 23, 1833.

Kellermann,
Francois Christophe, born at Strasbourg May 28, 1735. Served in Poland, and fought in the Netherlands and at Valmy. Honorary Marshal 1804, Duke of Valmy in 1808. Died a natural death September 13, 1820.

Lannes,
Jean, born at Lectoure April 11, 1769. Served in the Pyrenees, fought at Millesimo and Lodi, in Egypt, at Montebello and Marengo. Ambassador in Portugal. Fought in Germany in 1807, Spain in 1808. Marshal in 1804, and Duke of Montebello in 1808. Mortally wounded at Aspern May 22, and died May 31, 1809.

Lefebvre,
Francois Joseph, born October 25, 1755, at Ruffach. Fought under Pichegru, Hoche, Moreau and Jourdan in the Netherlands and in Germany, and with especial distinction at the battle of Stockach. Fought in the German campaigns of 1805-6-7, and at Eylau. Captured Dantzig after a prolonged siege. Served successfully in Spain, and was present at Abensburg, Eckmühl and Wagram. Commanded the Imperial Guard in the Russian campaign. Honorary Marshal in 1804, and Duke of Dantzig in 1807. Died September 4, 1820.

Macdonald,
Stephen James Joseph Alexander, born at Sedan, November 17, 1765. Entered the army in 1785, Captain in 1792, Colonel in 1793, General of Division in 1794, Governor of Rome in 1798, Ambassador Extraordinary to the Court of Copenhagen, 1801, created Marshal on the field of battle of Wagram, July 6, 1809, and Duke of Tarentum August 15 1809. For his services refer to the present volume. Macdonald died a natural death at Courcelles-le-Roi, September 7, 1840.

[He was made a Peer of France in 1814, Knight Grand Cross of the Order of St. Louis 1814, Governor of the Twenty-first Military Division 1814, Arch-Chancellor of the Legion of Honour 1815, and Major-General of the Royal Body Guard 1816.]

Marmont,
Auguste Frédéric Louis Viesse de, born at Châtillon-sur-Seine July 20, 1774. Fought at Toulon and with Napoleon in Italy, Egypt, Syria, and at Marengo, also in Germany in 1805-6-7 and 9. Opposed to Wellington at Salamanca, where he lost an arm. Returned to active service in time to be present at Lutzen, Bautzen, and Leipsic, and went through the campaign of 1814. Marshal in 1809, and Duke of Ragusa in the previous year. Died at Venice March 2, 1852, from natural causes.

Masséna,
Andréa, born at Nice May 6, 1756. Almost the ablest of the Marshals. Originally a sailor. He entered the army, and retired, after fourteen years' service, only an adjutant. Recalled and made General of Division in 1793. Fought in Italy and at Rivoli, and in Switzerland. Defeated Souvarof at Zurich. Defended Genoa. Defeated the Austrian forces in Italy in 1805, at Eylau in 1807, and at Landshut, Ebersberg, Eckmühl, Essling, Wagram and Znaim in 1809. During the next two years he was present in Portugal and Spain. Marshal in 1804, Duke of

Rivoli in 1808, Prince of Essling in 1810. Died a natural death April 4, 1817.

Moncey,

Bon Adrien Jeannot de, born at Besançon July 31, 1754. General of Division 1794. Fought in the Eastern Pyrenees, at Marengo, and in Eastern Spain, in 1808-9, in Russia 1812, in Germany 1813. Marshal in 1804, and Duke of Conegliano 1808. Imprisoned by Louis XVIII. for refusing to preside at the trial of Marshal Ney in 1815. Died a natural death April 20, 1842.

Mortier,

Edouard Adolphe Casimir Joseph, born at Cambrai February 13, 1768. Fought under Pichegru, Moreau and Masséna. Occupied Hanover in 1805, and took part in the battles of Central Europe during the two following years, and at Friedland. Transferred to Spain, defeated the Spaniards at Ocana, and afterwards took part in the Russian campaign, and in the Saxon campaign of 1813, and that of France in 1814. Intended to have been present in Belgium in 1815. Marshal in 1804, Chancellor of the Legion of Honour in the same year, Duke of Treviso in 1807. Assassinated July 28, 1835, by Fieschi.

Murat,

Joachim, born at Bastide Fortunière March 25, 1767. Originally an ecclesiastic. In the Egyptian and Italian campaigns. Married Caroline Bonaparte January 20, 1800. Governor of Paris. Took part at Marengo, Donauworth, and Austerlitz. Occupied Madrid in 1807. Marshal in 1804, High Admiral of France in 1805, Grand Duke of Berg and Cleves in 1806, King of Naples in 1808. Went through the Russian campaign, 1812, and was present at Dresden and Leipsic. Shot at Pizzo October 13, 1815.

Ney,

Michel, born January 10, 1769, at Sarre-Louis. Present at Neerwinde, Valenciennes, etc. Served under Kléber and Moreau, and captured Mannheim. Occupied Switzerland. Fought at Elchingen and Ulm, Eylau and Friedland. In 1808 went to Spain and Portugal, and in 1812 to Russia. Fought at Borodino, and commanded the rear-guard at the passage of the Beresina. Took a prominent part in the Saxon campaign of 1813, and in the battles in Champagne in the following year. Fought at Quatre Bras and Waterloo in 1815. Marshal in 1804, Duke of Elchingen in 1808, Prince of the Moskowa in 1813. Shot by

Louis XVIII. December 7, 1815.

Oudinot,
Nicolas Charles, born April 25, 1767, at Bar-le-Duc. Served under Hoche, Pichegru, Moreau and Masséna. Fought at Wagram and in the Russian campaign, and at Bautzen. Defeated by Bernadotte at Gross Beeren in 1813. Took part in the battles east of Paris in 1814. Count in 1804 or 1808, Marshal in 1809, Duke of Reggio in 1810. Died a natural death September 13, 1847.

Perignon,
Domenique Catherine, born at Toulouse May 31, 1754. Fought in Spain (and captured Rosas) and at Novi. Honorary Marshal in 1804, and Count in 1808. Died from natural causes December 25, 1818.

Poniatowski,
Josef Anton, Prince, born May 7, 1762, at Warsaw. Commanded the Polish troops in 1809. Took part in the Russian campaign, and was wounded at the battle of Leipsic. Marshal in October, 1813. Drowned in the Elster October 19, 1813.

St. Cyr,
Laurent Gouvion, born at Toul April 13, 1764. Fought on the Rhine, in Italy, in Spain, in the Russian campaign, and besieged at Dresden. Count in 1808, Marshal in 1812. Died a natural death March 17, 1830.

Sérurier,
Jean Matthieu Philibert, born at Laon December 8, 1742. Fought in the Pyrenees and at Mondovi and Cassano. Honorary Marshal in 1804, Count in 1808. Died a natural death December 21, 1819.

Soult,
Nicolas Jean de Dieu, born March 29, 1769, at St. Amand la Bastide. Served under Hoche, Jourdan, Marceau and Masséna. One of the ablest of the Marshals, and took a leading part at Austerlitz, Memmingen and Eylau. Fought at Corunna, Oporto, Albuera, also at Bautzen. Returned again to the Peninsula, and was engaged at the Pyrenees. Orthez and Toulouse. Marshal in 1804, Duke of Dalmatia in 1808. As Major-General took part at Ligny and Waterloo. Died November 26, 1851, from natural causes.

Suchet,
Louis Gabriel, born at Lyons March 2, 1770. Present at Toulon, and

served in Italy under Napoleon, Masséna, Joubert, Schérer and Brune, and on the Rhine. Took part in the campaign of 1805 and of 1807, and afterwards distinguished himself in Eastern Spain. Count in 1808, Marshal in 1811, Duke of Albufera da Valencia in 1812. Died a natural death January 3, 1826.

Victor,
Or Victor Perrin, was born at Marche, in Lorraine, December 7, 1764. Was present at Toulon, and served in the campaigns of Italy and Marengo, and at the Battle of Friedland. Sent to Holland in 1800, Governor of Louisiana in 1802, and Minister Plenipotentiary at Copenhagen 1805-6. Fought at Espinosa, Talavera and Barrosa, and besieged Cadiz. Took part in the battles of Witepsk, the Beresina, Dresden, Leipsic, Hanau, and those of the campaign of 1814. Marshal in 1807, and Duke of Belluno in the following year. Died a natural death March 1, 1841.

The Viceroy of Italy, Clarke Duke of Feltre, Junot Duke of Abrantes, and Duroc Duke of Friuli, were not Marshals of the First Napoleon.

Generals Clausel, Lauriston, Drouet d'Erlon, Reille, Gérard, Molitor, Mouton-Lobau, Clarke, Sebastiani, Excelmans. Harispe, Valée and Dode, became Marshals after the downfall of Napoleon.

Note:—
The dates given upon these pages do not in all instances correspond with those shown in the previous edition. Those in the last edition were compared and checked by three different works; those in the present edition are taken from the French Official List of Soulié. It is not certain, however, which are most authentic.

NOTES
GENERAL MACDONALD'S PASSAGE OF THE ALPS.
(CHAPTER 11)

Macdonald modestly gives so slight an outline of his exertions on this occasion that it is right to subjoin a few extracts on the subject from General Mathieu Dumas's *Recollections*

'In my first communications with my new General-in-chief, I foresaw how easy and agreeable I should find the duties that I had to perform about him; easy, because his foresight and activity left nothing to the Chief of his Staff, besides the care of well directing the execution of orders, always precise, always clearly expressed; and agreeable, because his frank and military manner was tempered and set off by a tone of the most pleasing urbanity, and by lively and instructive conversation, which invited and inspired confidence. An unerring *coup-d'oeil*, prompt resolution, much boldness and perseverance under the most trying circumstances, are the principal traits of character which General Macdonald manifested in this campaign.

'Being directed to open the march, I proceeded to Tusis, at the foot of the glaciers, with General Verrières, whom General Sorbier, commander of the artillery, had detached to prepare, under my direction, the roads for the passage and the means of conveyance. We arrived at Tusis on November 24, preceded by three companies of sappers, whose labour could not render the road beyond that village passable for carriages. All those of the artillery were taken to pieces and placed upon sledges of the country, which were narrower and lighter than those which we had had made. These sledges were drawn by oxen; the ammunition was loaded on the backs of mules; and as these means of conveyance, collected with so much difficulty, were still very insufficient, I gave orders to distribute to every soldier—already overburdened with the weight of his arms—his knapsack and his provisions for five days, ten packets of cartridges, besides the ordinary supply in the *cartouche*.

'On November 27, the weather appearing calm, I caused the column of cavalry to march, and to attempt to ascend the glacier of the Splügen. I had assembled the most experienced guides, who preceded the column, and set up poles to mark the way. The workmen who followed them swept away or trod down the snow. General Laboissière and myself encouraged them; they advanced with difficulty. The day was on the decline, and the column had scarcely got half-way up the mountain when the east wind suddenly rose. The guides and the workmen struggled on amidst clouds of snow and pulverized ice.

'An enormous avalanche loosing itself from the highest summit, rolling with a fearful noise, and gliding with the rapidity of lightning, carried off thirty dragoons at the head of the column, who, with their horses, were swept away with the torrent, dashed against the rock, and buried under the snow. I had just quitted General Laboissière, and was engaged in making the column more close. I was not above one hundred and fifty paces from the spot, and thought for a moment that the General and the officers who accompanied him had likewise been swept away by the avalanche; but I perceived them, with some dragoons and the guides, beyond the mass of snow, pursuing their way.

'I stopped the rest of the column, and made it fall back to the village. General Laboissière, finding himself in advance, separated from his troops, and almost alone, had no hope of safety but by reaching the summit of the mountain. He succeeded by the assistance of some vigorous countrymen, who conducted him to the hospital. Some of the dragoons who had been swallowed up by the avalanche were also extricated by the brave mountaineers.

'This fruitless attempt only doubled the ardour of the French. The remainder of the company of dragoons which had suffered so severe a loss desired again to form the head of the column, under the command of its Colonel (Cavaignac); but the hurricane continued three days with the same violence. The avalanches had in several places blocked up the path; the guides declared that the passage was entirely closed, and that with the greatest exertions it would not be possible to open it in less than a fortnight, and then only for the infantry. . . .

'The General-in-chief persisted in passing. The labourers of the country, the sappers of the army, and the grenadiers, after six hours' excessive labour, reached the summit; but finding between the glaciers a considerable accumulation of snow, over which the guides would not venture, all retreated, crying that the passage was closed up. General Macdonald, accompanied by Generals Sorbier and Pully, stopped them, brought back the grenadiers to the trace of the path, rallied the workmen and the guides, and himself sounding first of all, he made them pierce and clear away these walls of snow, in which many men were entombed.

'The storm was dreadful in the passage to the hospital, and on the *plateau* as far as the Cardinel; the column was several times divided; the 104th *Demi*-Brigade was almost entirely dispersed, and could not be rallied till two days afterwards. General Rey, with the reserve, closely followed the steps of General Macdonald; but General Vandamme, who was at some distance in the rear, could scarcely find any traces of them. He would have been obliged to give up all thoughts of passing if his workmen and soldiers, discouraged by dangers in appearance less glorious than those which they were accustomed to brave in battle, had not been supported by the example of their comrades, who had been animated by that of the commander-in-chief.

'This last day alone cost about a hundred men, who were lost in the snow or frozen to death during the march. Above a hundred horses and mules likewise perished, and many sledges were abandoned. Articles belonging to the artillery and camp equipage were picked up after the tempest. At length, on December 6, all the troops and the greater part of the artillery had passed the Splügen, and the headquarters were fixed at Chiavenna.'—General Count Mathieu Dumas's *Memoirs of his own Time*, vol. 2. (London: Bentley, 1839.)

The Emperor Napoleon's Return.

Chapter 37

The following is a contemporary account of the arrival of Napoleon at Fontainebleau in March, 1815:

'The number of national guards, volunteers, and other troops, collected at Melun to stop the march of Buonaparte, was not less than 100,000 men. The best spirit seemed to prevail amongst them. They appeared devoted to the cause of the King, and eager to meet and repel his antagonist. A powerful artillery strengthened their positions. Relying on their numbers, they had left the town, the rocks, and the forest of Fontainebleau unguarded, preferring the flat plains of Melun, where the whole of their army might act at once against the comparatively small band of the invader.

'On the 19th Buonaparte reached and occupied Fontainebleau without the least opposition. He had at that time with him only 15,000 veteran troops; but other divisions were either following him or advancing to support his right and left flanks on parallel lines of march.

'Ney, whose corps is stated to have amounted to 30,000 men, had previously communicated to the Court a declaration signed by the whole army under his command, both officers and privates, in which they stated *"that they respected him too much to deceive him; that they would not fight for Louis XVIII.; but that they would shed all their blood for Napoleon the Great."* This declaration did not entirely extinguish the hopes of the Bourbons. They still relied on the good disposition and numbers of the troops at Melun, and blinded by the addresses sent up from many garrisons and provinces at the very moment of their defection, still thought that their cause would be espoused by the nation as her own.

'Early on the morning of Monday, the 20th, preparations were made on both sides for the encounter which was expected to take place. The French army was drawn up *en étages* on three lines, the intervals and the flanks armed with batteries. The centre occupied the Paris road. The ground from Fontainebleau to Melun is a continual declivity, so that, on emerging from the forest, you have a clear view of the country before you, whilst, on the other hand, those below can easily descry whatever appears on the eminence.

'An awful silence, broken only at times by peals of martial music, intended to confirm the loyalty of the troops by repeating the royal airs of "*Vive Henri Quatre*" and "*La Belle Gabrielle*," or by the voice of the commanders and the march of divisions to their appointed ground, pervaded the King's army. All was anxious expectation; the chiefs conscious that a moment would decide the fate of the Bourbon dynasty, and the troops, perhaps, secretly awed at the thought of meeting in hostility the man whom they had been accustomed to obey. On the side of Fontainebleau no sound as of an army rushing to battle was heard. 'If the enemy was advancing, his troops evidently moved in silence. Perhaps his heart had failed him, and he had retreated during the night! If so, France was saved and Europe free.

'At length a light trampling of horses became audible. It approached; an open carriage, attended by a few *hussars* and dragoons, appeared on the skirts of the forest. It drove down the hills with the rapidity of lightning; it reached the advanced post. "*Vive l'Empereur!*" burst from the astonished soldiery. "Napoleon!—Napoleon the Great!" spread from rank to rank; for, bareheaded, Bertrand seated at his right, and Drouet at his left, Napoleon continued his course, now waving his hand, now opening his arms to the soldiers, whom he called "his friends, his companions in arms, whose honour, whose glories, whose country he now came to restore." All discipline was forgotten, disobeyed, and derided; the commanders-in-chief took to flight; thousands rushed towards Napoleon; acclamations rent the sky. At that moment his own Guard descended the hill, the Imperial March was played, the eagles were once more exhibited, and those whose deadly weapons were to have aimed at each other's life embraced as brothers, and joined in universal shouts. In the midst of these greetings did Napoleon pass through the whole of the royal army, pursuing his course to Paris, and arrived at 'eight o'clock in the evening at the Tuileries. It was not until the next morning that his arrival was generally known. He is said to have left his army behind him at Fontainebleau.'—*The Gentleman's Magazine*, March, 1815.

The *Château* of Courcelles-le-Roi

The letter in a bracket (A) at the side indicates the room in which the Duke of Tarentum passed away. His remains are deposited in the Cemetery of Père-la-Chaise.

ALSO FROM LEONAUR
AVAILABLE IN SOFTCOVER OR HARDCOVER WITH DUST JACKET

IRON TIMES WITH THE GUARDS *by An O. E. (G. P. A. Fildes)*—The Experiences of an Officer of the Coldstream Guards on the Western Front During the First World War.

THE GREAT WAR IN THE MIDDLE EAST: 1 *by W. T. Massey*—The Desert Campaigns & How Jerusalem Was Won---two classic accounts in one volume.

THE GREAT WAR IN THE MIDDLE EAST: 2 *by W. T. Massey*—Allenby's Final Triumph.

SMITH-DORRIEN *by Horace Smith-Dorrien*—Isandlwhana to the Great War.

1914 *by Sir John French*—The Early Campaigns of the Great War by the British Commander.

GRENADIER *by E. R. M. Fryer*—The Recollections of an Officer of the Grenadier Guards throughout the Great War on the Western Front.

BATTLE, CAPTURE & ESCAPE *by George Pearson*—The Experiences of a Canadian Light Infantryman During the Great War.

DIGGERS AT WAR *by R. Hugh Knyvett & G. P. Cuttriss*—"Over There" With the Australians by R. Hugh Knyvett and Over the Top With the Third Australian Division by G. P. Cuttriss. Accounts of Australians During the Great War in the Middle East, at Gallipoli and on the Western Front.

HEAVY FIGHTING BEFORE US *by George Brenton Laurie*—The Letters of an Officer of the Royal Irish Rifles on the Western Front During the Great War.

THE CAMELIERS *by Oliver Hogue*—A Classic Account of the Australians of the Imperial Camel Corps During the First World War in the Middle East.

RED DUST *by Donald Black*—A Classic Account of Australian Light Horsemen in Palestine During the First World War.

THE LEAN, BROWN MEN *by Angus Buchanan*—Experiences in East Africa During the Great War with the 25th Royal Fusiliers—the Legion of Frontiersmen.

THE NIGERIAN REGIMENT IN EAST AFRICA *by W. D. Downes*—On Campaign During the Great War 1916-1918.

THE 'DIE-HARDS' IN SIBERIA *by John Ward*—With the Middlesex Regiment Against the Bolsheviks 1918-19.

AVAILABLE ONLINE AT **www.leonaur.com**
AND FROM ALL GOOD BOOK STORES

ALSO FROM LEONAUR
AVAILABLE IN SOFTCOVER OR HARDCOVER WITH DUST JACKET

FARAWAY CAMPAIGN *by F. James*—Experiences of an Indian Army Cavalry Officer in Persia & Russia During the Great War.

REVOLT IN THE DESERT *by T. E. Lawrence*—An account of the experiences of one remarkable British officer's war from his own perspective.

MACHINE-GUN SQUADRON *by A. M. G.*—The 20th Machine Gunners from British Yeomanry Regiments in the Middle East Campaign of the First World War.

A GUNNER'S CRUSADE *by Antony Bluett*—The Campaign in the Desert, Palestine & Syria as Experienced by the Honourable Artillery Company During the Great War .

DESPATCH RIDER *by W. H. L. Watson*—The Experiences of a British Army Motorcycle Despatch Rider During the Opening Battles of the Great War in Europe.

TIGERS ALONG THE TIGRIS *by E. J. Thompson*—The Leicestershire Regiment in Mesopotamia During the First World War.

HEARTS & DRAGONS *by Charles R. M. F. Crutwell*—The 4th Royal Berkshire Regiment in France and Italy During the Great War, 1914-1918.

INFANTRY BRIGADE: 1914 *by John Ward*—The Diary of a Commander of the 15th Infantry Brigade, 5th Division, British Army, During the Retreat from Mons.

DOING OUR 'BIT' *by Ian Hay*—Two Classic Accounts of the Men of Kitchener's 'New Army' During the Great War including *The First 100,000 & All In It.*

AN EYE IN THE STORM *by Arthur Ruhl*—An American War Correspondent's Experiences of the First World War from the Western Front to Gallipoli-and Beyond.

STAND & FALL *by Joe Cassells*—With the Middlesex Regiment Against the Bolsheviks 1918-19.

RIFLEMAN MACGILL'S WAR *by Patrick MacGill*—A Soldier of the London Irish During the Great War in Europe including *The Amateur Army, The Red Horizon & The Great Push.*

WITH THE GUNS *by C. A. Rose & Hugh Dalton*—Two First Hand Accounts of British Gunners at War in Europe During World War 1- Three Years in France with the Guns and With the British Guns in Italy.

THE BUSH WAR DOCTOR *by Robert V. Dolbey*—The Experiences of a British Army Doctor During the East African Campaign of the First World War.

AVAILABLE ONLINE AT **www.leonaur.com**
AND FROM ALL GOOD BOOK STORES

ALSO FROM LEONAUR
AVAILABLE IN SOFTCOVER OR HARDCOVER WITH DUST JACKET

THE 9TH—THE KING'S (LIVERPOOL REGIMENT) IN THE GREAT WAR 1914 - 1918 by Enos H. G. Roberts—Mersey to mud—war and Liverpool men.

THE GAMBARDIER by Mark Severn—The experiences of a battery of Heavy artillery on the Western Front during the First World War.

FROM MESSINES TO THIRD YPRES by Thomas Floyd—A personal account of the First World War on the Western front by a 2/5th Lancashire Fusilier.

THE IRISH GUARDS IN THE GREAT WAR - VOLUME 1 by Rudyard Kipling—Edited and Compiled from Their Diaries and Papers—The First Battalion.

THE IRISH GUARDS IN THE GREAT WAR - VOLUME 1 by Rudyard Kipling—Edited and Compiled from Their Diaries and Papers—The Second Battalion.

ARMOURED CARS IN EDEN by K. Roosevelt—An American President's son serving in Rolls Royce armoured cars with the British in Mesopotamia & with the American Artillery in France during the First World War.

CHASSEUR OF 1914 by Marcel Dupont—Experiences of the twilight of the French Light Cavalry by a young officer during the early battles of the great war in Europe.

TROOP HORSE & TRENCH by R.A. Lloyd—The experiences of a British Lifeguardsman of the household cavalry fighting on the western front during the First World War 1914-18.

THE EAST AFRICAN MOUNTED RIFLES by C.J. Wilson—Experiences of the campaign in the East African bush during the First World War.

THE LONG PATROL by George Berrie—A Novel of Light Horsemen from Gallipoli to the Palestine campaign of the First World War.

THE FIGHTING CAMELIERS by Frank Reid—The exploits of the Imperial Camel Corps in the desert and Palestine campaigns of the First World War.

STEEL CHARIOTS IN THE DESERT by S. C. Rolls—The first world war experiences of a Rolls Royce armoured car driver with the Duke of Westminster in Libya and in Arabia with T.E. Lawrence.

WITH THE IMPERIAL CAMEL CORPS IN THE GREAT WAR by Geoffrey Inchbald—The story of a serving officer with the British 2nd battalion against the Senussi and during the Palestine campaign.

AVAILABLE ONLINE AT **www.leonaur.com**
AND FROM ALL GOOD BOOK STORES

www.ingramcontent.com/pod-product-compliance
Lightning Source LLC
Chambersburg PA
CBHW021959160426
43197CB00007B/183